Deadly Musings

Deadly Musings

VIOLENCE AND VERBAL
FORM IN AMERICAN FICTION

Michael Kowalewski

PRINCETON UNIVERSITY PRESS

PRINCETON, NEW JERSEY

Library of Congress Cataloging-in-Publication Data

Kowalewski, Michael.
Deadly musings : violence and verbal form in American fiction /
                      p.   cm.
Includes bibliographical references and index.
ISBN 0-691-06973-5
1. American fiction—History and criticism.   2. Violence in
literature.   3. Style, Literary.   4. Literary form.   I. Title.
PS374.V58K68   1993
813.009'355—dc20   92-36088

FOR CATHY

Contents

Acknowledgments

MANY PEOPLE have generously offered their time and advice in the past several years as this book took shape, first as a dissertation at Rutgers University in 1986 and then in several permutations thereafter. This study would never have been launched without the support and friendship of James Guetti. His presence in this book will, I hope, adequately suggest my personal and intellectual indebtedness to him. The debt is both for specific advice on the manuscript and for more generally teaching me—though I didn't feel I was being "taught"—that "accuracy counts for something."

Thomas R. Edwards deserves special thanks for numerous suggestions as to how the manuscript might be improved. His careful intelligence and his memories of going to drive-in movies both kept my spirits up. George Kearns persistently offered himself as "a hard wall to bounce off of," and I am grateful for his continuing interest in my work, whether in New Jersey, Turkey, or Scotland. George Levine, Andrew Welsh, and William Vesterman at Rutgers all took time out from other obligations to comment on portions of the manuscript, as, at Princeton, did Lee Mitchell and Marc Chénetier. They all have my gratitude. Barry Qualls and Linda Kozusko both offered indefatigable help and good cheer at Rutgers; Emory Elliott and A. Walton Litz offered sane counsel and moral support at Princeton—and they threw some good dinner parties too.

Behind all my work—if I'm lucky—lies the influence of Richard Poirier, whose criticism and classroom presence ensured that never again would American literature be the same. It has been my additional good fortune to study with a number of other extraordinarily talented and inspiring teachers: William H. Pritchard, G. Armour Craig, Christopher Ricks, Paul Fussell, David Kalstone, Elaine Showalter, and William Howarth all deserve a word of thanks. Each of them, in individual ways, quickened my sense of how inventively improbable good writing is and why the improbability matters. Pete Petersen, who first introduced me to American fiction as a sophomore at Shasta College and who let me work on this book in his office weekends in the spring of 1989, deserves special acknowledgment. More than one of the ideas in here sprang from discussions with him over a beer on summer nights in Redding. I also thought often while working on this project of Richard Dalrymple, James Loveall, and Ross Fetters at Shasta College, all of whom baffled and entranced me as a young student with their love of poetry, medieval romance, and B-movies. Their insight, companionship, and assistance of every sort have not been forgotten. They put me on the path of playfulness.

A Louis Bevier fellowship from the Rutgers Graduate School allowed me to finish the dissertation portion of this study, and I here record my gratitude. A sabbatical leave from Princeton University and a fellowship from the American Council of Learned Societies gave me time to revise and expand the manuscript in 1988–89. I am grateful for the support of both institutions. I also wish to thank the English department at U.C. Davis for granting me permission to use Shields Library during my sabbatical year.

A version of chapter 2 first appeared in the 1984 edition of *James Fenimore Cooper: His Country and His Art*, under the careful eye of George Test at SUNY Oneonta. Much of the argument of chapter 7 appeared in "On Flannery O'Connor" (*Raritan: A Quarterly Review* 10, no. 3 [Winter 1991]), while a portion of chapter 8 appeared in "For Once, Then, Pynchon" in *Texas Studies in Literature and Language* 28, no. 2 (Summer 1986). I thank Suzanne Hyman and the editorial board of *Raritan*, and the editorial board of *Texas Studies in Literature and Language* and the University of Texas Press for permission to republish.

Others have helped see this manuscript through in less visible but no less valuable ways. Robert Brown at Princeton University Press has been a more patient and supportive editor than I've had any right to expect. Lauren Oppenheim's help with the manuscript was scrupulously kind. Raymond Cooper (with an assist from Janet Mosholder) helped me escape death by double-density disk, Rick Jacobsen helped move books and files three thousand miles in the summer of 1988, Julie Kowalewski did some emergency photocopying after midnight one Fourth of July, and Carolyn Soule at Carleton College helped me master a new word-processing program. They all have my heartfelt thanks, as do my parents, Edward and Suzanne Kowalewski, and my grandparents, Mary and Gerald Thome, whose love and financial help have constantly steadied me. Nicholas and Sarah Kowalewski, who both showed up in the middle of this book's gestation, have my thanks for knowing when to disrupt Daddy's work schedule and bring him back to the Land of Legos.

As always, my greatest debt of gratitude is to my wife, Catherine Kowalewski, the reader I try hardest to be worthy of. Without her encouragement, her good spirits, and her patience, this book would never have been undertaken, much less finished. It is dedicated to her with "countless ties of love and thought."

Deadly Musings

Reading Violence, Making Sense

> All art is in a sense symbolic; but we say "stop thief" to the
> critic who deliberately transforms an artist's subtle symbol
> into a pedant's stale allegory—a thousand and one nights
> into a convention of shriners.
>
> —*Vladimir Nabokov*, Lectures on Literature

IN BEGINNING to think about American fiction, one could do worse than to
adopt Jake Barnes's more general proposal about life on a drunken night in
Pamplona: "I did not care what it was all about. All I wanted to know was how
to live in it. Maybe if you found out how to live in it you learned from that
what it was all about."[1] Jake's desire to learn eventually what life "is all about"
(though even this possibility is qualified by a "maybe") does not represent an
attempt to reduce, pacify, essentialize, or beautify his existence. It exemplifies
an impatience to get rid of all the "bright ideas" and "fine philosophies" by
means of which he spuriously convinces himself he is learning about life.

A skepticism this deep about interpretive schemes that only *seem* to make life
yield its meaning remains, of course, as potentially disillusioning as it is laudable. "The bill always came," Jake tells us sourly; "that was one of the swell
things you could count on."[2] Yet Jake, to his credit, is as wary of self-disgust
here as he is of what might prompt it. He wishes to discard all his "fine philosophies" not just to be rid of them, not just to see what life in some nihilistic
vacuum might be like. He seems to realize that even the irony so many readers
associate with *The Sun Also Rises* (with its famous deflationary last line) offers
but one more form of potential complacency, one more "bright idea" he must
finally avoid. (Jake's friend Bill Gorton intimates as much when he joshes him
about the Irony and Pity "they're mad about" in New York. "You ought to be
ironical the minute you get out of bed," Bill advises; "You ought to wake up
with your mouth full of pity."[3]) Jake at his most admirable, that is, resembles
the T. S. Eliot who six years later would resist "the use of irony [that gives] the
appearance of a philosophy of life, as something final and not instrumental."
Such a philosophy, Eliot contended, "seems to us an evasion of the difficulty of
living, where it pretends to be a kind of solution of it."[4]

Jake wants out of his ideas and philosophies because life, he feels, asks for
something better. Confronting "the difficulty of living" does not consist of
evading it; it entails making his accounts of that difficulty somehow account-

3

able *to* it. His previous ways of considering "what it was all about" were not "wrong," he concludes, merely satisfied with too little. Thus his resolve to live life rather than interpret it does not simplify or lessen the complexity of his existence. But it does help him realize that his experience will continue to elude and baffle him so long as he feels that it shouldn't, so long as he poses a demand that it hold still long enough to be "explained."

This may seem an odd prelude to a book whose ostensible subject is the presence of violence in American fiction. But Jake's concerns bear importantly upon my own because a desire to "live in" the complexity and detail of American fiction has shaped my investigation of the violence depicted there. It may seem a country-headed thing to say, but the only presence violence has in fiction is verbal. It comes to us not raw and in person, though the powerful illusion that it can is something I will be investigating. A fist, most of us will be pleased to hear, cannot burst through a page and into our face (though this also means we cannot, as readers, try to stop a rape or warn a child in a street about the speeding car headed its way).[5] Violence is always verbally mediated in novels and stories; it is not "there" in language except in the sense that it has been rendered, like a dress from a feed bag, out of it. Violence thus appears in fiction, like everything else with which it shares the page, as something *styled* (styled, not "stylized").

This does not mean, however, that style somehow exists independently of represented acts. Violence in American fiction is not best thought of as in any way separable from its conception in and as verbal form. Its imaginative status consists of the stylistic features not "with which it is endowed" but in which it is begotten. Thus violence per se concerns me less in this study than the imaginative dynamics and expressive forms by and through which it has been depicted. I wish to explore the representation of violence in American fiction only by way of exploring the nature of the verbal conditions—the muses, if you will—that make violence "possible" in certain American works.

American writers have persistently, almost obsessively, turned violence (and I refer here to depictions of physical violence or pain and its aftermath, not psychological violence or examples of metaphorical, "discursive" violence) into an imaginative resource. The resource it most readily provides is its usefulness as a plot device. Violence in American fiction frequently offers a vivid means of dramatizing or initiating some form of conflict and action: whether class or racial tensions, a novel-long search for revenge, or a permanent disruption of someone's view of the world (perhaps a reader's) as a stable or equitable place. Yet most critics are rightly dissatisfied with seeing something so potentially harrowing and gruesome as only a functional fictional device.

Violence in fiction cannot be understood "simply as violence," John Cawelti contends, "for its meaning depends on the place it plays in the overall structure of the action."[6] True enough, but I wish to go farther here, for violence depends for its "meaning" not only upon dramatic action but upon the more fundamental forms of verbal action and imaginative substance by which dramatic action is represented sentence by sentence and scene by scene. My goal is to explore the verbal equivalent of acting styles, as Robert Warshow describes them, in movie Westerns:

> Really, it is not violence at all which is the "point" of the Western movie, but a certain image of man, a style, which expresses itself most clearly in violence. Watch a child with his toy guns and you will see: what most interests him is not (as we so much fear) the fantasy of hurting others, but to work out how a man might look when he shoots or is shot. A hero is one who looks like a hero.
>
> Whatever the limitations of such an idea in experience, it has always been valid in art.[7]

The ways in which individual writers "work out" violence in their fiction directly determines the aesthetic force and perceptual impact that violence has. Thus what I have chosen to focus on (it forms indeed my principle of selection) are authors whose work includes extended depictions of violence, scenes that cannot be thought of as merely functional because their very length and energy outstrip whatever dramatic function they might be said to have initially served.

I use the word "served" here in the most conditional sense, for to say that violence *serves* a dramatic purpose is already to dictate how we might take it up as a subject. We end up with a significantly different angle of approach if we begin by thinking of violence, for instance, not as serving dramatic purposes but as both prompting and enacting stylistic prerogatives. I wish to think of fictional violence—to borrow some of Kenneth Burke's terminology in his startling essay "The Imagery of Killing"—not only in terms of a battle (the depicted action) but in terms of the battlefield itself, both the principles at work in the battle and the ground upon which it takes place:

> The battlefield . . . which permits rival contestants to join in battle, itself "transcends" their factionalism, being "superior" to it, and being "neutral" to their motives, though the conditions of the terrain may happen to favor one faction. The *principles* of war are not themselves warlike, and are ultimately reducible to universal principles of physics and dialectic.[8]

The principles that dictate the representation of violence in fiction consist of nothing more nor less than what a given author can do with words and with the governing assumptions (literary, psychological, or social) that underlie those words.

"Seeing the possibilities" of any medium, as Stanley Cavell asserts, involves seeing what can be done with it, seeing what can empower certain expressive properties with meaning. Thus in the history of movies (to take but one example), narrative films emerged, Cavell argues, because someone "saw the possibilities" of the technical "actualities of film mechanics" (modes of cutting, editing, shot selection, and so on). The very act of "seeing" such actualities, however, which many home movies and newsreels also contain, was inseparable from the realization of what would "give them *significance*":

> The first successful movies—i.e., the first moving pictures accepted as motion pictures—were not applications of a medium that was defined by given possibilities, but the *creation of a medium* by their giving significance to specific possibilities. Only the art itself can discover its possibilities, and the discovery of a new possibility is the discovery of a new medium. A medium is something through which or by means of which something specific gets done or said in particular ways.[9]

Cavell's remarks bear crucially upon my own concerns here because they reflect upon the nature of artistic expression and suggest the critical directions from which it can be most profitably studied. My interest lies in examining violent scenes as a part of the writing from which they emerge rather than in thematically tracing such scenes. The latter approach (which has been attempted before) tends to grant the fiction from which those scenes appear a stabilized rather than a mobile and self-renovating status; it tends to extract acts of violence and discuss them as ex post facto actions (whether explicit or "encoded"), which can then be analyzed or "thematized." I do not wish to impugn the value of such thematic studies, only to supplement them with criticism that proceeds from a different ground. The energy of verbal depiction in scenes of violence in American fiction is decidedly an energy in motion. We are likely to lose track of that imaginative energy, however, if we think of it as something other than generative, if we think of the presence of violence in fiction as somehow distinct from an author's discovery of how it can be *expressed*. It seems less fruitful, in other words, to think of fictional violence as something to which language is applied than to think of it as something that emerges from various attempts to give it imaginative form.

The assertion that fictional violence exists only by virtue of the imaginative shapings and transformations of an author's touch may be mistaken by some readers to mean that I find scenes of violence "self-referential," with no subject but their own language. This would be part of a larger complaint, I take it, that an attention to style in fiction somehow represents a displacement of reality, a relegation of the life and history of which violence forms a part to the status of discourse, a way of banishing the world by replacing it with "texts." This is not my intent. The possibility of someone's thus construing my motives, however, testifies to the difficulties of trying to map out the terrain I wish to explore.

The word "violence" is a catch-all term, a kind of verbal wooden nickel, used with such frequent ease that its actual indeterminate status appears almost self-evidently clear. Yet as John Fraser notes, "there is in fact no one thing, no chemically isolatable and analysable substance, that is violence, any more than there is one thing that is sex, even though it is easy to slip into talking as if there were."[10] The commonplace notion of violence, as the British political scientist W.J.M. MacKenzie suggests, negatively construes it as excessive and uncalled for, something from which, at least officially, we wish to dissociate ourselves and, in all likelihood, connect with someone else: "A Rugby correspondent paying tribute to a pack of forwards might call them 'rugged' or 'vigorous' or even 'forceful.' But to say 'violent' would be to say that they go beyond the limit of the rules as 'we' understand them. Violence is dangerous play."[11]

Violence is thus popularly understood as an act of aggression that is usually destructive, antisocial, and degrading in its consequences and that usually seems deliberate. "The rifle that misfires can kill violently," Jane Tompkins says, "but that's not the kind of thing we're concerned with when we think about violence as a moral issue. Intention has to be involved."[12] But in what ways might intention be involved here? Is violence an action or the "cause" of that action? Is violence an emotion or the result of that emotion? Is it a crime or a disease? And if a disease, what kind: mental or physical? Is it an individual behavioral aberration or a culturally determined reflex? The bewildering array of sociological, psychiatric, juridical, physiological, religious, political, and anthropological answers to questions like these do not, perhaps, affect our practical usage of the word or our ordinary conception of violence. They should, however, effectually erode any firm certainty we may have in thinking about what violence is and how we know about it.

A false or simpleminded clarity about such issues will simply augment the convenience with which we refer to "representations of violence" in fiction without ever questioning the provisionality of stating the matter that way. To use that phrase thoughtlessly is, in effect, already to insist upon an approach to the problem, or in fact to identify it as a "problem." To say that there are representations *of* violence in literature (or film) implies that there is a preexistent something out there, called violence, which is then presented to us via language (or a camera lens) in a novel or a short story (a horror film or a documentary). The truth of such a notion may be more provisional, more procedurally convenient than it first appears.

One can hardly argue that certain nonlinguistic or "nonfictional" acts and occasions we have come to call violent are not actually there, that knifings, rapes, murders, and drive-by shootings do not somehow exist. But how do they "exist" in *literature*? What imaginative conditions allow them to exist? And what happens when those experiences we designate as violent emerge as a part of the exigencies and shapings of verbal form? What I attempt to map out in exploring such questions is what might be called an *epistemology of violence*. I wish to explore not only the disturbing power that scenes of violence have for us but the imaginative sources and consequences of that power. Thus I have set for myself the task of considering not only the question of what we know about or can "make" of violence in fiction but the more reflexive matter of *how* we know what we know about it. I am less interested in what a particular author is "telling us" about violence than in what his depictions of it reveal about him as a writer, about his powers of sympathy and generosity, and about whom and what we are asked to be as readers when engaged with his work.

These matters cannot be fruitfully studied without a close, detailed attentiveness to the writing that brings fictional violence into being. Examining the depiction of violence in fiction involves, for the most part, a "description" of description. This is not to say that other compositional elements such as plot, dialogue, and character do not come into play in such scenes—they obviously do. But by and large violence in fiction is described or witnessed, and thus it consists of the depictive energies of style: the sounds and shapes of sentences, the movements and rhythms of syntax and imagery. These technical aspects of expression exist not for or by themselves but as the locatable signs of an author's imaginative presence in language, or of the attempt to establish (or abolish) such a presence. I am primarily concerned, then, not with the critical uses of violence as a theme but with the ways in which it has been imagined or "performed" in American fiction—the ways in which it exists not as an isolated element or subject but as the conformation, at a given moment, of a larger stylistic field of force. I wish to treat scenes of violence, to borrow the physicist Hermann Weyl's phrase for subatomic particles, as imaginative "energy knots."[13]

This brings me back to Jake Barnes, for Jake appeals to me as a model of critical independence and sensitivity because his human need to feel a part of life and his resolve to "learn how to live in it" remain more important than the theoretical possibility that these needs and resolves can never actually be fulfilled. This does not mean, it is worth repeating, that Jake has any illusions about simplifying his existence. But he does intend to scrutinize (and even, if necessary, dispense with) the means by which his life might be held to account. Jake seems to have a dawning awareness (to quote John Lennon's lovely remark) that life is what happens while we're busy making other plans. American fiction, too, is what happens while critics (myself included) are busy telling us what it's up to. The most admirable readers of that fiction do their best to "live in" the stories and the novels they consider. (This is not, it should be clear, the same as "living out" that fiction, affecting unconventional mores—living in a loft or sipping kirsch—in hopes of being taken for a character in a novel.) Such commendable readers are, I want to say, a pushover for the fiction they study. In a critical atmosphere thick with resistance to and paranoia about the ideological con games in society, such an assertion may seem at best provincial, at worst hopelessly obtuse. I intend it as neither. Living in the books they care about, remaining committed to an accurate description of their imaginative energies, does not mean that such readers are uncritical of them, nor does it mean that they necessarily think of them, in William Bennett's notorious phrase, as a legacy to be reclaimed. What it does mean is that they cannot help but tend and attend to such material admiringly as well as critically. This is less for personal reasons than, as Wendell Berry says, "in proper discharge of an obligation": "To pay attention is to come into the presence of a subject. In one of the root senses, it is to 'stretch toward' a subject, in a kind of aspiration. We speak of 'paying attention' because of a correct perception that attention is owed."[14]

"Why isn't there more talk about pleasure, about the excitement of witnessing a performance, about the excitement that goes into a performance of any kind?" The Frostean challenge Richard Poirier extended in 1971, in his remarkable book *The Performing Self*, lies as a motivating force behind this study. His call for a "close-up, detailed concern for performance, for enactment and execution in a work of art" seems more pertinent than ever, if only because so few people now seem willing to admit that "talking about the experience of any work of art is more difficult than talking about the theory of it, or the issues in it, or the history around it."[15] Such an approach in regards to literature is not, as I will demonstrate, "ahistorical" (to mention but one scarlet *A* of shame in contemporary criticism). Nor is it a thoughtless or escapist glorification of the "fun" in art. Instead, it represents a rigorous (though unsomber) investigation into the nature of literary expression, one which assumes that the shifty articulations of power in verbal artistry are best studied in their alloyed particularity. The kinds of questions such an approach poses—how is this novel reaching us? what relation does its author have to this material? how is his or her narrative authority established? what kind of complexity is in question here?—can be profitably answered only with some kind of text in front of us, some stage or page upon which a performer struggles to shape a self out of the recalcitrant expressive materials at his or her disposal.

"Imagining an audience for such criticism," Poirier asserts,

> the critic thinks not of a public with Issues and Topics at the ready, but rather of a group of like- minded people who find pleasure in certain intensive acts of looking and listening. Looking and listening to something with such a group, imaginary

or real, means checking out responses, pointing to particular features, asking detailed questions, sharing momentary excitements.[16]

The energy expended in such efforts to describe what we see, hear, and feel in a given story or novel will be too involved (too much the discharging of the debt we owe to what has moved us) to allow the dictates of critical fashion to carry much weight. Current temptations to willful obscurity, mock-apocalyptic authority, or pun-infested rhetorical "sexiness" in criticism will be seen, in the light of such efforts, for exactly what they are: critical concessions (like Sno-Kones and Mars bars) on sale only during intermission. Literary criticism is seldom as good—as flexible, attentive, and marveling—as it can be, but this testifies, ultimately, less to the unresponsiveness of critics than to the energy and inventiveness of what they attempt to describe. This study proceeds upon one fundamental conviction: the finest works of American fiction continue to move and entertain us because they continue to be better than what we have to say about them.

Here, as one kind of "proof," is a moment from *Moby-Dick* in which, as the chapter title would have it, Stubb kills a whale:

"Haul in—haul in!" cried Stubb to the bowsman; and, facing round towards the whale, all hands began pulling the boat up to him, while yet the boat was being towed on. Soon ranging up by his flank, Stubb . . . darted dart after dart into the flying fish. . . . The red tide now poured from all sides of the monster like brooks down a hill. His tormented body rolled not in brine but in blood, which bubbled and seethed for furlongs behind in their wake. The slanting sun playing upon this crimson pond in the sea, sent back its reflection into every face, so that they all glowed to each other like red men. And all the while, jet after jet of white smoke was agonizingly shot from the spiracle of the whale, and vehement puff after puff from the mouth of the excited headsman; as at every dart, hauling in upon his crooked lance (by the line attached to it), Stubb straightened it again and again, by a few rapid blows against the gunwale, then again and again sent it into the whale.

"Pull up—pull up!" he now cried to the bowsman, as the waning whale relaxed in his wrath. "Pull up!—close to!" and the boat ranged along the fish's flank. When reaching far over the bow, Stubb slowly churned his long sharp lance into the fish, and kept it there, carefully churning and churning, as if cautiously seeking to feel after some gold watch that the whale might have swallowed, and which he was fearful of breaking ere he could hook it out. But that gold watch he sought was the innermost life of the fish. And now it is struck; for, starting from his trance into that unspeakable thing called his "flurry," the monster horribly wallowed in his blood, overwrapped himself in impenetrable, mad, boiling spray, so that the imperilled craft, instantly dropping astern, had much ado blindly to struggle out from that phrensied twilight into the clear air of the day.

And now abating in his flurry, the whale once more rolled out into view; surging from side to side; spasmodically dilating and contracting his spout-hole, with sharp, cracking, agonized respirations. At last, gush after gush of clotted red gore, as if it had been purple lees of red wine, shot into the frighted air; and falling back again, ran dripping down his motionless flanks into the sea. His heart had burst!

"He's dead, Mr. Stubb," said Tashtego.

"Yes; both pipes smoked out!" and withdrawing his own from his mouth, Stubb scattered the dead ashes over the water; and, for a moment, stood thoughtfully eyeing the vast corpse he had made.[17]

American fiction is not for hemophobics. The energies of its performance are often as gut-wrenching or discomfiting as they are pleasurable, as heart-rending in pain as in lyric aspiration. They play themselves out not only on our pulses (to invoke John Keats's terms) but along our spines and in the pit of our stomachs. In studying fictional violence one must explore the power of words to sicken and befoul as well as freshen and redeem. This does not mean we have to surrender our moral intelligence in encountering scenes of violence, any more than Melville has surrendered his here. But it does mean that our responsiveness will be put to some fairly harsh tests. After such knowledge, what innocence?

Yet it is a sign of Melville's genius and humanity in this moment that he is not content with merely the "knowledge" of brutality. There is a terrifying vitality in the way he imagines this scene, and that itself forms one kind of imaginative counteragent to its bleak picture of monumental death. Of course, the monumentality of the whale itself offers the chance to turn its death here into a spectacle that could prove less moving than sensationalistic, less poignant than "heroic"—a depiction of suffering whose dimensions are too overwhelming to have the pathos of merely human pain (Lear on the heath, not a friend on an I.V. expiring slowly in the hospital). But Melville manages to invoke and combine the most moving of both possibilities here. He seems as far from glorifying this butchery as he is from caricaturing Stubb's participation in it.

The idiomatic reticence of Stubb and Tashtego at the end of this scene is in marked contrast to, first, the action and adrenaline of the chase, then the unbearable evocation of the dying whale's vulnerability and pain in simply trying to breathe, and finally, the Jacobean extravagance of a grotesque rain of "clotted red gore." Stubb's laconic rejoinder at the end here serves as one kind of response to this scene. His "thoughtful" eyes seem, for a moment at least, to regard this dead animal as not just the prize of venture capitalism but a "vast corpse" he has brutally "made." His action of emptying his pipe does not seem a funerary gesture on his part (it has simply gone out in the course of the chase), yet the imagistic parallels between whale and man Melville draws serve to attribute the dignity of that action to Stubb anyway. Melville can, that is, by simple deployments of imagery, suggest that a single feeling about this scene is insufficient. He can invest the most informal and unremarkable of gestures (the emptying of a pipe) with an austere formality expressive of both Stubb's character and the larger thematic dimensions of the novel as a whole.

Melville's respect for Stubb's inarticulate thoughts can be gentle and un-judgmental even as he gives full vent to his own fascinated horror at the slaughterous precision and efficiency with which this whale is killed. Yet even here, in the midst of a remarkable display of how words and images can them-selves resist conditioned reflexes in our language (the danger, in this case, of responding only single-mindedly to experience), Melville reminds us that words can also obstruct the very experience they designate. The word "flurry," with its connotations of sudden gusting snow, is not inadequate to the "un-speakability" of the "phrensied twilight" of showering blood and saltwater that the dying whale creates, but neither, Melville suggests, does it quite capture the experience itself.

There seems little point in pretending that American authors and their read-ers are not often as fascinated as they are horrified by instances of violence. A fully human view of life will have to admit not only to our commendable wish to look away from, say, a traffic accident, but also to the difficulty many have in trying to do so. It will have to acknowledge, that is, our deep-seated impulse to see or even vicariously experience what we know we should not (and will not) want to see. What can be most intriguing about such moments in fiction is that many authors feel they must account for an experience they in many ways wish they could "forget" or at least not imagine.

In this passage, what proves incongruously affecting is the unanticipated delicacy of Stubb's "slowly," "carefully," "cautiously" churning his sharpened lance in the whale as if fearful of breaking a fragile gold watch. In a way typical of *Moby-Dick*, this image exfoliates in several simultaneous dimensions. It serves to suggest the delicacy of the whale's life, which can be so easily broken or "cracked," as well as the incongruity that such fragility and vulnerability lie at the heart of a creature so massive and imposing. But as much as it reflects on the whale, the image also forms part of a frightened recognition of how easily Stubb's deadly impersonal expertise can be imagined as exactly its oppo-site, as discretion or a judicious caution that would normally protect and preserve.

The terrifying contrast of intimacy and brutality Melville notes in Stubb's actions is not dissimilar to his own apparent uneasiness in being able to de-scribe them. He goes so far as to pull the carpet out from under his own metaphor ("but that gold watch he sought was the innermost life of the fish"), as if he himself were momentarily anxious about his own impulse to trope all he touches. Simultaneously compelled and repulsed both by what he depicts and by his ability to depict it, Melville here resembles Joyce Carol Oates as she recalls an image "indelibly imprinted" in her memory, that of "the doomed South Korean lightweight [boxer] Duk Koo-Kim struggling [in his death match] to rise from the canvas after a blow of [Ray] Mancini's burst a blood vessel in his brain—as if his body possessed its own demonic will even at the threshold of death."[18] If Oates is haunted by this image (and who wouldn't be?), its indelibility is due not only to Koo-Kim's actions themselves but to the analogy that they so frighteningly suggest. Thus in one self-torturing sense, Oates herself, not just the aggressor Mancini, is "responsible" for the movements of Koo-Kim's fatally injured body: Oates cannot help what she has seen but neither, in a sense, can she help what it *seems like*. Posing the analogy of a "demonic will" with which a body might be possessed here is simply a way of trying to get something straight, to understand that by which one is haunted. "Getting it straight," however, does not release one from a sense of implicated horror; it merely measures the depth of the implication. Such matters should be, in Melville's words, unspeakable, but even he knows it is often only pretty to think so.[19]

Oates mentions this image in her compelling book on boxing, and her discussion there of the sudden complicitous "*frisson* of dread" that can affect a spectator watching a boxing match raises issues that will be repeatedly germane to this study:

> To watch boxing closely, and seriously, is to risk moments of what might be called animal panic—a sense not only that something very ugly is happening but that, by watching it, one is an accomplice. This awareness, or revelation, or weakness . . . can come at any instant, unanticipated and unbidden; though of course it tends to sweep over the viewer when he is watching a really violent match. I feel it as vertigo—breathlessness—a repugnance beyond language: a sheerly physical loathing. That it is also, or even primarily, self-loathing goes without saying.
>
> For boxing really isn't metaphor, it is the thing in itself. And my predilection for watching matches on tape, when the outcomes are known, doesn't alter the fact that, as the matches occurred, they occurred in the present tense, and for one time only. The rest is subterfuge—the intellectual's uneasy "control" of his material.[20]

The stakes in the boxing ring are significantly different from those in literature, as nobody actually dies in the latter. But as I will discuss more fully in regard to realism, such an assertion can be made to seem merely a part of our uneasy "control" of a given instance of violence, a way of mentally or emotionally accommodating scenes or actions whose qualities are more disturbing than it is comfortable for us to acknowledge. Gloucester doesn't really have his eyes put out in *King Lear*, but does "knowing" that make the scene any less unbearable?

"The sickness of any violent spectacle," David Bromwich says in a discussion of Fritz Lang's movie *The Big Heat*, "may not be that it is seen, as such" but that a reader or viewer's response "is organized around the pleasure of seeing it."[21] The feeling of being an accomplice in watching boxing and reading fiction would seem to differ, however, in that the ugliness of the physical violence Oates describes cannot be taken as metaphoric (or not, at least, for very long). Neither can it, so to speak, be attributed to an author. (We might have conspiracy theories about fixed fights, but they too would form part of a protective gesture here, a way of lessening or mitigating the shock of the violence seen.) In boxing, our complicity as a viewer, when it is felt as such, seems to stem from the *fact* of witnessing violence. Our very ability to watch suddenly seems a form of injustice. When boxing turns ugly we do not respond so much as we instinctively react. We see not a performance but a stark occurrence that cannot be "read" or construed in a different way and whose only structuring principle is temporal duration, the time it takes to throw or receive one shattering blow after another.

Such violent moments, as we shall see, have fascinated American authors. Those whose fiction we call realistic strive persistently for the illusion that the depicted action of a novel answers more to life (the physical forces of adrenaline and impact in a fight, for instance) than to an author at his desk. But even writers who are not primarily realistic in their imagining seem intrigued by actions that cannot, in life, be properly ascribed, that resist the attributions of significance or justification we may nevertheless try to impose upon them. The phrase "senseless violence" is worth considering in this regard. What we seem to mean by "senseless" is "motiveless," as when Coleridge speaks of Iago's "motive-less malignancy." But lack of motive forms only one component of a larger absence, one that might more precisely be termed "contextless," "uninterpretable," "unaccommodated," "unintelligible," perhaps even "selfless."

If we know, for instance, that a serial killer has repeatedly and brutally murdered others with indifference or even pleasure, we may be unable to conceive of a "self" capable of such actions, at least until someone (probably a psychiatrist) evokes its conceivability by "explaining" those actions. The killer's "self" does not seem to consist of his physical person. It would seem instead to exist more as the *possibility* of motivational coherence, as some imaginable source of motives and feelings or, as Robert Garis puts it, "a field for a moral activity":

The existence of a self behind or beneath or beyond or above visible and audible behaviour is the creation of our own act of imagination and faith; we create the self of others. Yet this creation is, in ordinary experience, so automatic, so habitual as hardly to deserve the name. The question hardly interests us until the habit is frustrated. . . . When an Adolf Eichmann, for instance, interrupts the mechanism of faith, we react by instituting a search for signs of that moral activity. We are not inquiring whether that activity has been carried on to good effect; we are already certain that it has not. We are inquiring whether that activity has taken place at all, whether, indeed, there actually is a field, a self, in which that activity could possibly take place.[22]

Hayden White and Leo Bersani and Ulysse Dutoit, among others, have discussed the normalizing and moralizing tendencies inherent in "narrativizing" modes of perception and thought and the implications such modes have in regards to artistic, historical, and psychiatric representation.[23] This is not the place to summarize the full extent of their engaging work, but in light of it we can see how previous critical considerations of fictional violence have assumed an almost inevitable shape.

With our everyday "creations" of others' selves so automatic a perceptual reflex, and with our practical sense that violence is gratuitous when it is unassimilable or uninterpretable, it would seem only natural that the proper study of fictional violence would consist of providing contexts within which to accommodate, assimilate, and "explain" such scenes. Anything less might itself seem gratuitous, a form of savoring the violence that a critical study claims to investigate. The liveliest and most discerning investigation yet written on represented violence, John Fraser's *Violence in the Arts*, falls prey to something like this criticism. Fraser's very ambitiousness in considering the widest possible range of both actual and represented violence (and the latter includes everything from horror movies and thrillers to paintings by Goya, Bosch, and Daumier) forces him, in the name of inclusiveness, to extract scenes of violence from their context and assemble a sort of anthology of atrocities, one that ends up giving the impression of a grim relish for the topic.

However helpful Fraser's book, that is, it sometimes resembles the colloquies in which ardent fans of Clint Eastwood or Charles Bronson movies sometimes engage, comparing notes about (and reenactments of) violent scenes.[24] One of the pitfalls awaiting a study like this is the temptation inadvertently to romanticize scenes of violence by taking a sort of bleak pride in their recalcitrance to moralizing. The danger consists of overemphasizing the specialness of violence in human experience as some kind of ultimate confrontation, some furious sign of "real" life.[25] The Scylla to this Charybdis consists of a tendency

15

in the opposite direction: a complacency in the face of fictional suffering and pain, a refusal to admit just how deep and frightening the impact of certain depictions of violence can actually be. An eagerness to argue too strenuously for the imaginative power of violence seems as unhelpful as the impulse to tame and domesticate that power by too glibly asserting that others romanticize it. An overwillingness to shock and provoke others seems as inhibitive as the pretense of unshockability.

A survey, even a partial survey such as this, of the ways in which violence has been depicted in American fiction provides more than the chance to focus upon particular scenes in individual novels and stories. It affords, in addition, a useful vantage from which to consider and evaluate the imaginative ambitions of that fiction and what criticism does to and with those ambitions, how it renders a subject like violence a "subject," an occasion for interpretation, a site for hermeneutic excavation. Much present criticism seems hampered by its tendency to change violence into Violence. It embues violence with the status of a metaphysical phenomenon (one around which we might arrange a colloquium or assemble a special issue of a journal) that can somehow be detached from the verbal circumstances that locate and bring it to life in the first place. The liabilities of such an approach are more than hypothetical. An overinsistence upon seeing the "meta" in the physical, as Arthur Krystal asserts, represents a distorting liability: "a drawback of gazing at the skull beneath the skin is that features in full view sometimes get overlooked."[26] The need to attribute some kind of interpretive significance to fictional violence frequently gets in the way of actually describing what is there in the first place.

One measure of the disturbing power that scenes of violence have for us is the fact that a descriptive investigation of *how* it has been represented in American fiction has not heretofore been attempted. Violence is so palpably and viscerally *there* in those works that an investigation of how it imaginatively takes shape might seem if not gratuitous then simply superfluous: why describe such scenes? Just read them and cringe. Yet to state matters baldly, violent scenes in American fiction are not only brutal, bleak, and gratuitous (though they are all of those, often unrelievedly). They are also, by turns, comic, witty, poignant, and sometimes, strangely enough, even terrifyingly beautiful. However deadly and lacerating these scenes often are, the verbal resourcefulness and forms of intensity they display and enact are too richly multiple to be ignored or watched from a distance. Criticism has not been in a position to attend properly to such matters, however, because it has tended to focus on the "why" and the "wherefore" of violence, on the sociocultural ideologies it purportedly exemplifies or encodes and the kinds of empathy or callousness our imaginative "complicity" in it promotes.

The violence depicted in American fiction can of course be seen as implicated in the social and political arrangements of a given era or in the personal obsessions of a particular author. But the usefulness of any study of such implications will be radically abbreviated if it misconstrues or oversimplifies the imaginative status of the very thing it declares to be implicated. A case in point is Richard Slotkin's investigation of how depictions of violence on the American frontier have exemplified competing cultural anxieties and conflicting visions of nature. "Our heroes and their narratives," he concludes,

> are an index to our character and our role in the universe. . . . Under the aspect of mythology and historical distance, the acts and motives of the woodchopper, the whale and bear hunter, the Indian fighter, and the deerslayer have an air of simplicity and purity that makes them seem finely heroic expressions of an admirable quality of the human spirit. They seem to stand on a commanding ridge, while we are still tangled in the complexities of the world and the wilderness. But their apparent independence of time and consequence is an illusion; a closely woven chain of time and consequence binds their world to ours. Set the statuesque figures and their piled trophies in motion through space and time, and a more familiar landscape emerges—the whale, buffalo, and bear hunted to the verge of extinction for pleasure in killing and "scalped" for fame and the profit in hides by men like Buffalo Bill; the buffalo meat left to rot, till acres of prairie were covered with heaps of whitening bones, and the bones then ground for fertilizer; the Indian debased, impoverished, and killed in return for his gifts; the land and its people, its "dark" people especially, economically exploited and wasted; the warfare between man and nature, between race and race, exalted as a kind of heroic ideal; the piles of wrecked and rusted cars, heaped like Tartar pyramids of death-cracked, weather-browned, rain-rotted skulls, to signify our passage through the land.[27]

This panorama of brutality and waste is both sobering and rhetorically effective and it serves to emphasize, as does the rest of Slotkin's lengthy book, the darker aspects of American individualism and initiative upon which many would prefer not to dwell. Yet whatever insight this passage offers about the "American character," the status of the "mythic" evidence marshaled for its claims is abstract and immaterial. In this sense Slotkin's paradigm, to adapt Denis Donoghue's comments on another critic, "seems to have preceded the need of it; it has an air of applied romance."[28]

Of course, Slotkin is dealing with more than simply literary material here, and I am not questioning the validity of his historical continuum of exploitative consequence. What I am calling attention to are the aerodynamics that allow for the rhetorical swoops and dips of this passage. The signs of American restiveness and remorseless exploitation here (acres of rotting buffalo corpses,

17

piles of wrecked cars) are taken as images sufficient in and of themselves to carry Slotkin's argument or at least to extend his grammar. And who would want to disagree? Certainly no one wants to look like an apologist for Buffalo Bill. Yet Slotkin's way of dealing with violence is as a represented fact, not a fact of representation. Or rather, he takes fictional instances of violence to be merely functional, bits of paraphrasable action that constitute part of an ideological "index," a plot or a narrative that we are to render intelligible by dint of interpretation.

Slotkin's indifference to how these scenes are actually depicted and to what verbal features distinguish them from or connect them with the rest of a text, makes him representative of a sizable portion of contemporary criticism. There is relatively scant attention paid today to how something is said in fiction. I refer here not just to some connoisseurship of *le mot juste* but to a more basic attentiveness to aural or auditory forms of imagining, a sensitivity to the idioms and rhythms of an author's voice rather than to merely what that voice represents. Critical energy is now more immediately engaged by and devoted to some image or aspect of represented life than by the verbal choices those images exemplify and the consequences attendant upon those choices. ("A criticism that loves imagery," Helen Vendler reminds us, "is likely to slight both phrasing and syntax."[29]) The effort to gain leverage on a text, to lift images from books and then subsume or "implicate" them within ideological categories (say, of race, gender, class, or ethnicity) seems ultimately less rewarding to me than an attention to the more subtle and revealing movements of mind by which a writer entertains and then resists and reimagines his own images and ideas. American fiction still seldom gets a *hearing* in contemporary criticism, though it sometimes seems to be on trial.

In this instance, Slotkin has a stake in keeping the heroes he treats "mythological," distant not only from our own time but from the novels in which their claims to legendary status might be complicated by an author's other motives. If Natty Bumppo, for instance, can be said to stand on a commanding ridge, it is because he stands free from both the entangled complexities of our own world and, more importantly, those of Cooper's narrative voice. So although I find Slotkin's book valuable as a study of the mythic components of the American character, its usefulness in regards to violence in American fiction seems to me more tenuous.[30]

In carefully watching and listening to the movements of certain authorial temperaments as construable in a given verbal performance, I will, I'm afraid, have little patience with criticism that operates, as it were, a week after the performance is over, when the special circumstances of a given verbal sequence have faded in memory or been negligently or willfully misapprehended. There can be no responsible critical speculations about violence in American fiction, about submerged ideologies and implied complicity, until and unless we carefully differentiate among the ways it has been conceived in and as verbal form, the ways it exists on the surface of particular novels and stories, *in*, not just beneath or behind, them. This calls for a resistance to any account that ignores or simplifies the inventive, troubled, or volatile features of a work in order to get better critical mileage. I wish to put violence back into texts, not abstract it out of them.

This study thus reverses the usual critical conceptions of violence and the interpretive models that support them. Violence in American fiction has generally been studied in a manner I would characterize as translative. It has been taken to be "about" something besides itself. Scenes of violence have been translated into psychosexual, mythic, or ideological vocabularies separate from and exterior to the writing by which those scenes are constituted. Critical focus has emphasized not the language or imaginative substance of fictional violence but thematic and ideological processes or circumstances that are conceived as being prior or parallel to it. Thus violence has been variously interpreted as a structuring metaphor for an American myth of regeneration (in Slotkin), a vehicle for dramatizing the working of racial prejudice (in Carolyn Karcher's *Shadow over the Promised Land*) or deromanticizing the myth of the Old South and invoking the salutary power of order (in Louise Gossett's *Violence in Recent Southern Fiction*), or an exemplification of divergent American conceptions of time and fate (in William Frohock's *The Novel of Violence in America*). In each case, fictional violence has been variously conceptualized as a kind of critical rosetta stone, one that provides thematic or ideological inscriptions, encryptings, or encodings that run parallel to or are embedded within violent scenes.[31]

Such approaches to literature are not entirely dissimilar to the more recent and general trend in literary studies to turn away from an attention to language as such in favor of placing literature within the larger contexts of history, politics, class and gender concerns, and cultural conditions of production. I sympathize with and applaud the motives behind this trend, which J. Hillis Miller rightly characterizes as a demand that we as critics be "ethically and politically responsible in our teaching and writing" and that we "grapple with realities rather than with the impalpabilities of theoretical abstractions."[32] Yet I find the critical consequences of those motives troublesome.

What current contextual approaches too often do is conceive of literary works as merely the puppets of processes outside of themselves. They render novels and stories subsidiary to the social or cultural conditions that supposedly "account" for them. They tend to see any given verbal occasion as dramatizing, or referable to, or the product of, such conditions, and they take those conditions to be more deserving of our interrogative energy than the language they are seen to originate and control. In fact, "the mere mention of broader social contexts" now often seems to function, as Noel Carroll puts it, "rather like the Seventh Cavalry did in old movies."[33] The problem with such arguments is that they frequently depend upon and confirm our assumptions, first, that we can indeed pinpoint such processes, and second, that they at least are clearly understood, that they are somehow less controversial, less marked with or by theoretical difficulties, than the texts they are brought in to resolve.

What this usually boils down to, in fact, is that we know far less about such extraliterary processes than we do about the present verbal instance for which they are meant to "account." Such contexts too often have, as James Guetti puts it, "the apparent solidity of things seen on a periphery."[34] The critics utilizing such contextualizing strategies thus frequently assume what we ask them to prove, they solicit assent as the price of admission to their insights. They ask us to disregard or attend only fleetingly to what appears on the page in favor of a novel's *real* significance, even if that goes against the imaginative grain of a work. "To see politics everywhere is one thing," Thomas R. Edwards asserts, "probably a salutary thing on the whole, but to see it there at the expense of the particular and obvious qualities of the object observed is [both] dangerous [and] impoverishing."[35]

This study aims not at debunking but at counterbalancing such approaches. I have purposefully run counter to the pervasive conception of criticism as a kind of interpretive alchemy, one meant to distill or refine ideological issues out of particular verbal occasions without considering the nature and imaginative properties of their source elements. The disconcerting and saddening notion in much contemporary criticism (and one that all the studies of violence I cite more or less perpetuate) is that criticism is to take shape as an interpretive act whose necessary precondition is a neglect and transformation of how an author says a thing. This is saddening because so little care is taken in watching or listening to an author's attempts to shape a voice in language. It is disconcerting because a close attention to the imaginative motions of those attempts offers, to my mind, the best chance we have of examining the literary workings of power and desire that most contextual critics set out to investigate in the first place.

It is a truism—or, in John Fraser's words, a sad-but-truism—in contemporary criticism that critical "description," in any neutral sense, is impossible, and that any description of a text's features and movements is already a *prescription*. Our terms, we hear, are already laden with value, interest, and perspective. They are always covertly ideological, we are told, and they predetermine the shape of our critical attention and dictate our choices of topic and focus. Our accounts of literature are never "preinterpretive," and the evidence we might marshal in trying to prove otherwise would be not neutral but simply already self-implicated.

All critical argument, to be sure, builds some kind of case; it always to some degree "creates" the text it encounters by establishing certain "facts" and ignoring others. Nevertheless, there are still readily apparent differences between critics who read for evidence to support an exterior or "buried" claim—who conceive of novels, in William Gass's words, "as platforms to speak from [or] middens from which may be scratched important messages for mankind"[36]—and those who attempt to describe their experience of a text from the inside out, from the midst of a story's verbal life and action. Those in the latter group will remain unwilling to discount, annul, or filter out the particularities and complications of the language that cues and controls their responses. This recalcitrance entails more than a curatorial displeasure in people leaving their fingerprints on "masterpieces." It exemplifies a far more fundamental misgiving, one grounded in the conviction that any attempt to reduce, purify, simplify, or otherwise ignore a writer's engagement with language represents not a tinkering with ornamental superfluities but the erasure of all a writer ever has in struggling to shape an identity in words.

My methodological model in this study is Ludwig Wittgenstein, especially the Wittgenstein of *Philosophical Investigations*, whose descriptive scrupulosity constantly serves to emphasize how many different things we do or can do with words, and what their effect on us in various situations *seems* to be. The fact that this "seeming" offers the only ground on which we can proceed does not, for Wittgenstein, constitute an epistemological inhibition. It simply represents a given, a wall against which a writer serves. His emphasis is always differentiating, calling attention to the multiple imaginative functions of verbal expressions and the linguistic contexts within which they gain their life. His dedication to describing that verbal life as precisely as he can is everywhere apparent. "Mere description," he says, "is so difficult because one believes that one needs to fill out the facts in order to understand them. It is as if one saw a screen with scattered colour-patches, and said: the way they are here they are unintelligible; they only make sense when one completes them into a shape.— Whereas I want to say: Here *is* the whole. (If you complete it, you falsify it.)"[37]

Adopting this descriptive model means, in practical terms, that I have not restricted my commentary on the fiction I consider to violent scenes, for I wish to describe how those scenes are situated within and controlled by the imaginative atmosphere established in a given piece of fiction. I have thus found it necessary at points to quote extensively, to evaluate as much of the language

21

of a given scene as I possibly can. This is a less minor point than it may seem. Many contemporary critical conceptions of what literature is (and of how we ought to discuss it) are enabled by critics' *not* quoting at length, by their variously "absorbing" texts, either through the use of ellipses or, more typically, by scissoring up and incorporating snippets of a passage into their own paraphrases in such a way that its imaginative status is altered and denatured in the retelling. This is less a matter of quoting out of context than an indication of how context is construed in the first place. Critical quotation is not, I wish to suggest, simply a subordinate technical device in interpretation. Our methods and styles of quotation themselves embody assumptions not only about what will count as evidence but about what it means for evidence to *count*. Simple decisions about critical quotation have, as I will show in relation to Cooper, Poe, Crane, and Hemingway, directly determined the way in which certain authors have been previously read and taught.

I have also tried to circumvent some of the pitfalls distinctive to certain previous examinations of style in literature. I have attempted to avoid critical terms that tend to absorb and ultimately replace the verbal phenomena they seek to describe. I have also tried to avoid the temptation to make style "mean" in certain circular, preordained ways—ways designed to prop up interpretive fictions of "organic" unity and coherence. I resist, that is, the duty of a critic as Jean-Paul Sartre formulated it over fifty years ago: "A fictional technique always relates back to the novelist's metaphysics. The critic's task is to define the latter before evaluating the former."[38] This temptation consists of taking what we know of a writer outside of his works and reading it back into his style, thus "discovering" in the style what we already know. What this amounts to is a subordination of an author's imagination to a prior metaphysics or moral code or personal obsession, one his or her writing cannot then challenge or ignore or simply grow weary of, but merely express and exemplify. (In regards to Hemingway in particular the limits of this approach will be made apparent.)

This doubling-back to find substantiation in a writer's work of dicta spelled out elsewhere in letters, essays, interviews, or biographies usually entails siphoning off our attention from a particular passage or work under consideration. Though I will occasionally allude to such extratextual material, I do so only in order to expand upon tendencies exfoliated in the writing itself. My concern is with the aesthetic attitudes visible and implied in a given performance rather than with speculations about their biographical or social origins. I begin with the assumption that style reflects less a view of the world than the mind's form of address in considering it. It exemplifies, most fundamentally, an attitude toward writing, a concern (in every sense) with what a person can do with words. Stylistic choices represent more than a writer's means of imagining life. They also evince how he wishes to stand in relation to his characters and thus how he stands in relation to the pain and suffering they undergo, by which he can, in turn, seem appalled or indifferent or even amused.

My aim in this study, as a consequence of such convictions, is not to be encyclopedic but to be descriptively sufficient in a limited number of cases. I leave exhaustiveness, in the words of an eminent Bulgarian essayist, to those who have no other recourse. Given the hundreds of American novels and stories that include violence there can be no question of choosing the "right" texts, and there are, of course, distinguished bodies of achievement upon which this study does not touch. My selection of authors was guided by the wish to display an array of works that would suggest just how diversified the range of stylistic environments from which fictional violence emerges actually is. The substantial—and in Cooper and Faulkner's case, prodigious—output of all the authors I consider has also made limitation mandatory, and I have not hesitated to be selective according to my own tastes. My hope, of course, is that my critical methods and forms of attention, will have some usefulness beyond the material I examine here and that they will prove illuminating in regard to certain other works and authors as well.

These essays offer less an argumentative progression than an extended attempt to articulate a rough scale of fictional effects upon which each of the authors I treat might be placed. At one end of this hypothetical scale would be the purest example of "straight" realism, of an "unvoiced" narrative that is experienced as formless, as devoid of the felt presence of a forming author, and that implicitly invites us to mis-take the formlessness of its verbal action for some kind of nonverbal life. At the other end of the scale would be the richest possible example of a novel or a story that is conspicuously "voiced," whose author flaunts the wordiness of his words, and who constantly and variously reminds us that we are never out of a verbal orbit in reading his work. The realistic violence such fiction includes will be largely, perhaps even completely, absorbed and denatured and denied an imaginative autonomy more compelling than its generative fuel of verbal display. Leaving the ends of this scale deliberately hypothetical and utopian will provide room for a more flexible responsiveness with which to consider the run of a given text's verbal life.

It will also help correct the fairly prevalent notion that fictional violence is or should be treated as if it were primarily realistic. Though realism forms a powerful descriptive mode in American fiction, not all the violence in that fiction has been realistically depicted. I begin by describing the narrative conditions that need to obtain in order for violence to seem realistic. Then, author by author, I detail what happens when those conditions are variously altered

23

and leavened by the workings of fictional voice. Many of the works under consideration here challenge the conception of verbal "life" that the academic intelligence extracts from the language of fiction. They implicitly question and test current critical notions that language always signifies or communicates or "means" something—or, with a deconstructive twist, that it always wants to but never quite can. Violent scenes are particularly useful in this regard because they are always, to some degree, violent. They can never, it would seem, entirely shake the specter of realism, the signifying or conceptualizing power of words to conjure up vivid illusions of nonverbal life.

But that specter, that one aspect of language, can always be *made*, in critical discussion of a work, to cancel out the other motives and effects of which our verbal imaginations are capable. By taking the capacity of language to signify or "mean" as its most intimate possibility, its only imaginative function (or by relying upon that conception in order to deconstruct it), we frequently fail to recognize how often such capacities do not characterize our experience of words, how often certain fictional conditions make meaning or communication or signification a sufferance or a courtesy rather than an obligation. Scant critical attention has been paid to what happens when a "real" subject like violence takes shape in writing that, as William Carlos Williams puts it, is not "dissociated from natural objects and specified meanings" but "liberated from the usual quality of that meaning by transposition into another medium, the imagination."[39] Because fictional violence is elsewhere so disturbing, so "unliberated" from morbid realism, adequate descriptions of what it is like when it is not primarily realistic are more difficult, but also more rewarding. The true focus of this book is, of necessity, the language of American fiction, its shapings and deshapings, its imaginative processes and effects. A study of our ambivalence about violence, of how we are both fascinated with and repulsed by it is, for me, a study of how refreshingly heterogeneous depictions of violence are in American fiction and of how they resist and elude most of our critical methods of accounting for their power.

Invisible Ink

VIOLENCE AND REALISTIC IMAGINING

"IF IT SOUNDS like writing, I rewrite it": so Elmore "Dutch" Leonard, writer of crime fiction and author of dozens of novels and screenplays, once declared in an interview.[1] He did no more than echo a long line of American writers, not all of them novelists, who have agreed—if not publicly in *Newsweek* interviews, then implicitly, in the imaginative energies of their work—with Walt Whitman's assertion, in his preface to the 1855 edition of *Leaves of Grass*, that "the greatest poet" "swears to his art, I will not be meddlesome, I will not have in my writing any elegance or effect or originality to hang in the way between me and the rest like curtains. I will have nothing hang in the way between, not the richest curtains. What I tell I tell for precisely what it is."[2] As with Whitman's formulation here, realism is defined at least as much by what it avoids as by what it champions. An author interested in realistic effects will strive, that is, not only to "capture" life but to capture it in ways that other literary methods, with their elegant curtains, simply can't.

We understand realism best, Warner Berthoff rightly contends, "by seeing what it opposes": "As a measure of virtue 'realism' has regularly been put forward in response to a sentiment of something acutely unsatisfactory in existing literary conventions and hence also of something repugnant in the settled contemporary practice of the *activity* of literature within the vast institutional conspiracy that at any given moment we call society."[3] "I tried to write this book the way lives are being lived," John Steinbeck said of *The Grapes of Wrath*, "not the way books are written." "I've done my damndest to rip a reader's nerves to rags."[4] The recourse to violent analogies in describing the aims of realistic fiction offers one hint as to why violence itself is so frequently a subject in that fiction. The process of "ripping a reader's nerves to rags" is felt to be an activity continuous with life, not books, and thus depictions of realistic violence offer riveting examples of how writers imagine the kind of intensity such "life" supposedly entails. Vividly evoked scenes of violence offer a crucial means by which a novelist can shatter social complacency or literary convention.

The novelistic "uses" of realistic violence, however, cannot be easily separated from the imaginative means by which that violence takes shape and by which realism is more generally defined. Literary realism originates in a demand that fiction, in a given historical moment, should more conscientiously include what it has tended to overlook (new characters, new economic classes, new social quandaries, new landscapes, new dialogue). But as Berthoff suggests, the introduction of such new subject matter is not enough, by itself, to satisfy that demand successfully. New material must be rendered in ways that seem "real," which is to say, ways that no longer seem "literary" in a pejorative sense. But how is that process verbally effected? What shape do such new renderings assume? How does an impatience with the very idea of literature (and the verbal conventions that comprise it) become a stylistic imperative?

To assert, as has often been done, that one of the cardinal features of realism is the absence of an explaining commentator (either an author or his stand-in) who shapes, alters, directs, or misdirects a reader's perceptions and judgments, begins—but only begins—to account for the aesthetic force of realistic effects in fiction. As Wayne Booth reminds us, the "convenient distinction between 'showing,' which is artistic, and 'telling,' which is inartistic" has become more a schematic orthodoxy than a fruitful critical discrimination.[5] The imaginative substance and verbal action of what replaces a self-effaced author still remain largely unexplored. The very possibility of realism in fictional description depends upon writing that generates and sustains the illusion of realistic action and life, and that illusion springs from the verbal effects that are kept from impinging upon it as well as from those that initiate it.

Elmore Leonard's remark is apt for my purposes because it emphasizes that what often makes writing seem like "writing" (and thus not, the logic goes, like life) is *sound*. For Leonard, an accomplished realism involves more than simply rejecting or revitalizing outmoded diction or certain representational conventions. It involves a much more basic struggle with and ambivalence toward the expressive properties of language capable of being conventionalized in the first place. In the best tradition of the American writers whose fictional sequences and effects I am terming "realistic," Leonard makes a literary virtue out of not sounding "literary." He promulgates an adverse relationship not to language so much as to the sounded presence of words.

But perhaps it would be more accurate to say that Leonard declares himself in favor of what the sounds of writing obscure. Hearing words is not the same as seeing through them to an illusion of life. If we are to imaginatively hear anything in a realistic narrative it should be not the sound of descriptive language but the sound of what it describes: the honk of a horn, music on a radio, or the sound of someone cocking a gun. To deemphasize the auditory presence of words on the page is to accentuate what we can imaginatively see and sense in passing through or beyond them. Whitman's meddlesome curtains of "style," in such a view, are to be either torn away or somehow rendered invisible.

This subordination of language to life in realism is crucially connected to its creation of an illusion of temporal purity. Realistic fiction must invoke and accentuate what Ian Watt calls a "minutely discriminated time-scale," a chronology that is plausible and internally consistent within its imaginative setting.[6] But more than this, the imagined seconds or seasons of a realistic novel must seem more important and palpable than the actual time it takes us to read about them. For a verbal sequence to seem realistic, we must seem to be seeing the colors, details, and visual textures of a fictional world, sensing its physical qualities and conditions, and watching and listening to its characters. But we must also seem to be doing this in "real" time. The events and actions we imaginatively witness must seem to obey their own laws of cause, duration, and consequence, not those a writer quietly creates and manipulates. The more our imaginative energy as readers is channeled into the physical properties and temporal contingencies of a realistic fictional world, the less we pay attention to the words and rhythms that evoke them. The more life we seem to see in a realistic sequence, the less verbally "adulterated" or upholstered its world seems to be:

> He laughed as if he had said something funny. He slapped his thighs. He was standing in a strange way, leaning back against the car as if he were balancing himself. He wasn't tall, only an inch or so taller than she would be if she came down to him. Connie liked the way he dressed, which was the way all of them dressed: tight faded jeans stuffed into black, scuffed boots, a belt that pulled his waist in and showed how lean he was, and a white pull-over shirt that was a little soiled and showed the hard small muscles of his arms and shoulders. He looked as if he probably did hard work, lifting and carrying things. Even his neck looked muscular. And his face was a familiar face, somehow: the jaw and chin and cheeks slightly darkened because he hadn't shaved for a day or two, and the nose long and hawklike, sniffing as if she were a treat he was going to gobble up and it was all a joke.[7]

This is a moment from Joyce Carol Oates's story "Where Are You Going, Where Have You Been?" and the man Connie is scrutinizing here is Arnold Friend, who has just pulled up in his gold-painted convertible and his mirror sunglasses. Friend is given to us as a succession of individual visual details and a series of descriptive possibilities: he leans against the car "*as if* he were balancing himself," he looks "*as if* he probably did hard work," and he sniffs at Connie "*as if* she were a treat." The grammar that keeps those details and possibilities coming one after the other is unremarkable. Its rhythm consists of short, abrupt, irresolute units that are not allowed to draw attention to themselves. They are not allowed to gain an assurance or energy that would be greater than the "information," the imagistic variety and change, they provide. What we are offered is less a rhythm than an informational conveyor belt, the grammatical equivalent of the mechanical impulsion that starts and follows a line of falling dominoes.

As throughout the rest of the story, the more we know about Friend here, the less we know about how to take him—or where he is going to take Connie. But the sense of danger and psychological instability we come to feel in regard to this character is due to more than his ominous preview, for Connie, of what lies ahead for the two of them. ("I'm always nice at first, the first time. I'll hold you so tight you won't think you have to try to get away or pretend anything because you'll know you can't. And I'll come inside you where it's all secret and you'll give in to me and you'll love me."[8]) It also results from the fragmentary verbal form of Oates's prose. This paragraph runs somewhat smoother than what we often find in realistic sequences, but it still serves to render Friend strange by means of its perceptually fractured vision, its grammatical list of one visual item after another.

By one set of standards this is simply successful writing. A good writer, Mark Twain once asserted, "accustoms himself to writing short sentences as a rule": "At times he may indulge himself with a long one, but he will make sure that there are no folds in it, no vaguenesses, no parenthetical interruptions of its view as a whole; when he is done with it, it won't be a sea-serpent, with half its arches under the water, it will be a torchlight procession."[9] Realistic narrative form consistently assumes the verbal shape of a "torchlight procession," a series of details that seem to emerge from and offer proof of the world in which they exist. These perceptual fragments seem completely natural and plausible within a given scene because they do not seem to have been shaped or manipulated or preselected by an author. In fact, because they seem part of an evoked scene rather than themselves a part of the evocation, they may actually seem unavailable for authorial manipulation. Toto has no chance in such moments (or so it seems) to pull back the curtain and reveal the Great Oz.

The details of realistic fiction "exist," as Roland Barthes reminds us, within the context of the traditional conviction "that the 'real' is assumed not to need any independent justification, that it is powerful enough to negate any notion of 'function,' that it can be expressed without there being any need for it to be integrated into a structure, and that the *having-been-there* of things is a sufficient reason for speaking of them."[10] The illusion in the passage above is that a real car and man somehow precede the words that have created them, thereby licensing Oates to render or re-present them in any number of ways, rather than call attention to this particular rendition. There may in fact have been for Oates an actual man and car upon which she modeled those in her story. Yet even if there were, they form no part of a reader's experience of this scene.[11] Our experience of her story results from and is prompted by its verbal arrangement, an arrangement that allows us to ascribe to represented life an imaginative reality that is in fact an effect of the story's style.

The traditional conception of realism as "mimetic," as offering an imitation or simulacrum of life, seems inadequate in describing the imaginative status and power of effects such as those I am examining here.[12] The realism of such descriptions is attributable not to their subject but to the way in which that subject is taken up. It involves more than a respect for empirical reality. It comprises a fascination with the imaginative process by which something can be made to seem empirical, a fascination with the actions of a prose that can make physical and sensory details seem justified because they seem self-evident. Their plausibility is made to seem referential (in Barthes's terms) rather than aesthetic or discursive. Such details seem to be what they are because there is so little else they might be: least of all "just" words.

This illusion of course, like all illusions, is conjured, and it is the verbal action and form responsible for it, rather than the ideological purpose it might be said to express or fulfill, that concerns me here. The indispensable prerequisite for realistic imagining is that we feel we are operating by ourselves, moving off and away from language toward something real. The purity of what we imaginatively see, sense, and intuit must seem as inevitable, unpredictable, and "possible" as something we might happen upon in life. And that illusion of representational purity depends upon language and a grammar that are undistinctive, anonymous, and self-effacing. Its effectiveness is measured by its lack of verbal "interference" or, if you will, verbal static. Realistic sequences are meant to seem verbally empty in order that they can be imagistically flooded by a reader. Their verbal insubstantiality allows for a referential volume and depth. Words are meant to fade and attenuate in realistic descriptions, as the world comes rushing in.

Again, the detail, psychology, and action of that fiction seem part of the world rather than part of a book, because they seem innocent of authorial tampering, of extraneous ascriptions of function, structure, or form. They seem to evoke life rather than present us with writing because their constituent details appear to be self-sufficiently disparate, random, and unarranged. The language of realistic fiction seems "real" not because it mimetically represents life with a neutral exactitude but because the words of a realistic sequence encourage us to see and feel life somewhere beyond them. They encourage our action upon and away from them—action that seems warranted because there are no conspicuous signs of an author's having descriptively acted before we arrived. We visualize Arnold Friend's "black, scuffed boots" and "the hard small muscles of his arms and shoulders" (or have the confidence that we could visualize them if we took the time) to the extent that we move off and away from the words *scuffed*, *hard*, and *small* and into the images they evoke in this context. That process of visualization is subverted if we linger over the imaginative presence of those words *as words*: if we stop, for instance, to listen to the sound of the word *scuffed*.

What keeps us from hovering over and hanging onto the words of a realistic sequence is the narrative form that keeps them in motion. The itemization of bits and fragments of perceptual information typical of such sequences is, by definition, incomplete. An author, no matter how exhaustive or ambitious his descriptions, could never include every detail about a particular place, person, or action (nor would most authors care to include everything).[13]

This narrative incompletion, however, is not experienced as a deficiency or a perceptual deficit in realistic sequences. The incomplete form of those sequences takes shape instead as an imaginative insufficiency upon which a reader is invited to act. Their fragmentary form—composed of a surplus of perceptual details and a grammar that keeps them moving—is experienced, as James Guetti argues, "as an absence of form," one whose "felt substance seems in obvious ways not merely to depend upon but to be inseparable from what a reader does with it."[14] The plethora of perceptual information in realistic fiction, Guetti says, encourages us to "smooth the story out, to break it down to something handier and neater than this list of details, to reduce it in volume by somehow changing its state from a mixture of separate things to a more homogenous solution."[15]

Yet the very formlessness of realistic narrative militates against our efforts to reshape it. For if realistic sequences seem realistic because their self-evidencing, self-justifying nature seems to make them impervious to authorial manipulation, the same holds true for a reader. The details of a realistic sequence will seem simply (or complexly) present to the degree that they resist our efforts to make something out of them or to endow them with some kind of significance. Realistic narrative, as Guetti says, is full "of the sort of perceptual detail that ought to become 'information,' detail that would seem potentially processable into some significant reduction of itself." But because a realistic narrative typically assumes the form of a "narrative nonstructure that tends to evoke problem-solving responses in a reader but that does not satisfy them," it continues to resist "significant rephrasing" and to maintain its own terms and conditions against translation.[16] Realistic fiction, that is, largely baffles our efforts to complete a world we have only just been invited to piece together. Its claims on our attention are continuing because most of us can neither resist nor fully "answer" that imaginative invitation.

Noel Carroll has recently characterized a spectator's perceptual vantage in relation to movies in a way that bears upon my concerns here. Instead of contending, as others have, that watching a film somehow involves a simultaneous process of both believing and disbelieving what we see, Carroll asserts that

> our mode of attention is better characterized by way of two, simultaneous, *noncon-flicting* modes of awareness: a *focal* mode, directed at what is being represented, and a *subsidiary* mode, through which we remain constantly aware that what is before us is a representation. . . . these states of consciousness—focal and subsidiary—are not contradictory states of belief such that one of them must be disavowed in order . . . to maintain equilibrium.[17]

Carroll's remarks are useful here as a preliminary description of our response to fictional (rather than cinematic) representations, if we conceive of the modes of attention he proposes as flexible and constantly mobile. In that sense, these modes need not disavow one another; they can be said to coexist.

But in relation to realistic sequences, their coexistence will be both uneasy and conflicting, because the imaginative motives of such sequences do not tend toward or result in equilibrium. A focal attention to the illusion of reality evoked by realistic narratives is established not because but *as* our attention to words is rendered subsidiary. Thus the "subsidiary" mode of our response is less a component than an imaginative motion, less a peripheral form of attention than an action of self-diminishment that participates in and exemplifies its own imaginative eclipse.

A reader's impulse to act upon a narrative is incited by language that seems to be unformed or untouched by an author. Thus our exertion of imaginative will and agency seem not only desirable but necessitated by the language of a realistic text. The more the language of realistic sequences seems to refer to nonlinguistic objects and actions—the more words seem to offer themselves as "reality," the imaginative reality into which we are cued to translate them— the less it sounds like "writing" as Elmore Leonard disparagingly conceives of it. The felt presence of an author responsible for that writing would disrupt the illusion that we ourselves are creating a fictional world or, more precisely, reading it into existence. Our awareness of that author depends crucially upon whether he channels his narrative energies into the imagined properties of his fictional world (leaving the impression that that world is simply *there*, "unauthored" or "unvoiced," and that our imaginative progress through it is thus free

31

and independent) or whether he directs those energies elsewhere. It depends upon whether he makes us cognizant of his language as language (print on a page with a sounded presence) or as a collection of signs—signs not so much of "real" experience but of the necessity of moving or pointing toward it. The difference here is not that between a mirror and a lamp so much as that between, say, Burma Shave and an echo.

Realistic effects in fiction do not thus result simply from an author's attending to the details of everyday life. Those details have to be arranged so as to encourage a reader to mis-take the experience of a particular kind of verbal interaction for some extratextual aspect of life. But in order for that creative mis-taking to occur, a writer must, paradoxically, conjure the illusion that he is not writing. All his imaginative energy must be self-effacing or, in a more positive light, life-enhancing. The authority of realistic representations as I am describing them resides always in their adequacy to an illusion of life, not to the elegance, shape, tone, length, pitch, or rhythm of words.

There is no denying that most readers (at least some of the time) have some kind of subsidiary awareness, in Carroll's terms, of the artificial basis of their illusions. But such an assertion prompts more questions than it may seem to answer. For while we may always seem to "know," by virtue of the fact that we are reading a novel, that someone else has authored a scene, if that scene is realistic, our reading experience largely belies and transcends any such knowledge. We can argue that the imaginative power of realistic effects is illusory. But we have not thereby accounted for why we do not always *experience* such imaginative effects as illusory. We have not explained how it is that what is always secondhand can come to seem so immediate. We have not accounted, that is, for why we wince in reading scenes of realistic violence.

The appetite in contemporary criticism for evidences of "textuality" in fiction—which are now routinely (sometimes gleefully) offered as signs of the referential instability and self-subversion of language—leaves it particularly unsuited for describing the imaginatively engulfing effects of realism. The assumption by poststructuralist theory that language produces rather than reflects reality has tended, Amy Kaplan notes, to locate "the power of realistic texts precisely in their ability to deconstruct their own claims to referentiality" and expose their own fictionality.[18] We have, as a consequence, no suitable vocabulary for discussing the capacity of realistic sequences to evade any imaginative *sense* of textuality. Nor at present do we have an animated sense of why the verbal action of realistic sequences is not imaginatively processed as "verbal." Literary criticism has largely forfeited its capacity to describe the imaginative dynamics of realism adequately. We have lost our sense that the introduction of realism into literature was, as Tom Wolfe puts it, "like the introduction of electricity into engineering." "It was realism," Wolfe claims, "that created the 'absorbing' or 'gripping' quality that is peculiar to the novel, the quality that makes the reader feel that he has been pulled not only into the setting of the story but also into the minds and central nervous systems of the characters."[19]

Of course, we can always refuse to be "beguiled" by a realistic sequence and highlight the verbal coordinates from which it can never free itself. "The economical doing of anything will look like a sequence of tricks if we retrace it slowly," Hugh Kenner says. But, Kenner affirms, "if, having tied a bowline by tracing the diagram, we watch an expert tie it with just two gestures, we may be tempted to say he has employed a trick with his middle finger; whereas he simply understands the knot."[20] No serious thinker about these matters would suggest that an "average" reader's imagination functions like that of Don Quixote or Tom Sawyer: a person who too insistently forgets that he is reading a book and becomes so preoccupied with the projected reality of a fiction that he mistakes it for life. (Realistic novels are full of such characters, and they are usually depicted derogatorily as either comical or pathetically deluded.[21]) Yet the epistemological "mistake" such a reader makes is but an excessive form of the less extreme process of perceptual mis-taking that I am locating as the central dynamic of realistic imagining. A more balanced reader may not *physically* act upon a realistic narrative (by pulling a fly rod out of the closet, for instance, after reading a story about fishing). But he will, nevertheless, have been imaginatively acting upon that narrative all along in a way only less absolute than, not different in kind from, that of an "imbalanced" reader.

THE KIND OF NARRATIVE I am referring to here as realistic, it should by now be clear, is not necessarily the product, or to be treated as the product, of a school of thought outside of its own writing—one delineated, say, in an author's prefaces, critical essays, or personal letters. Neither is it chronologically restricted to American fiction in or about the 1880s or 1890s, there to be contrasted with romanticism or naturalism. It is not my purpose here to position something called "realistic discourse" within a typology of other discourses. I am concerned, rather, with the verbal arrangements responsible for what I have called realistic imagining, an imagining that may be sustained for the entire length of a narrative or granted only an intermittent life in a novel, a scene, or a paragraph.

Realism has become a notoriously elusive, often overly convenient term because criticism has tended to treat it as something other than the effort by writers to open and release certain representational capacities in language, something other than the effort to find what will evocatively suffice. Its usefulness as a critical term has been hampered in two obvious ways. First, discussions of realism often founder on the question of what reality *is* and whether or not it can be known or made accessible to language. Second, realism is an unwieldy term because it connotes more a literary project than a literary practice, and thus it prompts merely generic thinking about itself.

The problem with thinking about realism as a genre or a literary project is that it encourages criticism to separate the more explicitly thematic elements of a fictional work from its expressive conventions. Or rather, it encourages an overly emphatic focus on ideological conventions and implications as somehow apart or detachable from the verbal conventions and conditions that create and then often alter them. Realistic effects are often achieved in the fiction of writers who are not committed to a "realism" explicitly formulated in their prefaces and letters, and writers so committed do not always, in fact, achieve them. Professing to value such effects is obviously not the same as rendering them.

Even classic American realism, as Kaplan and others have shown, was less a "seamless" practice than "an anxious and contradictory mode which both articulates and combats the growing sense of unreality at the heart of middle-class life."[22] Daniel Borus has noted the paradoxical "dual imperative" of classic American realism, which required an author to be both "out of and in the text": "At the same time that the narrator refrains from editorial comment on the action, the realist author . . . [sets] in motion a distinct set of values that animate the text."[23] This theoretical tension or inconsistency within realist theory (which is evident in contemporary forms of realism as well) concerns me less than the stylistic means by which we are made to forget about it. What interests me, to borrow some of Richard Rorty's terms,[24] are the "low-practical" rather than the "high-theoretical" concerns of realism. My description of how realistic imagining seems to function is not based on empirical research into the actual reception of realistic novels by numbers of readers.[25] This is partly because it would be extremely difficult, if not impossible, to measure the *quality* (as opposed to, say, the sociological aspects) of that reception accurately. My focus is on the imaginative substance and action of realistic imagining and on the particular verbal features (grammar, syntax, diction, and so on) that are designed to engender and sustain it.

Realistic fiction manifests the desire of certain authors to evoke an imaginative world in words whose substantiality seems more than verbal, and this desire is implemented, I have been suggesting, in certain characteristic ways. Realistic fiction contains a set of implicit directions, as it were, about the appropriate manner in which it is to be imagined. However difficult it may be to describe the felt quality of realistic imagining adequately, the causal elements that trigger it in fiction can be examined and specified. But this descrip-tion is, we should keep in mind, an ex post facto account; the prerequisite of realistic imagining is that we not dwell on such matters *while we are reading*.

Realistic narratives as I am discussing them here are those narratives whose verbal conditions insistently strive for the illusion of stylelessness and temporal purity. The authors of these stories and sequences want, so it would seem, to do away with language altogether, to free themselves from the very means by which they intimate that such freedom is necessary and suggest that it might be possible. The only justification for the words in a realistic sequence lies in their imagined referentiality, their devotion to some experience beyond, behind, or on the other side of language. Realistic imagining is prompted by language designed to create the illusion that it *is* what it triggers—an explosion out the barrel rather than the hammer and powder that cause it. A realistic sequence constantly attests to the richness, the complexity, the *unrepresentability* of real-ity by evoking all that language can point to but never itself substantiate.

Thus, the implicit avowal by realistic fiction that words cannot themselves body forth actual life is less a denigration of the insufficiencies of language than an affirmation of the power, the autonomy, the overwhelming sufficiency of the reality that necessitates such language: language designed to be self-dissolv-ing, to summon up an illusion of life even as it disposes of itself. Realistic fiction tries to employ only those fictional devices that will take us away from words and into the imagined world they evoke. ("The difference between the almost right word and the right word," Twain asserts in "The Art of Author-ship," is "the difference between the lightning-bug and the lightning."[26]) The primary goal of realistic fiction is to convince us of what might be awkwardly termed the "unverbalness" of its reality. It is writing made to persuade us that *as language* it is simply beside the point, most successful when it is not or is least itself.

Again, some may object that the very fact that we are reading print on a page would constantly seem to repudiate the force of the imaginative dynamics I am describing here. Isn't the illusion of representational purity always a matter of substituting one kind of language for another, not of replacing language with life? "There are no style-less works of art," Susan Sontag reminds us, "only works of art belonging to different, more or less complex stylistic traditions and conventions."[27] Realistic novels, we might feel compelled to assert (in showing that we are not naive or easily duped readers), themselves manifest the sheer impossibility of language ever attaining a wished-for condition of unmediated commerce between mind and matter. Prose cannot, as Paul West puts it, "turn to the sun, like a plant, or wither without actually falling off its stem, or spawn tapeworms in its interior. It will not oxidize except through the material body of its vehicle: ink and paper."[28] Furthermore, realistic fiction is, after all, always authored, always selectively assembled; it always forms, in some sense, what George Levine calls "a subtle disguised version" of a writer's own desires.[29]

Much recent criticism has variously emphasized these assertions with an exclusionary partiality that seems troubling because it prematurely dismisses what might be more closely examined. The contention that realistic fiction exemplifies a writer's disguised desires, for instance, can turn into an inflexible insistence that we read that fiction against its imaginative grain so as to unmask such desires. Our primary role as critics, in such a view, is to stand back from the textual power of books (to use Robert Scholes's terms) in order to make our own judgments about them.[30] The problem with such conceptions of "textual power" (and the kind of reading they encourage) is that they frequently settle for fairly simplistic accounts of the sounds and images and idioms of the writing under consideration. They tend to iron out the life and particularity of a given verbal occasion as a way of exalting the alleged forms of power and coercion that such occasions are said merely to support or be implicated within. It may in fact be possible (as Bill Nichols, one of the shrewdest critics of documentary films, says about that cinematic genre) to hear the "voice of [a] textual system" as distinct from "the sounds and images of the evidence it adduces." But this possibility is effected, he notes, only by means of "a vigorous, active and retroactive reading."[31] Nichols sees this intellectual "resistance" as a positive form of response. I see it as a frequent excuse for an inattention to style in literary works, one that reduces the complexities of imaginative response to the status of "evidence" for prior claims about a "textual system."

"My suspicion," Roger Sale says, "is that one reason realistic fiction has never received the attention it deserves is that it is not easy to describe its ways and means, and that the more obviously eccentric, experimental, high-flying fictions often make and keep their lofty critical status because they are easier to describe and appreciate. One is always tempted to say that a realistic novel is just there."[32] Construing the language of realistic fiction to be simple and straightforward, criticism attempts to "rescue" or complicate it by investigating the social and cultural determinants of realism.[33] These critical accounts are often interesting and useful and they have permanently unsettled our conviction that a realistic novel is "just there" in the sense of being a preinterpretive *take* on life or that it is somehow unimplicated in the historical specificities of its time. But such studies often reach their conclusions by pulling back from the imaginative motions of our reading experience in order to emphasize something else: cultural modes of production, gender stereotypes, or a political unconscious. The process of securing a critical purchase on a realistic novel or story, that is, often entails ignoring or misconstruing the verbal action and substance of what is purportedly being examined: too often there is no *there* there, in such accounts, to investigate.

So while I would not presume to assert that social, literary-historical, or psychosexual considerations are irrelevant to the study of realistic fiction, I would suggest that even as an aggregate such considerations are insufficient for a careful study of the actual verbal phenomena of that fiction. I am keying my usage of the term *realistic* to the note William Empson more generally sounded some fifty years ago: "literature, in so far as it is a living matter, demands a sense, not so much of what is really there, as of what is necessary to carry a particular situation 'off.'"[34] The writer of realistic fiction, as well as the critic who considers his work, requires the kind of knowledge Ansel Adams said an architect needed to have. An architect need not know "the complexities of steel manufacture," Adams asserted; all he needs is the "knowledge of *what steel will do*" and the "confidence that it will do it."[35]

THE DESIRE for the fictional immediacy of realism has been present in narratives that are not themselves realistic in the way I mean the term. A chapter in Harriet Beecher Stowe's *Uncle Tom's Cabin* entitled "In Which It Appears That a Senator Is but a Man," for instance, offers a parable about the issues I have been discussing. Senator Bird, Stowe tells us, is well known in the Ohio state legislature as a strong supporter of "more stringent resolutions against escaping fugitives [and] their harborers and abettors." Yet when he is touched by the plight of the fugitive Eliza and helps her to escape, Stowe is not without an explanation. "He was as bold as a lion" about the "sentimental weakness of those who would put the welfare of a few miserable fugitives before great state interests,"

> and "mightily convinced" not only himself, but everybody that heard him;—but then his idea of a fugitive was only an idea of the letters that spell the word,—or, at the most, the image of a little newspaper picture of a man with a stick and a bundle, with "Ran away from the subscriber" under it. The magic of the real presence of distress,—the imploring human eye, the frail trembling hand, the despairing appeal of helpless agony,—these he had never tried. He had never thought a fugitive might be a hapless mother, a defenceless child,—like that one which was now wearing his lost boy's little well-known cap; and so as our poor senator was not stone or steel,—as he was man, and a downright noble-hearted one, too—he was, as everybody must see, in a sad case for his patriotism.[36]

Stowe here presents a familiar and justified complaint (one we might hear voiced today by William Safire) about the emptiness of political rhetoric and its catchwords: a rhetoric that is nonreferential, mere language, an "idea" of the letters that spell words. But in proposing to supply the "magic of the real presence of distress"—and one is tempted to ask, What price such magic?—Stowe offers up some formulaic and nonreferential options herself. Just what is "the despairing appeal of helpless agony" other than a literary phrase? Stowe can suggest how the associational or signifying power of language can be nullified and how a three-dimensional reality can be flattened into a cliché or print on a page. But she cannot suggest this without implicating her own abstract and formulaic language.

Fortunately, none of this stops Stowe from writing, for she is convinced that her readers will see through phrases about frail and trembling hands to more than stick figures in newspaper ads. Her earnest, direct appeals to a reader's sympathy constituted for her, as Robyn Warhol reminds us, a kind of realistic technique, part of a "literary attempt to represent a recognizable world" that would convince a reader that her Christian, antislavery message was "not only true, but of personal importance to each actual reader, him- or herself."[37] Of course, intending to work magic among readers is not the same as fulfilling such an intention. This is one reason *Uncle Tom's Cabin* remains, as Stephen Railton puts it, both "powerfully radical and perfectly conventional." "Stowe and her readers united in prizing the ability to see the reality that was not there," Railton argues, "whether that was the hand of Providence, maternal sovereignty, or Little Eva." They saw a character through Stowe's verbal gauze of euphemism, cliché, and abstraction (which we now see as "the pattern of pieties by which they understood reality") because "they had agreed beforehand on the meaning and validity of these terms."[38]

Thus Stowe could rely on the force of implicit agreements with her readers to carry much of the representational "work" of her novel. She establishes a paradigm for later writers in her feeling that she can effectively bypass, with a sweep of the wand, the verbal status of her account of "the anguish and despair that are, at this very moment, riving thousands of hearts, shattering thousands of families, and driving a helpless and sensitive race to frenzy and despair" (p. 514). Stowe's motives, if not the verbal result of those motives, are thus the same as those behind all realistic imagining. In a way typical of realistic writers, she continues to let the world be too much with her. She continues to imagine (or pretend to imagine) that the fact of suffering and human emotion are themselves powerful enough to transform the preconditions and representational pitfalls of language.

The powerful appeal that realistic fiction has for us stems, at least partially, from an ambivalence about reading literature in the first place. There is, of course, a kind of imaginative thrill or satisfaction as we read in being convinced that we have seen life. We read realistic fiction in part because of a vivid interest in the world around us and because we enjoy or believe in the value of literary as well as journalistic or sociological or scientific investigations of that world. We are often charmed by and imaginatively assent to the illusion of life that realistic fiction evokes precisely because it does not seem fictional or "literary." It often seems familiar or recognizable (or so we wish to contend when we are finished reading), full of people and places and dialogue whose plausibility we enjoy encountering or think it important that we know about.

But we also read realistic fiction to reassure ourselves that the books we read are not too bookish, that we are not insulated from a world that does not conceive of or judge itself in literary terms. We read realistic fiction so that we can convince ourselves, at least part of the time, that we are not what one of Robert Frost's speakers calls "the fool of books." The popular imperative that we "face facts" or "be realistic" usually means, "in the American metaphysic," that we align ourselves with a reality that is, as Lionel Trilling puts it, "always material reality, hard, resistant, unformed, impenetrable, and unpleasant. And that mind alone is felt trustworthy which most resembles this reality by most nearly reproducing the sensations it affords."[39] When the "whole romance and ideal of life" disappear for Augustine St. Clare, what remains for Stowe is an italicized reality: "the *real* remained,—the *real*, like the flat, bare, oozy tide-mud, when the blue sparkling wave, with all its company of gliding boats and white-winged ships, its music of oars and chiming waters, has gone down, and there it lies, flat, slimy, bare,—exceedingly real" (p. 185).

This equation of reality, in American fiction, with the recalcitrant and the unpleasant holds out the promise of a life free from illusions and self-decep-tions. It also institutes a kind of conceptual hierarchy with "reality" placed strategically over dreams, idealism, and abstractions, over "nerds," "eggheads," and the "academic" (as sportscasters use that term). It guarantees that certain experiences within the realm of "reality" will seem more *real* than others. Certain experiences will be less susceptible to the romanticization and inter-ventions of Whitman's "meddlesome" authors. They will be purer than the language that attempts to represent them.

The idea that "reality" is synonymous with hard materiality (with brutality, suffering, and violence) is accorded such credibility in American fiction, it should come as no surprise that realistic narratives often specialize in violent scenes. This continuing fascination with violence cannot, I think, be adequately accounted for by "historicizing" it, by attributing it to the shaping exigencies of a given historical moment. Writers as temperamentally distinct and as sepa-rated in time as Stowe, Steinbeck, Joyce Carol Oates, Elmore Leonard, and, as we will see, Richard Wright and Tom Wolfe, all propose in varying but

39

analogous ways that the intensity and tension of violent actions ("the magic of the real presence of distress") validates a reality separate from the world of books and language. Neither are these authors alone. When "the interest of the narrative is languid," Frank Norris declares in his 1903 essay "Simplicity in Art," "we are willing to watch the author's ingenuity in the matter of scrolls and fretwork and mosaics-rococo work. But when *the catastrophe comes*, when the narrative swings clear upon its pivot and we are lifted with it from out the world of our surroundings, we want to forget the author. We want no adjectives to blur our substantives. The substantives may now speak for themselves" (my emphasis).[40] Thirty-eight years later, when James Agee proposes "to pry intimately into the lives of an undefended and appallingly damaged group of human beings," his only goal, he says, is "to perceive simply the cruel radiance of what is." "If I could do it," he says,

> I'd do no writing at all here. It would be photographs; the rest would be fragments of cloth, bits of cotton, lumps of earth, records of speech, pieces of wood and iron, phials of odors, plates of food and of excrement. Booksellers would consider it quite a novelty; critics would murmur, yes, but is it art; and I could trust a majority of you to use it as you would a parlor game.
>
> A piece of the body torn out by the roots might be more to the point.
>
> As it is, though, I'll do what little I can in writing.[41]

Realistic imagining frequently takes shape as an act of imaginative violence against language and books. And if realistic fiction is more generally committed to exposing purportedly false notions of human behavior or beauty or desire—many perpetuated, it is felt, by the influence of previous literature—then violence, as a kind of ultimate, untranscendable physical fact (a piece of the body torn out by the roots), becomes an important imaginative resource, a final repudiation of everything comfortably accommodated in literary terms. The success of violent scenes, with their ability to shock and terrify, becomes a measure of how imaginatively powerful language can be—if we conceive of verbal power in the way realistic writers do, if we focus only on the signifying potential of words. We are not likely to appreciate that imaginative power, however, unless and until we adequately explore how it springs from certain stylistic choices, certain forms of verbal action. What inspirits the language of realistic depictions of violence, as some examples from Richard Wright and Tom Wolfe suggest, is less the metaphysics than what we might call the *physics* of "presence."

THE MOST NOTORIOUS scene in *Native Son* and perhaps in all of Richard Wright's fiction depicts Bigger Thomas disposing of the body of Mary Dalton (the daughter of Bigger's rich white employer), whom he has accidentally smothered. It is a powerful, disgustingly graphic moment, which is exactly what Wright wanted it to be. We need not look for evidence of this outside the novel itself, but Wright's explanation of his motives in a pamphlet entitled "How 'Bigger' Was Born" (which he wrote just after he finished the novel in 1940) is relevant here. He asserts that two "events" accelerated the process of transforming the idea of Bigger Thomas into a character and a novel. The first was a stint as a worker at the South Side Boys' Club in Chicago, where hypocritical "rich folk" paid to distract black youngsters with "ping-pong, checkers, swimming, marbles and baseball" in order to keep them off the streets and away from nearby "valuable white property."[42] The second event was "more personal and subtle." Wright had just published a book of short stories entitled *Uncle Tom's Children* which he now considered "an awfully naïve mistake": "I found that I had written a book which even bankers' daughters could read and weep over and feel good about. I swore to myself that if I ever wrote another book, no one would weep over it; that it would be so hard and deep that they would have to face it without the consolation of tears. It was this that made me get to work in dead earnest" (p. 874). This "dead" earnestness takes on a disturbing literalness if we think in terms of the novel: Mary Dalton thus in one way becoming for Wright the audience for his first book, a "banker's daughter" upon whom to wreak his revenge. But I am more interested here in how Wright conceives of a story too "deep" for tears.

"Art, for Wright," Henry Louis Gates notes, "always remains referential": "Wright sees fiction not as a model of reality but as a representative bit of it, a literal report of the real."[43] Thus the effort to render a "hard and deep" fictional world consists for him primarily of the effort to make us "face it," to make us imaginatively visualize it in its supposed purity, unsentimentalized and unpleasant. Wright's commitment to making us "see" Bigger Thomas and the "indescribable . . . huge, roaring, dirty, noisy, raw, stark, brutal" city (p. 872) where he lives is the commitment, in the best realistic tradition, to employing only that language which will prompt us to see right through it to imagined events and feel their imaginative palpability. "In the writing of scene after scene," Wright says, "I was guided by but one criterion: to tell the truth as I saw it and felt it. . . . And always I tried to *render, depict*, not merely to tell the story. If a thing was cold, I tried to make the reader *feel* cold, and not just tell about it" (pp. 877, 878).

The decision to "not just tell about it" here forms the equivalent of Whitman's contempt for the curtains of style; for both these authors the truth is what counts, and the truth is nonverbal. The language describing that truth should function to camouflage itself in the very act of imaginatively substantiating what it depicts. This process occurs so naturally in fiction because it capitalizes, as Guetti suggests, upon a more general epistemological predisposition. "To 'see' through words is conceived not as one of the functions of the mind, but as the main function, that of understanding itself. . . . As far as our verbal imagination is concerned, there seem not to be five senses, but one: seeing, in permanent association with knowing, appears to include and to dominate the rest, so much so that it may seem the only important business of words and the mind."[44] Visual potential does not necessarily inhere in language (though some words "appear to gravitate toward their subject," as William Gass puts it, "like flies settle on sugar"[45]). Rather, visual energy and sensory evocativeness are sparked by a particular kind of grammar and stylistic devices that make us feel that what we are imaginatively witnessing in a piece of writing is "real," not linguistic. Realistic imagining usually partakes of a visual process of imaginative substantiation, but it can appeal to our other senses as well. We frequently refer to the "mind's eye" in criticism but seldom to the mind's ear, the mind's nose, or the mind's sense of taste and touch. As readers of realistic fiction we probably should, for we often find such imaginative senses acknowledged and solicited there:

> BRRRRRRRIIIIIIIIIIIIIIIIIINNG!
> An alarm clock clanged in the dark and silent room. A bed spring creaked. A woman's voice sang out impatiently:
> "Bigger, shut that thing off!"
> A surly grunt sounded above the tinny ring of metal. Naked feet swished dryly across the planks in the wooden floor and the clang ceased abruptly.
> "Turn on the light, Bigger."
> "Awright," came a sleepy mumble.
> Light flooded the room and revealed a black boy standing in a narrow space between two iron beds, rubbing his eyes with the backs of his hands. (P. 447)

The opening word of Wright's novel is not a word at all but the denotation of a sound, a sound that means nothing in itself until we find out, instantly, that it comes from an alarm clock. It is extremely difficult to describe what we do in reading this, how it is that we provide a mental context in which the illusion of sound imaginatively materializes by being connected with its source. Does the illusion of a sound spring more from the signboard transcription "BRRRRRRRIIIIIIIIIIIIIIIIIIINNG" or from our being told that an alarm clock and not a telephone or doorbell has just "clanged"? When we read that Bigger says "Awright" we do not, or rather we are not supposed to, think Aha, Wright is trying to do dialogue. We hear Bigger's answer pronounced in the silence of our reading imagination and continue on to the next line, the next bit of sensory information. We find here, as Robert Alter says we usually find in realistic novels, "a tacit agreement between both author and audience" that the verbal conventions of the sequence are to be "a transparent medium even in their conspicuousness; for our chief interest is in the personages and events they convey to us, not in the nature and status of the artifice."[46]

The details of this scene have obviously been selected and perhaps even verbally fondled by an author. But as we imaginatively "take in" or ingest one perceptual fragment after another we do not feel the presence of an author making comments about this room. We ourselves seem to author this scene. We move from one verbal item to the next as if they were there for the picking, and as we try to piece them together, the presence of something we can imaginatively see, hear, and maybe even touch (in a creaking bedspring), begins to materialize. As is usual with our experience of realistic sequences, we are convinced that what we are "sensing" here, what our imaginative senses are conjuring up, is "real." It seems real both because the language of the scene— as verbal fact, as print on a page—is self-obliterating or figuratively invisible as our eye swings from line to line, and because the grammar here provides a current of imagistic freshness and change. We think of fiction as realistic when we are made to feel, as we read, that we are continually on our way (without an author's help) to more life—more images and sense impressions. That continuous stream of images, dialogue, and sensory impressions seems new and self-renewing because it seems unformed and undigested, and our typical action as readers is to attempt to shape the apparent formlessness of this fictional world. We attempt to transform it in our minds from being just a messy collage of actions and sensations to being something we can coherently see and sense.

Wright articulates the sine qua non of realistic narratives as I am describing them:

> For the most part the novel is rendered in the present; I wanted the reader to feel that Bigger's story was happening *now*, like a play upon the stage or a movie unfolding upon the screen. Action follows action, as in a prize fight. Wherever possible, I told of Bigger's life in close-up, slow-motion, giving the feel of the grain in the passing of time. I had long had the feeling that this was the best way to "enclose" the reader's mind in a new world, to blot out all reality except that which I was giving him. (Pp. 878–79)

The connection between a sense of temporal immediacy (action following action "as in a prize fight") and the illusion of visual presence (close-ups and slow-motion effects) is a given for Wright and other realistic writers. "Giving us reality" means erasing any felt sense of an authorial presence, of a camera-

43

man holding the camera. That process depends crucially upon an illusion of "real" time, of the "pure" temporal motion or *grain* that governs life, and not the internal rhythms and duration of sentences.

We do not need to be told, if *Native Son* succeeds in the way Wright intends it to, that some of the incidents in the novel "are but fictionalized versions of the Robert Nixon case and rewrites of news stories from the *Chicago Tribune*" (p. 875), for they will *feel* like nonfictional accounts. The fictional pool halls and streetcars and slum buildings with their twelve-inch-long rats will all exist for us as elements of an imagistic progression we are meant to visualize as we would actual facts. Here is Wright's rendering of Bigger's escape from the Dalton house just after the detectives have discovered Mary's bones in the furnace:

> [Bigger] reached the top of the steps and breathed deeply, his lungs aching from holding themselves full of air so long. He stole to the door of his room and opened it and went in and pulled on the light. He turned to the window and put his hands under the upper ledge and lifted; he felt a cold rush of air laden with snow. He heard muffled shouts downstairs and the inside of his stomach glowed white-hot. He ran to the door and locked it and then turned out the light. He groped to the window and climbed into it, feeling again the chilling blast of snowy wind. With his feet upon the bottom ledge, his legs bent under him, his sweaty body shaken by wind, he looked into the snow and tried to see the ground below; but he could not. Then he leaped, headlong, sensing his body twisting in the icy air as he hurtled. His eyes were shut and his hands were clenched as his body turned, sailing through the snow. He was in the air a moment; then he hit. It seemed at first that he hit softly, but the shock of it went through him, up his back to his head and he lay buried in a cold pile of snow, dazed. Snow was in his mouth, eyes, ears; snow was seeping down his back. His hands were wet and cold. Then he felt all of the muscles of his body contract violently, caught in a spasm of reflex action, and at the same time he felt his groin laved with warm water. It was his urine. He had not been able to control the muscles of his hot body against the chilled assault of the wet snow over all his skin. He lifted his head, blinking his eyes, and looked above him. He sneezed. He was himself now; he struggled against the snow, pushing it away from him. He got to his feet, one at a time, and pulled himself out. He walked, then tried to run; but he felt too weak. He went down Drexel Boulevard, not knowing just where he was heading, but knowing that he had to get out of this white neighborhood. (Pp. 651–52)

What about this sequence strikes us as realistic? Its presentation, someone might say, of a deflationary, antiheroic fact. Bigger has, in the urgency of the escape, wet his pants. Thus we are provided, I suppose, with one more reminder that Bigger Thomas is not Ahab or, for that matter, Isabel Archer, that he is not a three-dimensional or complicated or "literary" character here, just a body subject to embarrassing physical reactions and the promptings of instinct ("just . . . knowing that he had to get out of this white neighborhood"). But how are we made to feel this way? What kind of narrative dynamic allows us to think we have a typical realistic moment here that we can label "deflationary" and fit into a thematic patterning of this and perhaps other novels? What is it that makes us feel that Bigger *has* wet his pants, that the experience of reading "at the same time he felt his groin laved with warm water. It was his urine" has a distinctly different effect from our saying "he wet his pants"?

It has to do, first, with a deflationary syntax, a syntax that resists any kind of established rhythm or grammatical expansiveness and that provides us instead with a series of small verbal scraps. Sentences are crimped and folded, factored up into sensory units, like the individual frames on a strip of film: "It seemed at first that he hit softly, but the shock of it went through him, up his back to his head and he lay buried in a cold pile of snow, dazed." The narrator here is so unobtrusive—both so restrained and unnoticed as a voice and so closely aligned with and dominated by Bigger's perspective—that his descriptions often deliver what seem like first-person impressions. The whole passage seems imaginatively black and white, visual but not strikingly visual. This seeming colorlessness has less to do with the fact that the snowscape into which Bigger leaps is bleakly monochromatic than with the neutralization of Wright's narrative voice. The monosyllabic simplicity of his writing seems built for imaginative speed, streamlined to cut down on verbal drag. We are to keep moving, this style implies, and to do that we must forget about the words that Wright's undistracting grammar keeps in motion. The scene seems real because we follow its progress, we feel the passage of time as we connect the temporal links of the sequence: "[Bigger] reached the top of the stairs . . . He stole to the door . . . He turned to the window . . . He heard muffled shouts . . . then turned out the light" and so on. The choppy, arhythmic step of the prose functions like a kind of verbal stenography: we record or process a multitude of discrete actions or images the better to move more quickly, to keep up with the events in the fictional world we are following and imaginatively enacting.

The sense of emergency or breathlessness in this moment stems in part from the nature of the depicted action. We expect escape scenes to be tense, to convey a heightened awareness of time, crucial time, passing. But realistic fiction always operates, to a more or less evident degree, as a propellant temporal pressure, a forward momentum that invites a reader to render a fictional sequence intelligible by moving through it, by imaginatively following, digesting, and, in the process, internalizing its signifying action. In the case of *Native Son* this is often a terrifying process, as we find in the scene I referred to earlier: Bigger's disposal of Mary Dalton's corpse, which will not entirely fit in the Dalton furnace:

> He got his knife from his pocket and opened it and stood by the furnace, looking at Mary's white throat. Could he do it? He had to. Would there be blood? Oh, Lord! He looked round with a haunted and pleading look in his eyes. He saw a pile of old newspapers stacked carefully in a corner. He got a thick wad of them and held them under the head. He touched the sharp blade to the throat, just touched it, as if expecting the knife to cut the white flesh of itself, as if he did not have to put pressure behind it. Wistfully, he gazed at the edge of the blade resting on the white skin; the gleaming metal reflected the tremulous fury of the coals. Yes; he *had* to. Gently, he sawed the blade into the flesh and struck a bone. He gritted his teeth and cut harder. As yet there was no blood anywhere but on the knife. But the bone made it difficult. Sweat crawled down his back. Then blood crept outward in widening circles of pink on the newspapers, spreading quickly now. He whacked at the bone with the knife. The head hung limply on the newspapers, the curly black hair dragging about in blood. He whacked harder, but the head would not come off.
>
> He paused, hysterical. He wanted to run from the basement and go as far as possible from the sight of this bloody throat. But he could not. He must not. He *had* to burn this girl. With eyes glazed, with nerves tingling with excitement, he looked about the basement. He saw a hatchet. *Yes!* That would do it. He spread a neat layer of newspapers beneath the head, so that the blood would not drip on the floor. He got the hatchet, held the head at a slanting angle with his left hand and, after pausing in an attitude of prayer, sent the blade of the hatchet into the bone of the throat with all the strength of his body. The head rolled off.
>
> He was not crying, but his lips were trembling and his chest was heaving. He wanted to lie down upon the floor and sleep off the horror of this thing. But he had to get out of here. Quickly, he wrapped the head in the newspapers and used the wad to push the bloody trunk of the body deeper into the furnace. Then he shoved the head in. The hatchet went next. (Pp. 531–32)

It is difficult to identify what, precisely, makes for the palpable, even visceral terror we feel in reading this sequence. (Our potential disgust—if we step back from our narrative motion—at Wright's making us watch Bigger here, at his need to shock "bankers' daughters," is obviously far easier to understand.) In responding to realistic depictions of violence we often feel indignant for our own sake as much as for a character's. We feel vulnerable not only because the vulnerability of the human body has just been graphically emphasized but because we feel that someone else has the power to shock us, the ability to capitalize upon our usual ways of imaginatively involving ourselves in fiction. We are forced to realize that the visual-sensory bias of realistic fiction that can render all the attractions of a seemingly recognizable world, can also be manipulatively unpleasant.

As the sequence develops here (and to do it perceptual justice I would have had to quote all three pages) our response takes the form of a tension that springs from our dawning realization—as we have experienced in how many horror movies or thrillers?—of what is actually going to happen. Our normal action of imaginatively seeing and sensing, that is, of following and acting upon a realistic narrative, is transformed into an anxiety about seeing too much, a feeling that we may be about to wince, or turn away our heads, or in the classic movie-theater gesture, cover our eyes. The image of an audience member partially covering his eyes, peeping through the gaps of his fingers, seems to me perfectly emblematic of how realistic depictions of violence successfully function. Our revulsion at seeing other people (or ourselves as projected in them) get hurt is countered by our desire to see what is happening, to stay "informed," to continue our attempt to understand and put together a fictional world. We want it both ways. And because we do, it clearly becomes reductive either to conclude dismissively that the scene is "simply" disgusting or to pretend that we have not been shocked, that we are, after all, only reading a book. Being disgusted or unshocked by such scenes are obviously different kinds of responses, but they are both "realistic" responses, both reactions that the language of realistic fiction is calculated to elicit. If we are disturbed or dismayed by what has happened then we have obviously yielded to the power of a realistic effect. If we feel called upon to say that we are mistaken in getting too upset in this instance; that there is no violence here, just words on a page; that life is not the same thing as fiction—that too is a realistic response. We obviously feel we have been presented with something it is important we declare is not real, and this declaration simply comprises another way of trying to establish our imaginative control of a text: an action, we have seen, that realistic fiction encourages by seeming pure and simply *there* for us to respond to and attempt to render intelligible.

But how do we respond here if we are not dismissive? How are we made to feel disgusted, as I am, by Bigger's actions? Is it a matter of the psychological dynamics of the scene, of our feeling the cruel irony, as Jerry Bryant suggests, that "Bigger's behavior seems out of proportion to the apparent danger" facing him and that Jan (Mary's boyfriend), were he in the same position, would realize this? Wright "does not allow us to applaud Bigger as an incipient revolutionary stoutly defending his manhood," Bryant asserts, he does not "try to morally justify Bigger's actions."[47] But Bryant also feels that the excessiveness of Bigger's reaction proves a point Wright wants to make:

> The intensity of [Bigger's] feelings expresses the entire set of circumstances that has shaped Bigger's response. . . . The extremity of his reaction to Mrs. Dalton is in direct proportion to the completeness with which he has internalized the taboo [of interracial rape]. . . . He does not accomplish the deed unfeelingly, or with a relish of revenge against the white race. He does it out of desperation for safety.[48]

Whatever the reasons for Bigger's actions, they largely cease to matter once he begins to saw and hack through the neck of Mary's corpse. The terror and disgust caused by that action become more powerful than our desire to keep reading, more powerful than the narrative itself. (Wright ends the first of the novel's three "books" just a page after this description.) The scene becomes an imaginative entity unto itself, something that stands out from the rest of the novel in a way few other moments do, something we refer to and vividly recall in having read the book. The scene becomes, in effect, what Bigger (with Wright closely at his shoulder) later wishes it could be: "He wished that he had the power to say what he had done without fear of being arrested; he wished that he could be an idea in their minds; that his black face and the image of his smothering Mary and cutting off her head and burning her could hover before their eyes as a terrible picture of reality which they could see and feel and yet not destroy" (p. 565).

Criticism of the novel seems to have felt this but never, so far as I know, to have explained why, to have accounted for how such terror and revulsion are brought about. There seems to be a direct ratio (and this holds true for the criticism that addresses violence in realistic writers more generally, not just in Wright) between the imaginative intensity of a violent scene and our unwillingness to talk about the violence itself. The more graphic and disturbing scenes of realistic violence are, the more critics feel the need to translate or paraphrase them in thematic or ideological terms and say they are "about" something else. Thus critics of *Native Son* assert that Bigger's murder of Mary Dalton represents an "act of metaphysical reprisal" ("The whites conspire to ignore his human presence. Very well, then, let them ignore the presence of a white corpse!");[49] or that it offers a "clear" sign that the white world is the cause of "violent desires and reactions";[50] or that it represents an existential gesture, an "expression of rebellion" against the encroachments "upon the self" of "an immoral world"[51] or an index to the "romantic" and "naturalistic" aspects of Bigger's identity;[52] or that the very "gusto" of the description, "the great attention to the details of physical destruction reveal[s] a terrible attempt to break out of the cage" of sexual mythologizing and paranoia with which whites have invested black males.[53]

Laura Tanner usefully revises such criticism by suggesting that part of the reason critics "come to see Mary's murder as an assault against an enslaving system of value rather than a fearful reflex response to a potentially dangerous situation," is that we do not sufficiently discriminate between Bigger and the narrator's interpretive "reading" of him throughout the novel.[54] If we respond in the way we are encouraged to in this scene we will, in effect, be simply agreeing with the sentiments of Buckley, the hysterical prosecuting bigot of the novel's courtroom sequence: "Your Honor, literally I shrink from the mere recital of this dastardly crime. I cannot speak of it without feeling somehow contaminated by the mere telling of it. A bloody crime has that power! It is that steeped and dyed with repellent contagion" (p. 829). Yet critics like James Baldwin shrink as well "from the mere recital of this dastardly crime" by translating it into an indictment of white America or an existential object lesson, neither of which readings Bigger's "haunted and pleading look" in the scene bears out. ("Could he do it? He had to. Would there be blood? Oh, Lord! . . . He wanted to lie down upon the floor and sleep off the horror of this thing. But he had to get out of here . . .")

It is to Wright's credit that he keeps the explicit editorializing that mars the last section of the novel (in the figure of Max the lawyer) out of this scene. He does not explore Bigger's motivations for violence here or explicitly insist upon the killing as a racially charged metaphor. Wright capitalizes less on white or black fantasies of violence or violation than on the imaginative capacities of realistic fiction. He recognizes that the power of a "bloody crime," of what Bigger calls "a terrible picture of reality" that we can "see and feel and yet not destroy," consists of its power to cripple interpretive effort. We can try to "destroy" or ignore the power of realistic representation by confusing it with what it represents and attributing that to black depravity (like Buckley) or the savagery of white prejudice (like some later critics). Yet either way we are responding realistically—we are reacting to Wright's ability to render Bigger's actions "real"—without addressing the nature of the writing that prompts us to do so.

THE QUESTION remains: What makes for the seeming reality of Bigger's actions in the decapitation scene? While we may feel certain we are seeing a violent act here, that certainty cannot, for most of us, stem from our relating the fictional sequence to an actual event: few of us have, fortunately, ever witnessed such a gruesome event. Yet that fact does not make Wright's fictional account seem any less real. The unnerving illusion of palpability and imaginative substantiality here is not, I think, accounted for by a mimetic model of correspondence, by the idea that we mentally correlate Wright's language with some kind of sensory information from our own experience. Precisely the opposite. The very unfamiliarity of this violence—the fact that we do *not*, in the terms of our experience outside of novels, know what it is like—impels us to work all the more avidly to understand it, to render it intelligible. And it is as a result of our imaginative "work" as readers, our action of following and imaginatively translating the sequence's verbal cues, that its terror for us arises. We cannot be disgusted or terrified—at least not in the way we are in this scene—by what we *recognize*, by what we can perceptually accommodate. The more we imaginatively follow the rhythms of Wright's realistic prose—which is to say, the more we work to see something strange in this moment, something unfamiliar, something we have never seen before—the more the imaginative substance of that event becomes palpable without our being able to understand it any more fully. This imaginative intractability, we can infer, was precisely the effect for which Wright was striving. Bigger "was more important," he asserted, "than what any person, white or black, would say or try to make of him, more important than any political analysis designed to explain or deny him, more important, even, than my own sense of fear, shame, and diffidence" (pp. 869–70).

Sequences of realistic violence encourage us to exert a pressure of intelligibility upon something that cannot be adequately rendered intelligible. They cannot be "read" (in the sense of understood, interpreted, deciphered) because we are convinced that they are being so insistently *witnessed*. Acting as a translator, to put it another way, leaves us no time to learn a third language:

> Gently, he sawed the blade into the flesh and struck a bone. He gritted his teeth and cut harder. As yet there was no blood anywhere but on the knife. But the bone made it difficult. Sweat crawled down his back. Then blood crept outward in widening circles of pink on the newspapers, the curly black hair dragging about in blood. He whacked harder, but the head would not come off.

"Blood crept outward in widening circles of pink on the newspapers": the potent visual force of this image seems to spring from the fact that while we may not know what blood (as opposed to, say, water or dog urine) looks like as it spreads absorptively through a wad of newspapers, somebody else seems to know quite precisely. This is not to say that we are aware of that authorial "somebody" here, however, for he has vanished into the imagination of these wet, widening circles. The natural laws of porosity and absorption seem responsible for this image, not the language of Richard Wright.

We do not need to "know" about such natural laws and physical properties to be convinced that what we are seeing is "real." What we have to be persuaded of is that the imaginative possibility of such natural phenomena is more compelling than the language of their description. Our imaginative enactment of that possibility seems real not because we know, in some nonfictional way, about what we are mentally envisioning here but because the imaginative action responsible for our envisioning it is our own. Wright's violence in this scene seems real, therefore, because it remains strange and unfamiliar, despite our imaginative work to familiarize ourselves with it. The shapelessness of his narrative (grammatically fractured and verbally unadorned, as realistic writing generally is) keeps that strangeness preeminent and encourages us all the more to explore and possess such unknown perceptual territory.

The will to imaginative "possession" in realistic fiction, the will to "see" and understand a world in its pages, is so ardently encouraged that its violence does not have to be graphically represented in order to be terrifying. Take, for example, the early fight between Bigger and Gus in Doc's pool hall:

> "Get up! I ain't going to ask you no more!"
> Slowly, Gus stood. Bigger held the open blade [of his knife] an inch from Gus's lips.
> "Lick it," Bigger said, his body tingling with elation.
> Gus's eyes filled with tears.
> "Lick it, I said! You think I'm playing?"
> Gus looked round the room without moving his head, just rolling his eyes in a mute appeal for help. But no one moved. Bigger's left fist was slowly lifting to strike. Gus's lips moved toward the knife; he stuck out his tongue and touched the blade. Gus's lips quivered and tears streamed down his cheeks.
> "Hahahaha," Doc laughed.
> "Aw, leave 'im alone," Jack called. (P. 481)

Gus's humiliation here and the idea of how easily a tongue can be sliced open are enough to unnerve us without our being gratuitously subjected to the nasty sensory details. The "idea" of violence—of what it is actually like—empowers its depiction in a realistic mode, whether that depiction is explicit or not. But it is the imaginative palpability with which realistic fiction infuses that idea, rather than some outside knowledge we may have of actual violence, which prompts us to imagine it. And that act of imagining on a reader's part (an activity that realistic narratives constantly invite) constitutes *in itself* the imaginative substance of that violence.

In reading sequences of realistic violence we are engaged in an imaginative activity that is not unique to violent scenes; we could as quickly be moving off and imaginatively "applying" the language that realistically describes a sunset or a dinner party or a stroll through a park in the spring. What makes scenes of violence seem to exaggerate the nature of visual-sensory imagining, what makes them seem particularly potent ghosts in realism's closet, is the fact that what they imaginatively bring alive are actions and events that are not only disquieting but, for most of us, frighteningly unfamiliar as well. It would probably offer little consolation to inform a reader who has just been upset by a scene of realistic violence—who has accepted the imaginative terms with which such scenes are enacted—that his response is largely self-induced, that the violence is largely of his own invention. But consoling or not, this seems to be the case. It is, of course, Wright's writing that makes us respond the way we do, but the function of that writing all along has been to make us forget that he (or rather, he and we together), not "life," has determined what we are seeing. Our awareness of violence in realistic fiction depends crucially upon our not being aware, *as we read*, of an author using language or altering fictional time in order to create that violence. The insistence by realistic narratives that we see life, that we never be imaginatively immobilized, that the informational power line never be cut, forms an insistence that words are to be subordinated to that "information," that they do not matter, that they do not interfere, that they do not, perhaps, even exist.

Up to this point I have used the terms "realistic fiction" and "realistic narrative" interchangeably, but I would like to suggest, by way of some examples from Tom Wolfe's book *The Right Stuff* (1979), that realistic narratives do not necessarily have to be fictional. Wolfe is useful for my purposes because *The Right Stuff* is science "fiction," a fictionalized account of the Mercury Space Program. Though its spine is labeled "nonfiction," the book comprises the equivalent of what television programmers call "docudrama." Some have questioned the accuracy of Wolfe's methods,[55] but he contends that he has simply played Boswell to NASA's Dr. Johnson, gathering factual information from declassified files in the Houston Space Center and from numerous conversations with various "pilots and non-pilots who were intimately involved in the beginning of the era of manned rocket flight in America."[56] Wolfe's task is to be as vividly detailed and realistic a historian as possible. "Improbable as some of Tom's tales seem," former astronaut Mike Collins is quoted as saying in one of the many promotional blurbs at the front of the paperback edition, "I know he's telling it like it was."

"Telling it like it was" means more than simply transcribing historical incidents. The book treats subjects familiar to many in Wolfe's audience: the Sputnik hysteria, Mercury launches, aircraft-carrier recoveries of space capsules, *Life* articles about the astronauts and their wives, John Glenn's ticker-tape welcome in New York City. But Wolfe makes these events *seem* strange—familiar but still, somehow, improbable. Improbability is the thematic frequency of this and much of Wolfe's work. He displays a dazzling knowledge in this book of rocket mechanics and cockpit layouts, the sound barrier, and astronaut training devices. But he invokes this knowledge so as to suggest the gap between the astonishing sophistication of modern aerial technology and the libidinous, venturesome, grinning men who use it.

These two thematic aspects emerge from two narrative techniques. The first consists of Wolfe's research, the "history" of the book: his knowledge not only of technology but of Air Force barrooms and low-rent housing, test-pilot pay salaries and corporate journalism. Like threading the back streets of Malta or Venice with Thomas Pynchon, the narrative detail about Pancho's Happy Bottom Riding Club and the centrifuge trainer seems "real" because we do not know about such matters and are intrigued by how much better than we Wolfe seems to know them. The second technique, more recognizably fictional, is related to that knowledge and has become a trademark of Wolfe's writing. The flashy verbal wattage of his narrative voice (what Morris Dickstein calls his "first-person baroque"[57]) is used to paraphrase what any number of people are feeling but not saying in a particular scene. That voice is often too overbearing, too insistently ironic or acrobatically knowing, to make for the kind of realistic or unvoiced effects I have been discussing. But it also frequently submerges its descriptive energies in a scene itself via the psychological ventriloquism of free indirect discourse. Wolfe's verbal imagination is more hyperactive, more committed to self-consciously novel imagery, than Wright's, but it partakes of the same realistic representational mode. *The Right Stuff* seems realistic, that is, not because Wolfe is recording historical fact but because he makes it read like realistic fiction.

The highly visual and sensory bias of that fiction allows us, in Wolfe's book, to see more than "great lubricated hunks of beef on paper plates" at a barbeque in the Houston Coliseum (p. 299). There is, for example, what greets Pete Conrad as he searches for a wrecked plane five pages into the book. It is Conrad's "first duty assignment" as a "squadron safety officer," and as the search helicopter lands in the Florida "rot-bog of pine trunks, scum slicks, dead dodder vines, and mosquito eggs" he is nauseated by the smell of what has, in the military euphemism, been "burned beyond recognition": "When airplane fuel exploded, it created a heat so intense that everything but the hardest metals not only *burned*—everything of rubber, plastic, celluloid, wood, leather, cloth, flesh, gristle, calcium, horn, hair, blood, and protoplasm—it not only burned, it gave up the ghost in the form of every stricken putrid gas known to chemistry. One could smell the horror" (p. 5). We may not know exactly what to smell here imaginatively, but the force of novelty in saying "One could smell the horror" after such a list of scientific-sounding items whets our sensory appetite. It must be quite a smell if Wolfe can talk about it that way. We work all the harder to imagine and understand a heat so intense it can burn blood.

Conrad is wading in swamp water up to his armpits when he reaches the plane, "which was an SNJ,"

> he found the fuselage burned and blistered and dug into the swamp with one wing sheared off and the cockpit canopy smashed. In the front seat was all that was left of his friend Bud Jennings. Bud Jennings, an amiable fellow, a promising young fighter pilot, was now a horrible roasted hulk—with no head. His head was completely gone, apparently torn off the spinal column like a pineapple off a stalk, except that it was nowhere to be found.
>
> Conrad stood there soaking wet in the swamp bog, wondering what the hell to do. It was a struggle to move twenty feet in this freaking muck. Every time he looked up, he was looking into a delirium of limbs, vines, dappled shadows, and a chopped-up white light that came through the tree-tops—the ubiquitous screen of trees with a thousand little places where the sun peeked through. Nevertheless, he started wading back out into the muck and the scum, and others followed. He kept looking up. Gradually he could make it out. Up in the treetops there was a pattern of broken limbs where the SNJ had come crashing through. It was like a tunnel through the treetops. Conrad and the others began splashing through the swamp, following the strange path ninety or a hundred feet above them. It took a sharp turn. That must have been where the wing broke off. The trail veered to one side and started downward. They kept looking up and wading through the muck. Then they stopped. There was a great green sap wound up there in the middle of a tree trunk. It was odd. Near the huge gash was . . . tree disease . . . some sort of brownish lumpy sac up in the branches, such as you see in trees infested by bagworms, and there were yellowish curds on the branches around it, as if the disease had caused the sap to ooze out and fester and congeal—except that it couldn't be sap because it was streaked with blood. In the next instant—Conrad didn't have to say a word. Each man could see it all. The lumpy sac was the cloth liner of a flight helmet, with the earphones attached to it. The curds were Bud Jennings's brains. The tree trunk had smashed through the cockpit canopy of the SNJ and knocked Bud Jennings's head to pieces like a melon. (Pp. 5–6)

This sequence is, to my mind, definitively realistic. Wolfe, like Pete Conrad, does not "have to say a word" here, or so it seems. The reality of what has happened seems all too evident, too terrifying for language. Before Wolfe tells us about it, what the searchers see is so frighteningly *there* that no alternative to the silence of sheer terror or hopeless disgust seems possible. For those in the scene to hunt for words to describe it would be inappropriate as well as futile. The last few sentences of the sequence seem traceable to no authorial origin. They form the verbal equivalent of a cinematic "pan," a movement in silence from the men to what they now realize is up in these branches. Wolfe's highly sensory description of Jennings's "head" does not feel metaphorically constructed or fictional because the image that evokes it appears so suddenly. Its sensory palpability surprises us with its instant force, like a landscape suddenly lit by lightning: "The curds were Bud Jennings's brains." Nothing could be more terrifying because nothing could be more simply put. The power to make language seem to evoke something here remains entirely disproportionate to the means by which that power is exercised. The simpler the language, the more powerful the evocative sense that blossoms behind it. The narrower the grammatical neck of the bottle, the more effective the genii it emits.

As the messy sense impression of Bud Jennings's "brains" floods our imagination, as it entirely occupies our imaginative vision for a moment and blocks out everything else, it is difficult to describe how unaware we are of the words on a page that evoke it. What we imaginatively sense here, what the idea of yellowish curds (or a pineapple ripped forcibly from its stalk) so suddenly evokes, seems to snap into palpable focus, to borrow a phrase from Paul West, at the speed of ionization. There is no conceptual lag, no chance for us to wonder how such a verbal effect has been achieved or who is responsible for it. The sense of instantly evoked life seems to occur simultaneously with the negation of our awareness of the words that compose it. There seems to be no causal priority here, for the negation of the words' presence *as words* seems less to "cause" imaginative seeing than to represent simply a different aspect of the same imaginative action.

How we actually see an imaginative "image" here is perhaps an unanswerable question (or rather, one for cognitive scientists, not literary critics, to answer). Again, most of us have never seen a wrecked airplane nor, surely, a decapitated pilot. So what seems real to us in this scene cannot seem so because it is mimetic, because we know what a smeared brain looks like and thus can apply that knowledge to our imaginative experience. Various details may seem mimetic ("curds," a melon, a pineapple) but they are more aptly described as metaphoric. Their palpability for us stems more from our having cooked a meal or gone grocery shopping than from an idea of how fragile a human head is.

When such commonplace things as, say, fruit or cottage cheese are incorporated into a phrase like "the curds were Bud Jennings's brains," however, their very familiarity makes them seem all the more strange and terrifying. Wolfe's reference to easily recognizable objects here seems to ensure our understanding of them. Yet the metaphoric context in which those objects are evoked serves to render them unintelligible—part of something we have yet to understand. That this process epitomizes the imaginative dynamic of realistic imagining is by now, I hope, clear. Not only is realistic narrative form experienced as formless and unstructured, it poses a resistance to a reader's attempts to give it form. "It can only maintain itself by resisting for a certain time, for whatever its imaginative duration, one's efforts to see it," Guetti says, "while simultaneously making the seeing of it the crucial imaginative issue."[58] Our imaginative efforts to see the grisly remains of Jennings's head are no different in kind (however much more disturbing) than our efforts to see the other visual items in the scene, like the "dappled shadows, and a chopped-up white light that came through the tree-tops." All are spurred on by a chopped-up grammar that keeps feeding us more information, more sensory data. But that writing keeps encouraging us to digest this imaginative information at the same time that it resists those very attempts at mental digestion.

The process by which Pete Conrad gradually "makes out" what he sees provides a kind of paradigm for a reader's own action in a realistic narrative. We, like Conrad, move from one detail, one conjecture to another like the bouncing ball in an old television singalong. First we see a tree scar, then some tree disease (or is it?), then a brownish sac that looks like something else—and it all seems "odd," unformed, unexplained as of yet. Conrad's wish to make sense of these details is satisfied. He finds out, morbidly, what all this is leading to, and so does a reader. But we are "looking into" a pattern of rhetorical units, not a pattern of broken tree limbs. The reality of this scene for a reader is composed not of blood or crushed flight helmets but of the consecutive disposition of narrative information—information that does not seem "verbal" because we are imaginatively prompted to transform it into something else. We are invited to mis-take a fabric of contributive verbal events for a more repulsive event beyond it.

The realism of this early scene of violence helps establish some of the thematic bases from which Wolfe will operate. It introduces the indecorous gap between military euphemisms and what they actually describe. It also conveys both the awesome power of aeronautical technology and a frighteningly antiheroic sense of what can happen to a human body should something go wrong with it. That modern rocket aircraft is extremely dangerous comprises, of course, the main point of Wolfe's investigation of "the right stuff." If men were not killed in the brutal way Bud Jennings is, if that kind of risk were not known to exist, the nonchalance of those possessing Wolfe's mysterious, unspoken quality would be simply gratuitous. But all these thematic aspects can be extracted only when we step back from our reading experience, from what has convinced us that the violence Wolfe presents is real. We can understand the psychological dynamics of "the right stuff," that is, only when we comprehend its attendant dangers—dangers that themselves result, at least for *us*, from a realistic narrative dynamic.

Wolfe's merger of realistic imagining with free indirect discourse is perhaps best illustrated by a scene late in the book in which Chuck Yeager, a seasoned test pilot, goes on a training run with a new jet airplane he hopes to use the next day in setting "a new world record for altitude achieved by a ship taking off under its own power" (p. 355). The sequence goes on for six pages and is difficult to excerpt because of Wolfe's use of ellipses. Yeager takes the jet up to 104,000 feet—twenty miles up—before the aerodynamic pressure at that altitude causes the ship to start "spinning right over its center of gravity, like a pinwheel on a stick" (p. 357). Yeager slows the jet down with a parachute but he cannot sufficiently stabilize it and he is forced to eject himself explosively from the cockpit while going "about 175" miles per hour. He is blown free of the ejection seat but remains near it in midair. As Yeager begins to fall earthward, the ejection socket beneath the seat dribbles out the remains of its rocket propellant:

> In this infinitely expanded few seconds the lines stream out and Yeager and the rocket seat and the glowing red socket sail through the air together . . . and now the seat is drifting above him . . . into the chute lines! . . . The seat is nestled in the chute lines . . . dribbling lava out of the socket . . . eating through the lines . . . An infinite second . . . He's jerked up by the shoulders . . . it's the chute opening and the canopy filling . . . in that very instant *the lava*—it smashes into the visor of his helmet . . . Something slices through his left eye . . . He's knocked silly . . . He can't see a goddamned thing . . . The burning snaps him to . . . His left eye is gushing blood . . . It's pouring down inside the lid and down his face and his face is on fire . . . Jesus Christ! . . . the seat rig . . . The jerk of the parachute had suddenly slowed his speed, but the seat kept falling . . . It had fallen out of the chute lines and the butt end crashed into his visor . . . 180 pounds of metal . . . a double visor . . . the goddamned thing has smashed through both layers . . . He's burning! . . . There's rocket lava inside the helmet . . . The seat has fallen away . . . He can't see . . . blood pouring out of his left eye and there's smoke inside the helmet . . . Rubber! . . . It's the seal between the helmet and the pressure suit . . . It's burning up . . . The propellant won't quit . . . A tremendous *whoosh* . . . He can feel the rush . . . He can even hear it . . . The whole left side of the helmet is full of flames . . . A sheet of flame goes up his neck and the side of his face . . . The oxygen! . . . The propellant has burned through the rubber seal, setting off the pressure suit's

automatic oxygen system . . . The integrity of the circuit has been violated and it
rushes oxygen to the helmet, to the pilot's face . . . A hundred percent oxygen!
Christ! . . . It turns the lava into an inferno . . . Everything that can burn is on fire
. . . everything else is melting . . . Even with the hole smashed in the visor the
helmet is full of smoke . . . He's choking . . . blinded . . . The left side of his head
is on fire . . . He's suffocating . . . He brings up his left hand . . . He has on
pressure-suit gloves locked and taped to the sleeve . . . He jams his hand in through
the hole in the visor and tries to create an air scoop with it to bring air to his mouth
. . . The flames . . . They're all over it . . . They go to work on the glove where it
touches his face . . . They devour it . . . His index finger is burning up . . . His
goddamned finger is burning! . . . But he doesn't move it . . . Get some air! . . .
Nothing else matters . . . He's gulping smoke . . . He has to get the visor open . . .
It's twisted . . . He's encased in a little broken globe dying in a cloud of his own
fried flesh . . . The stench of it! . . . rubber and a human hide . . . He has to get the
visor open . . . It's that or nothing, no two ways about it . . . It's smashed all to hell
. . . He jams both fingers underneath . . . It's a tremendous effort . . . It lifts . . .
Salvation! . . . Like a sea the air carries it all away, the smoke, the flames . . . The
fire is out. He can breathe. He can see out of his right eye. The desert, the mes-
quite, the motherless Joshua trees are rising slowly toward him . . . He can't open
his left eye . . . Now he can feel the pain . . . Half his head is broiled . . . That isn't
the worst of it . . . The damned finger! . . . Jesus! . . . (Pp. 359–60)

This sequence seems to me the culmination, or at least one kind of culmination, of realistic imagining as I have been describing it. The urgency and tension of this set of "infinitely expanded few seconds" are so intensely felt that
they result in nothing less than the breakdown and fracture of "ordinary" grammar. The scene is temporally overdetermined and pressurized to the point that
Wolfe's language seems subject to nothing but the dictates of time: it comprises a purely temporal sequence. In few other fictional moments I know of
are we so strongly induced to feel, in Wright's words, "the grain in the passing
of time." The dissolution and disruption of narrative form here make the *idea*
of grammar seem a gratuitous nicety, a pathetic, pointless sign of composure
in the face of the intensity with which nonlinguistic action and pain seem
tensed and explosive behind the words of this sequence.

Karl Marx's assertion that arrangements or structures reveal themselves
principally at the moment and in the act of breakdown applies tellingly here
not to political but to narrative structure. What this sequence provides, in an
unusually unadulterated form, is the essential imaginative functioning of realistic fiction, devoid of even the sparing embellishments that an author like
Wright might confer. The unflagging drive of these ellipses allows only for the

itemization of one visual or sensory detail after another, each beaded and strung upon the thinnest of grammatical skeins. The sequence can do nothing but end; its details cannot be rephrased or rearranged. Wolfe invokes no sense of verbal leisure or measure or resonance. The force of such forward-driving narrative momentum makes the action here seem *soundless*, both the action in the scene itself and the verbal action that brings it to us. It is as if we were watching a film in which the soundtrack has suddenly, purposefully, been turned off or turned down so that the only noise seeping in is the sound of Yeager's seat hitting his helmet visor or the *whoosh* of his pressure-suit's oxygen system.[59]

Yet the strange, distanced sense of our watching the silent motions of Yeager's body as he tries to free his helmet (as if he were a small, plummeting dot on a wide screen of sky) alternates startlingly with the urgency of Yeager's own sensations. The sheer terror of his choking helplessness, pain, vulnerability, and his determination to save himself are all paraphrased for us as he falls noiselessly toward the California desert: "His index finger is burning up . . . His goddamned finger is burning! . . . But he doesn't move it . . . Get some air! . . . Nothing else matters . . . He's gulping smoke." Our inability as readers to ease the fright or the tension of this sequence forms the ultimate testimonial to its realism. It seems imaginatively "pure" (unaltered and unalterable) and unvoiced in a way that can make us long for the comforts of a verbal intelligence to shape and form this kind of visual concentration and sequential pressure. In Wolfe's hands the typical perceptual structure of realistic fiction becomes a syntax of fear. The raw terror of this and other scenes of realistic violence in fiction owes everything to the raw and unaccommodating nature of its representational mode.

WHAT AN EXAMINATION of realistic violence in fiction suggests is that the act of representation itself is more powerful and unfamiliar than what we say it ends up representing. Realistic imagining operates not by reproducing but by inventing "reality." If we dispense with, or at least radically qualify, the notion of representation as mimesis (as a verbal mirror, a kind of pledge of allegiance to reality) we may be able to consider more precisely how the act of representing the world is always, in some way, the act of creating it. This is not, at least not from my perspective, the same as asserting that the world does not exist outside of language, that everything is, with a flourish, always already a text. If we refuse to make a kind of metaphysics out of the illusion of intense physicality in realistic violence, if we do not try to separate the illusion of that physicality from the verbal circumstances that locate and bring it to life in the first place, we can begin to understand representation not as a means of representing something but as the imagination of what is representable, and how.

Critics usually presume, in thinking about fictional depictions of violent acts, that those acts are already "out there," simply waiting to be re-presented and described. This seems to me mistaken. Literary occurrences of violence are not the result, exclusively, of either actual violence or of verbal representation. They result from fusions of the two, from the specific verbal means by which certain stylistic contexts express something that may or may not appear to resemble nonverbal objects and events. Substituting the idea of "conveyability" for that of "representation" may help us begin to describe the verbal conditions that must prevail if a fictional depiction of violence is to seem "violent" in the way we normally use that term.

As I have tried to suggest, such depictions must seem real in a way for which we cannot entirely account. The illusion of that reality is generated by a certain kind of narrative structure or "nonstructure," one that assumes the shape of a sequentially energetic stream of imagistic variety and change and that is kept in motion by an arhythmic, deflationary, temporally "pure" grammar that keeps allowing for more images, more action, more fragmentary specificity to appear. Such narratives, in their absence of the felt presence of a forming author, seem untouched or "unevoked" by any voice or consciousness outside themselves, which is what calls our visual-sensory imaginative bias into play. Realistic imagining works to camouflage language as reality by nullifying our awareness of artifice, of words on a page, and of an author, the artificer who prepared them. The temporal continuity and self-effacing language we find in realistic fiction grant it the illusion of representational purity and license a reader's action upon and away from the verbal components of that illusion. The more convinced we are that nonfictional life is expanding or exploding behind a realistic sequence, the harder we work to understand it, the harder we try to make nonfictional sense of a fictional world.

Our imaginative action in making the language of realistic narratives seem to refer to something beyond itself resembles that of the child in the Tim O'Brien novel who looks for the cold in the air conditioner, sure that there must be "a little box inside the machine where all the cold is stored up."[60] Our imaginative action in such a search seems "real" because it is our own, because it appears to be free and autonomous. We believe in the detail and texture of realistic fiction because we have worked to give it imaginative substance and make it into something "more." The writing in such fiction has of course been prearranged so as to encourage us to do so, but we are not aware of this as we read. Our narrative motion must seem unhindered and necessary in order for it to seem real.

Under, and only under, such verbal conditions can violence in fiction seem like actual violence, like the violence of a drive-by shooting or an urban mugging, the violence of an assassination or a traffic accident. Realistic scenes of violence, as we experience them, seem violent whether we like it or not, and we act accordingly. Disgust, fascination, shock, even titillation in the face of such scenes all partake of the same responsive posture: the treatment of a fictional event as if it were real, as if it were actually happening. One can understand why critics might react strongly to realistic fictional violence without pausing to consider what motivates that response: the stakes seem too high for reflection. We seem to be dealing with life, not books—and suffering, damaged life at that.

But why critics should typically treat a fictional incidence of violence they consider "real" in a way they would seldom treat an act of real violence—why we should, for instance, treat a decapitation as an encoded image of socially inscribed sexual anxiety—is a bit more perplexing, and a bit less susceptible to the supposition of charitable motives. Whether intentionally or not, such critical attempts usually end up diverting attention away from what presumably sparked or arrested our interest to begin with: the power of certain representational contrivances to provide the illusion of nonfictional life. They do so in order to interpret scenes of violence rather than to describe them, to fit them into "a reading" rather than to discuss what reading them is *like*. They also tend to treat all violence in fiction as if it had been realistically depicted.

Yet if violence as such cannot exist in fiction outside of realistic or unvoiced narratives, what happens when it appears, as it more usually does in American fiction, in "voiced" narratives, in novels and stories that revel in the pleasures and powers of fictional voice? What happens when the language of violent scenes does not primarily evoke them realistically, when it dilutes or disregards potentially realistic energies in favor of more readily apparent artifice, when it tranquilizes the perceptual contingency and incompletion of realistic narrative form? What happens, to put it another way, when Huck Finn tells us why "looking at the new moon over your left shoulder is one of the carelessest and foolishest things a body can do"? "Old Hank Bunker done it once," Huck says, "and bragged about it; and in less than two years he got drunk and fell off of the shot tower and spread himself out so that he was just a kind of layer, as you may say; and they slid him edgeways between two barn doors for a coffin, and buried him so, so they say, but I didn't see it. Pap told me."[61]

Fictional voice, whether that of an author or, ostensibly, a character, usually works as a kind of shock absorber or verbal painkiller. It provides a conspicuous reminder that we are safely or at least recognizably within a verbal circuit—a world of words. Yet no depiction of violence can ever be entirely nonviolent. Even the comic decapitations and tortures of a Monty Python film can never entirely disassociate themselves from what they are parodying. What never quite ceases to haunt verbal depictions of violence is not the specter of *différance*, of endlessly deferred meaning, but the signifying energy of language (its everyday capacity to communicate, "mean," and "refer") that generates realistic imagining. Still, our ability to beat an imaginative path through certain usages of language, and to make that movement seem both free and immediate, does not keep the jungle from thickening or refusing entry elsewhere. So while we may be tempted to assert that realistic narratives provide us with violence itself, while other narratives give us fictional "likenesses," neither assertion is entirely accurate. Realistic narratives invariably include what seem to be fictional or "literary" effects, and more self-conscious or self-resonating narratives are seldom without a kind of realistic fallout. But by starting with one type of fictional imagination of violence, that which seems to relinquish its interest in fiction altogether, I hope to suggest how many other imaginative versions there actually are. There seems a great deal yet to tell about the ways violence has been told in American fiction.

James Fenimore Cooper

VIOLENCE AND THE LANGUAGE OF ROMANCE

The style of some authors has variety in it, but Cooper's
style is remarkable for the absence of this feature. Cooper's
style is always grand and stately and noble. Style may be
likened to an army, the author to its general, the book to
the campaign. Some authors proportion an attacking force
to the strength or weakness, the importance or unimpor-
tance, of the object to be attacked; but Cooper doesn't. It
doesn't make any difference to Cooper whether the object
of attack is one hundred thousand men or a cow; he hurls
his entire force against it. He comes thundering down with
all his battalions at his back, cavalry in the van, artillery on
the flanks, infantry massed in the middle, forty bands bray-
ing, a thousand banners streaming in the wind . . . Cooper's
style is grand, awful, beautiful; but it is sacred to Cooper,
it is his very own, and no student of the Veterinary College
of Arizona will be allowed to filch it from him.
—*Mark Twain, "Cooper's Prose Style," in* Letters from
the Earth

[*The Deerslayer*] is a gem of a book. Or a bit of perfect
paste.

And myself, I like a bit of perfect paste in a perfect setting, so long as I am not fooled by pretense of reality. . . .
Of course it never rains: it is never cold and muddy and
dreary: no one has wet feet or toothache: no one ever feels
filthy, when they can't wash for a week. God knows what
the women would really have looked like, for they fled
through the wilds without soap, comb, or towel. They
breakfasted off a chunk of meat, or nothing, lunched the
same, and supped the same.

Yet at every moment they are elegant, perfect ladies, in
correct toilet.

63

Which isn't quite fair. You need only go camping for a
week, and you'll see.

But it is a myth, not a realistic tale. Read it as a lovely
myth. Lake Glimmerglass.

—*D. H. Lawrence,* Studies in Classic American Literature

POKING FUN at James Fenimore Cooper's *The Deerslayer* has traditionally been
a kind of literary *rite de passage* for other authors. The novel is, for Lawrence,
one of Cooper's "lovely half-lies"; for Twain, just "a literary delirium tre-
mens."[1] Lawrence is temperamentally incapable of doing what he recom-
mends: reading the novel as "a kind of yearning myth" and not a realistic tale.[2]
Both he and Twain measure Cooper's performance against the standard of
what Lawrence calls "actuality." Both prefer and value realistic fiction, or at
least they value it enough to crow over Cooper. Their particular brands of
intemperate response rely upon a comic hyperbole or a smug wryness more
interested in its own deprecatory force than in an attentive scrutiny of Cooper's novel.

The impatience implicit in their responses to the novel suggests, beyond the
ease of their flippancies, the depth of their commitment to a realistic aesthetic.
That commitment entails more than simply an adherence to what Twain's
prankster-persona in "Fenimore Cooper's Literary Offenses" teasingly refers to
as the "nineteen rules governing literary art in the domain of romantic fiction"
(eighteen of which he says Cooper violates). It also entails an antagonism
toward what Richard Poirier calls an "artificiality" in Cooper's writing, a "com-
pulsive and also inadvertent imitation . . . which exerts a pressure of accommodation on visionary moments."[3] The determining force of this stylistic accommodation exerts a pressure not just on visionary moments, however, but
on everything within Cooper's reach. The depiction of violence in *The Deerslayer* provides a telling example of how "romance," at least in Cooper's case,
involves and invokes a different order of imaginative perception from that we
find in realistic fiction.

Realistic fiction as I have described it in the previous chapter consists of
writing in which a particular kind of self-effacing verbal action is meant to
disguise itself as "life." Realistic narratives strive to be imaginatively self-
sufficient beyond their words, to invoke the imagistic variety that the illusion
of imagined life requires. That illusion can only be sustained when our attention is distracted away from the language that invokes it. The words of a
realistic sequence, James Guetti asserts, are "like a treadmill slipping away

beneath us, and we have to keep moving on them and away from each of them as they occur. In this way they are not a presence but an action; their substance consists of the motion of self-neglect, of leading beyond themselves."[4] Nothing in a realistic sequence is to remind us that someone remains backstage designing and manipulating effects. The more successful that sequence, the more it offers its language as "reality" and implicitly denies that there is any authorial user of language contriving that reality.

Fictional romance, on the other hand, does not generally display a compulsiveness about disguising its status as fiction. It remains easily recognizable first because of what Richard Chase calls its "penchant for the marvelous, the sensational, the legendary, and in general the heightened effect."[5] But more than that, romance expresses that penchant in specifiable verbal ways; it renders its heightened effects in particular narrative forms. Romance depends upon a storytelling voice or a narrative manner that presents its effects and events but is never consumed or extinguished by them. One analogy here might be that the language of realistic fiction functions like a window through which we imagine we are seeing life, while the language of romance, its storytelling voice, presents us with a stained-glass window whose opacity we cannot see through—an opacity necessary for its own effects. The formalized and formulaic language of romance, like a plate of stained glass, should be judged for what it is and not, as it were, as a "failed" or unsuccessful window.

Harold Martin rightly asserts that the "heaviness" we associate with the language of romance is due to the "telling" relationship it establishes between an author and his reader. The reader is encouraged to be passive rather than active, to listen to a narrative voice fashion an obvious fiction rather than to engage in what I have called realistic imagining. "The total effect" of such language, Martin says, "is to blunt action, to distribute the energy of action throughout the sentence, rather than to focus it for striking effect."[6] This does not mean, of course, that Cooper's historical romances are without action or conflict. They have appealed to many readers for precisely that reason: they are full of skirmishes, confrontations, last stands, and hair-breadth escapes. But these events do not occur in a verbal vacuum. The imaginative status of the events and characters in Cooper's fiction is indissolubly wed to the writing out of which they emerge. Twain and Lawrence both freely accept this precondition and proceed, accordingly, to smirk in entertaining but ultimately wrongheaded ways. Later critics, on the other hand, have tried to "rescue" Cooper from his writing by acting as if it somehow did not exist, as if the themes they find "encoded" in Cooper's novels or the "cultural work" they see exemplified there are somehow conveniently free of the accommodating pressures that Cooper's style exerts upon them.

COOPER'S NARRATIVE hallmark is a verbal luxuriousness out of proportion to the actions and characters it describes. It is a hallmark that generations of students have complained of as "wordy" or "too literary" (complaints that teachers usually tend to deflect or to acknowledge fleetingly before diving into what "really matters" in his fiction). I wish to propose a different critical stance here, one that takes the presence of this verbal excess—which Twain derogatorily calls "surplusage"[7]—as the central, refractory component of Cooper's writing, one with fundamental consequences for his more explicitly delineated themes. Yet however apparent this stylistic tendency is to *us*, we must remember that Cooper viewed the function of fiction in quite another way. Whereas a late-twentieth-century reader is likely to find Cooper's syntactical elaborations a constant reminder that he is reading a romance, Cooper himself considered his writing to be a species of realistic fiction, as is evidenced in the last sentence of *The Deerslayer*: "We live in a world of transgressions and selfishness, and no pictures that represent us otherwise can be true, though happily, for human nature, gleamings of that pure spirit in whose likeness man has been fashioned, are to be seen, relieving its deformities, and mitigating if not excusing its crimes."[8]

This sounds like nonfictional prose and not only because it has an expository function here. There is an assurance (which might pass as resignation) in this narrative voice that allows it to speak unabashedly about "the world" and "human nature." Cooper offers a final apologia here for the moral orientation of what he considers realistic writing: that which includes both pure and depraved characters, both deformity and "relief." Though we live in a world full of the likes of Tom Hutter, Briarthorn, Hurry Harry, and Captain Warley, Cooper implies, we are not without our Deerslayers and Hetty Hutters—characters who possess, in the words of his preface to *The Leather-Stocking Tales*, "little of civilization but its highest principles as they are exhibited in the uneducated" (p. 490).

But Cooper also implies that there is an aesthetic parallel to these moral coordinates: though we live in the midst of "transgressions and selfishness," thank goodness we can still identify them as such. The moral vocabulary he relies upon here, as throughout the novel, bears about the same relation to realistic fiction as the "pure spirit in whose likeness man has been fashioned" bears to actual people. The depiction of that pure spirit requires not only the qualities that Deerslayer exemplifies but the moral vocabulary that allows Cooper to create their exemplification in the first place: "Deerslayer stood at the end of the pallet, leaning on Killdeer, unharmed in person; all the fine martial ardor that had so lately glowed in his countenance having given place to the usual look of honesty and benevolence, qualities of which the expression was now softened by manly regret and pity" (p. 1010). By the time we reach this point in the novel (chap. 31) we still may not know what "honesty and benevolence" look like glowing in someone's "countenance," but we can be sure—if we have accepted the imaginative conditions established in the novel—that we are supposed to know. The "usual look" of Deerslayer is no look at all in terms of visual specification; it consists, instead, of Cooper's usual way of describing it.

The verbal formulas and syntactical labyrinths that comprise that descriptive process (and the descriptive dynamic of romance more generally) are, as Martin notes, "entirely consistent with the fictional method itself. The reader is being told, rather than shown, and the economy of telling—the arrangement of information by logical relations—is conventionally a generous one."[9] The workings of this verbal generosity enable Cooper to mix, sometimes implausibly, what Natty calls "ra'al" speech with what Twain calls "the showiest kind of booktalk."[10] Listen to Hurry Harry, for instance, as he chastises Deerslayer for his inexperience in worldly affairs: "You've never yet heard the crack of an angry rifle, and let me tell you, 'tis as different from the persuasion of one of your venison speeches, as the laugh of Judith Hutter, in her best humor, is from the scolding of a Dutch housekeeper on the Mohawk" (p. 578).

Hurry Harry, along with the other characters in the book, is less a character than a rhetorical occasion and he should be treated as such. Such an assertion, however, may be seen as a concession—which it is not—to the charge that Cooper's work is now just children's literature to be read, as Leslie Fiedler puts it, "in large print and embellished with pictures."[11] Critics trying to protect Cooper from such assessments often wound themselves with their own shields, for they try to defend themselves against critical terms they do not challenge in the first place. Allan Nevins, for instance, in a short afterword to a paperback edition of *The Deerslayer*, attempts to overturn the common complaint that Cooper could not depict a "true woman" and that he "gave his readers colorless, namby-pamby heroines instead of the resourceful, intrepid women and daughters of our real frontier." But he does so not by asserting that Cooper had other aims in mind but rather by dubiously emphasizing Judith Hutter's "strength," "enterprise," and "true womanliness" of speech.[12]

"Where the American novelist was successful enough to create genuine art," Marius Bewley asserts, "it will usually be found that it is a deep and emotional concern with abstractions which is the controlling factor in the motives and organization of his work."[13] Cooper's characters are, in effect, abstractions: fictional blanks, whose reality seems highly, if not exclusively rhetorical. Although Judith, of all the characters, seems to gain a psychological depth denied the others, she too finally becomes simply the woman-who-cannot-marry-

Deerslayer. We are never made to feel there is any extended motivational coherence to her personality because the book has no language with which it might be engineered. Judith forms, as it were, the human equivalent of the "dark, Rembrandt-looking hemlocks, 'quivering aspens,' and melancholy pines" (p. 514) that fringe the eastern shore of Lake Glimmerglass—trees that stem less from naturalistic perception than from Cooper's familiarity with previous artistic conventions of the picturesque. If there are moments when Judith appears to gain a touch of psychological complexity (when she reads her mother's letters from the chest, for instance, or insists that Tom Hutter be buried on the lake-bottom at a distance from her mother) she still conducts herself, as Poirier says, "like a refugee from the novels of Jane Austen or, even more, of Thackeray or Scott."[14] She resides in a novel where the narrative voice can verbally attenuate and dismantle what little realistic identity she has, in an aside: "All her feelings as a woman, and as a woman who, for the first time in her life, was beginning to submit to that sentiment which has so much influence on the happiness or misery of her sex, revolted at the cruel fate that she fancied Deerslayer was drawing upon himself" (p. 866).

Poirier rightly interprets Cooper's inability to complicate his imagination of Judith as a consequence of his extravagance in imagining Deerslayer. Cooper, like Melville, needed to "believe in the possibility that the self can expand not merely in the presence of natural force but also in the company of other people, that the self can carry on polite conversation and be [at the same time] something as non-human as a 'transparent eyeball.'"[15] But the inadvertent constraints to which such an ambivalent commitment subjects Cooper's hero, in moments when Deerslayer is forced to express himself and his ideals within social situations made familiar by the novel of manners, exert a distorting pressure of social and psychological accommodation on his character. The legendary dimensions of Cooper's conception of Deerslayer are expansive enough to make the available means of dramatically realizing them often seem either compromising or decorous.

Deerslayer is at his most impressive, Poirier notes, when he is "described rather than self-articulated":

> When we think of the Leather-Stocking Tales years after reading them we forget the hero's dialogue and remember him as one of the great creations of American fiction. . . . silent, marvelously alert, capable of irresistible mechanical proficiency without explanatory claptrap, the servant of principles the more eloquent for being vaguely defined, and with a will undisrupted by muddled personal feelings of sexual love or the desire for gain.[16]

But this distant remembrance of Deerslayer, no matter how appealing, results in a lopsided, partial view. For in seeing this character as a version of the

American Adam, we too often forget, in Poirier's words, "the Sunday School prize essayist who emerges from the dialogue."[17] What we recognize in much of that dialogue, of course, is the seepage of Cooper's own fictional voice into the narrative, which is another way of saying that Deerslayer's conception as a character is, in effect, adulterated by its verbal origins.

Cooper's writing brings with it its own intricate network of literary references, formulas, and social conventions, all of which are marked by their own prehistory and all of which often inadvertently immobilize the very dream of freedom Cooper attempts to embody in Deerslayer. Not only does the novel's "society" fail to provide room for Deerslayer, Cooper himself indicates his inability to make imaginative provisions for such a figure. The question of whom Deerslayer might properly marry, for example, is only as pressing as the terms in which it can be asked. Cooper's language carries with it the signs and sounds of a psychology and literary decorum adopted from the very society Deerslayer is often meant to contest. One has only to consider why the novel is inconceivable (given its present imaginative ambitions) as a first-person narrative, to see that its titular hero gains his mythic dimensions by the extent to which he escapes not from the Iroquois, Hurry Harry, or encroaching settlers but from Cooper's narrative voice. Deerslayer struggles, so to speak, against the idea of his own nature implicit in Cooper's language; he tries to step out of the shadow cast in the novel by Cooper's writing. An analogy to a contemporary film that dramatizes a similar situation may be helpful here. "I'm not bad," the sultry femme fatale Jessica says in *Who Framed Roger Rabbit* (1988), "I'm just drawn that way." I don't *really* talk like this, Natty might say, I'm just written that way. The password is "Fenimore sent me." It seems appropriate that one of Leatherstocking's most original attributes as a character—his laugh (which expresses "exultation, mirth, and irony," as Cooper puts it in *The Pioneers*[18])—is, we are told repeatedly, *silent*.

WHAT LAWRENCE TAKES to be "the essential keyboard of Cooper's soul"—the dramatization of "THE WIGWAM *vs.* MY HOTEL" and "CHINGACHGOOK *vs.* MY WIFE"[19]—remains more evident in the *sounds* of Cooper's prose than in its more explicitly "thematic" tensions. This, for instance, is what it sounds like to enter, and exit, from one of Cooper's forests:

> Whatever may be the changes produced by man, the eternal round of the seasons is unbroken. Summer and winter, seed time and harvest, return in their stated order, with a sublime precision, affording to man one of the noblest of all the occasions he enjoys of proving the high powers of his farreaching mind, in compassing the laws that control their exact uniformity, and in calculating their never ending revolutions. Centuries of summer suns had warmed the tops of the same

69

noble oaks and pines, sending their heats even to the tenacious roots, when voices were heard calling to each other, in the depths of a forest, of which the leafy surface lay bathed in the brilliant light of a cloudless day in June, while the trunks of the trees rose in gloomy grandeur in the shades beneath. The calls were in different tones, evidently proceeding from two men who had lost their way, and were searching in different directions for their path. At length a shout proclaimed success, and presently a man of gigantic mould broke out of the tangled labyrinth of a small swamp, emerging into an opening that appeared to have been formed partly by the ravages of the wind, and partly by those of fire. This little area, which afforded a good view of the sky, although it was pretty well filled with dead trees, lay on the side of one of the high hills, or low mountains, into which nearly the whole surface of the adjacent country was broken.

"Here is room to breathe in!" exclaimed the liberated forester as soon as he found himself under a clear sky, shaking his huge frame like a mastiff that has just escaped from a snowbank. "Hurrah! Deerslayer, here is daylight, at last, and yonder is the lake." (Pp. 496–97)

Philip Fisher, in his highly original study *Hard Facts*, argues that this first appearance of the characters, as they break free into a clearing, is offered "almost as a moment of original creation." He finds this moment of breaking free from the entanglements of nature emblematic of Cooper's "definition of American freedom as the freedom of the just-released captive," but that freedom is purchased only by "the sum total of human violence expended in the novel." This scene, Fisher says, miniaturizes the early stages of national history Cooper imagines from his vantage in 1840. Writing at the conclusion of the Jacksonian Indian Removal, he looks back to see the origins of a now manifest history of white predation, the "ravaged" clearing Americans have made of an original wilderness.[20]

Fisher's points are well taken, yet the most important features of the novel (and this scene) in his account take place on a level of symbolic enactment remarkably unconstrained by and independent of the verbal means by which they are rendered. His focus is upon how "Cooper 'made up' the wilderness" and "the killing of the Indian" by "lodging" certain details, settings, and characters "in the imagination of the American and European world."[21] But what is the role of Cooper's writing in this process of imaginative "lodging" or "cultural incorporation"? The danger of overemphasizing the workings of a "national self-imagination" in any novelist's work is that a discussion of the means by which it is condensed in a text (one of Fisher's favorite analogies) may proceed without a full regard for the imaginative status of the condensation. We may end up, that is, with a national self-imagination free of the very texts that are supposed to constitute the evidence of its existence. We may end up with a compass rather than with the ship it is supposed to steer.

The cultural consequences of dramatic action in Cooper's novel are themselves preceded by the social constraints of the language in which action is imagined. The gap between description and action we so often encounter in Cooper's frontier romances remains more than simply a stylistic trait we can either satirize or defend. It cannot be easily wished or edited away and it fundamentally determines the imaginative status of the thematic tensions these novels present. Whatever the dramatic focus of *The Deerslayer*, the "stated order" of its writing, like the seasons in the passage above, remains unbroken and proclaims its status as literary utterance.

Warren Motley has noted that Cooper frequently controls his material more "by his tone than by the plotting of a narrative line."[22] Cooper's verbal expansiveness and broadening syntax in this passage express less a botanical knowledge of forests than an acknowledgment of the woods as a source of moral lessons. The "eternal rounds of the seasons" are first alluded to not so their praises can be sung but because they afford a noble occasion for dramatizing "the high powers" of man's "far-reaching mind, in compassing the laws that control their exact uniformity, and in calculating their never ending revolutions." This disquisitional tone, however, seems incapable of achieving the kind of rhetorical effect Cooper desires. He drops it in the next sentence and then verbally attempts to enact what he has, like a legal brief, just argued. When we hear that "centuries of summer suns had warmed the tops of the same noble oaks and pines," aural rhythm has replaced moral annotation. Voices call in "a" forest on "a" cloudless June day, surrounded by the trunks of "the" trees (you know, the noble oaks). (Cooper can on occasion "reel off lists of native trees," Fiedler notes, but his woods usually "contain not oaks or beeches or maples, only unnamed archetypal trees, the tree-ish conceptual trees children draw."[23]) The scene takes on a grand anonymity and seems forever caught and suspended in the mythic resonances of phrasings meant to be heard rather than seen ("summer suns," "tenacious roots," "gloomy grandeur").

Yet this is not a scene out of Faulkner's "The Bear." What keeps the language from settling into the kind of rich narrative rhythm we associate with that story is the sudden reappearance of Cooper's prosaic formulas: "At length a shout proclaimed success." A way of singing about the wilderness, that is, quickly reverts back to a ceremonious way of talking about it. This alternation between two divergent narrative impulses continues throughout the novel. One side of Cooper's imagination wants Hurry Harry raw, shaking himself off like a snow-covered mastiff and cheering for daylight; the other side, stiffened and decorous, makes him, with a mild-mannered pun, "the liberated forester." Both

71

impulses or voices use formulaic language but one forms the voice of the settlements, as it were, and the other the voice of the woods.

Twain was painfully and painstakingly sensitive to only the former voice, to the sounds of Cooper's genteel volubility, and he was temperamentally incapable of doing anything but lampooning such verbal fluency. Twain's remarks are, of course, unfair, even when we acknowledge that his "sulphurous grumbling over Cooper," in Sydney Krause's words, is not the work of "a responsible citizen like Samuel Clemens" but of "a hoodwinking persona who . . . is not always entitled to the horror he exhibits and is not the unsuspecting reader he pretends to be."[24] Yet it remains to be understood that Twain's exuberant satire of Cooper's style is shrewd as well as nastily dismissive. His remarks, when drained of their pejorative venom are, in fact, critically astute:

> Cooper's word-sense was singularly dull. When a person has a poor ear for music he will flat and sharp right along without knowing it. He keeps near the tune, but it is *not* the tune. When a person has a poor ear for words, the result is a literary flatting and sharping; you perceive what he is intending to say, but you also perceive that he doesn't *say* it. This is Cooper. He was not a word-musician.[25]

Twain is often right about Cooper, but he is not right in the ways he thinks he is. While Twain's general appraisal of Cooper's literary merit is, in Krause's words, "a bacchanal of sophistry,"[26] he does emphasize Cooper's ability to "flat and sharp right along," to establish a rhythmic continuity, whether or not Twain thinks it is out of key. Twain rightly contends that we perceive Cooper's language *as language* and not, as in realistic imagining, as a sustained illusion of reality. In Twain's own terms, Cooper actually *is* a word-musician; he does create a sound in his prose that we cannot ignore, one that rises from what Martin calls his "serried banks of balanced clauses."[27] The problem is that the sound of Cooper's writing simply does not happen to suit Twain's taste.

Cooper's stylistic fluency is evident in the smallest details of his prose as well as in his larger conceptions of psychology or landscape. He can, for instance, transform the act of dining into "doing justice to the viands," he can turn the sun into "the great luminary" or a bullet into "a fatal messenger," and he can make a loon into one of the "feathered inmates of the wilderness." His ability to invoke high diction in this way forms just a small part of how his romances establish a verbal continuity, a stabilized narrative manner that can inspect the instep of an Indian or rhapsodize about an uncharted continent in much the same way.

An example of this can be seen in Cooper's addresses to the reader, which are generally meant to serve as narrative anchorage points, moments in which to regroup after a digression or places from which to tack off in a new direction:

Here we shall leave him [Hurry Harry] to recover his strength and the due circulation of his blood, while we proceed with the narrative of events that crowd upon
us too fast to admit of any postponement. (P. 829)

We have written much, but in vain, concerning this extraordinary being [Deer-
slayer], if the reader require now to be told, that, untutored as he was in the
learning of the world, and simple as he ever showed himself to be in all matters
touching the subtleties of conventional taste, he was a man of strong, native, poetical feeling. (P. 758)

Deerslayer and the Delaware took their rest in the Ark, where we shall leave them
enjoying the deep sleep of the honest, the healthful and fearless, to return to the girl
we have last seen in the midst of the forest. (P. 648)

Rivenoak quietly took the seat we have mentioned, and, after a short pause, he
commenced a dialogue, which we translate, as usual, for the benefit of those readers who have not studied the North American languages. (P. 774)

The motives behind these various statements are not, of course, all the same.
The force of all of them, however, is to impose a narrative drag in the novel,
an animated condition of delay. The first, for instance, enacts a postponement
while telling us we cannot afford to have one, while the second lengthily
provides the very explanation it deems unnecessary. We can recognize in all
these examples the same verbal manner at work, that of a well-barbered,
slightly cumbersome, deliberating sensibility, actively committed to preserv-
ing the "due circulation" of its imaginative processes.

"A man of strong, native, poetical feeling" seems sure to be treated to "the
deep sleep" of "the healthful and fearless" because both are part of the same
narrative rhythm, the product of the same fictionalizing voice. That voice
makes an avowal of realistic motives all the more literary for having been so
avowed. Thus, to remind readers that Rivenoak "commenced a dialogue,
which we translate, as usual" is not meant to stigmatize those readers who have
not boned up on Algonquin or Iroquois dialects but to emphasize, or intend to
emphasize, that we are privy to a "translated" moment. Yet however much
Cooper may have wanted this kind of aside to complicate a reader's response
to a dramatic situation, such remarks frequently end up leaving him at the
mercy of the kinds of embarrassment Twain is eager to initiate.

The sheer volume of what Cooper's inflationary syntax can bring within its
grasp is seen as smothering by some of his critics. Arthur Mizener, for example, claims that Cooper's interpolative "sermons,"

like everything else in Cooper's novels, are written in an insensitive, mechanical
version of the genteel style of the eighteenth century. Even at the most dramatic

73

and emotional moments, Cooper does not deviate from this rather dry and pompous style. . . . its orderly, dispassionate, reasonable tone is incongruous with the
passionately romantic subject matter it is often required to express.

Written as they are in this style the sermons in *The Deerslayer* may seem to
modern readers both awkward interruptions of the narrative and dull in themselves, but Cooper's instinct is right; it is the moral drama of his novels that gives
them their power.[28]

Mizener can conceive of Cooper's subject matter in the novel—Indians, escapes and chases, natural scenery, religious halfwits—as "passionately romantic" only when he separates it from Cooper's "orderly, dispassionate, [and]
reasonable" verbal manner. "Dramatic and emotional moments" exist in *The
Deerslayer* for Mizener not because of but in spite of Cooper's gentility. Yet
in looking for something to defend in Cooper ("moral drama"), Mizener implies that we can, in effect, evaporate Cooper's language and ignore its weight
of countervailing social contract by locating what he says it imaginatively suffocates. Mizener fails to notice, that is, how the dry gentility of Cooper's style
integrally determines how that drama is created and perceived.

Mizener's remarks form something of a paradigm for later critical approaches to Cooper's work like that of Fisher and Richard Slotkin. The latter
asserts that Deerslayer is "a kind of priest of the woodlands, a figure out of
primitive mythology or out of Flint's portrait of Boone as the hunter acolyte
of the forest, whose deeds are contained by a moral spirit that transforms them
into acts of devotion."[29] But the agency of containment that Slotkin vaguely
terms a "moral spirit" here seems somehow to exist outside of the language by
which that spirit is embodied and is itself contained and predetermined. The
primitive woodland figures Slotkin mentions here hover, like holographic images, behind the well-dressed, smiling, public man who emerges from the
novel's narrative voice.

For better or for worse, Cooper's verbal manner remains unavailable to the
kind of editing Mizener, Fisher, Slotkin, and others wish to impose, though the
conspicuous use of ellipses in much critical quotation from Cooper's work
often helps such approaches seem tenable. Cooper's style operates not mathe-
matically (narrative minus genteel style equaling moral drama or hunter-aco-
lytes) but chemically, introducing imaginative conditions that largely render
our ways of processing realistic fiction inapplicable. The social and literary
premises embedded in Cooper's language have, by the time we encounter
them, already prefigured his dramatic capacities and representational range.

By establishing a set of verbal circumstances that invoke the legitimacy of
fictional language, of convention and special indulgence rather than the realis-

tic legitimacy of words used to signify something beyond themselves, Cooper alters our sense of what can or cannot happen in his novel. If we accept this, we can freely admit to the special kind of literary pleasure afforded by Hetty Hutter's kneeling for an "Our Father," unharmed, in front of an upreared brown bear, by Deerslayer's catching tomahawks by the handle when they are thrown at him, or by Hurry Harry's being dragged, as he hangs onto a rope by his teeth, in the water behind the Ark. Cooper's novel, that is, inhabits a self-contained world, freed from any necessity for our translating it or applying it to an aspect of our own experience.

Henry James aptly describes the kind of imaginative license we yield to a romance, as it depressurizes a realistic bias, in his well-known preface to *The American*:

> The only *general* attribute of projected romance that I can see, the only one that fits all its cases, is the fact of the kind of experience with which it deals—experience liberated, so to speak; experience disengaged, disembroiled, disencumbered, exempt from the conditions that we usually know to attach to it and, if we wish so to put the matter, drag upon it, and operating in a medium which relieves it, in a particular interest, of the inconvenience of a *related*, a measurable state, a state subject to all our vulgar communities. . . . The balloon of experience is in fact of course tied to the earth, and under that necessity we swing, thanks to a rope of remarkable length, in the more or less commodious car of the imagination; but it is by the rope we know where we are, and from the moment that cable is cut we are at large and unrelated: we only swing apart from the globe—though remaining as exhilarated, naturally, as we like, especially when all goes well. The art of the romancer is, "for the fun of it," insidiously to cut the cable, to cut it without our detecting him.[30]

If Cooper is at times easily detected cutting the cable, he is less hampered than James by qualms about "vulgar communities," or the need for such a phrase. The verbal "balloon" of a Cooper romance is never entirely free of its earthly moorings, its "measurable" or realistic extensions, just as, if it comes to that, there is a real geographical model for Lake Glimmerglass. But the atmospheric conditions in *The Deerslayer* are not conducive to realistic accountability. Cooper establishes a verbal equilibrium whose imaginative artificiality remains greater than any of the single elements scattered along its narrative surface, including scenes of violence.

When incidents involving murder, scalping, or torture occur within what we recognize as a distinctly verbal or fictional context, the visual and sensory efficiency of what might otherwise become highly graphic or disturbing is largely discounted. This does not mean such scenes cannot be affecting. But "seeing" an act of violence in a film or a novel involves an entirely different response from being told about it. And though all verbal representations of such acts are "told" in the sense of being re-presented in language, not all of them involve the same representational energies. Our responses to examples of violence in fiction depend upon whether a text presents us with the illusion of an event or with a voice that describes that event.

A descriptive voice clearly dominates the depiction of what greets Hetty and Judith Hutter after the Mingos have futilely chased them on the lake. The women regain the previously occupied "castle" where the Indians were holding their father. Hetty sees him in his room and says that "he seems to be overtaken with liquor now":

> "That is strange!—[Judith says] Would the savages have drunk with him, and then leave him behind? But tis a grievous sight to a child, Hetty, to witness such a failing in a parent, and we will not go near him 'till he wakes."
>
> A groan from the inner room, however, changed this resolution, and the girls ventured near a parent, whom it was no unusual thing for them to find in a condition that lowers a man to the level of brutes. He was seated, reclining in a corner of the narrow room, with his shoulders supported by the angle, and his head fallen heavily on his chest. Judith moved forward, with a sudden impulse, and removed a canvass cap that was forced so low on his head as to conceal his face, and indeed all but his shoulders. The instant this obstacle was taken away, the quivering and raw flesh, the bared veins and muscles, and all the other disgusting signs of mortality, as they are revealed by tearing away the skin, showed he had been scalped, though still living. (P. 835)

In the verbal terms of the passage it is not Tom Hutter but "a parent, whom it was no unusual thing for them to find in a condition that lowers a man to the level of brutes" that has been scalped. A parent, we might add, whom it is no unusual thing to find so periphrastically described throughout the novel. Tom Hutter remains imaginatively invisible here: merely something covered with a canvas cap.

"The quivering and raw flesh, the bared veins and muscles": nothing about this description is necessarily connected, in a visual way, with Tom Hutter. It could apply to a dissected frog. Cooper attempts visually to detail a palpitating mess that refuses to resolve itself into something we can imaginatively see. His phrases about Hutter's scalped head seem to provoke or tempt a flash of visual or sensory potential that is then dampened first by its "laboratory" language and then by the quickness with which Cooper's narrative manner is again reestablished. The visual ambivalence of one moment in the sentence's rhythmic stride gets quickly assumed into the fabric of an obviously fictional formulation: "and all the other disgusting signs of mortality as they are revealed by tearing away the skin." So has Tom Hutter been scalped or not? He obviously has, but the action occurs within the verbal confines of a romance that keeps its description from visually impinging upon us. We imaginatively process its effect in much the same way we accept Deerslayer's bringing down two Mingos with one shot: by granting them both a fictional validity that has no extension into nor contingency upon our own experience.

That suspension of disbelief, however, is not Cooper's. A scalped head seems disgusting to him as much because it can allow for realistic description (for "bared veins" rather than for the "signs of mortality") as because it reveals an inhumane or barbaric practice. The shudder in the last sentence of the passage, which ends chapter 20, arises in response to a side of Cooper's verbal imagination that seems out of place in this novel. The force of Cooper's disquisitional Augustan style immediately absorbs this tiny visual rupture and reinstates the verbal frequency established in the rest of the novel. Instead of providing an example of what Wayne Franklin calls "the bite" of Cooper's realism in *The Deerslayer* (which he says "upsets what otherwise might become a pure dream"[31]) the language of this moment allows the controlling power of the narrative voice to be reinstated. That voice opens the next chapter, unabated:

> The reader must imagine the horror that daughters would experience, at unexpectedly beholding the shocking spectacle that was placed before the eyes of Judith and Esther, as related in the close of the last chapter. We shall pass over the first emotions, the first acts of filial piety, and proceed with the narrative, by imagining rather than relating most of the revolting features of the scene. The mutilated and ragged head was bound up, the unseemly blood was wiped from the face of the sufferer, the other appliances required by appearances and care were resorted to, and there was time to enquire into the more serious circumstances of the case. (P. 836)

The reemergence of sanitized euphemisms here ("quivering and raw flesh" having changed into "the revolting features of the scene") and Cooper's insistence on returning to an explicitly acknowledged fictional context—one with readers, chapters, and a proceeding narrative—make the previous realistic details seem an unfortunate, almost illicit narrative lapse. He now calls what momentarily fascinated him "a shocking spectacle," one whose "revolting features" are morally as well as physically "unseemly." Our further interest in them, he implies, can only be gratuitous and morbid. Yet Cooper can now "pass over" the scene (and tell us he is passing it over) precisely because he knows his reader will vividly imagine its revolting details without more of his

77

help. The physical "fact" of a scalping seems to lie just off the edge of the page, and Cooper officially refuses that action his representational sanction. He reminds us, first, that our motives in wanting to see more are at best questionable, and second, that there are "more serious circumstances" to attend to here. There is, after all, a story to tell.

The potentially realistic details in the description of Tom Hutter's scalping are further muffled by the time Deerslayer is a captive in the Mingo camp and confronted by the Panther, "a grim chief" whose brother-in-law Deerslayer has killed:

> "Dog of the palefaces!" [the Panther] exclaimed in Iroquois, "go yell among the curs of your own evil hunting grounds!"
>
> The denunciation was accompanied by an appropriate action. Even while speaking his arm was lifted, and the tomahawk hurled. Luckily the loud tones of the speaker had drawn the eye of Deerslayer towards him, else would that moment have probably closed his career. So great was the dexterity with which this dangerous weapon was thrown, and so deadly the intent, that it would have riven the scull of the prisoner, had not he stretched forth an arm, and caught the handle in one of its turns, with a readiness quite as remarkable, as the skill with which the missile had been hurled. The projectile force was so great, notwithstanding, that when Deerslayer's arm was arrested, his hand was raised above and behind his own head, and in the very attitude necessary to return the attack. It is not certain whether the circumstance of finding himself unexpectedly in this menacing posture and armed, tempted the young man to retaliate, or whether sudden resentment overcame his forbearance and prudence. His eye kindled, however, and a small red spot appeared on each cheek, while he cast all his energy into the effort of his arm and threw back the weapon at his assailant. The unexpectedness of this blow contributed to its success, the Panther neither raising an arm, nor bending his head to avoid it. The keen little axe struck the victim in a perpendicular line with the nose, literally braining him on the spot. Sallying forward, as the serpent darts at its enemy even while receiving its own death wound, this man of powerful frame, fell his length into the open area formed by the circle, quivering in death. A common rush to his relief left the captive, for a single instant, quite without the crowd, and, willing to make one desperate effort for life, he bounded off, with the activity of a deer. There was but a breathless instant, when the whole band, old and young, women and children, abandoning the lifeless body of the Panther, where it lay, raised the yell of alarm and followed in pursuit. (Pp. 955–56)

Twain and other readers' first response to the unexpectedness of this description may have been laughter. The death of the Panther seems to bother Cooper much less than Hutter's scalping. There is no talk of the "disgusting signs of mortality," but that is partly because the Indian here is so quickly and neatly deprived of mortality.[32] At the climactic moment Cooper turns the tomahawk into "the keen little axe" (with what sounds like admiration for its efficiency) and its actual impact into an idiomatic phrase: "literally braining him on the spot." Such an expression, in its very contradictoriness (since "braining" someone is so obviously a figurative rather than a literal action) seems the perfect example of how Cooper's style functions. Yet what may be even more characteristic of Cooper's manner here is the earnestness we hear in "literally," as if no other phrase but "braining him on the spot" could convey a precise sense of what has happened.

In the dramatic setup here Cooper plays the role of a narrative sportscaster, speculating on contingencies that never materialize and admiringly sizing up both opponents. From the same spectatorial distance, Cooper then guesses at Deerslayer's motives in throwing the tomahawk back, notices that "a small red spot appeared on each cheek" and fashions a metaphor for the quite literal downfall of the Panther. How a man with a tomahawk stuck in his head "sallies forward" like a darting snake, even as he heavily collapses at full length, is a question for Twain to ask. Yet Twain would undoubtedly turn this moment into parodic farce, which is not at all what it is meant to be. In the same way that much of the fun in watching someone imitate, say, Ronald Reagan resides in the fact that the impersonator is *not* the person he is pretending to be, the inadvertent literary pleasure of this scene arises to the extent that mimesis has been upstaged. There is, obviously, nothing amusing about people getting struck by axes in life, but there can be about the fact that they get struck, in this theatrical and bloodless a fashion, quite naturally in a Cooper romance. Cooper refuses to let the realistic details of violent scenes untrack the verbal continuities of his Leatherstocking novels. His narrative, too, abandons "the lifeless body of the Panther" here (if not quite with "the activity of a deer") and continues on its action-packed, storytelling way.

REALISTIC FICTION often makes a highly visual-sensory description of violence a climactic event whose shock or terror is made imaginatively palpable because we are unaware of the language of its description. The insistence that we see through language to grisly particulars is an insistence that words are less important than what they can imaginatively evoke. Violence in Cooper's novels, however, emerges from the even rhythms and moral vocabulary of his writing, which tend to absorb and neutralize whatever realistic descriptive impulses they may prompt. Our awareness of verbal artifice in reading Cooper attenuates the realistic substantiality of his violence. Cooper's knives, at least in this novel, have no edges.

79

Later in the book, when Deerslayer is tortured by being tied to a tree and having tomahawks thrown within inches of his head (in one case pinning some of his hair to the bark of the tree) he does not, of course, flinch or close his eyes. When the Indians shoot at him while he is thus bound he seems even more insouciant:

> Shot after shot was made; all the bullets coming in close proximity to the Deer-slayer's head, without touching it. Still no one could detect even the twitching of a muscle on the part of the captive, or the slightest winking of an eye. This indom-itable resolution, which so much exceeded everything of its kind that any present had before witnessed, might be referred to three distinct causes. The first was resignation to his fate, blended with natural steadiness of deportment; for our hero had calmly made up his mind that he must die, and preferred this mode to any other; the second was his great familiarity with this particular weapon, which de-prived it of all the terror that is usually connected with the mere form of the danger; and the third was this familiarity carried out in practice, to a degree so nice as to enable the intended victim to tell, within an inch, the precise spot where each bullet must strike, for he calculated its range by looking in at the bore of the piece. (P. 986)

This is a novel in which "indomitable resolution" can not only be appealed to as an emotional attribute but phrased as such and accounted for by three-part explanations. Cooper is, after all, describing not Deerslayer but *the* Deer-slayer, a figure Fiedler aptly calls a sinless "Faust in buckskins" aglow in legend-ary, if formulaic, glory.[33]

Realistic fiction attempts to subvert and explode all such examples of narra-tive equilibrium, which is why it customarily presents us with depictions of violence that seem raw and unaccommodated. But when scenes of violence are deprived of a realistic dynamic and set in inhospitable, or rather overly hospita-ble verbal contexts, they provide a useful example of how our experience of reading romance distinctly differs from that of reading realistic fiction. To participate we have to set aside our more common habits of visual imagining and accept the verbal conditions an author establishes. Cooper seems less in-terested in dramatically staging scenes than in telling us about them, in layering the sentences that describe them with a kind of verbal Styrofoam. We can have an opinion about his style, but it seems particularly ungenerous to judge it inappropriately in terms of realistic fiction.

Critics attempting to "rescue" Cooper from the opprobrium heaped upon him by Twain and Lawrence, however, often err just as badly in another direction by neglecting the writing that forms such an integral part of Cooper's lasting appeal. There seems to be a missing middle ground in the criticism of

Cooper's work, a perspective from which to defend the value of his fiction without simply turning his characters and landscapes into ideograms that are somehow independent of the writing from which they arise. To read *The Deer-slayer* without recourse to ellipses, without the need for thematically editing or visually focusing its language, is to confront the novel on its own verbal turf: in the imaginative extravagance that governs its fictional life. It is also to gain a vantage on those critics, outside of Twain's Veterinary College of Arizona, who keep trying either to protect Cooper from his own style or tendentiously to "filch it from him."

Poe's Violence

GANGRENOUS PROTOCOL

> [Wordsworth] was to blame in wearing away his youth in
> contemplation with the end of poeticizing in his manhood.
> With the increase of his judgment the light which should
> make it apparent has faded away. His judgment conse-
> quently is too correct. This may not be understood,—but
> the old Goths of Germany would have understood it, who
> used to debate matters of importance to their State twice,
> once when drunk, and once when sober—sober that they
> might not be deficient in formality—drunk lest they should
> be destitute of vigor.
>
> —*Edgar Allan Poe, "Letter to B———"*

"IT WOULD be difficult for me to take Poe up," Allen Tate remarked in 1949,
" 'study' him, and proceed to a critical judgment."[1] The prospect of taking Poe
up forty odd years later seems no less difficult or problematic, for he still seems
as odd as he was ingenious, as neurotic as he was impetuous and original. Poe's
life and work offer a logjam of temperamental contradictions, a complicated
braid of heterogenous impulses, attributes, and posturings. Something like a
cross between William Blake and O. Henry, Poe was a poetic visionary who
tried to master the American magazine fiction market of the 1830s and 1840s.
Poe's literary criticism was notorious in his time for its display of a fastidious,
multilingual urbanity and a brassy disdain for what he considered trash. (He
once complained of "this trumpery declamation, this maudlin sentiment, this
metaphor run-mad, this twaddling verbiage, this halting and doggrel rhythm,
this unintelligible rant and cant" in Cornelius Mathews's poem *Wakondah*.[2] Yet
this acerbity was also interspersed with eager self-promotions and hyperbolic
overestimations of friends' work (especially that of women poets in whom he
took an amorous interest).

"Poe enjoyed the world of literary journalism," Julian Symons asserts, and
"took pleasure in drubbing nonentities." Yet "at the same time . . . he despised
it." Poe's attitudes toward his own fiction were equally unstable. His "hack-
work and the pieces he regarded seriously interpenetrated each other," Symons

says, "and he was so avid for praise that he was prepared to applaud almost any friendly criticism, no matter how ill-judged or foolish."[3] Moreover, Poe was avid for such praise at the same time that he was commendably trying, as Edmund Wilson says, "to curb the tendency of Americans to overrate or over-praise their own books," "fighting a rear-guard action against the over-inflation of British reputations and the British injustice to American writers," and attempting "to break down the monopolistic instincts of the New Englanders, who tended to act as a clique and to keep out New Yorkers and Southerners."[4] With such multifarious ambitions, it is hardly surprising that Poe's work is often approached today with skepticism, a skepticism heightened by the French exaltation of what Leslie Fiedler calls "*Edgairpo*," a *poète maudit* and "French *symboliste*, once-removed."[5] (Baudelaire, we are told, was in the habit of making his morning prayers to God and to Edgar Poe.)

"The psychology of the pretender is always a factor to be reckoned with in Poe";[6] "that an air of conscious falsification—trickery, prestidigitation, humbug—has always hung about the name of Poe and his productions is undeniable";[7] "Poe's nature was histrionic";[8] Poe's style "seems always something half borrowed, half patched" and makes his reader "suspicious of the grandiose interpretations the stories perversely invite":[9] such are the assertions routinely encountered in Poe criticism. But these assessments sometimes tend to be rhetorical throwaways, obligatory disclaimers that do not then sidetrack the extravagant critical claims for Poe's work that follow them. "The association between the acting style of Vincent Price and the styles of Poe," Harold Bloom quips, "is alas not gratuitous, and indeed is an instance of deep crying out unto deep." Bloom's pejorative appraisal, however, is itself as gratuitous as his "alas" here, for he goes on to claim that Poe's "bad writing"—with "its palpable squalors" and "awful diction"—does not matter, for "the tale somehow is stronger than its telling": "Poe's diction scarcely distracts us from our retelling, to ourselves, his bizarre myths. There is a dreadful universalism pervading Poe's weird tales."[10]

Poe's work embodies "a hymn to negativity," Bloom says, a dark, demonic refutation of the pragmatic Emersonian vision of American self-reliance. This scarcely represents a new critical take on Poe's writing but what interests me here is the fact that for Bloom, Poe's "dreadful universalism" (a phrase that sounds like it might be *in* rather than about a Poe story) is somehow stronger than the language that effectively suffocates it. As with criticism of Cooper, style exists not as a crucial shaping agent but as a peripheral element that impedes a recognition of more important matters. An impatience with style becomes in Poe studies a requisite prelude to high claims about what Bloom calls the "psychological dynamics and mythic reverberations" encrypted or encoded in his stories.[11] The notion of the critic as a kind of exegetical resurrection man exhuming "mythic reverberations" would no doubt have appealed to Poe, but it proves fairly unhelpful in describing the imaginative conditions at work in his writing. The question with Poe, as Walter Bezanson aptly puts it, "is how much flummery one will endure in exchange for his special vision."[12] It is possible, I think, to read Poe's work without simply jeering at it as cheap Gothic Pablum or transforming it into what Symons calls "a wonderful academic property, a kind of palace of symbolic marvels in which [we] can roam endlessly, forever making new discoveries."[13] But we cannot do this by sundering Poe's flummery and his special vision: the two are joined at the spine in his fiction.

"POE IS the transitional figure in modern literature," Tate argues, "because he discovered our great subject, the disintegration of personality, but kept it in a language that had developed in [an eighteenth-century] tradition of unity and order. . . . He is at the parting of the ways; the two terms of his conflict are thus more prominent than they would appear to be in a writer, or in an age, fully committed to either extreme."[14] The conflict in Poe's work between psychological disintegration and a genteel descriptive tradition offers an interesting contrast to Cooper's fiction. As we have seen, the artificiality of Cooper's writing, the felt weight of its literary authority, directly determines the representational force of what it depicts—whether the wilderness, alien cultures, or scenes of violence. It ensures that such subjects will not gain an imaginative substantiality more autonomous than the language that descriptively stabilizes and controls them. The very verbal means by which Cooper ostensibly celebrates savage or aboriginal aspects of human behavior render them safely "intelligible," free from any menacing moments of imaginative illegibility.

Poe's narrative manner—with its inflationary syntax, genteel self-assurance, and euphemistic diction ("we never get a pint or quart or gallon of wine from Poe," Gordon Weaver notes, "we get 'a decanter'. . . . [or] 'a gobletful'"[15])—often seems reminiscent of Cooper. But the drama of Poe's stories typically accentuates the tenuousness of such verbal equanimity. In some cases a rational narrative voice is found to be that of a self-admitted madman. In others, a tone of reasonableness is suddenly disrupted by paranoia or by nightmarish images of necrophilism, incest, physical decay, and violence. The rationalistic cadences of a narrative voice are often sustained in Poe's stories for the sole pleasure of watching them run for cover when the irrational or the fantastic unexpectedly intrudes. Rationality does not always crumble: the narrator of "The Fall of the House of Usher" flees "aghast" in the story's last paragraph, yet his terror does not prevent him from staying for the credits, as it were: he looks back in time to catch a glimpse of *Apocalypse Now.* But in general, when a discourse of rationality collapses in Poe's fiction the spectacle is meant to afford something like the "primitive gratifications," in Susan Sontag's words, of watching expensive sets come crashing down in disaster films.[16]

A crucial question in approaching Poe's work is, To what degree is he manipulatively aware of what he attempts in his fiction? "As a writer," Judith Sunderland notes,

> Poe has been condemned for producing an art that is cold and calculating; on the other hand, he has been condemned for a compulsiveness and obsession that severely limited his work by leaving him only barely in control. In the first case, the artist is cast in the role of victimizer; in the second, in that of a hapless victim. Both states occur in his fictions, and there is some danger in attributing either one or both of them to Poe himself.[17]

The respective dangers are those of naiveté or overdetermination. Either we take Poe to be a Roderick Usher at the mercy of his own morbidly acute senses and lack of moral energy or a crafty Montresor who knows that all it takes to get Fortunato into the family vaults is a hint that if he is busy Montresor can always consult his rival Luchresi.

The notion that Poe is "fundamentally a bad or tawdry stylist," James Gargano argues, "is based, ultimately, on the untenable and often unanalyzed assumption that Poe and his narrators are identical literary twins and that he must be held responsible for all their wild or perfervid utterances; their shrieks and groans are too often conceived as emanating from Poe himself."[18] True enough, but Gargano goes on to assert that "the structure of many of Poe's stories clearly reveals an ironical and comprehensive intelligence . . . ordering events so as to establish a vision of life and character which the narrator's very inadequacies help to 'prove.'" Yet to assert that Poe "is conscious of the abnormalities of his narrators" does not necessarily mean that he wishes only to expose "the intellectual ruses through which they strive, only too earnestly, to justify themselves."[19] The issue of whether or not Poe condones such ruses should not keep us from noting how often he delights more in the earnestness of the confessional rhetoric of his first-person tales than in the self-condemnation that earnestness supposedly dramatizes. Henry James's charge that an enthusiasm for Poe's work "is the mark of a decidedly primitive stage of reflection" can be quickly countered but not by simply asserting that Poe intends to slap the wrists of his febrile narrators. Such a defense neglects the "imp of the perverse" in Poe's writing.

The notion of perversity is usually considered in relation to Poe's work in the way he proposed it: as a psychological principle, "one of the primitive impulses of the human heart," as he puts it in "The Black Cat," an "unfathomable longing of the soul to vex itself—to offer violence to its own nature—to do wrong for the wrong's sake only" (p. 599). Poe typically accentuates this notion because it allows him to investigate a fundamental component of human behavior overlooked by the phrenologists and "all the moralists who have preceded them" (p. 826). Yet it is characteristic that he describes this most irrational of impulses in the most exaggeratedly rationalistic of terms. The narrator of "The Imp of the Perverse," for instance, begins his story less as a narrator than as a guest lecturer:

> It cannot be denied that phrenology, and in great measure, all metaphysicianism, have been concocted *àpriori*. The intellectual or logical man, rather than the understanding or observant man, set himself to imagine designs—to dictate purposes to God. Having thus fathomed to his satisfaction, the intentions of Jehovah, out of these intentions he built his innumerable systems of mind. In the matter of phrenology, for example, we first determined, naturally enough, that it was the design of the Deity that man should eat. We then assigned to man an organ of alimentiveness, and this organ is the scourge with which the Deity compels man, will-I nill-I, into eating. Secondly, having settled it to be God's will [and so forth]. (P. 826)

Poe's topic is not spurious but he addresses his subject here in the same overdetermined way that the prefect of the Parisian police searches the Minister D's apartment in "The Purloined Letter": probing seat cushions with "fine long needles" and examining the jointings and gluing of "every description of furniture, by the aid of a most powerful microscope" (p. 685).

The speaker in "The Imp of the Perverse" (whether a man or a woman we cannot tell) turns out to be imprisoned and is waiting to be hung for having murdered a nameless victim by means of a poisoned candlestick (no evidence, the perfect crime). Addressing an unidentified "you," he says that he has "said thus much" (four pages on perversity), "that in some measure I may answer your question, that I may explain to you why I am here, . . . Had I not been thus prolix, you might either have misunderstood me altogether; or with the rabble, you might have fancied me mad" (p. 830). Though the narrator claims to be a victim of the imp of the perverse, he appears to be entirely amoral. He inherits his victim's estate but there is no indication that he kills him in order to gain the inheritance,[20] nor does he reveal his guilt here because of remorse for his crime. What beckons him "on to death" is not "the very ghost of him whom I murdered" but the "imp," his own "casual self-suggestion, that I might possibly be fool enough to confess the murder of which I had been guilty" (p. 831).

The most immediate impulse of perversity that the narrator indulges, however, is not self-betrayal but "prolixity," which eventually takes shape as an argumentative example:

There lives no man who at some period, has not been tormented, for example, by an earnest desire to tantalize a listener by circumlocution. The speaker is aware that he displeases; he has every intention to please; he is usually curt, precise, and clear; the most laconic and luminous language is struggling for utterance upon his tongue; it is only with difficulty that he restrains himself from giving it flow; he dreads and deprecates the anger of him whom he addresses; yet, the thought strikes him, that by certain involutions and parentheses, this anger may be engendered. That single thought is enough. The impulse increases to a wish, the wish to a desire, the desire to an uncontrollable longing, and the longing, (to the deep regret and mortification of the speaker, and in defiance of all consequences,) is indulged. (P. 828)

Is Poe being self-consciously and ironically prolix here to demonstrate the narrator's point?[21] Or is he simply so enthralled with the notion of perversity that he remains unaware of the speaker's own "involutions and parentheses"? It seems characteristic of Poe to take ideas that were controversial or outlandish in his own time and pour them through a rationalistic sieve in his fiction— though the sieve, as we shall see, often has a fairly loose rhetorical mesh. "How, then, am I mad?" asks the narrator of "The Tell-Tale Heart," epitomizing the narrative strategy of much of Poe's fiction: "Hearken! and observe how healthily—how calmly I can tell you the whole story" (p. 555). Mental health is frequently equated (both by Poe's narrators and by Poe himself) with what seems to be verbal equanimity, with a rationalistic ability to "healthily" describe a marvelous, thrilling, or horrific experience.

Julian Symons distinguishes two analogous aspects of Poe's fictional sensibility, which he labels "Visionary Poe" and "Logical Poe":

For Visionary Poe, any art worth the name was in search of something different from, and finer than, ordinary reality. Logical Poe, however, believed that all literary effects were explicable, and that by the exercise of logic you could take a work of literature apart like a clock, and see how it functioned. . . . Visionary Poe was concerned with the nature of art, with man's relationship to God, with the connection between beauty and death. Logical Poe was given the task of making a living, playing jokes, evolving hoaxes, creating and solving puzzles and cryptograms, and in the end creating the detective story. . . . The horror stories were written by Visionary Poe, but Logical Poe was always breathing over his shoulder.[22]

If we think of Symons's terms here as characterizing two rhetorical impulses in Poe's work (and ignore the way Visionary and Logical Poe start to sound like Laurel and Hardy), we can see that they apply to more than the difference between, say, the mind that writes "The Raven" and that which writes "The Philosophy of Composition" to account for it. They describe as well the varying descriptive modes that interact sentence by sentence within the same story.

In "A Descent into the Maelström," for instance, Visionary Poe offers us High Romantic descriptions of a Norwegian fisherman's journey into a maelstrom, a "howling Phlegethon" (p. 436) with moonlit, jet-black walls whirling at a forty-five-degree angle and with "a thick mist" at the bottom, "over which hung a magnificent rainbow, like that narrow and tottering bridge which Mussulmen say is the only pathway between Time and Eternity" (p. 445). Logical Poe, on the other hand, provides in the same story, sometimes the same paragraph, quotations from the *Encyclopedia Britannica*, mock-scientific talk about the "gyratory motion of the subsided vortices" (p. 434), a pedantic distinction between the use of the words *cylinder* and *sphere*, and a footnote that says, "See Archimedes, 'De Incidentibus in Fluido.'—lib. 2" (a work that, as one critic has pointed out, is fictional[23]).

It is possible to argue that the imaginative bonding of the discursive sensibilities represented by Visionary and Logical Poe is "cultural" in origin. As Roland Barthes puts it,

> the mixture of the strange and the scientific had its high-point in the part of the nineteenth century to which Poe, broadly speaking, belongs: there was great enthusiasm for observing the supernatural scientifically (magnetism, spiritism, telepathy, etc.); the supernatural adopts a scientific, rationalistic alibi; the cry from the heart of that positivist age runs thus: if only one could believe scientifically in immortality![24]

Yet while Poe seems keenly aware of these cultural ambivalences, a quick example from *The Narrative of Arthur Gordon Pym* shows that he seems interested in them as much for their promise of fictional capital as for any deeper psychological impulse to which they might answer.

Poe frequently establishes a narrative voice whose verbal function is wordily to detail a wordless experience. He delights, for example, in language that describes, at length, a character's inability to speak, as when Pym, forsaken and debilitated in the hold of the *Grampus*, unexpectedly hears his name called by his friend Augustus Barnard—a sure sign, it seems, that he will soon be rescued:

> So unexpected was anything of the kind, and so intense was the emotion excited within me by the sound, that I endeavoured in vain to reply. My powers of speech totally failed, and, in an agony of terror lest my friend should conclude me dead, and return without attempting to reach me, I stood up between the crates near the door of the box, trembling convulsively, and gasping and struggling for utterance. Had a thousand worlds depended upon a syllable, I could not have spoken it. . . . Shall I ever forget my feelings at this moment? He was going—my friend—my companion, from whom I had a right to expect so much—he was going—he would

abandon me—he was gone! He would leave me to perish miserably, to expire in the most horrible and loathsome of dungeons—and one word—one little syllable would save me—yet that single syllable I could not utter! I felt, I am sure, more than ten thousand times the agonies of death itself. My brain reeled, and I fell, deadly sick, against the end of the box.

As I fell, the carving-knife was shaken out from the waist-band of my pantaloons, and dropped with a rattling sound to the floor. Never did any strain of the richest melody come so sweetly to my ears! With the intensest anxiety I listened to ascertain the effect of the noise upon Augustus. (Pp. 1038–39)

In one sense, the verbal extravagance here of Pym the narrator is a perfect match for the emotional agitation of Pym the character. It offers one more example of what Robert Irwin calls "the essential precariousness, both logical and ontological, of the narrative act" in Poe's fiction.[25] But the fact that Pym's agitation explicitly incapacitates speech here lends an inadvertently parodic dimension to the narrator's volubility. This is not so much because Pym neglects to think of making some kind of nonverbal noise (to bang against some lumber, for instance), or because his very ability to tell the story indicates that he will be rescued. Rather, Pym the character's agitation is amusing because the verbal form of this "agony of terror" is self-titillating, even for the narrator who has survived the moment. "Ten thousand times the agonies of death itself" exemplifies precisely what Pym, with his self-described "enthusiastic temperament, and somewhat gloomy, although glowing imagination" (p. 1018), has wanted in this novel from the start. What initially enlisted his feelings "in behalf of the life of a seaman" was his paradoxically hopeful vision of hopelessness, "of shipwreck and famine; of death or captivity among barbarian hordes; of a lifetime dragged out in sorrow and tears, upon some gray and desolate rock, in an ocean unapproachable and unknown" (p. 1018).

One critic has suggested that we can take Pym's "excessive romantic wallowing in his own emotions" throughout the novel as an implicit sign of Poe's taking satiric aim at Pym.[26] Yet Pym is so infused with Poe's fictional presence—both in his longing for squalid and horrible encounters and in the rationalistic suasions meant to atone for that longing—that he cannot avoid surrendering his self to his author's style. Indeed the "self" outside that style remains so diminished (Arthur Gordon Pym's very name offering a rhythmic echo of Edgar Allan Poe[27]) it is actually unavailable for surrender in the first place. Pym epitomizes the Poe narrator, James M. Cox rightly asserts, because "he has no tragic sense. . . . All he can do is experience sensations" and attempt to shock himself into life with lurid imaginings. Because "perversity constitutes the root of his identity," Cox says, Pym "compulsively thrusts himself upon our consciousness, forcing us to dissociate from rather than to identify with

89

him. . . . [until] we are brought round to the position of watching the narrator himself."[28] The wording of Pym's visions of shipwreck and death echoes the novel's title page and suggests that the contemporary factual accounts by whalers, traders, and explorers Poe consulted in writing *Pym* exhilarated him largely as verbal opportunities—ways of writing about "exotic" subject matter. He wanted to use captivity and voyages across the Rockies, to the South Pole, or into a Norwegian maelstrom as fictional subject matter, but he also wanted to use them in a manner that authorized him to invoke phrases such as "atrocious butchery," "incredible adventures," and "an ocean unapproachable and unknown." The imaginative hybridization that ensues when this exoticized verbal license arises amid the rationalistic and rationalizing intonations of his narrators is present in Poe's scenes of violence, and the results, as we shall see, are curiously compelling.

"POE CAN laugh," Judith Sunderland asserts, "and among the most disturbing things about reading him is that one is never sure when he is laughing and when he is not."[29] Neither can we be quite sure when Poe is laughing at *us* rather than at a character, as we can see in the burlesque with which any study of violence in Poe—and perhaps any study of Poe, period—should begin: "How to Write a Blackwood Article." Like "The Imp of the Perverse," this story consists of an essay-sketch with an attached story. But the narrator of this tale, Signora Psyche Zenobia, provides not a "lecture" but details about her personal appearance, her enemies, and her professional activities. Poe satirizes Zenobia as a vain and dizzy literary parvenu. She consults with Mr. Blackwood who provides her with literary rules to follow in writing one of the "miscellaneous articles"—those that "come under the head of . . . the *bizarreries* (whatever that may mean) and what every body else calls the *intensities*" (p. 280)—for his *Blackwood's Edinburgh Magazine*, an important British literary magazine that published sensational stories Poe himself admired. She then writes a story called "A Predicament" in which she comically misapplies Blackwood's advice.

Poe's humor is modeled, as Symons says, on the "raw, often crude joking" that was part of a self-consciously coarse American comic tradition, one that used "a buttonholing, this-will-amaze-you style" and "an abundance of appalling puns."[30] (There are characters in Poe's fiction, for instance, with names such as Thingum Bob, Slyass, Touch-and-go Bullet-head, Bibulus O'Bumper, and Ferdinand Fitz-Fossillus Feltspar. His story of "The Devil in the Belfry" is set in the Dutch borough of Vondervotteimittiss.) What we frequently encounter in Poe's stories is the fictional equivalent of his horselaughs in "Letter to B——," in which he parenthetically interrupts a quotation from Wordsworth's preface to *Lyrical Ballads*:

"Those who have been accustomed to the phraseology of modern writers, if they persist in reading this book to a conclusion (*impossible!*) will, no doubt, have to struggle with feelings of awkwardness; (ha! ha! ha!) they will look round for poetry (ha! ha! ha! ha!) and will be induced to inquire by what species of courtesy these attempts have been permitted to assume that title." Ha! ha! ha! ha! ha! (p. 10)

In "How to Write a Blackwood Article," what corresponds to the parenthetical guffaws here is the fact that Zenobia is the corresponding secretary for "P.R.E.T.T.Y.B.L.U.E.B.A.T.C.H—that is to say, Philadelphia, Regular, Exchange, Tea, Total, Young, Belles, Lettres, Universal, Experimental, Bibliographical, Association, To, Civilize, Humanity" (p. 279). As if this were not laborious enough, Zenobia then says that when she adds these initials to her name, "Dr. Moneypenny will have it that our initials give our true character— but for my life I can't see what he means" (p. 279). A page later Poe has Blackwood answer the popular contention that Coleridge wrote *Confessions of an English Opium Eater* by asserting that "it was composed by my pet baboon, Juniper, over a rummer of Hollands and water, 'hot, without sugar'" (p. 281).

Not only are these squibs characteristic of Poe's heavy-handed satire, they are offered in the spirit of Blackwood's enumerated rules in this sketch for composing "a genuine . . . article of the sensation stamp": "Sensations are the great things after all. Should you ever be drowned or hung, be sure and make note of your sensations—they will be worth to you ten guineas a sheet. If you wish to write forcibly, Miss Zenobia, pay minute attention to the sensations" (p. 281):

> "The first thing requisite is to get yourself into such a scrape as no one ever got into before. The oven, for instance,—that was a good hit. But if you have no oven, or big bell, at hand, and if you cannot conveniently tumble out of a balloon, or be swallowed up in an earthquake, or get stuck fast in a chimney, you will have to be contented with simply imagining some similar misadventure. I should prefer, however, that you have the actual fact to bear you out. Nothing so well assists the fancy, as an experimental knowledge of the matter in hand. 'Truth is strange,' you know, 'stranger than fiction'—besides being more to the purpose."
>
> Here I assured him I had an excellent pair of garters, and would go and hang myself forthwith. (P. 282)

Poe here takes fictional techniques that he himself uses constantly in his serious stories—a preoccupation with bodily sensations, unusual narrative circumstances, and mock-factuality—and projects them onto others in order to parody them as stylistic abuses.

Blackwood next describes various ways in which "the tone, or manner" of the narration can be established, noting "the tone laconic," "the tone elevated,

diffusive and interjectional," and "the tone heterogeneous" ("made up of everything deep, great, odd, piquant, pertinent and pretty" [p. 283]). He also discusses "the tone metaphysical":

> If you know any big words this is your chance for them. Talk of the Ionic and
> Eleatic schools—of Archytas, Gorgias and Alcmœon. Say something about objec-
> tivity and subjectivity. Be sure and abuse a man called Locke. Turn up your nose
> at things in general, and when you let slip anything a little *too* absurd, you need not
> be at the trouble of scratching it out, but just add a foot-note, and say that you are
> indebted for the above profound observation to the "*Kritik der reinen Vernunft,*" or
> to the "*Metaphysische Anfangsgrunde der Naturwissenschaft.*" This will look erudite
> and—and—and frank." (Pp. 282–83)

Blackwood finishes up by suggesting that if it is inconvenient for her "to—to—
get [herself] drowned, or—choked with a chicken-bone," "a couple of very
excellent bull dogs in the yard" will oblige her ("I say—Tom!—Peter!—Dick
you villain!" [p. 287]). She flees to write "A Predicament" in the tone heterogenous.

Set in Edina (or Edinburgh), the story is written in the first person with
Zenobia as narrator. She is accompanied by her one-eyed poodle, Diana, who
is "not more than five inches in height" but whose head is "somewhat bigger
than her body" (p. 288), and her aged black servant, Pompey, who is "three
feet in height," corpulent, and has bow-legs: "Nature had endowed him with
no neck, and had placed his ankles (as usual with that race) in the middle of the
upper portion of the feet" (p. 289). Poe's racism and antiabolitionist sentiments are often explicit in his writing, and when Zenobia seizes this tottering,
minstrel-show retainer "furiously by the wool with both hands" and tears out
"a vast quantity of the black, and crisp, and curling material" (p. 291), it was
undoubtedly meant to provoke a bigoted snicker in certain members of his
audience. But Pompey is only a peripheral figure in this sketch, and his "op-
pressor" is about to lose more than a chunk of her scalp.

Zenobia climbs to the inner belfry chamber of a Gothic cathedral and, standing on Pompey's shoulders, sticks her head through an aperture in the tower
wall for a view of the city. Thus begins her "lamentable adventure":

> I observed that the aperture through which I had thrust my head was an opening in
> the dial-plate of a gigantic clock, and must have appeared, from the street, as a large
> keyhole, such as we see in the face of French watches. No doubt the true object was
> to admit the arm of an attendant, to adjust, when necessary, the hands of the clock
> from within. I observed also, with surprise, the immense size of these hands, the
> longest of which could not have been less than ten feet in length, and, where
> broadest, eight or nine inches in breadth. They were of solid steel apparently, and

their edges appeared to be sharp. Having noticed these particulars, and some others, I again turned my eyes upon the glorious prospect below, and soon became
absorbed in contemplation. (P. 292)

Poe's comparison of this huge dial-plate to a French watch helps us visualize
what the steeple clock looks like and it helps, by contrast, to establish its
immensity. He is often at his best when conjuring up images of vast marvels,
whether deep, niter-encrusted catacombs; the "range of vapour" like "a limitless cataract, rolling silently into the sea from some immense and far-distant
rampart in the heaven" at the end of *Pym* (p. 1179); or the gigantic, white
sandstone cliffs in *The Journal of Julius Rodman*, that rise up from the Missouri
River, crisscrossed with "a variety of lines" that "a fertile fancy" might take to
be "hieroglyphical" carvings (pp. 1246–47). These magnified images, however,
are usually set in relief against a welter of rationalistic details. Like so many
Poe narrators, Zenobia here precisely notices "particulars" to which she presently gives little heed but whose importance she will soon be made to acknowledge.

"Deeply absorbed" in the "heavenly scenery" beneath her, Zenobia fails at
first to notice that "the huge, glittering, scimetar-like minute-hand of the
clock" has, she shrieks in italics, "*descended upon my neck.*" She struggles to "force
upwards the ponderous iron bar" but soon realizes that she "might as well have
tried to lift the cathedral itself" (p. 293).

> The ponderous and terrific *Scythe of Time* (for I now discovered the literal import
> of that classical phrase) had not stopped, nor was it likely to stop in its career.
> Down and still down it came. It had already buried its sharp edge a full inch in my
> flesh, and my sensations grew indistinct and confused. At one time I fancied myself
> in Philadelphia with the stately Dr. Moneypenny, at another in the back parlor of
> Mr. Blackwood receiving his invaluable instructions. And then again the sweet
> recollection of better and earlier times came over me, and I thought of that happy
> period when the world was not all a desert, and Pompey not altogether cruel.
>
> The ticking of the machinery amused me. *Amused me*, I say, for my sensations
> now bordered upon perfect happiness, and the most trifling circumstances afforded
> me pleasure. The eternal *click-clack, click-clack, click-clack*, of the clock was the most
> melodious of music in my ears, and occasionally even put me in mind of the
> grateful sermonic harangues of Dr. Ollapod. (Pp. 293–94)

Zenobia's attention to her sensations as the clock-hand buries "its sharp edge
a full inch in her neck" and her mock-astonishment at the pleasure "the most
trifling circumstances" afford are echoed and anticipated by several other Poe
narrators: Pym, for instance, who notes that his stuporous delirium in the hold
of the *Grampus* is "attended with the most distressing spasmodic action of the

chest" (p. 1036). Oddly enough, what Poe is parodying here is the "dynamic of intensification," as Douglas Robinson calls it, at work in Poe's most effective stories, a dynamic "developed not through character and event but through the accumulation of details and the horrific though strangely lyrical intensification of both environmental threats and the narrator's sensations."[31]

After Zenobia quotes some "exquisite verses" from Cervantes, she is quickly presented with "a new horror, one indeed sufficient to startle the strongest nerves":

> My eyes, from the cruel pressure of the machine, were absolutely starting from their sockets. While I was thinking how I should possibly manage without them, one actually tumbled out of my head, and, rolling down the steep side of the steeple, lodged in the rain gutter which ran along the eaves of the main building. The loss of the eye was not so much as the insolent air of independence and contempt with which it regarded me after it was out. There it lay in the gutter just under my nose, and the airs it gave itself would have been ridiculous had they not been disgusting. Such a winking and blinking were never before seen. This behaviour on the part of my eye in the gutter was not only irritating on account of its manifest insolence and shameful ingratitude, but was also exceedingly inconvenient on account of the sympathy which always exists between two eyes of the same head, however far apart. I was forced, in a manner, to wink and to blink, whether I would or not, in exact concert with the scoundrelly thing that lay just under my nose. I was presently relieved, however, by the dropping out of the other eye. In falling it took the same direction (possibly a concerted plot) as its fellow. Both rolled out of the gutter together, and in truth I was very glad to get rid of them.
>
> The bar was now four inches and a half deep in my neck, and there was only a little bit of skin to cut through. My sensations were those of entire happiness, for I felt that in a few minutes, at farthest, I should be relieved from my disagreeable situation. And in this expectation I was not at all deceived. At twenty-five minutes past five in the afternoon precisely, the huge minute-hand had proceeded sufficiently far on its terrible revolution to severe the small remainder of my neck. I was not sorry to see the head which had occasioned me so much embarrassment at length make a final separation from my body. It first rolled down the side of the steeple, then lodged, for a few seconds, in the gutter, and then made its way, with a plunge, into the middle of the street. (Pp. 294–95)

The physical impossibility of a headless (and thus lidless) eye "winking and blinking" and of Zenobia's "seeing" the separation of her head from her body (unless we hypothesize that her ousted eyeballs watch the decapitated head as it falls[32]) is entertained in the final paragraphs of the tale with a mordant humor worthy of Alfred Hitchcock or David Lynch. Zenobia attempts to take a pinch of snuff before becoming aware of her "peculiar deficiency," whereupon she throws her snuffbox down at the head, which "took a pinch with great satisfaction," "smiled me an acknowledgement in return," and "made me a speech which I could hear but indistinctly without ears" (p. 296).

Symons notes what he calls an "element of unconscious sadism" in Poe's comedy here: "the Signora Psyche Zenobia is no doubt a tiresome woman, but is it funny that her head should be cut off by a clock hand?"[33] Poe does not grant Zenobia a fictional substantiality, however, that actually allows her to become susceptible to realistic pain. Within the context of a story in which a character can feel socially snubbed by one of her dislodged eyeballs, Zenobia's beheading has about the same imaginative status as one of the sketch's inauspicious puns. Poe seems less interested in wreaking vengeance on a "bluestocking" (especially one who so obligingly injures her black servant) than in displaying his complete mastery of the fictional conventions that he himself utilizes elsewhere. The cruelty of the story is neutralized or "de-realized" not only by the absurdity of the events it depicts but by the way Zenobia's preposterous narration deprives her tale's violence of the realistic verbal dynamic that might otherwise prove so disquieting.

"How to Write a Blackwood Article" resembles what John Fraser calls "idea jokes" (manic one-liners like "but apart from that, Mrs. Lincoln, how did you enjoy the play?"):

> They are nasty, of course, but that is their point. They are a form of counter-aggression. They affront all the American liberal-suburbanizing pressures making for uniform, unrelaxed postures of Sympathy, Pity, Good Works, and so on—pressures, in other words, towards a bland, ego-suppressing, and essentially not-thought-through niceness. . . . [Yet such jokes] are only endurable because of the very mechanism that makes them funny, namely that the mind, directed at first towards real people or kinds of people, recognizes almost instantaneously that what is really under attack is certain other kinds of people thinking about them, and so veers away from a serious contemplation of the objects themselves.[34]

Fraser seems right to a point here. A listener veers away from a serious contemplation of these jokes and their fictional cousins but not, I think, because he recognizes that what is "really under attack" are certain kinds of people thinking about certain kinds of victims. What such jokes dramatize (rather than attack) seems to be the personality of the joke-teller, a person whom we feel fairly certain would not actually, for instance, stick babies into blenders. Our assurance in such matters seems to stem from the very fact that the joke is being told, for startling violations of etiquette or a behavioral norm can only be entertaining when those norms are otherwise in force. In fiction this imagi-

native condition depends upon our listening to a narrative or authorial intelligence rather than upon our reading through words to the illusion of an unauthored world, as we do in realistic imagining. Most of Poe's stories have
narrators who describe the events they participate in or witness. But as with
Cooper, the events Poe's narrators describe gain an imaginative substantiality
(and, in scenes of violence, a capacity to disturb us) only to the extent that they
break free of the verbal and psychological earmarks of those narrators and of
Poe behind them.[35]

Like so many of the other injuries, wounds, and physical indignities in his
fiction (e.g., Dirk Peters's accidentally pulling a putrescent leg off Augustus
Barnard's corpse in *Pym*, or the final scene in "The Facts in the Case of
M. Valdemar," in which the patient's de-mesmerized body collapses, in less
than a minute, into a "nearly liquid mass of loathesome—of detestable putrid-
ity" [p. 892]), Zenobia's beheading exercises Poe's obsession with the physical
immediacies of violence and decay. It is an obsession he usually disguises by a
show of puritanical right-mindedness, by a quick labeling of its fictional results
as "loathesome," "horrid," or "detestable." We might see this obsessiveness,
like Bloom, as part of Poe's peculiarly Southern genius for nightmarish, anti-
Emersonian "negativity and opposition."[36] Or, like Fraser, we might see it as
an example of a more general suspicion of the body in American literature
("perhaps because it is the body that most ineluctably sets limits to individual
human ambitions, however sublime or generous"[37]). But whatever the interpretive context in which it is placed, the violence and grotesquerie in Poe's
fiction coexist with a rhetoric of "ratiocination" designed first to invite such
disruptions and then to stare them down.

"How to write a Blackwood Article" was published in 1838, the same year
that the first portions of *Pym* were appearing and four years before the story
that most nearly resembles it, "The Pit and the Pendulum." Brian Harding, in
noting the similarities between those two stories, asserts that "a parodic treatment of a fictional theme did not, for Poe, preclude a serious reworking of
theme and effect."[38] As we have seen, however, "How to Write a Blackwood
Article" parodies not merely "a fictional theme" but nearly every stylistic technique Poe employed in his serious stories. David Reynolds says that this sketch
and story caricature "the directionless sensationalism" of a subversive strain of
American humor popular at the time (the dropping out of eyes was, for instance, a repeated image in violent American humor).[39] But again, Poe was not
parodying subject matter alone, and Reynolds substantiates his notion that
"Poe's comic theory and practice" formed "a direct rhetorical response to a
popular American humor he found simultaneously fascinating and disturbing"

only by saying that the comic violence of this sketch "is exaggerated to such a degree that it becomes distanced and therefore harmless." The story's harmlessness, in Reynolds's view, is attributable to its exaggerated "contraventions of perceived reality."[40]

The story's interest, I think, springs from more than this, for it encourages us to rethink the effects other Poe stories achieve and to reconsider the mechanistic theories of composition Poe delineates in "The Philosophy of Composition," an essay that many would otherwise regard, in T. S. Eliot's words, as "a hoax, or a piece of self-deception."[41] Is it possible to take Poe's other fiction seriously once we are aware of his canniness about the artificiality of effects now critically touted as psychologically penetrating and dreadfully universal? It is, but we should be conscientious about stressing Poe's extraordinary self-consciousness. (Imagine Ernest Hemingway writing *The Torrents of Spring* knowing that no matter how cleverly disguised, it was largely self-parodic.)

That self-consciousness is also apparent in the overdetermined "textuality" of Poe's fiction, its impishly self-declared status as verbal artifice.[42] Many of his stories are presented as manuscripts or written monologues complete with elaborate editorial embroiderings and mock-documentation (which strengthen our sense of Poe's narrative control even as they call it into playful question). His tales are also often set in exotic settings straight out of other books. "Nothing is more characteristic of Poe," Paul Fussell notes, "than the ease with which, in his fictions, he escapes Baltimore to occupy imaginatively and plausibly such scenes as Eton, Oxford or the back streets of Paris."[43] The action of his tales is often foreshadowed by epigraphs or paralleled within a story by a reading of, for instance, the "Mad Trist" of Sir Launcelot Canning. Likewise, his subject matter itself frequently comprises some kind of printed or written text, whether a cryptogram, printed crime-witness reports, a scrap of paper with a note scrawled in blood, a stolen letter, or a forged envelope. Egaeus, the narrator of "Berenice," might stand as the perfect emblem for a Poe story: he is born in the library.

In a letter to Thomas White, the owner of the Richmond *Southern Literary Messenger*, Poe argues that the literary magazines "which have attained celebrity" have done so on the strength of stories "*similar in nature*" to "Berenice" (which White had recently published). This "nature," Poe says, consists of "the ludicrous heightened into the grotesque: the fearful coloured into the horrible: the witty exaggerated into the burlesque: the singular wrought out into the strange and mystical." Poe's emphasis upon one imaginative condition being heightened, colored, exaggerated, or wrought into another reveals his preoccupation with narrative technique: "originality is an essential in these things— great attention must be paid to style, and much labor spent in their composition, or they will degenerate into the turgid or the absurd." By Poe's own conception, style alone is what redeems a story from being in "bad taste." Yet it is typical of Poe that in the same letter he asserts that whether or not a story like "Berenice" is in bad taste "is little to the purpose": "to be appreciated you must be *read*, and these things are invariably sought after with avidity." He then encourages White to ignore "critiques" of this kind of fiction and to remember that the ultimate worth of a story "will be estimated better by the circulation of the Magazine than by any comments upon its contents."[44]

Poe wishes to curry favor with a potential publisher in this letter and thus he purposefully stresses the financial advantages of his artistic views. Yet all of Poe's fiction represents "a complex adjustment," as Leslie Fiedler puts it, "between his desire to mock his audience and to be accepted by it."[45] Even when Poe's fiction is successfully original it seems to be so in quotations marks, it seems implicitly to acknowledge its proximity to "the turgid or the absurd" which is the stylistic flip-side of its success. Poe uses the word "phantasmagoric," Gordon Weaver rightly asserts, "not because it denotes much, but because it suggests, connotes [and] sounds appropriate to the kinds of 'reality' Poe means to persuade us to accept."[46] The same holds true for Poe's characters. In the midst of the conspicuously literary features trussing and draping Poe's fiction, his characters are granted a fictional substantiality that approximates that conjured by the word "phantasmagoric." Poe often seems to care less about his characters than he does about the kinds of fictional effects they make possible. Thus we cannot be entirely certain, in moments of violence, whether the victims in Poe's tales are ever more than so many Psyche Zenobias—figures designed to be entertainingly brutalized. As "How to Write a Blackwood Article" demonstrates, Poe is often willing to disrupt belabored displays of arcane erudition with anecdotes about beheadings and literary baboons.

A similar impulse surfaces in "Hop-Frog," a tale concerning a jester's revenge on the king he serves. The story is told by an unidentified first-person narrator who remains separate from the action. Hop-Frog is a crippled dwarf abducted from a nearby province. He moves with "a sort of interjectional gait—something between a leap and a wriggle, a movement that afforded illimitable amusement" to the king (p. 900), and he has "a set of large, powerful, and very repulsive teeth" (p. 903). Although he can "move only with great pain and difficulty along a road or floor" due to "the distortion of his legs," "the prodigious muscular power which nature seemed to have bestowed upon his arms, by way of compensation for deficiency in the lower limbs, enabled him to perform many feats of wonderful dexterity, where trees or ropes were in question, or anything else to climb. At such exercises he certainly much more resembled a squirrel, or a small monkey, than a frog." Joining Hop-Frog in the court is Trippetta, a young girl who was also abducted by the king's conquering generals and with whom he has "a close intimacy" (p. 900).

The king, on the other hand, is quite the opposite of "the two little captives" (p. 900). He "seemed to live only for joking": "About the refinements, or, as he called them, the 'ghosts' of wit, the king troubled himself very little. He had an especial admiration for *breadth* in a jest, and would often put up with *length,* for the sake of it. Over-niceties wearied him. He would have preferred Rabelais's 'Gargantua,' to the 'Zadig' of Voltaire: and, upon the whole, practical jokes suited his taste far better than verbal ones" (p. 899). Over-niceties may weary the king, but they do not fatigue Poe's narrator as he tells of Hop-Frog's humiliation when the king consults him about what costumes he and his ministers should wear to a masquerade ball:

> Hop-Frog was not fond of wine; for it excited the poor cripple almost to madness; and madness is no comfortable feeling. But the king loved his practical jokes, and took pleasure in forcing Hop-Frog to drink and (as the king called it) "to be merry."
>
> "Come here, Hop-Frog," said he, as the jester and his friend entered the room: "swallow this bumper to the health of your absent friends [here Hop-Frog sighed,] and then let us have the benefit of your invention. We want characters—*characters,* man—something novel—out of the way. We are wearied with this everlasting sameness. Come, drink! the wine will brighten your wits."
>
> Hop-Frog endeavored, as usual, to get up a jest in reply to these advances from the king; but the effort was too much. It happened to be the poor dwarf's birthday, and the command to drink to his "absent friends" forced the tears to his eyes. Many large, bitter drops fell into the goblet as he took it, humbly, from the hand of the tyrant.
>
> "Ah! ha! ha! ha!" roared the latter, as the dwarf reluctantly drained the beaker. "See what a glass of good wine can do! Why, your eyes are shining already!"
>
> Poor fellow! his large eyes *gleamed,* rather than shone; for the effect of wine on his excitable brain was not more powerful than instantaneous. He placed the goblet nervously on the table, and looked round upon the company with a half-insane stare. They all seemed highly amused at the success of the king's "*joke.*" (Pp. 901–2)

Poe's placement of the word "joke" in both quotation marks and italics suggests, obviously, that the narrator does not approve of the king's sense of humor. It also ominously hints that the king's just desserts *may* be just a few pages away. The image of Hop-Frog's crying for his "absent friends" on his birthday ("Poor fellow!") is almost as touching as it is manipulative in playing upon a reader's heart-strings. But if "madness," as the narrator tells us with winning earnestness, "is no comfortable feeling," Poe soon indirectly lets us know that Hop-Frog can fend for himself. When Trippetta intercedes on his behalf, the king shoves her away and "throws the contents of the brimming goblet in her face" (p. 902). Whereas Hop-Frog's eyes gleamed in italics above there now comes "a low, but harsh and protracted *grating* sound," a noise that one of the king's lovably obtuse courtiers contends is the result of "the parrot at the window, whetting his bill upon his cage-wires" (p. 903) and not, as the king suspects, Hop-Frog gritting his teeth. ("That's what you think!" Poe's narrator fairly cackles here.)

Hop-Frog proposes that the king and his seven ministers come to the masquerade habited as the "Eight Chained Ourang-Outangs." The men are "encased" in "tight-fitting stockinet shirts and drawers" that have been saturated with tar and plastered with flax, and they are chained "after the fashion adopted, at the present day, by those who capture Chimpanzees, or other large apes, in Borneo" (p. 905). The masquerading apes rush into the hall at midnight, causing several women to swoon, "and had not the king taken the precaution to exclude all weapons from the saloon, his party might soon have expiated their frolic in their blood" (p. 906). Hop-Frog has a different expiation in mind. He hooks the men's chains to a "chandelier-chain," grabs a flambeau from one of the "fifty or sixty" caryatids in the hall, and clings to the chain a few feet above the king's head, screaming "*I* shall soon find out who they are!" (p. 907). The chain flies "violently up for about thirty feet—dragging with it the dismayed and struggling ourang-outangs, and leaving them suspended in mid-air between the sky-light and the floor." In the "dead silence, of about a minute's duration," the grating sound is heard again, but this time, the narrator tells us, "there could be no question as to *whence* the sound issued."

> It came from the fang-like teeth of the dwarf, who ground them and gnashed them as he foamed at the mouth, and glared, with an expression of maniacal rage, into the upturned countenances of the king and his seven companions.
>
> "Ah, ha!" said at length the infuriated jester. "Ah, ha! I begin to see who these people *are*, now!" Here, pretending to scrutinize the king more closely, he held the flambeau to the flaxen coat which enveloped him, and which instantly burst into a sheet of vivid flame. In less than a minute the whole eight ourang-outangs were blazing fiercely, amid the shrieks of the multitude who gazed at them from below, horror-stricken, and without the power to render them the slightest assistance. (P. 907)

Poe spectacularly undermines the previous conventions of victimization he has established, transforming the pathetic cripple who weeps at the thought of his "absent friends," and with whom a reader might sympathize, into a foaming, fang-gnashing maniac.

100

The magnitude of Hop-Frog's act of vengeance outstrips its ostensible cause and the reader is forced to reconsider his first appraisal of Hop-Frog. If we read the story as an autobiographical fantasy of revenge (which is tempting), we run the risk of ignoring how Poe purposefully emphasizes Hop-Frog's "repulsive" and "maniacal" qualities. We also risk ignoring the complication at the end of the story:

> "I now see *distinctly*, [Hop-Frog] said, "what manner of people these maskers are. They are a great king and his seven privy-councillors—a king who does not scruple to strike a defenceless girl, and his seven councillors who abet him in the outrage. As for myself, I am simply Hop-Frog, the jester—and *this is my last jest*."
>
> Owing to the high combustibility of both the flax and the tar to which it adhered, the dwarf had scarcely made an end of his brief speech before the work of vengeance was complete. The eight corpses swung in their chains, a fetid, blackened, hideous, and indistinguishable mass. The cripple hurled his torch at them, clambered leisurely to the ceiling, and disappeared through the sky-light.
>
> It is supposed that Trippetta, stationed on the roof of the saloon, had been the accomplice of her friend in his fiery revenge, and that, together, they effected their escape to their own country: for neither was seen again. (P. 908)

The problem with finding a "moral" in this story ("he who lives by the crude joke dies by the crude joke"?) is that it distracts us from the zany incongruity of Hop-Frog's first saying "I am simply Hop-Frog, the jester," and then adding "*and this is my last jest*," which, so italicized, utterly erases his claim to being "simply" anything. If we take Hop-Frog's final words as Poe's condemnation of his character's poor, befuddled sense of just retribution, then we have to consider why Poe does not end the story with those words, why he goes on to make the last paragraph rife with fairy-tale overtones as Hop-Frog and Trippetta head off for the politically enlightened precincts of "their own country." As elsewhere, Poe seems to take a desperate delight in phrases like "a fetid, blackened, hideous, and indistinguishable mass" precisely because his narrator's self-declared horror and repulsion raise a rhetorical screen behind which he can remain as amoral as the Hop-Frog who "leisurely" clambers away through the skylight. Hop-Frog's ostensible explanation for why he has committed his crime does not exonerate him. Instead, it effectively laughs in the face of a reader who sentimentally sympathized with him earlier in the story. Poe seems entirely aware that the story's final image of chained burn victims will be far more indelibly printed in the reader's imagination than the reasons for its occurrence.

Poe's willingness to brutalize characters for the sake of an indelible effect is further apparent in the first chapter of *Pym*, in which Pym and Augustus Barnard's sloop, the Ariel, is run down and crushed by a whale ship. Pym passes out before the moment of impact, but he wakes up on board the whaler (the Penguin), and "the mystery of our being in existence was soon explained." Pym was thrown from the sloop upon impact and was later found by the mate of the Penguin, who launched a rescue boat in the teeth of the storm:

> The body of a man was seen to be affixed in the most singular manner to the smooth and shining bottom (the Penguin was coppered and copper-fastened), and beating violently against it with every movement of the hull. After several ineffectual effforts, made during the lurches of the ship, and at the imminent risk of swamping the boat, I was finally disengaged from my perilous situation and taken on board—for the body proved to be my own. It appeared that one of the timber-bolts having started and broken a passage through the copper, it had arrested my progress as I passed under the ship, and fastened me in so extraordinary a manner to her bottom. The head of the bolt had made its way through the collar of the green baize jacket I had on, and through the back part of my neck, forcing itself out between two sinews and just below the right ear. I was immediately put to bed—although life seemed to be totally extinct. There was no surgeon on board. The captain, however, treated me with every attention—to make amends, I presume, in the eyes of his crew, for his atrocious behaviour in the previous portion of the adventure. (P. 1015)

Walter Bezanson calls this "one of Poe's better 'night scenes'—wild, impossible, violent, yet precisely detailed. The fake seamanship and Pym's unlikely endurance fall away before an apocalyptic vision of the self, spread-eagled against the hull, nailed to the copper sheathing, and drowned again and again."[47] There is so little realistic room for Pym the character in this moment that his underwater crucifixion does seem to present a symbolic "vision of the self" being repeatedly drowned. But Pym's fake seamanship and mock-factual specificity do not "fall away" from his description. They cannot cover for the fact that a reader's disbelief here is not so much suspended (in the words of J.R.R. Tolkien) as "hanged, drawn and quartered."[48] The anatomical precision of the bolt's "forcing itself out between two sinews and just below the right ear" makes the image seem at least as gratuitously painful as it is apocalyptic. Yet Pym seems no more engaged with the details of his impalement than he is with the captain's "atrocious behaviour in the previous portion of the adventure." His acknowledged status as the teller of a tale, of an adventure with "previous portions," works against the realism he so constantly attempts to establish.

"One must ask," as Sunderland puts it, if "Poe really intended *Pym* to be other than it is, an illustration of the process of creation and destruction of literary form."[49] Yet if we pursue this question too gravely we will miss the fun (whether intentional or not) of Pym's informing us that "the wound in my neck, although of an ugly appearance, proved of little real consequence, and I soon recovered from its effects."

> The Penguin got into port about nine o'clock in the morning, after encountering one of the severest gales ever experienced off Nantucket. Both Augustus and myself managed to appear at Mr. Barnard's in time for breakfast—which, luckily, was somewhat late, owing to the party over night. I suppose all at the table were too much fatigued themselves to notice our jaded appearance—of course, it would not have borne a very rigid scrutiny. Schoolboys, however, can accomplish wonders in the way of deception, and I verily believe not one of our friends in Nantucket had the slightest suspicion that the terrible story told by some sailors in town of their having run down a vessel at sea and drowned some thirty or forty poor devils, had reference either to the Ariel, my companion, or myself. We two have since very frequently talked the matter over—but never without a shudder. (P. 1017)

It is typical of Poe that Pym's quiet smile about the exaggerated report of "some thirty or forty poor devils" being drowned at sea is meant to certify his own veracity and to distract us from Pym's own "wonders" of deception.

Poe's narrators seldom seem able to tell their tales without a shudder, which leaves Poe susceptible to Wayne Booth's criticism that his narrative voice, "like the voice of the commentator in a bad documentary film," is often "divorced from the effect of his own rhetoric." "For Poe's special kind of morbid horror, a psychological detail, as conveyed by an emotionally charged adjective, is more effective than mere sensual description in any form."[50] But as Poe's scenes of violence make clear, he often lovingly lingers over the sensory details of death or injury: the inch-by-inch progress of a decapitating clock-hand or the precise location at which an iron bolt forces its way through a human neck. And he often does this in the same paragraph in which he also, for instance, invokes abstract Gothic superlatives about a "horror more horrible for being vague, and [a] terror more terrible from ambiguity" (p. 232).

This mixture of imaginative tendencies within Poe's verbal temperament dominates his fiction, and his stories tend to become truly terrifying only to the extent that the events they describe linger just outside his representational reach.[51] This is not to say, however, that Poe's language and his fictional self-consciousness should be quickly dismissed or that they form simply a barrier to what is most engaging about his work. We cannot fully appreciate the imaginative extravagance of images and events in Poe's fiction if we study it in a verbal vacuum, for that extravagance is no sooner evoked than it is imaginatively altered and busily tacked down with narrative footnotes and parenthetical explanations. Frank appraisals of the imaginative extremes at work in Poe's fiction are scarce, perhaps because those who enjoy his work still feel it must be defended against claims that "Poe is the poet of unripe boys and unsound men."[52] But as scenes of violence in Poe's fiction suggest, an inattention to his style offers not a sound means of defense but a critical evasion, one that can only weaken our appreciation of the alternately wondrous and pettifogging legerdemain of American literature's imp of the perverse.

Violence and Style in Stephen Crane's Fiction

> It can never be satisfied, the mind, never.
> —*Wallace Stevens, "The Well Dressed Man with a Beard"*

"THERE ARE writing men," Stephen Crane wrote in 1897, "who, in some stories, dash over three miles at a headlong pace, and in an adjacent story move like a boat being sailed over ploughed fields."[1] Crane is remarking upon what his friend Harold Frederick successfully avoids in establishing a "perfect evenness of craft" in his fiction. He was generous in finding such "evenness" a worthy quality, for it constitutes an expressive condition Crane himself seemed temperamentally incapable of achieving. The alternating dramatic styles that Crane says Frederick avoids from story to story aptly characterize his own work, sentence by sentence. Criticism of Crane's fiction continues to pay lip service to its intriguingly uneven qualities, but it tends to treat that unevenness as a secondary characteristic, one blithely subordinated to what are construed as more important themes. The odd expressive masonry of his fiction tends to be neglected in favor of scenic perspectives from a distance.

The habit of finding Crane's work ironic, for instance, often involves ignoring verbal occasions (like the narrator's remark, in "One Dash—Horses," that "a 44-caliber revolver can make a hole large enough for little boys to shoot marbles through" [p. 736]), in which "irony" seems an inadequate term. Similarly, seeing his work as "impressionistic," a term incessantly applied after Joseph Conrad and Edward Garnett first used the tag, frequently results in either peripheral lectures on the state of the visual arts in the 1880s and 1890s or in vague descriptive efforts that Crane himself probably would have parodied.[2] Despite lengthening bibliographies and dauntingly dense new studies of his work,[3] the life of Crane's language still seems insufficiently appreciated. Scenes of violence in his fiction provide some of the most valuable occasions for suggesting just how freshly unsatisfied and stylistically mercurial his work is. They also help demonstrate that many critics, in the very act of conceptualizing Crane's themes, often annul the imaginative exorbitance of his stories.

Amy Kaplan, in a discerning essay on how Crane represents the violence of war in *The Red Badge of Courage*, notes that he "decontextualizes" the Civil War, not only by stripping it of a recognizable political context but by subverting and parodying previous plots, symbols, and conventions of narrative coherence that comfortably accommodated the war. "Although *The Red Badge of Courage* is about the growth of a youth," Kaplan says, "it does not tell the story of a self that evolves from cumulative experience; rather it displays a self that must be repeatedly improvised before the observer," a self that is "highly theatrical, and thus inherently tentative and unstable." Such "improvisations," she adds, characterize not only Crane's characters but his own "bold strokes" and "theatrical style" as a narrator.[4] Yet the narrative bravura Kaplan rightly highlights in Crane becomes, even as she defines it, a "thematized" element of his writing that is ancillary to rather than the expressive *source* of what we might later be tempted to identify as a theme. Crane's style, in *Red Badge* and elsewhere, cannot be seen as solely a revision of previous literary representations, if only because the verbal inventiveness of those revisions too often outstrips their ostensible function. Crane's expressive theatrics cannot be subsumed within a given interpretation of his work, Raymond Carney warns, without inadvertently making his fiction seem "less complex, less nuanced, less intricately and subtly troubled" than it actually is.[5]

The volatile play of styles in his writing does not simply annotate a character's actions. It directly determines the substance from which "character," psychology, or a notion of the self might be fashioned in the first place. "Making sense" of Crane's work seems less crucial than understanding how he himself frequently baffles that process. We have to *listen* to his writing take shape, rather than assume that its shape is already there to be thematically paraphrased. But what does that effort entail? How does listening in on Crane's work differ from "interpreting" it? What (to narrow the range of the inquiry) does violence *sound like* in Crane's fiction?

Long celebrated for its "nervousness" and "dash," Crane's writing typically consists of short sentences, and its rhythm tends to be choppy and abrupt. "Unwilling to see relations between events as they were presumed by the fictional structures of his contemporaries" and impatient with literary styles he identified "with the false and badly written," Crane, Frank Bergon notes, "most noticeably abandons long, complex sentences possessing clear transitions."[6] When his sentences do lengthen and extend they are typically composed of short, condensed rhetorical units that are often full of the imagistic variety and perceptual detail we associate with realism. But there is also another aspect of Crane's writing that resists critical labeling. Within and juxtaposed with his realistic imagining, we also encounter a very different kind of verbal temperament, one that inclines to stiff abstractions, visual blockages, dead metaphors, and explicitly contorted syntax. "The character of the deliberate," John Berryman argues, is conspicuous in Crane's fiction. Crane's writing is "flexible, swift, abrupt, and nervous," Berryman says, but it also has "an unexampled capacity for stasis": "Color is high, but we observe the blank absence of the orotund, the moulded, which is Crane's most powerful response to the prose tradition he declined to inherit."[7]

We can best understand this capacity for imaginative numbness or stasis in Crane's prose by examining what it halts and opposes:

> When [the correspondent] came to the surface he was conscious of little but the noisy water. Afterward he saw his companions in the sea. The oiler was ahead in the race. He was swimming strongly and rapidly. Off to the correspondent's left, the cook's great white and corked back bulged out of the water, and in the rear the captain was hanging with his one good hand to the keel of the overturned dingey.
>
> There is a certain immovable quality to a shore, and the correspondent wondered at it amid the confusion of the sea . . . ("The Open Boat," p. 907)

The first paragraph here presents an itemized succession of sensory details, and as is typical with realistic sequences, the reader moves quickly over and through such language in an attempt to gain imaginative traction, to see something here. The start of the second paragraph seems, in part, a continuation of that process of visualization. The reference to the immobility of the shore serves to emphasize "the confusion of the sea," which will soon send the correspondent, on a "piece of life-preserver," "down the incline of a wave as if he were on a hand-sled" (p. 907). The correspondent "wonders" at the shore's immovable quality because its very solidity seems a mirage from his vertiginous perspective among the rolling swells.

Yet characteristically here, the sound of Crane's writing works against its imagistic function. Following so closely upon the quick progression of perceptual details in the first paragraph, this phrase—"there is a certain immovable quality to a shore"—itself manifests, by contrast, a certain immovability and initiates a slowing of the sequence's pace. This distanced reflection (offered almost as an odd proverb or a truism) comes from a narrator who continues to call momentary time-outs from the narrative action in "The Open Boat." Crane's aphoristic aside—a sign of what one critic calls his fondness for "the locution that launches the statement"[8]—does not sidetrack his realism here, but its mock-judiciousness stiffens and affectedly heightens its verbal effect.

This kind of unexpected rhetorical heightening is not always so evanescent or so quickly subordinated to Crane's realism. It is in fact a mild example of the radical indecisiveness of Crane's verbal behavior and of the divided motives that accompany that behavior. The double-mindedness that many critics have noted in the workings of Crane's irony is present in fictional effects that are not best, or at least adequately, thought of as "ironic." These effects spring, to use

Kenneth Burke's phrase, from "a perspective by incongruity."[9] That incongruity arises in part from the interactions of two contrasting viewpoints, interactions that are both complex and ephemeral. Narrative viewpoints in Crane seem less established than provisionally occupied and then abandoned. His work consistently displays what David Halliburton terms "a complex perspectivism" in which, by turns, we see characters and then see *with* them.[10]

What has not been adequately addressed in Crane criticism, however, is that the way in which these narrative shifts rhetorically register in his work crucially effects the fluctuating vantages the stories offer. Crane's irony, that is, springs not simply from the interactions of two narrative viewpoints but from the "languages" by which those viewpoints are entertained. We hear a narrative voice in "The Open Boat," as Halliburton asserts, that tells us "what the men cannot say because it knows what they cannot know, or knows at least that of which they are not for the moment aware."[11] But this narrative "knowledge" does not somehow exist apart from its stylistic articulation, which variously alters the ways in which we might construe it as knowledge. What we "know" in Crane's fiction is not always the same as what we hear. A narrative voice in his writing does not always constitute a view-point (a stabilized vantage from which a view might be had or from which a self might be imagined).[12]

To read Crane well we must sufficiently acknowledge the constant and unrelieved oscillation between, in James Guetti's terms, his "rhetoric of realism" and his "rhetoric of fiction" (or what I will also call his rhetorical imagination). Crane's commitment to narrative as "both realistic sequence and fictional arrangement" offers not just "two sets of technical possibilities," Guetti asserts, but conflicting moral allegiances as well: for "from one side or the other, either words are bad and action good or vice-versa."[13] Crane's realism entails an implicit loyalty to the authority of lived experience and practical action, while his rhetoric of fiction, which is interwoven with that realism, invokes the legitimacy of fictional imagining, of verbal artifice and authorial voice. The fluctuations between self-diminishing and self-aggrandizing verbal postures form a stylistic signature in nearly all Crane's work.

A flexible critical vocabulary is crucial in attempting to describe the expressive dartings and cross-currents of Crane's imagination. If we use terms like the "rhetoric of realism" and the "rhetoric of fiction" not as absolutes but as ends of a scale between which any given Crane story constantly slides and readjusts itself, their critical value will be more apparent. They help highlight Crane's simultaneous adherence to and critique of realistic forms of expression:

> The little boat, lifted by each towering sea, and splashed viciously by the crests, made progress that in the absence of sea-weed was not apparent to those in her. She

seemed just a wee thing wallowing, miraculously, top-up, at the mercy of five oceans. Occasionally, a great spread of water, like white flames, swarmed into her.

"Bail her, cook," said the captain, serenely.

"All right, Captain," said the cheerful cook. (P. 890)

A reader attuned to and appreciative of only Crane's realism might imaginatively "process" this paragraph as follows: "The little boat, lifted and splashed by each swell seemed just a tiny, wallowing thing flooded by occasional waves." The sense of foaming motion and splash in Crane's image of waves "swarming" like a "spread" of "white flames" is so sudden and imaginatively tactile that it seems to block out and erase the formal and mannered language that precedes it. To be told that the little boat here is "lifted by each towering sea" is not just to emphasize the precariousness and danger of such a "wee thing" (with its "six inches of gunwale" [p. 885] separating the men from water and then sharks). It is to emphasize it in such a way that there seems no time or justification for being told that the boat "made progress that in the absence of sea-weed was not apparent to those in her." What works against the realistic pressure of that emphasis, or what stands in such contrast to it, is less a narrative perspective—a different angle of vision from that of the men—than the sound of language suggestive of some other viewpoint. The fact that the men do not know the boat is moving might, in other circumstances, be a realistic detail, one more pertinent indication of their preoccupied state of mind. But the verbal means by which we are informed of this are not neutral or self-effacing here—quite the opposite. "Made progress that in the absence of sea-weed": this is the unexpected but characteristic Crane touch, one whose dry and mock-precise phrasing seems playfully at odds with the realism against which it is suddenly foregrounded. The verbal intelligence behind such a formulation not only conveys information, it also, in effect, stops to listen to itself do so.[14]

In general, the energy and drive that inhere in Crane's curt and telegraphic grammar establish an ostensibly realistic function for his writing. Thus the tendency of his rhetorical imaginings to default on that function, to sound off when they should be seen through, seems to compromise their fictional presence. Their imaginative substance seems faltering and attenuated. They seem less images than narrative concessions: verbal processes that are merely entertained rather than imaginatively sanctioned. The incongruity they strike with Crane's realism seems to guarantee their imaginative eclipse. His rhetorical imaginings come to seem like so many clay pigeons, launched only so that the story's realism can shatter them convincingly. Their claims to fictional legitimacy appear ephemeral or peripheral because the reinstatement of Crane's realistic imagining, with its grammar of action and color, seems inevitable.

But again, that inevitability is only apparent. If such lapses of realistic imagining were unusual in Crane's work, we might be tempted to treat them as a "lapse," as carelessness or perhaps some kind of period mannerism to be tolerated charitably. But far from seeming an aberration or a sign of carelessness in Crane's narratives, his rhetoric of fiction itself often seems to establish a story's normative dimension. It is as consistently invoked, discontinued, and then reinvoked as is the rhetoric of realism in Crane's work:

> the three were silent, save for a trifle of hemming and hawing. To express any particular optimism at this time they felt to be childish and stupid, but they all doubtless possessed this sense of the situation in their mind [the captain's sense that they have little chance of surviving]. A young man thinks doggedly at such times. On the other hand, the ethics of their condition was decidedly against any open suggestion of hopelessness. So they were silent. (P. 888)

> The wind slowly died away. The cook and the correspondent were not now obliged to slave in order to hold high the oar. But the waves continued their old impetuous swooping at the dingey, and the little craft, no longer under way, struggled woundily over them. The oiler or the correspondent took the oars again. (P. 891)

> It is fair to say here that there was not a life-saving station within twenty miles in either direction, but the men did not know this fact and in consequence they made dark and opprobrious remarks concerning the eyesight of the nation's life-savers. Four scowling men sat in the dingey and surpassed records in the invention of epithets. (P. 893)

Each of these passages makes a claim for realism, telling us when the men have to row, why they do not voice their opinions, or that they curse unrestrainedly. Yet none of them convey the realistic effects Crane is capable of elsewhere in "The Open Boat."

The rhetorical gestures in these passages are protean and complex, ranging from mock-heroic teasing ("not now obliged to slave in order to hold high the oar") to foppish erudition ("in consequence they made dark and opprobrious remarks") and formulaic phrasing (as in the waves' "old impetuous swooping"). What they all share is a verbal distinctiveness. They are all the products of an authorial voice that insists upon its literary autonomy, its capacity for generating language that sounds like something we might find in literature, in other books. There are young men thinking doggedly and little crafts struggling woundily all through Crane's fiction. The people and objects in his work are continually described in such a way that they seem less people or objects than verbal occasions, individual pretexts for a particular way of writing.

To say, for instance, that the men are "surpassing records in the invention of epithets" is not merely to note that they are cursing but to note it in a waggishly mocking manner. Two pages before, these same characters were described as feeling a "subtle brotherhood of men" that the correspondent "who had been taught to be cynical of men, knew even at the time was the best experience of his life" (p. 890). Now Crane seems wryly amused at their not knowing (and how could they?) that there is no life-saving station for twenty miles in either direction. Instead of the captain, the oiler, the cook, and the correspondent, we are presented with "four scowling men" in a dinghy: a literary formula with the imaginative status of a cartoon. The author who informs us that the men "made dark and opprobrious remarks concerning the eyesight of the nation's life-savers" seems entirely removed, for the moment, from any sense of the men's physical exhaustion and discomfort. He seems to pride himself on the parodic inappropriateness of this description. Crane knows, or so it is intimated, what the men are actually saying as they curse, and how that might shock some contemporary readers.[15] But at the same time he camouflages that knowingness with what advertises itself as a Nimble Wit, and the dynamics of that literary misnaming momentarily displace and diminish the importance of the story's dramatic situation and the realism that has helped establish it.

"In the wan light," Crane tells us early in the story, "the faces of the men must have been gray. Their eyes must have glinted in strange ways as they gazed steadily astern. Viewed from a balcony, the whole thing would doubtlessly have been weirdly picturesque. But the men in the boat had no time to see it, and if they had had leisure there were other things to occupy their minds" (p. 886). "The Open Boat" and Crane's fiction in general are full of "weirdly picturesque" effects. But they are also full of contexts that implicitly denigrate those effects, contexts that make the very possibility of a balcony perspective seem an inappropriate, even irrelevant form of narrative "leisure." Crane's ambivalent allegiance to a vantage other than that the men occupy is apparent in his phrasing here. Crane speculates about what "the whole thing" must have looked like even as he first refuses to substantiate that speculation and then abruptly suggests that it is frivolous in any case. His statement that the men's eyes "*must* have glinted in strange ways" (as if the narrator did not know) offers an example of what Berryman calls Crane's "refusal to guarantee," which has "the effect of obliterating with silent contempt half of what one thinks one knows."[16] It would seem to indicate Crane's interest in the men's perspective and in the story's realism. But the focus and the depth of that interest are at least partially belied by a note of what is if not contemptuousness then at least a curious equivocation.[17]

Throughout the story Crane's odd rhetorical effects displace and even parody his resolve to depict the physical and psychological situation of the men accurately. That displacement is effected not only by perspectival shifts in the narrative but by various invocations of a self-consciously "crafty" or artful prose that suggest other perspectives without always stopping to establish them. We are often aware, that is, of weirdly picturesque effects in Crane's fiction without our being told each time that they are the product of a view from some imaginary balcony. They seem "picturesque" (and this is only one word we might use in describing these moments) because they do not seem realistic. Their picturesqueness has its inception in the lapsing of the narrative's realism.

Reading Crane is a bit like wearing glasses in a cold climate; there is a continuous fogging and clearing of your vision as you enter and leave heated buildings. Yet to put the matter this way is misleading, for the verbal action that works against his realism is felt not as a failed attempt at realistic imagining but as part of an entirely different perceptual mode, one in which we are made aware of the sounded presence of words. When we are not seeing through language to imagined life in Crane's fiction, we are listening to an authorial voice fashioning a conceit, stiffening its syntax, mimicking a literary convention, or employing a purposefully audacious word.[18]

Yet even the term "voice" in relation to Crane's work is problematic and fails to describe its idiosyncrasies sufficiently. Because his rhetorical imagination establishes itself only in contrast to his realism, its presence is felt as obstructive and self-mimicking rather than self-sustaining. His fictional voice has none of the resonance, energy, or range we find in, say, Melville, Faulkner, or Conrad. It is both less assured and less self-substantial in its imaginative halts and waverings. Thus even when the rhetorical aspects of Crane's work are established, they are less musically compelling than stiff, jocular, and purposefully awkward. They seem an imaginatively "imported" presence and Crane seems, in Berryman's words, "a rhetorician who refused to be one."[19]

These ambivalent imaginative allegiances directly determine the impact of Crane's scenes of violence. War and other occasions of dramatic tension and violence are peculiarly apt preoccupations for him because they mirror, in a larger way, the embattled imaginative conditions he preferred, moment by moment, in his fiction. Tony Tanner rightly suggests that Crane's imagination may be "more death-drawn, death-scared, death-haunted than that of any other American writer."[20] But this obsession continually takes shape in both intriguing and unanticipated verbal forms. What we repeatedly find in his writing, to borrow a phrase from "Death and the Child," are "manners erect by the side of death" (p. 958).

THE SHORTNESS of Crane's career, Warner Berthoff argues, "and that ripeness of individual sensibility in his style from the first—the basis of Howells's remark that Crane had sprung into life 'fully armed'—make chronology and questions of development nearly immaterial in his case."[21] The truth of this statement is borne out in Crane's first published Sullivan County tale, "Killing His Bear" (1892), a story that while far from his most accomplished work, still displays the unique complexities of his writing.

The sketch, one of what Crane once called the "little grotesque tales of the woods which I wrote when I was clever,"[22] opens with a "little man" (who anonymously figures throughout the Sullivan County vignettes) waiting for his dog to flush a bear out of the woods:

> In a field of snow some green pines huddled together and sang in quavers as the wind whirled among the gullies and ridges. Icicles dangled from the trees' beards, and fine dusts of snow lay upon their brows. On the ridge-top a dismal choir of hemlocks crooned over one that had fallen. The dying sun created a dim purple and flame-colored tumult on the horizon's edge and then sank until level crimson beams struck the trees. As the red rays retreated, armies of shadows stole forward. A gray, ponderous stillness came heavily in the steps of the sun. A little man stood under the quavering pines. He was muffled to the nose in fur and wool, and a hideous cap was pulled tightly over his ears. His cold and impatient feet had stamped a small platform of hard snow beneath him. A black-barrelled rifle lay in the hollow of his arm. His eyes, watery from incessant glaring, swept over the snowfields in front of him. His body felt numb and bloodless, and soft curses came forth and froze on the icy wind. The shadows crept about his feet until he was merely a blurred blackness, with keen eyes. (P. 506)

There is enough sensory "data" in this moment (level beams of sunlight, a platform of hard, stamped snow, a black-barreled rifle posed on an arm) for us to begin to visualize the scene. A reader may also, in his perceptual progress, hit a phrase such as "a hideous cap" and go right through it imaginatively, to see how it is pulled down tightly over the little man's ears. But if our visual attention does waver on that "hideous," to what might we be attending? Is Crane suggesting that the little man has a debased taste in caps? Perhaps, but it also seems that a cap can be hideous in this scene for the same reason that a "dismal choir of hemlocks" can croon "over one that had fallen": they both answer to a certain descriptive impulse, they both remain part of a fictitious world populated by such vaguely sinister conceits.

Berryman has noted that the "ferocity" of Crane's prose, "whether intended or casual, seems primitive. His animism is like nothing else in civilized literature."[23] Everything about the passage above seems actively, hyperbolically quickened and alive. Pines huddle and sing in quavers, hemlocks croon, the sun dies and creates a tumult, armies of shadows steal forward, and—by this time, almost understandably—soft curses come forth, like a vulnerable animal, and freeze "*on* the wind." The imaginative atmosphere is dense and metaphorically crowded. In fact, the verbal melodrama nearly obliterates the ostensible subject of the scene, leaving him "merely a blurred blackness." The final effect is one of menacing natural sentience, but the source of that malevolent potential is not nature but an imagistically hyperactive narrator. If any of the metaphors or personifications in this paragraph seem conceptually vital, it is due as much to a general tone of imaginative aggression as to any one particular conceit. Yet if we label this kind of verbal behavior "animistic" or "primitive," we should also note that it is extremely conventional. The passage is full of stock-phrases: "a dismal choir," "crimson beams," "armies of shadows," "steps of the sun," and "keen eyes" (eyes that just were, realistically enough, "watery from incessant glaring"). What for me epitomizes the strangeness of Crane's effects here is the way he enlivens, or attempts to enliven, what sounds like a literary formula— "quavering pines"—by informing us beforehand that these pines are actually capable of singing "in quavers," like the tremolo of an opera singer. That enlivening remains an entirely abstract and conceptual matter, for pines sing in quavers only in a metaphoric world, an imaginative realm separate from one where a man's "cold and impatient feet" can stamp "a small platform of hard snow beneath him."

This mixing of literary formulas and abstract conceits with the illusion of imagined life is kept up throughout the sketch. The little man hears the cry of the dog, which has, at first, "a strange vindictiveness and bloodthirstiness in it. Then it grew mournful as the wailing of a lost thing, as, perhaps, the dog gained on a fleeing bear. A hound, as he nears large game, has the griefs of the world on his shoulders and his baying tells of the approach of death. He is sorry he came" (p. 506). A hound, a bear, and the "approach of death": we have, it would seem, all the elements of a dramatic scene. But there is no "dog" here, only the voice of an authorial Lao-tsu telling us what a hound undergoes when he nears large game. Crane's mock-proverb is entertainingly inappropriate here both because of its sudden tone of profundity and because "the griefs of the world" is so shopworn and conventional, and thus so purposefully unrevealing a phrase. Yet in two sentences, the little man's "fancy" will be fixed on "the panting foam-spattered hound, cantering with his hot nose to the ground in the rear of the bear, which runs as easily and as swiftly as a rabbit, through brush, timber and swale." This startling example of the visual-sensory potency of Crane's prose would seem capable of swiftly establishing a descriptive norm in the story. But Crane's realistic detail, as Willa Cather noted, was highly selective: "If he saw one thing that engaged him in a room, he mentioned it. If he saw one thing in a landscape that thrilled him, he put it on paper, but he never tried to make a faithful report of everything else within his field of vision. . . . He is rather the best of our writers in what is called 'description' because he is the least describing."[24] The realism here is quickly discontinued as we are told that in the little man's fancy, "swift pictures of himself in a thousand attitudes under a thousand combinations of circumstances, killing a thousand bears, passed panoramically through him" (p. 507). The bear and the dog's movement in space are replicated in the sensorium of the little man, who listens "so tremendously that he [can] hear his blood surge in his veins" (p. 507).

The mock-grandiloquence of this mental panorama sounds like an ironic setup, as if the man is soon to prove himself pathetically incapable of heroic action. Still, Crane's irony seems strangely free-floating and untargeted: "The thicket opened and a great bear, indistinct and vague in the shadows, bounded into the little man's view, and came terrifically across the open snowfield. The little man stood like an image. The bear did not 'shamble' nor 'wobble'; there was no awkwardness in his gait; he ran like a frightened kitten. It would be an endless chase for the lithe-limbed hound in the rear" (p. 507). In pausing to correct faulty notions of how a bear actually moves, Crane deflates the descriptive magnitude such notions confer—it will be no "panoramic" act to kill a bear running "like a frightened kitten." But after taking time to revise others' descriptively imprecise language, the formulaic slickness of the phrase "lithe-limbed hound" works against the narrator's own caution about proper words. What chases this frightened bear-kitten is no longer a "panting, foam-spattered hound" but a mock-heroic epithet.

This odd amalgamation of realistic and rhetorical imaginings continues in the sketch's final sequence:

On [the bear] came, directly toward the little man. The animal heard only the crying behind him. He knew nothing of the thing with death in its hands standing motionless in the shadows before him.

Slowly the little man changed his aim until it rested where the head of the approaching shadowy mass must be. It was a wee motion, made with steady nerves and a soundless swaying of the rifle-barrel; but the bear heard, or saw, and knew. The animal whirled swiftly and started in a new direction with an amazing burst of speed. Its side was toward the little man now. His rifle-barrel was searching swiftly over the dark shape. Under the fore-shoulder was the place. A chance to pierce the heart, sever an artery or pass through the lungs. The little man saw swirling fur over his gun-barrel. The earth faded to nothing. Only space and the game, the aim and the hunter. Mad emotions, powerful to rock worlds, hurled through the little man, but did not shake his tiniest nerve.

When the rifle cracked it shook his soul to a profound depth. Creation rocked and the bear stumbled.

The little man sprang forward with a roar. He scrambled hastily in the bear's track. The splash of red, now dim, threw a faint, timid beam on a kindred shade on the snow. The little man bounded in the air.

"Hit!" he yelled, and ran on. Some hundreds of yards forward he came to a dead bear with his nose in the snow. Blood was oozing slowly from a wound under the shoulder, and the snow about was sprinkled with blood. A mad froth lay in the animal's open mouth and his limbs were twisted from agony.

The little man yelled again and sprang forward, waving his hat as if he were leading the cheering of thousands. He ran up and kicked the ribs of the bear. Upon his face was the smile of a successful lover. (Pp. 507–8)

The narrative perspective shifts restlessly here. We are told, sequentially, of what the bear hears, then what he does not see; we are given the man's perspective as he aims, the bear's response to that, and then the sighting down the gun-barrel; finally, we are told what the man feels before the narrator settles into a third-person omniscience. The perspectival shifts seem to arise almost naturally from the short sentences and corrugated rhythm of the passage, which intensify the scene's temporal determination, the urgency of passing time.

Yet even when the realistic focus of the writing loosens, the prose is still jerky and arhythmic:

The earth faded to nothing. Only space and the game, the aim and the hunter. Mad emotions, powerful to rock worlds, hurled through the little man, but did not shake his tiniest nerve.

When the rifle cracked it shook his soul to a profound depth. Creation rocked and the bear stumbled. The little man sprang forward with a roar.

The sequential momentum of the passage, which is continually springing forward, does not give creation a chance to rock or the earth to fade. There is no imaginative breathing room for such cosmic concerns because the rhythmic constriction here flattens the psychological depth of what the little man feels. Similarly, the anonymity of "a dead bear with his nose in the snow," when the drama demands more descriptive particularity, works at least two ways. It emphasizes the finality of the bear's death (as do the realistic details about the animal's oozing blood and "mad froth"). But it also makes the hunter's feelings of accomplishment seem self-inflated and gratuitous. The man "comes to" a dead bear, as if he might have come to some other animal and as if he had nothing to do with killing this one.

"Killing His Bear" displays stylistic earmarks that will, to a greater or lesser extent, characterize the rest of Crane's writing and the violence it includes. The narrator attempts to remain true to the perspectival and emotional experience of the hunt and then he ironically annotates that experience, suggesting the "littleness" of this anonymous hunter's activities. He simultaneously provides a rhetoric or a vocabulary that allows for an artery to be severed or a lung to be punctured, and one that has a "timid beam" of sunlight falling not on blood but on another verbal formula, "a kindred shade on the snow." The uneasy coexistence of these two modes of imagining makes the irony of the passage's last paragraph more dodgy than it may initially appear. In terms of the narrative action, the man has simply yelled, waved his hat, and kicked the bear. We know nothing of what he is thinking at this moment because the narrator watches him from the outside. By saying that the man waves his hat (that "hideous cap" of his) "as if he were leading the cheering of thousands," Crane implies that this is what the man thinks he is doing, and it makes him seem both callous and callow. Thus the narrator's avowal that "upon his face was the smile of the successful lover" might seem at first to mean "the smile of sexual conquest." The word "successful," coming as it does after the man kicks the bear in contempt or glee, suggests an air of prideful reproach. Yet what we are given in the last sentence is less a smile, an actual facial expression, than a phrase describing it, a phrase that sounds at first familiar and intelligible. We may be tempted to ignore its verbal smoothness because it ends the story and thereby gains a certain intelligibility and force. But it remains as visually non-specific and *heard* a phrase as "lithe-limbed" or "the griefs of the world." Is "the smile of sexual conquest" a leer? A grin? A simper?

Crane seems to be making fun of his character *as a character*, as a fictional construct, rather than as an actual person who likes to kill animals. That is, part of the amusement the little man affords stems from his status as an explicitly fictional creation rather than as a character who is made to seem like someone we might know or meet. The little man does not exemplify the psychology of a "successful lover," he just serves as a screen upon which the smile of such a person can be projected. The narrator seems uninterested in "knowing" what this man is thinking in the last paragraph because there seems to be no psychological process there to be known. The man's psychology is strangely corporealized: mental pictures pass through him panoramically and emotions hurl through him, the cry of the dog "pierces" his ears, his blood "surges" audibly in his veins, and the smile of the successful lover is *upon* his face, like a picture hung upon a wall. The conceptual blankness of Crane's rhetorical imagination—the blank absence of the orotund and the molded, in Berryman's terms—seems thus to extend into the psychology of his characters.

Maggie: A Girl of the Streets (1893) dramatizes this same conceptual process in its opening scene, in which violence is portrayed as being emblematic of the squalor of urban life in the Bowery. The novel was published the year after "Killing His Bear," and it shares many stylistic affinities with the earlier tale. Once again, the imaginative substance of Crane's characters is directly determined by his technical experiments:

> A very little boy stood upon a heap of gravel for the honor of Rum Alley. He was throwing stones at howling urchins from Devil's Row who were circling madly about the heap and pelting at him.
>
> His infantile countenance was livid with fury. His small body was writhing in the delivery of great, crimson oaths.
>
> "Run, Jimmie, run! Dey'll get yehs," screamed a retreating Rum Alley child.
>
> "Naw," responded Jimmie with a valiant roar, "dese micks can't make me run."
>
> Howls of renewed wrath went up from Devil's Row throats. Tattered gamins on the right made a furious assault on the gravel heap. On their small, convulsed faces there shone the grins of true assassins. As they charged, they threw stones and cursed in shrill chorus.
>
> The little champion of Rum Alley stumbled precipitately down the other side. His coat had been torn to shreds in a scuffle, and his hat was gone. He had bruises on twenty parts of his body, and blood was dripping from a cut in his head. His wan features wore a look of a tiny, insane demon.
>
> On the ground, children from Devil's Row closed in on their antagonist. He crooked his left arm defensively about his head and fought with cursing fury. The little boys ran to and fro, dodging, hurling stones and swearing in barbaric trebles.
>
> From a window of an apartment house that upreared its form from amid squat, ignorant stables, there leaned a curious woman. Some laborers, unloading a scow at a dock at the river, paused for a moment and regarded the fight. The engineer of a passive tugboat hung lazily to a railing and watched. Over on the Island, a worm of yellow convicts came from the shadow of a grey ominous building and crawled slowly along the river's bank.
>
> A stone had smashed into Jimmie's mouth. Blood was bubbling over his chin and down upon his ragged shirt. Tears made furrows on his dirt-stained cheeks. His thin legs had begun to tremble and turn weak, causing his small body to reel. His roaring curses of the first part of the fight had changed to a blasphemous chatter.
>
> In the yells of the whirling mob of Devil's Row children there were notes of joy like songs of triumphant savagery. The little boys seemed to leer gloatingly at the blood upon the other child's face. (Pp. 7–8)

We are given no insight here into how Jimmie or the Devil's Row boys actually feel. It is not Jimmie but rather his "infantile countenance" that is "livid with fury": "his wan features *wore* a look of a tiny, insane demon." On the "small, convulsed faces" of the other boys "there *shone the grins* of true assassins" and at the end of the sequence they "*seemed* to leer gloatingly" at Jimmie's bloody face. All we know about the inner feelings of these boys is discernible from and inscribed upon their faces. They seem to have no interiorized psychological dimension, because instead of offering symptoms of an internal mental process, their facial features display an oddly externalized "psychology." (Later in the novel this facial inscription becomes even more palpable in relation to one of Jimmie's ex-girlfriends. "In repose," Crane says, "her features had a shadowy look that was like a sardonic grin, as if some one had sketched with cruel forefinger indelible lines about her mouth" [p. 64].)

We cannot "read" Crane's characters in the same way we read, say, James's or Twain's, any more than we can successfully characterize the language of his fiction by pointing only to its realistic qualities. As Lee Mitchell notes, Crane, like Theodore Dreiser, Jack London, and Frank Norris, "rejected the very category of the 'self'" and created "characters who seem little more than occasions for passing events."[25] The "events" that momentarily constitute these characters, however, often consist less of emotions and desires than of particular ways of writing. Thus the boys' psychology in this instance seems "inscribed" not only because of metaphors of inscription but because their facial features become a *verbal* site, one described in glibly conventional rather than realistic terms. The "look of a tiny, insane demon" and "the grins of true assassins" are less facial expressions than formulaic linguistic ones. These phrases do not work toward visual definition, they fulfill a descriptive need. The faces of the boys, like Rum Alley itself, form a kind of verbal parchment upon which to indite stock-phrases.[26] Their faces bear the same relation to an inner psychology that the passage's verbal formulas bear to the realism of a stone's smashing into Jimmie's mouth and the blood bubbling over his chin.

The mock-heroic phrasing with which this scene is glutted—"howling urchins," "valiant roar," "barbaric trebles," "the little champion," "songs of triumphant savagery"—establishes in part an ironic context for this gang fracas. Donald Pizer argues that an idea of honor keeps the participants in this fight from knowing "they are engaged in a vicious and petty scuffle." Crane's irony, he says, "emerges out of the difference between a value that one imposes on experience and the nature of experience itself. His ironic method is to project into the scene the values of its participants in order to underline the difference between their values and reality."[27] Crane's irony here does seem to emerge out of the difference between "a value that one imposes on experience and the nature of experience itself" or, more precisely, out of the difference between Crane's mock-chivalric and realistic language. But the imposed values in this scene are not those of the participants—at least not as it is now worded. Tom Sawyer might use this kind of chivalric vocabulary in "playing robber" according to the dictates of *Don Quixote*. But as the speech idioms in this moment are meant to attest, that vocabulary is entirely lost upon Jimmie and the other boys. Crane caricatures "honor" not as a value projected by the participants here but as an idea whose inappropriateness can be exposed when superimposed upon poverty and violence.

Crane's use of mock-heroic phrasing operates, in this instance, in a way similar to Alexander Pope's in "The Rape of the Lock." The same imaginative dynamic that makes Belinda's or Jimmie's actions seem comparatively small and insignificant also indirectly implies that the heroic vocabulary that forms the standard of comparison may itself be suspect as a descriptive mode. Furthermore, Crane does not see this fight as only "a vicious and petty scuffle": vicious, yes, but not necessarily petty. He seems to remember or know what can seem at stake for those involved in such boyhood fights. Yet at the same time, Crane also seems remotely amused by the descriptive possibilities the situation affords. What seems to engage him about this fight is not simply its social or psychological aspects but the verbal opportunities it affords: the chance, say, for "tattered gamins on the right" to make "a furious assault on the gravel heap."

The element of pathos in Crane's irony is usually counterbalanced, as Berryman asserts, by an element of irony in his pathos. Crane is "simultaneously *at war with* the people he creates and *on their* side," and he "displays each of these attitudes so forcibly that the reader feels he is himself being made a fool of. . . . God knows [the distresses of his characters] are real enough; one feels them, and at the same time one is made to feel even more strongly that the character has to run a gauntlet to the author's sympathy. . . . Crane never rests. He is always fighting the thing out with himself."[28] Crane's irony seems peculiarly appropriate in scenes of violence, for it offers an imaginative analogue for the pulse of engagement and withdrawal war and fights involve. Crane seems fully resolved to describe the tensed sequential immediacy of violent scenes and the physical toll they exact. But in various ways, in the midst of that tension and action, he continually reminds us of other perspectives. "War takes a long time," Crane wrote in an 1897 newspaper sketch from the Greco-Turkish war. "The swiftness of chronological order of battle is not correct. A man has time to get shaved, or to lunch or to take a bath often in battles the descriptions of which read like a whirlwind" (p. 936).

In the opening of *Maggie*, the narrative equivalent of the time to eat lunch consists of a shift in perspective (one characteristic of Crane's scenes of violence more generally) to the spectators of the fight—the laborers, the engineer, and the "curious woman" who watch from a distance. The listless, inhumane indifference of the onlookers is emphasized, along with the torpid squalor of the boys' surroundings. The "worm of yellow convicts" on Blackwell's Island (which, it is implied, the boys will soon be joining) does not seem to notice the fight going on across the river. This frame for the action offers a kind of "balcony view" à la "The Open Boat," a new perspective on the fight that subsumes it within a social context and perhaps a social critique. But once again, that perspective is only momentary. It is dropped in the wake of the sudden shift back to realistic imagining (the smash of a stone), which will itself, in three sentences, be eclipsed by another rhetorical mode. Out of Jimmie's mouth will come not more bubbling blood but "blasphemous chatter," another verbal formula.

Crane's imaginative restlessness continues to operate, though to colder effect, as Jimmie and Blue Billie start to fight:

> They struck at each other, clinched, and rolled over on the cobble stones.
>
> "Smash 'im, Jimmie, kick deh damn guts out of 'im," yelled Pete, the lad with the chronic sneer, in tones of delight.
>
> The small combatants pounded and kicked, scratched and tore. They began to weep and their curses struggled in their throats with sobs. The other boys clasped their hands and wriggled their legs in excitement. They formed a bobbing circle about the pair.
>
> A tiny spectator was suddenly agitated.
>
> "Cheese it, Jimmie, cheese it! Here comes yer fader," he yelled.
>
> The circle of little boys instantly parted. They drew away and waited in ecstatic awe for that which was about to happen. The two little boys fighting in the modes of four thousand years ago, did not hear the warning. (P. 9)

Pete's "tones of delight" here and the onlookers' bobbing observational adrenaline seem increasingly grim as the two boys' "curses [struggle] in their throats with sobs." Their crying attests both to their pain and to their underlying incomprehension as to why they are fighting—though they refuse, in cold, childish fury, to stop. Crane's assertion that the boys are "fighting in the modes of four thousand years ago" suggests a historical continuum for this kind of instinctual cruelty. It is certainly the kind of detail that has prompted critics to refer to Crane's writing as "naturalistic," as bleakly cognizant of man's will to aggression. Yet that phrase is also stiff and decorous and at odds with its dramatic occasion. Crane's realism often quickly wins our sympathy for his characters, as when the boys are crying and cursing at the same time or when Jimmie's front teeth are smashed with a stone. But his odd, formalized narrative remoteness also often displays what we might paradoxically term an active or performed indifference to his characters, to his writing, perhaps even to himself.

Take for example the descriptive conceit in *Maggie* that arises in the course of a preacher's sermon to some men gathered in a mission church:

> While they got warm at the stove, he told his hearers just where he calculated they stood with the Lord. Many of the sinners were impatient over the pictured depths of their degradation. They were waiting for soup-tickets.
>
> A reader of words of wind-demons might have been able to see the portions of a dialogue pass to and fro between the exhorter and his hearers.
>
> "You are damned," said the preacher. And the reader of sounds might have seen the reply go forth from the ragged people: "Where's our soup?" (P. 20)

We can, with such a passage, understand the force of Wright Morris's contention that Crane was "as conscious of his attempt to make it new as Joyce or Pound."[29] The notion of "a reader of words of wind-demons" is not only decidedly strange, it is strange in such a way that it subverts the ostensible irony of this moment. When we ignore the conceit, Crane seems to be invoking a hard-boiled cynicism about mission preachers and an implied sympathy for those waiting for soup. But the "portions of dialogue" that pass back and forth here like banners of dialogue in an editorial cartoon, stress the almost comic predictability of not only the preacher's insensitivity but the ragged people's needs as well. Crane obviously wants to lampoon the preacher's hypocrisy, but he does not do it by simply exciting compassion for the hungry or by inducing social guilt in the reader. In fact, Crane satirizes the realistic means by which social misery itself can be conveyed. He often writes, Alan Trachtenberg notes, from "a curiously asocial perspective," as a kind of social "phenomenologist."[30] The larger dramatizations of unrelatedness in *Maggie*—the gap between rich and poor, between Bowery men and women, and between an inappropriately theatrical morality and the sordid physical conditions it is used to defend against[31]—seem but magnifications of Crane's discontinuous imaginative impulses. Once again, his larger thematic concerns seem to spring directly from the volatile play of styles we find more locally in his writing.

BECAUSE CRANE so continually lets one style, one form of verbal imagining, be intruded upon by other styles it could not otherwise accommodate, his fiction always seems to go beyond simply telling a story. It involves discovering, in the course of a scene or a sentence, how to hold together elements that would otherwise tend to destroy one another. Crane refuses to reduce the multitude of competing sounds in his writing to a predominant tone. He "often lets his prose attempt to stimulate more response than [his dramatic] situations themselves seem to warrant," Bergon notes, and in doing so he constantly calls into question the descriptive norms that underlie *any* expressive practice.[32] Nearly all the narrative vantages and expressive styles in his fiction seem provisional, established only so they can eventually be revamped or dismissed. Crane's fictional voice thus remains unmistakable and his naturalism, as Sydney Krause says, can be "precious and obvious" one moment and "stark and symbolic" the next.[33] Crane's relationship to previous literature, especially writing that he reacts against, is both complex and ambiguous. His scorn for sentimentality is equaled only by his verbal appetite for stiff, unwieldy literary formulas and stock vocabularies, as we can see in "The Blue Hotel."

A large part of that story's function is to expose the inappropriateness of Eastern dime-novel versions of the Wild West, to puncture the notion the Swede apparently has that he is (in the words of the Easterner) "right out in the middle of it—the shootin' and stabbin' and all" (p. 809). Crane satirizes the descriptive conventions of the Western that precede the story. When Scully follows the Swede upstairs at the hotel, for example,

> Scully's wrinkled visage showed grimly in the light of the small lamp he carried. This yellow effulgence, streaming upward, colored only his prominent features, and left his eyes, for instance, in mysterious shadow. He resembled a murderer.
> "Man, man!" he exclaimed, "have you gone daffy?"
> "Oh, no! Oh, no!" rejoined the other. "There are people in this world who know pretty nearly as much as you do—understand?" (P. 806)

"Wrinkled visage" and "yellow effulgence" purposefully exaggerate the menacing overtones that are then further subverted by the mock-precision of saying the lamplight leaves Scully's "eyes, *for instance*, in mysterious shadow." Scully resembles a murderer here only to the extent that Crane's language resembles previous writing about murderers with their lamplit features in shadowy relief. Crane's "very style of exaggeration," as George Monteiro says, "serves to convey the notion of a 'West' that lives only in overstatement."[34]

But the story offers more than the deflation of a literary myth, and the Swede's otherworldly rejoinder here makes both Scully's colloquialism and Crane's descriptive hyperbole seem somehow inappropriate and peripheral. The Swede seems as elusive and unknown a quantity at this point in the story as he does earlier when Crane says "he *resembled* a badly frightened man" (p. 801, my emphasis). To offer up a descriptive possibility at the same time that one identifies it as merely a possibility is to call attention not only to what an analogy enables but to what it refuses to allow. The Swede's cryptic statements and his unexplained paranoia help establish the story's strange dramatic edginess, to which Crane's rhythm also contributes:

As the men trooped heavily back into the front room, the two little windows presented views of a turmoiling sea of snow. The huge arms of the wind were making attempts—mighty, circular, futile—to embrace the flakes as they sped. A gate-post like a still man with a blanched face stood aghast amid this profligate fury. In a hearty voice Scully announced the presence of a blizzard. The guests of the blue hotel, lighting their pipes, assented with grunts of lazy masculine contentment. No island of the sea could be exempt in the degree of this little room with its humming stove. Johnnie, son of Scully, in a tone which defined his opinion of his ability as a card-player, challenged the old farmer of both gray and sandy whiskers to a game of High-Five. The farmer agreed with a contemptuous and bitter scoff. They sat close to the stove, and squared their knees under a wide board. The cowboy and the Easterner watched the game with interest. The Swede remained near the window, aloof, but with a countenance that showed signs of an inexplicable excitement. (P. 801)

Typically here, the narrative action does not match or seem to demand the verbal activity of its description. The two card players here are less characters than mock-heroic formulas ("Johnnie, son of Scully" and "the old farmer of both gray and sandy whiskers"). Similarly, the cartoon nightmare of a simile that precedes Scully's announcement about the blizzard makes it seem cheerfully inane. If the sequence read

two little windows presented views of a turmoiling sea of snow. In a hearty voice Scully announced the presence of a blizzard . . . ,

we would have an example of straight realistic description. It is the two intervening sentences that add the conspicuous Crane touch. The hyperbolic adjectives—"mighty," "futile," "blanched," "aghast," "profligate"—invoke a verbal melodrama that seems all the more eccentric and shadowy for its contrast with the men's unattending "grunts of lazy masculine contentment." The Swede's "inexplicable excitement" as he hovers on the edges of this scene comes to seem connected with Crane's strange, unexpected verbal gestures. It is as if the Swede's psychology had a verbal correlative, as if he himself were somehow capable of reading the story in which he appears, or at least being aware of the huge-armed wind and the blanched men that precede him on the page.

Crane's verbal activity continues to exceed the requirements of dramatic action in the fight between Johnnie and the Swede (one of the longest sequences of violence in Crane's fiction). The opening moments of the fight are self-consciously arranged as a spectacle, one in which "crowd shots" emphasize the excitement and "the fury of the fight" by showing the kind of response it engenders:[35]

The arrangements were swiftly made. The two men faced each other, obedient to the harsh commands of Scully, whose face, in the subtly luminous gloom, could be seen set in the austere impersonal lines that are pictured on the countenances of the Roman veterans. The Easterner's teeth were chattering, and he was hopping up and down like a mechanical toy. The cowboy stood rock-like.

The contestants had not stripped off any clothing. Each was in his ordinary attire. Their fists were up, and they eyed each other in a calm that had the elements of leonine cruelty in it.

During this pause, the Easterner's mind, like a film, took lasting impressions of three men—the iron-nerved master of the ceremony; the Swede, pale, motionless, terrible; and Johnnie, serene yet ferocious, brutish yet heroic. The entire prelude had in it a tragedy greater than the tragedy of action, and this aspect was accentuated by the long mellow cry of the blizzard, as it sped the tumbling and wailing flakes into the black abyss of the south.

"Now!" said Scully.

The two combatants leaped forward and crashed together like bullocks. There was heard the cushioned sound of blows, and of a curse squeezing out from between the tight teeth of one.

As for the spectators, the Easterner's pent-up breath exploded from him with a pop of relief, absolute relief from the tension of the preliminaries. The cowboy bounded into the air with a yowl. Scully was immovable as from supreme amazement and fear at the fury of the fight which he himself had permitted and arranged. (Pp. 816–17)

Crane asserts that "the entire prelude had in it a tragedy greater than the tragedy of action," but it is difficult to identify his tone. He again uses heroic formulas ("leonine cruelty," "the iron-nerved master of the ceremony," the fighters crashing together "like bullocks") but they are not as elaborately and inappropriately heightened as in the opening scene of *Maggie*. On the other hand, Johnnie seems hopelessly versatile as he is, by turns, "serene yet ferocious, brutish yet heroic"; the Easterner's "hopping up and down like a mechanical toy" (with anxiety as well as cold?) and his "pop of relief" as his "pent-up breath" explodes, are comically diminishing details; and "the austere impersonal lines" set in Scully's face, as "on the countenances of the Roman veterans," may be either mock-hyperbole or descriptive earnestness on Crane's part.

Despite the Easterner's mind working "like a film," there is little realistic detail to this point, outside of "the cushioned sound of blows":

For a time the encounter in the darkness was such a perplexity of flying arms that it presented no more detail than would a swiftly-revolving wheel. Occasionally a face, as if illumined by a flash of light, would shine out, ghastly and marked with pink spots. A moment later, the men might have been known as shadows, if it were not for the involuntary utterance of oaths that came from them in whispers.

Suddenly a holocaust of warlike desire caught the cowboy, and he bolted forward with the speed of a broncho. "Go it, Johnnie; go it! Kill him! Kill him!" . . . The cowboy's face was contorted like one of those agony-masks in museums.

"Keep still," said Scully icily.

Then there was a sudden loud grunt, incomplete, cut-short, and Johnnie's body swung away from the Swede and fell with sickening heaviness to the grass. The cowboy was barely in time to prevent the mad Swede from flinging himself upon his prone adversary. "No, you don't," said the cowboy, interposing an arm. "Wait a second."

Scully was at his son's side. "Johnnie! Johnnie, me boy?" His voice had a quality of melancholy tenderness. "Johnnie? Can you go on with it?" He looked anxiously down into the bloody pulpy face of his son.

There was a moment of silence, and then Johnnie answered in his ordinary voice: "Yes, I—it—yes."

Assisted by his father he struggled to his feet. "Wait a bit now till you git your wind," said the old man. (Pp. 817–18)

Scully's anxious peering into the "bloody pulpy face of his son" forms the most disturbing detail here, not only because of its sensory vividness but because Scully's tortured concern for his son (which has to be suppressed in the interests of a fair fight) is apparent before it is described as "melancholy tenderness." Most of the physical details of the fight, however, are visually nonspecific. "A perplexity of flying arms" conveys a sense of confused entanglement that seems purposefully blurred and indistinct. So too, the pinwheel faces that occasionally "shine out, ghastly and marked with pink spots" seem deliberately striking, another of Crane's self-consciously bizarre conceits. They belong to the rhetorical impulse that has the cowboy "caught" in "a holocaust of warlike desire" and his face "contorted like one of those agony-masks in museums." Yet in the midst of such rhetorical imagining, Crane's realism—his ability to evoke a powerful sense of pain and imaginative motion by simply saying "Johnnie's body swung away from the Swede and fell with sickening heaviness to the grass"—continues to strike a stark contrast.

At the end of the sequence, the battered Johnnie can hold his own only momentarily before the Swede attacks with "berserk abandon" amid "another perplexity of flying arms":

Johnnie's body again swung away and fell, even as a bundle might fall from a roof. The Swede instantly staggered to a little wind-waved tree and leaned upon it, breathing like an engine, while his savage and flame-lit eyes roamed from face to face as the men bent over Johnnie. There was a splendor of isolation in his situation at this time which the Easterner felt once when, lifting his eyes from the man on the ground, he beheld that mysterious and lonely figure, waiting.

"Are you any good yet, Johnnie?" asked Scully in a broken voice.

The son gasped and opened his eyes languidly. After a moment he answered: "No—I ain't—any good—any—more." Then, from shame and bodily ill, he began to weep, the tears furrowing down through the blood-stains on his face. "He was too—too—too heavy for me."

Scully straightened and addressed the waiting figure. "Stranger," he said, evenly, "it's all up with our side." Then his voice changed into that vibrant huskiness which is commonly the tone of the most simple and deadly announcements. "Johnnie is whipped." (Pp. 818–19)

Unlike in "The Open Boat," where a view from a balcony is hypothesized and then impatiently dismissed, Crane does not diminish the picturesque "splendor" of the Swede as he leans, with his "savage and flame-lit eyes," against "a little wind-waved tree." But neither does he ignore the ugly physical price exacted from Johnnie, whose tears furrow "down through the blood-stains on his face." Crane wants it both ways. He wants both the "mysterious and lonely figure, waiting" and the battered and weeping boy. He maintains a moral neutrality in depicting this fight, but not a verbal neutrality. The painful realism of Johnnie's body hitting the grass "with sickening heaviness" coexists with pops of relief and savage, flame-lit eyes. The imaginative tension that stems from this kind of juxtaposed incongruity results more from incessantly mobile verbal processes than from simple shifts in narrative perspective. But that tension is not here best described as ironic, unless it establishes an irony at the expense of the story itself.

In "The Blue Hotel" the narrator flamboyantly withdraws from his story when the Swede leaves the hotel after the fight and struggles into Fort Romper in a prairie blizzard with his face "fresh from the pounding of Johnnie's fists":

We picture the world as thick with conquering and elate humanity, but here, with the bugles of the tempest pealing, it was hard to imagine a peopled earth. One viewed the existence of man then as a marvel, and conceded a glamour of wonder to these lice which were caused to cling to a whirling, fire-smote, ice-locked, disease-stricken, space-lost bulb. The conceit of man was explained by this storm to be the very engine of life. One was a coxcomb not to die in it. However, the Swede found a saloon. (P. 822)

The telescoping diminishment of this image of the world as a lost, stricken "bulb" has often been cited as one of the definitive instances of American naturalism. It is taken to offer a philosophical perspective (this is a view from a balcony on the moon) that characterizes one side of Crane's imagination and generates his "cosmic" ironies. Yet even this grand ratio of man to universe is not unambiguously proffered: Crane's rhetorical haughtiness in fashioning it turns into a clever delicacy that scolds us as "coxcombs."

There is a perpetual "however" in Crane's style, instanced not only in shifts of perspective but in the constant modulations of his narrative voice that alter and qualify the imaginative force of those perspectives. Imperious, cynical notions of men reduced to the status of lice are "explained" in a language whose affectation and formulaic abstraction ("the bugles of the tempest pealing," "conceded a glamour of wonder") would offer a rhetorical impediment, in any other writer, to so radically deflating a conception of the world. "Except by a kind of parodic mimicry," Warner Berthoff contends, the "barrage of self-generating images and inward conceits" in Crane's fiction scarcely refer "to each other or to the narrative events they coexist with."[36] No two descriptive postures seem entirely incapable of sharing the page in Crane's work, despite their differing, often contradictory claims to imaginative legitimacy. The effect of this verbal interweaving is to open up imaginative gaps in his writing, so that reading his work resembles jumping from stone to stone in crossing a stream.

The Swede demands that the other men in the bar have a drink with him in honor of his having "whipped a man tonight." When the gambler "kindly" refuses for all of them, the Swede goes wild:

> The barkeeper dashed around the corner of his bar. There was a great tumult, and then was seen a long blade in the hand of the gambler. It shot forward, and a human body, this citadel of virtue, wisdom, power, was pierced as easily as if it had been a melon. The Swede fell with a cry of supreme astonishment.
>
> The prominent merchants and the district-attorney must have at once tumbled out of the place backward. The bartender found himself hanging limply to the arm of a chair and gazing into the eyes of a murderer.
>
> "Henry," said the latter, as he wiped his knife on one of the towels that hung beneath the bar-rail, "you tell 'em where to find me. I'll be home, waiting for 'em." Then he vanished. A moment afterward the barkeeper was in the street dinning through the storm for help, and, moreover, companionship.
>
> The corpse of the Swede, alone in the saloon, had its eyes fixed upon a dreadful legend that dwelt a-top of the cash-machine. "This registers the amount of your purchase." (P. 826)

"The Swede fell with a cry of supreme astonishment": this may be as cold a gesture on Crane's part as the gambler's calmly wiping off his knife on a bar towel. If we take the Swede's "astonishment" to be not so much physical shock as a final realization of his own boorishness and self-delusions, then Crane has simply brutalized his character for the sake of a dramatic comeuppance. Such a possibility is strongly present here, for in one sense the Swede's death does represent his "purchase." He begs for his death, Berryman asserts, "buys it" with his "excess of fear and then his pretentiousness and even his over-protest against a boy's cheating in a game where no money was at stake. There is nothing accidental in the murder of this Swede except that it was the gambler who committed it and he gets a light sentence."[37]

But Berryman does not suggest the full power of the last image of this sequence. The narrator seems as indifferent to the notion that a human body is a "citadel of virtue, wisdom, [and] power" as he is to whether or not the merchants and the district attorney actually did tumble "out of the place backward." Saying that they "*must* have at once tumbled out" is similar to asserting that "the bartender found himself hanging limply to the arm of a chair." No one, Crane included, seems to know what is happening in the midst of this disorientation and disrupted causation. The legend upon which the dead Swede's eyes are fixed is "dreadful" precisely because of its neutrality, its resistance to narrative significance. It seems the perfect epitaph for the Swede because the very familiarity of its words makes them seem strange and mysterious here. In the same way the bartender finds himself gazing into the anonymous "eyes of a murderer," the corpse's eyes stare at this blank, anonymous "language" of a cash-machine, language exempted, as so often in Crane, from any *necessary* relationship to its dramatic context. The cash-machine legend represents the culminating example of the verbal formulas that rhetorically "register" with such an incongruous force throughout Crane's fiction.

THE INTEREST in Crane's writing resides in the intersection of his disaffiliated rhetorical impulses, his connection of otherwise unconnectable forms of verbal imagining. The stylistic vacillations in his work between immediate engagement and indifferent withdrawal alter its imaginative substance in a way aptly emblematized by an incident he records during the Greco-Turkish war: "The [Greek] reserves coming up passed a wayside shrine. The men paused to cross themselves and pray. A shell struck the shrine and demolished it. The men in the rear of the column were obliged to pray to the spot where the shrine had been" (p. 936). Crane constantly establishes one course of verbal action and then, in effect, demolishes it. His most vivid realistic sequences are often peppered with words and locutions whose formal, inert, or ceremonious qualities stand like roadblocks in the narrative path. The visual-sensory power of Crane's realism, by its very nature, makes his rhetorical imagining seem pejoratively artificial, a series of verbal obstacles to be circumvented. Yet Crane's

129

use of "fake" or "dead" verbal formulas is itself so pervasive as to seem almost "institutionalized," as Guetti puts it:

> If we suppose, because he is so consistent in this, that it is what he wants to do, the effect is then often one of a strange and indeterminate irony in which he sometimes seems to be making fun of his characters, or of his story, or of himself as a writer and sometimes to be deliberately muting and damping his own visual energy or insisting on a faded archaic literary legitimacy for fictional movements that are in fact strong and novel.[38]

The "strange and indeterminate irony" that springs from Crane's writing often makes him seem cold and remote in scenes of violence, and his narrative behavior does at times anticipate and prefigure that of Flannery O'Connor. But that remoteness is noticeable only because it strikes such an odd contrast with the compassion implicit in his realistic renderings of suffering slum children, army regulars, and black stable hands. Crane's imaginative ambivalence is such that a reader continually encounters both his sympathetic acknowledgment of, for example, "that helpless beseeching for assistance which comes with supreme pain" (p. 648) and a narrative composure or disinterest in the face of such pain that seems preternaturally unagitated, even parodic. Crane appears to be of two minds, at least two minds, about nearly everything in his fiction. Acutely sensitive to his own procedures as a writer, nothing seems to fulfill the full range of his imagination for anything more than the time being. He seems skeptical about most subjects, even the motives for his own skepticism. The violence that appears as the ex post facto subject of his work seems but the larger exemplification of the violence of his crossed fictional motives—motives that continue to make Crane a stranger and more unexpected writer than many readers remember. Like the maimed soldiers who populate his war fiction, Crane's writing wavers between death and life, between the imaginative extremes of dead and living languages, and forms itself a kind of wounded music.

The Purity of Execution in Hemingway's Fiction

> *Old Lady*: You know I like you less and less the more
> I know you.
>   Madame, it is always a mistake to know an author.
> —*Death in the Afternoon*

THERE IS a long tradition of disliking Hemingway's work—one matched, in venerability, only by Hemingway's irascible depictions of those who object as frustrated schoolmarms. Much of the disapproval is aimed at his preoccupation with violence. Many commentators on his work have sensed "with increasing certainty after the shotgun blast in 1961," Frederick Crews says, that "the writer whose imagination reverted to goring, maiming, crucifixion, exploded body parts, and agonies of childbirth was by no means a simple realist of the out-of-doors."[1] Yet long before Hemingway's suicide, critics like D. S. Savage (in 1948) were complaining about the "crude, violent action" they found in his fiction. Explanations for this violence were not long to seek. It arose from the need to alleviate a state of "psychic vacuity," Savage contended: "the more violent the activity, the greater the relief from the sickening vertigo of bore-dom" that afflicted his characters. Violence cannot produce "a convincing sense of meaningfulness," Savage continued, but "it can at any rate produce an illu-sory [and depraved] sense of *life*" thrown up against "the stark, black negation of the void."[2] He quotes, in attempting to prove his point, from the opening scene of *To Have and Have Not*:

> The other fellow pulled the one who was hit back by the legs to behind the wagon, and I saw the nigger getting his face down on the paving to give them another burst. Then I saw old Pancho come around the corner of the wagon and step into the lee of the horse that was still up. He stepped clear of the horse, his face white as a dirty sheet, and got the chauffeur with the big Luger he had; holding it in both hands to keep it steady. He shot twice over the nigger's head, coming on, and once low.
>   He hit a tire on the car because I saw dust blowing in a spurt on the street as the air came out, and at ten feet the nigger shot him in the belly with the Tommy gun, with what must have been the last shot in it because I saw him throw it down, and old Pancho sat down hard and went over forwards. He was trying to come up, still holding on to the Luger, only he couldn't get his head up, when the nigger took the

shot gun that was lying against the wheel of the car by the chauffeur and blew the side of his head off. Some nigger.[3]

What is "crude" here is less the violence than the perhaps self-consciously slovenly prose that portrays it. While the violence in this moment is random, disturbing, and explicit—most of us would probably rather not see Brian De Palma film this scene in slow motion—the language of its depiction seems not only uncharacteristic of Hemingway (as does most of this novel) but fairly tame as well. As it is actually presented this scene is bloodless and its relatively low impact upon a reader's sensibilities can be traced to its verbal features. Its realism is considerably dampened by Harry Morgan's rather uninspired narration, by the triviality, for example, of the phrase "white as a dirty sheet." Raymond Chandler's disparaging remark about Dashiell Hammett's style—"it had no overtones, left no echo, evoked no image beyond a distant hill"[4]—might well apply to Morgan's narration here. The details do not help deepen the visual aspects of this scene so much as they convey Morgan's terse impression of them. This scene has none of the distressing, pathetic force of Albert Tracy's (third-person) death later in the novel from the burst of a Thompson gun "so close to his chest that the bullets whocked like three slaps": "Albert slid down on his knees, his eyes wide, his mouth open. He looked like he was still trying to say, 'Don't!'" (*HHN*, p. 153).

Pancho does not kill the chauffeur above—he "gets" him, as one might hit a moving duck in a shooting gallery—and what little realistic force there is in the idiomatic phrase "blew the side of his head off" is muted even further by Morgan's grim wisecrack: "Some nigger." That remark is something like the kind of parting shot with which Philip Marlowe exits paragraphs, and the "talkiness" of Hemingway's represented violence here actually resembles that of Chandler. But Marlowe's remarks in a similar situation would establish his verbal authority over flustering circumstances with more flamboyance. His slick one-liners—"Dead men are heavier than broken hearts," "the sunshine was as empty as a headwaiter's smile"—do not solve anything, James Guetti aptly says, "but they sound as if they do." They do "what punch lines do to jokes"; they help establish Marlowe's verbal adeptness as a weapon that can transform the confusions of a case into his own "private mental property."[5] Harry Morgan's voice is not quite so combat-ready, but his description of Pancho's killing is reminiscent of Marlowe's verbal tactics. Both represent a way of talking about violence that tells us not only about a witnessed event but about the verbal character of the witness who describes it. One of the things Harry Morgan *has*, in an alternative gloss on the novel's title, is the verbal ability to talk his way through violent scenes in alternating tones of sympathy and brutality.[6] Hemingway's writing in this novel represents less a "cold and spiritless" contempt of "human values and of human life," in Savage's terms, than one kind of unsuccessful experiment with verbal toughness.[7]

Unfortunately, Savage's inattention to the writing in this scene is still fairly representative of Hemingway criticism. Though current methods of exploring Hemingway's fascination with violence, suffering, and pain now tend to ground themselves in psychobiography or "constructions of masculinity" rather than in references to the void, neither the new nor the old approaches to violence in his work actually confront it. Suppositions about the why and the wherefore of Hemingway's violence seldom lead to an examination of its imaginative substance and the formal properties responsible for it. This seems regrettable, for as Harry Levin noted years ago, it is Hemingway's "verbal skepticism which leads toward what some critics have called his moral nihilism," and not the other way around.[8] Yet critics have consistently interpreted Hemingway's life or moral codes as being "responsible for" his verbal attitudes in order to ensure that critical accounts of his style accord with some preordained sense of the author (and this was largely the case even before the appearance of the Big Biographies in 1969 and thereafter). Biographical genuflections have not only impaired our awareness of the nature and function of his writing, they have often willfully misconstrued it by subordinating his verbal behavior to extratextual concerns. Scenes of violence in Hemingway's fiction afford a telling vantage from which to discern what kind of perceptual seismograph we find wavering in his work. The vantage is useful because it suggests that the motions and effects of Hemingway's fiction have more to do with writing than with bulls, marlin, dynamite, and moral codes. His fiction, as E. M. Halliday once noted, is full of verbal facets that are usually missed, "or if not missed, then sensed too vaguely for critical description,"[9] when his realism alone is overemphasized.

WHEN CAROLINE GORDON and Allen Tate wished, in 1950, to convey a sense of Hemingway's style, they quoted Henry James on De Maupassant: "Nothing can exceed the masculine firmness, the quiet force of his style, in which every phrase is a close sequence, every epithet a paying piece, and the ground is completely cleared of the vague, the ready-made and the second-best. Less than any one today does he beat the air; more than any one does he hit out from the shoulder."[10] This seems a happy parallelism, first because it defines the "quiet force" of Hemingway's style in terms of what it has been "cleared of," and second because James depends upon the moral claims of masculinity as the basis for his praise. Conceptions of Hemingway's "masculine" style often have more to do with his biographical posturings than with his prose. Thus when Gordon and Tate go on to refashion a complaint James had about De Maupassant ("Hemingway's characters reflect, but they do not reflect deeply enough") they help augment what was, even forty-odd years ago, an irritated ambivalence about Hemingway's literary expressions of masculinity.[11] Hemingway may not beat the air, but he repeatedly thumps on his chest. Or so we have been led to believe.

The problem here is one Delmore Schwartz helped identify but then himself exacerbated. Writing five years after Gordon and Tate, Schwartz noted that *Time* magazine had, in 1954, reported the award of the Nobel Prize to Hemingway under the rubric of *Heroes* instead of *Books*, proclaiming that the winner was "a globe-trotting expert on bullfights, booze, women, wars, big game hunting, deep sea fishing, and courage." When *Time* added that Hemingway's "personality had made as deep an impression upon the public as his books," Schwartz says that it would be more appropriate to say the deep impression Hemingway made upon the public (as the first American author ever to enjoy "the kind of limelight accorded a Hollywood film star") was due to the personality encountered in, not outside of his writing. "The famous maxim, the style is the man," Schwartz said, must be altered in Hemingway's case, for with him "the style is the personality."[12]

But Schwartz does not warn readers to beware of approaching Hemingway's work in the mythic exhaust of his public persona. Instead, he subordinates Hemingway's writing to the purposes it supposedly serves rather than imagining that those "purposes" might actually spring from the prose itself. The argumentative road from here—the tollway of cultural context—is fairly predictable. The "reticence, understatement, and toughness" of Hemingway's style represent "the expression of the moral code at the heart of his writing," Schwartz argues, a code that derives from "the American masculine ideal" that stretches back "to the pioneer on the frontier and [includes] the strong silent man of the Hollywood Western."[13] Schwartz's view here is not "wrong," but it is excessively partial and insufficient. First, he conceives of Hemingway's writing as subordinate to a prior moral code—one it cannot contest or disregard or simply grow weary of, but must tirelessly express and exemplify. Second, he describes that style exclusively in terms of "reticence, understatement, and toughness" and not its myriad other qualities. Schwartz's expectations as to what the particular experience of Hemingway's work should properly be cause him to ignore or repudiate other discernible features of that work. E. L. Doctorow's complaints about the posthumous editing of the voluminous manuscript for Hemingway's novel *The Garden of Eden* apply as well to this critical method. "The truth about editing the work of a dead writer," Doctorow asserts, "is that you can only cut to affirm his strengths, to reiterate the strategies of style for which he is known; whereas he himself may have been writing to transcend them."[14]

That the approach to Hemingway Schwartz exemplifies still forms something of a critical norm can be glimpsed in Frederick Crews's decree (in praising Kenneth Lynn's biography) that Hemingway's "locker-room, know-it-all side," "his claim to definitive expertise on every male topic from boxing and hunting through battle tactics," and his "suffocating need to be right about everything" all spring from "the psychic needs of a boy growing up in the shadow of an older sister [Ursula] with whom he was constantly paired and compared."[15] Once again, a prior thematic concern (here, the instabilities of male identity) predetermines a stylistic "consequence" or "result." As with Schwartz's characterization, the process of centralizing this theme, which exists on the periphery of the text (and thus must be given greater visibility lest an unwary reader "miss" it), is taken as justification for preconstruing Hemingway's style.

Hemingway's narrators, it is true, can be said to lay claim to "definitive expertise" on various subjects, and we are given information in his work on "male" topics such as hunting and fishing. But in what way are we given it? What kind of rhetorical characteristics and narrative impulses are critics referring to when they speak of Hemingway's "cult of macho sporting values and stoic mannerisms?" In Crews's case, some fairly high-flying psychological speculations rest upon a shopworn notion of "Hemingway's famous tight-lipped style," a notion whose very fame should make us suspicious of its accuracy.[16] How much, we might ask, are the perennial complaints about the limits and "narrowness" of Hemingway's subject matter merely displaced complaints about his supposedly "narrow" style (as if there were only one)? What may actually be narrow and narrowing here is less Hemingway's style than certain proprietary critical accounts of it, accounts prejudicial in the end to Hemingway's imaginative range.

It has been a longstanding critical truism that brevity is the most powerful attribute of Hemingway's fiction. Hemingway, many continue to believe, is the great understater. His predilection for understatement and indirection and the tough-mindedness we associate with certain displays of verbal reticence in his fiction are taken to be symptomatic of an obsession with self-control. "Troubled feelings," Lynn tells us, are packed beneath the surfaces of his stories "like dynamite beneath a bridge." Hemingway's "characteristic shuttling between mute physical details and irritable, elliptical conversation," Crews avows, "is hauntingly suggestive."[17] But Crews, Lynn, and those they follow are only half-right, it seems to me, in their characterization of Hemingway's fiction. Hemingway and his characters do often refrain from speaking at length. But the reverse is also true. He and they often say a great deal about not very much, about savoring canned peaches, digging worms, cutting wood, or packing trout in ferns. Hemingway once told Lincoln Steffens that he had to quit being a journalist because he became too fascinated with "cablese," the highly compressed idiom of the transatlantic cable.[18] It seems unlikely, Richard Peterson aptly remarks, that Hemingway would be preoccupied with "devices for understating and deflating" if he himself did not have a tendency for stylistic expansiveness and overstatement.[19] Hemingway may give us only the tip of the iceberg in certain highly charged emotional moments, but he often goes on at length about narrative incidents whose significance is not always readily apparent. Far from being offered up as "mute," the physical details of these incidents can take on an important, meandering imaginative life of their own, one that may attest to more than just an author's fondness for outdoor scenes.

Examples of Hemingway's "tight-lipped style" are easier to locate than they probably should be, and they can be said to define a kind of norm against which other sorts of imaginative perception are allowed to play. His work remains committed to realistic effect, and it features what Halliday terms a chiaroscuro of irony, a constant reminder of the "gap between expectation and fulfillment, pretense and fact, intention and action, the message sent and the message received, the way things are thought or ought to be and the way things are."[20] Here is an oft-noted paragraph from the end of "On the Quai at Smyrna": "The Greeks were nice chaps too. When they evacuated they had all their baggage animals they couldn't take off with them so they just broke their forelegs and dumped them into the shallow water. All those mules with their forelegs broken pushed over into the shallow water. It was all a pleasant business. My word yes a most pleasant business" (*SS*, p. 88).

This moment epitomizes one kind of irony for which Hemingway's work is celebrated. The grammatical breakdown in repetition here ("just broke their forelegs . . . with their forelegs broken") intimates how meager the forms of response are for such tortured realities. In the face of the heartlessness of the Greeks' "just" breaking the mules' forelegs, all one can do is simply repeat what one saw, grammatical niceties be damned. Some readers may see Hemingway satirizing the disdainful, stiff-lipped British euphemisms of his narrator here, as if this sarcastic loftiness exemplified a baffled attempt to hold what the narrator is describing at arm's length. But what allows us to feel he is discrediting one kind of response to that violence? He seems to endorse the coded, class-bound verbal reflexes of this British speaker, whose sarcasm serves as a form of self-protection.[21] This does not mean the crippled mules' pain is ignored here: certainly not. But the tough or "strong" response that pain calls forth from this speaker leaves little room for our doubts about *its* authority and potential complacency. What is insufficiently acknowledged here by Hemingway is the difficulty of knowing just how to respond properly in the face of such suffering.

For the most part Hemingway learned in the twenties (and then later forgot) to weed out this sort of self-protective virility. He could much more effectively assert, for instance, that "at the start of the winter came the permanent rain and with the rain came the cholera. But it was checked and in the end only seven thousand died of it in the army" (FA, p. 4). The "only" in the last sentence has been repeatedly characterized as bitterly, even viciously ironic, which implies far too active an emotional cast to the narrative voice. Frederick Henry (if his voice is substantial enough in this moment to be distinguished from that of his author) sounds not ironic but unmoved here, though he seems cognizant of the fact that he shouldn't be. His voice is as distant from bitterness as it is from consolation. Its wan neutrality is unmarred by the implicit self-congratulation about not wincing audible in the previous example. In the face of such a vast spectacle of human waste, this tone implicitly asks, what would a proper expression of outrage consist of? Henry's benumbed and uninflected remark suggests, in Robert Frost's words, that "anything more than the truth would have seemed too weak."

Even the examples of what is supposed to be most Hemingwayesque about Hemingway's fiction are often actually too complex to be adequately described by the adjectives that have traditionally been used to characterize his style: "simple," "lean," "clean," "hard," "laconic," "tough," "spare," "terse," "clipped," "guarded," "bare," "colloquial," "impassive," "austere," "clear-cut," "lucid," and "crystalline." These critical terms are relatively neutral in contrast with the adjectives designed to do what Gordon and Tate, Schwartz and Crews all do: to define Hemingway's style in the shadow of its implied opposite. Words such as "unadorned," "reticent," "unobtrusive," "guarded," "understated," "pared-down," "noncommittal," "nonliterary," "unemphatic," "restrained," "stripped-down," "unsentimental," "no-nonsense," "tight-lipped," and so on, all endow his style with a subterranean motive. They suggest a realm of experience avoided more than one actually invoked. The popularity of this conception owes much to Hemingway himself, who often loudly contended that the very idea of "literature" (safely handcuffed in quotation marks) was something he deliberately set out to avoid. He often acknowledged its presence only by way of wringing its neck, by designating it as something his self-proclaimed "shock-proof shit-detector" was designed to help search out and destroy.[22]

Hemingway's constant adjurations to know "truly what you really feel, rather than what you [are] supposed to feel, and [have] been taught to feel" (DA, p. 2) suggest just how strenuously determined he was to avoid "literary" experience (in the negative, sterilely bookish sense). On the one hand, the process of knowing something "truly" involves an almost paranoid solicitude about weeding out prepackaged emotion and socially inculcated perception in favor of original insight. On the other hand, the paranoia pays off, for Hemingway remains confident that by dint of rigorous self-scrutiny and self-censorship we can ensure that the authentic self is not, ultimately, implicated in society and that language can express inner perceptions uncontaminated by the outside world. That this autonomous self and the kind of authentic seeing it fosters can only, he felt, be established when one is socially alienated and outraged by corrupt perceptual practices simply helps a writer define what he is ethically bound to despise.[23]

Richard Peterson has usefully explored the ways in which "true" experience in Hemingway's fiction is often obviously identified by what it *isn't*, which suggests one reason why his work is full of phonies, complainers, and incompetent doctors, bullfighters, tourists, hunters, and writers.[24] Nearly all the distinctions made between true and false experience in Hemingway's work have moral and literary implications. Frederick Henry's famous denigration of politically expedient abstractions like "sacred, glorious, and sacrifice and the expression in vain" defines what alone has "dignity" by contrast: "the concrete names of villages, the numbers of roads, the names of rivers, the numbers of regiments and the dates" (*FA*, pp. 184–85). Hemingway writes off "the big empty words," as Hugh Kenner puts it, by returning to "the small full words, small because Saxon and rooted, full because intimate with physical sensation, the ground, the knowable."[25]

Hemingway's characters often feel a visceral reaction toward fakery or affectation that constitutes a kind of aesthetic heartburn. Jake Barnes, for instance, admires Pedro Romero's "purity of line" in a bullfight because of what it successfully avoids: "Romero never made any contortions, always it was straight and pure and natural in line. The others twisted themselves like corkscrews, their elbows raised, and leaned against the flanks of the bull after his horns had passed, to give a faked look of danger. Afterward, all that was faked turned bad and gave an unpleasant feeling" (*SAR*, p. 168). Similarly, Krebs in "Soldier's Home" "acquired the nausea in regard to experience that is the result of untruth or exaggeration." Because "his town had heard too many atrocity stories to be thrilled by actualities," Krebs "found that to be listened to at all he had to lie, and after he had done this twice he, too, had a reaction against the war and against talking about it" (*SS*, pp. 146, 145).[26] The ethical severity of constantly adhering to the "right" perception can become slightly ludicrous at times, as exemplified in one of Colonel Cantwell's attempts to circumvent the arty and the pretentious in *Across the River and into the Trees*. When tempted to call some fishing boats "picturesque" the colonel corrects himself: "The hell with picturesque. They are just damned beautiful" (*ART*, p. 34). Hemingway's early insistence upon true perception degenerates here into a fussy quibble about permissible description (the laudable phrase in this case being acceptable only, as Levin notes, "with the 'damned' to take off the curse").[27] Hemingway's early attempts to see with an unillusioned eye have become, in this later work, a petulantly disillusioned reflex, a prescriptive rather than a descriptive action.[28]

What concerns me here, however, is less the relative success with which Hemingway avoids the precious, the pompous, the high-flown, and the effusively emotional, than the critical practice this avoidance has been taken to legitimize. It is here that the critical tendentiousness of conceiving of Hemingway's "tight-lipped" style comes into sharpest focus. For when critics move from a fairly neutral description of its properties (spare, bare, lean) to one that defines those features by way of what they avoid or omit, chances are their attention will focus upon speculations about the nature of the omission. It is in this sense that Hemingway's various statements about his "theory" of omission have, in my opinion, unwittingly done more harm to the way his work has been subsequently read than any other single factor. Critics have, by and large, consistently construed and defined the surfaces of his stories by what supposedly lies beneath them. They have tended to interpret all his fiction, that is, in the way in which we are invited to read "Hills like White Elephants," whose silences and conversational evasions and descriptions of landscape prompt us to gloss indefinite pronouns and fill in unarticulated emotions.

Hemingway's thinking about his own work as a writer actually proves far more interesting than the critical practice it has tended to encourage. "If it is any use to know it," he once said, "I always try to write on the principle of the iceberg. There is seven-eighths of it underwater for every part that shows. Anything you know you can eliminate and it only strengthens your iceberg. It is the part that doesn't show. If a writer omits something because he does not know it then there is a hole in the story."[29] A writer cannot omit what he does not know, Hemingway says, or he will end up with "a hole" in his story, when what he wants, in effect, is a black hole, a subject or event whose presence is determinable only because of the way energy disappears toward its unseen center. If Hemingway had known of black holes he might have preferred them, as a figure, to an iceberg, for a black hole cannot be "exposed" by critical frogmen diving underwater to examine its underside: our knowledge of it is limited to a description of the energy patterns that disappear into its otherwise invisible structure.

Of course, in the best of Hemingway's works readers are not given enough information to know exactly what has been submerged; they are allowed only the feeling that something lurks in the background. Yet "lurks" seems an inappropriate word here, for Hemingway's contention is that the omitted portion of a story, if successful, will not redirect our attention but rather "strengthen the story and make people feel something more than they [understand it]" (*MF*, p. 75). The effectiveness of such stories depends upon our *not knowing*, exactly, how we are played upon, upon our *feeling* something rather than merely understanding it. This seems to have been conveniently forgotten. What Hemingway has omitted is supposed to be provocative rather than merely provoking. It is designed to generate a powerful sense of impalpability rather than simply pose a challenge to solve and reduce it; thus our efforts to "complete" or understand such stories falsify much of the effect for which they strive.[30]

Hemingway's critics continue to overlook what is "visible" in his fictional icebergs in favor of tropes of submergence. Even shrewd and inventive readers such as Hugh Kenner can fall prey to a skewed view of Hemingway's writing, one that has fairly wide-reaching implications for much of the now immense critical annotation of his work. Kenner admires the "refreshing closeness" of Hemingway's prose to physical experience and sees his fictional achievement as that of setting down words "so sparely that we can see past them" to the kinesthetic shocks and satisfactions of life.[31] Hemingway's writing, that is, both initiates and sustains realistic imagining. But because Kenner conceives of Hemingway's writing as "a rhetoric of evasion," what he "sees" beyond spare words is not just life but also what a story supposedly points to but does not mention. This "rhetoric of evasion" invites us to see the stories in *In Our Time*, for instance, as "distinguished by a lyric economy never eloquent about its *real* causes" (my emphasis). Similarly, "Big Two-Hearted River" resembles the Parable of the Sower, in Kenner's opinion, because its narrative content is so simple that "we are meant to realize there is more to it than it seems."[32]

The obvious question here is whether simplicity always implies something more. Must verbal reticence be figured as an act of avoidance? And under what conditions are we "meant to realize" that secondary levels of implication inevitably loom behind or beneath a story? There is an implied conception of literature in the idea that certain forms of simplicity oblige us to get beyond them ("real" literature had better be about something more than just a trout stream or, for that matter, whaling). There is also a conception of a reader. For if "Big Two-Hearted River," for instance, is "only" a story about fishing and camping, then it will only appeal to would-be backpackers who wish to know what size leader Nick uses or how to bone up on their flycasting technique. I am not particularly anxious to rescue the story for this implied reader (though I certainly would not want to deny him or her access to it either). What is of consequence here is Kenner's notion that literature is either 1) practical, simple, and thus eminently dismissable, or 2) something "more," something with more important fish to fry. Kenner's sense of what can legitimately constitute that "more" sometimes seems prohibitive rather than enabling. He tries to authorize his sense of what a true story is and what a good reader is not by grafting it back onto Hemingway's intentions. If "we are *meant* to realize there is more to [a story] than it seems," the author is obviously fashioning something like a parable, and you'd better perk up, reader, for an act of translation is in order. This particular argument is buttressed by an entire view of the 1920s that seems somewhat questionable: "It was a decade of Writing, a craft with a mystique; and what the writer got down 'truly'—Hemingway's signature is on that adverb—would last: which means, it would turn into a symbol."[33]

This is a telling characterization, for the passage Kenner alludes to here is Hemingway's famous avowal that if a writer could capture "the real thing, the sequence of motion and fact which made [an] emotion" it would "be as valid in a year or two or in ten years or, with luck and if you stated it purely enough, always" (*DA*, p. 2). Yet there is no notion on Hemingway's part, no matter how strongly some critics may wish to find it, that something lasts because it "turns into a symbol." In fact, Hemingway once explicitly warned John Dos Passos about his projected U.S.A. trilogy: "don't let youself slip and get any perfect characters in. . . . Keep them people, people, people, and don't let them get to be symbols."[34] The symbolization (or parablization) that Kenner seeks serves to limit rather than announce the merits of Hemingway's writing, because it dictates the way a sentence or a paragraph can be *serious*: that is, symbolic, and not "just" simple. This critical perspective offers to honor Hemingway's prose only when it is seen through an interpretative glass darkly.

"Big Two-Hearted River" is surely the right story with which to test the efficacy of such criticism, for readers have been puzzled by Nick Adams's behavior or, more precisely, the language that describes it, since it first appeared:

> Nick was happy as he crawled inside the tent. He had not been unhappy all day. This was different though. Now things were done. There had been this to do. Now it was done. It had been a hard trip. He was very tired. That was done. He had made his camp. He was settled. Nothing could touch him. It was a good place to camp. He was there, in the good place. He was in his home where he had made it. Now he was hungry. (*SS*, p. 215)

Actually, readers have not been nearly puzzled enough by this kind of writing and by its effect, in James M. Cox's words, of "nothing strangely happening."[35] The typical response consists of first assuming that the odd rhythm and obstinate repetition of this prose are signs that we are now learning something

141

about Nick's consciousness or psychology. No one, the argument goes, talks or "thinks" like this (if we can call it thinking) without having some reason for doing so. All this emphasis upon what is "happy" and "good" obviously represents an attempt on Nick's part to "choke" off the "needs" the narrator says he has left behind him at the start of the story. With that assumed, of course, it is psychiatric open season and critics scramble for all manner of speculation about what it is that Nick (and, quite automatically, his author) must be trying to escape: whether war and its wounds (Edmund Wilson, Philip Young, Hugh Kenner, Shelley Fisher Fishkin) or upsetting memories of Hemingway's 1919 fight with his mother (Kenneth Lynn).[36]

The justification for looking around and behind words like *good* and *happy* presumably has to do with what Levin calls the "heavy load of subjective implication" they carry. Like the words *fine* and *nice* and *lovely*, Levin says, they do not describe but evaluate; they form not a stimulus but "a projected response, a projection of the narrator's euphoria in a given situation. Hemingway, in effect, is saying to the reader: *Having wonderful time. Wish you were here.*"[37] Levin too reads this kind of language as the projection of a character's psychology, and he continues the same odd circularity of other critics here. "Odd" because there is so little recognition that the nonspecific character of the words in this passage serves to baffle the very psychological translations critics try to wrest from them. Apparently, impediments to critical paraphrase are to be taken as a warrant for ever more strenuous acts of translation. The less explicit "information" these words convey, the more we are to mine them for their subjective implications. The more singsongy their resistance to psychological specification, the harder we are to work at rendering them intelligible.

Yet the urge to generate intelligibility here, to "make sense" of Nick, to get somewhere with and through him by conceiving of this verbal behavior as a reflection of his own concerns, may tell us more about *our* motives than about his. There is no necessity, that is, to "read" this writing psychologically or even physiologically (as the breakdown of a connected flow of inner language when one is, like Nick, "very tired"). Those are certainly options available to us. But nothing about this writing compels us to translate or interpret it rather than to *listen* to it. The requirements this language fulfills, the needs it answers to, are at least as much rhythmic as psychological. The need to go on at such length about so little may not be a need at all but, instead, its satisfaction. Hemingway's concerns may dominate this passage more than Nick's—a concern not with unpleasant memories but with the possibility of using certain words to fill a certain cadence. "It was a good place to camp. He was there, in the good place. He was in his home where he had made it": this is not solely a way of "thinking," it is also a way of writing or, more accurately, the way an author listens to himself write. No critic I know of except Guetti has had the perceptive audacity to suggest that it may be Hemingway rather than Nick who is having a wonderful time and wishing you were here.[38]

That few have been willing to think of Hemingway's writing in this way has largely to do with some early critical bullies who helped intimidate readers of his work by accusing them of being politically obtuse. I am thinking here specifically of Wyndham Lewis, for it was primarily his charge that Hemingway's characters were "dull-witted, bovine, monosyllabic simpleton[s]" "of a few words and fewer ideas" that led Malcolm Cowley and then, more flagrantly, Philip Young to assure us that there was "a terrible panic . . . just barely under control" in Hemingway's style—and the race was off.[39] The assumption on Lewis's part that simple sentences imply a simple subject (or even a simple approach to a subject) was never seriously questioned. The upshot of his sportive critical sneering was that later critics felt impelled to defend Hemingway on intellectual grounds, to protect his writing from parody, to do everything they could to convince others that passages like the one above did not *really* show Hemingway "steining away for all he is worth" (for Lewis's primary complaint was that Hemingway was imitating Stein's "*faux-naif* prattle," her "infantile, dull-witted, dreamy stutter").[40]

In other words, subsequent critics have decided to fight fire with fire, to unquestioningly accept Lewis's demand that language be psychologically complex (in the specific ways he defines) and then defend Hemingway's work on those grounds. Thus if it is Hemingway rather than Nick who talks like this, we had better look into *his* problems. If there are no compelling "reasons" for such verbal behavior, then it comprises either "failed" writing or a dramatized symptom of Nick's failure to assemble his own thoughts. The critical appetite for intelligibility at any cost is such that an inadequate critical method can be projected onto a story and then viewed as a dramatized inadequacy on the part of the fiction itself.

A more sensible way to proceed here might be to assert, as William Pritchard does, that much of Hemingway's writing is "poised on the edge of the stylistically ludicrous," that "Hemingway's low-mimetic, 'noble' style is but an inch away from the bathetic."[41] (Nick tells us at one point in the story that "he liked to open cans.") But this too may be giving too much to the psychological, and Pritchard comes closer to what I want to emphasize when he acknowledges that Hemingway's "crafty, 'dumb,' sentences," with their minimal verbs and repetitions "appeal to our ears while suspending our urge to find 'meanings' in them." For while it is certainly not illegitimate to find

143

psychological import in Hemingway's writing, an overinsistence upon "seeing through" his words, either to an illusion of life or into a character's mind, has weakened our sense of the multifarious ways in which it plays to our ear.

Listen to Nick Adams watch trout:

> The river was there. It swirled against the log spiles of the bridge. Nick looked down into the clear, brown water, colored from the pebbly bottom, and watched the trout keeping themselves steady in the current with wavering fins. As he watched them they changed their positions by quick angles, only to hold steady in the fast water again. Nick watched them a long time.
>
> He watched them holding themselves with their noses into the current, many trout in deep, fast moving water, slightly distorted as he watched far down through the glassy convex surface of the pool, its surface pushing and swelling smooth against the resistance of the log-driven piles of the bridge. At the bottom of the pool were the big trout. Nick did not see them at first. Then he saw them at the bottom of the pool, big trout looking to hold themselves on the gravel bottom in a varying mist of gravel and sand, raised in spurts by the current. (*SS*, p. 209)

This is remarkable writing and not only because it entranced me and many other college freshman long before anyone pointed out how numerous and excruciating were the drafts Hemingway went through in achieving passages like this. The best question to ask a freshman here (or the freshman in ourselves, always a good guide to follow) would be, Why the second paragraph? What does it tell us that we have not already learned from the first? What would we lose if we were to delete it? What has happened to our famous iceberg here? Why is the inverted seven-eighths of its expressive energy now towering over its mundane subject matter?

The only new information we are given in the second paragraph is that the gravel and sand on the streambed are being raised in spurts by the current. Surely Hemingway, master of the laconic and the omitted excess, could have suggested this more economically. If these later sentences do not further realistic specification, what is their expressive justification? If we are ingenious we might notice that the trout are "looking to hold themselves on the bottom" and wonder about Nick's looking at the trout looking. But that merely misconstrues the idiomatic force of "looking to do something," as if Nick were trying to figure out the *intentions* of these trout, maybe even trying to see their eyes. All we may be able to "make" of this second paragraph is that it emphasizes, indeed refuses to let go of, the fact of Nick's watching. We are "meant to realize" that it must be somehow important that Nick spends so much time looking at these fish (a realization seemingly confirmed on the next page when we learn that "Nick's heart tightened as the trout moved. He felt all the old feeling"). Proceeding thus, Young established what is still the standard reading of this passage by interpreting Nick's long gaze as a search for an analogue for the self: "Nick goes about his business exactly as if he were a trout keeping himself steady in the current" and "there are now several deep pools in [his] personality—where in the shadows lurk the 'big ones.'"[42] What such a reading ignores is the echoing reverberation of this passage, which, while written in a simple language Nick himself would understand, is also replete with an expressive mastery of which he is innocent: not the "mastery" of repression but that of verbal recurrence, reduplication, and expansion. This moment may have less to do with expressions of character, in other words, than with the larger expressive necessities of Hemingway's verbal sensibility.

Some readers may take this passage to represent simply a delighted evocation of sensory vividness, of glassy convex surfaces and mists of gravel. Certainly, few writers (though Joan Didion comes to mind) have been capable of more memorably evoking the sensory properties of land, sea, and weather, or vivid kinetic sensation like "the rush and the sudden swoop" Nick feels while skiing down a mountain in "Cross-Country Snow": a thrill that "plucked Nick's mind out and left him only the wonderful flying, dropping sensation in his body" (SS, p. 183). Still, the passage above is only partially realistic. It does not pluck our minds out so much as it eases and guides them in. The justification for the writing here has as much to do with riding out a rhythm, with completing a self-enclosed verbal movement, as it does with accurately portraying a rustic bridge and stream.

Thus while it is possible to connect this writing with Nick or to see it as a realistic evocation of place, either of those options, if too exclusively insisted upon, will miss the powerful promptings to *hear* this passage rather than to visualize or psychologically translate it. These aural prompts (which are unmistakable to my ear) arise partly because there is so little new to see in the second paragraph. The progressive sense of the sequence seems to falter and drift. Yet to put the matter that way is to define this effect in the negative: as a lapse in the visual motives that sponsor imagistic novelty and change rather than as an access to a new kind of imaginative energy. Instead of conceiving of a sharp focus "going soft" here, we might more accurately note that what additional information we are given in the second paragraph does not *sound* new. "Fast water" becomes only "fast moving water," the trout "keeping themselves steady in the current" are still "holding themselves with their noses into the current," and so on. More important, when we hear the insistent repetition of

> At *the bottom of the pool* were the *big trout*. Nick did not see them at first. Then he saw them at *the bottom of the pool, big trout* . . .

145

we know we are listening to music. An interesting indication of this is the fact that if we were trying to visualize Nick's actions, we might pause in our reading after "Nick did not see them at first." We might, that is, try to mimic the fictional time of the story, to afford Nick the chance to adjust his vision and see the fish; or at least we might find this perceptual mimicry an appropriate action a second time through the story. That we do not stop, that we move right on to the next phrase here, is the sharpest indication that we have given ourselves over to the time not of imagined life but of verbal cadence and repetition.

Yet to say "given ourselves over" may be to overstate the matter, just as the terms "hypnotic" or even "incantatory" as they are sometimes applied to this sort of effect seem only partly sufficient. The interweavings, the constant recoveries and conversions from visual-realistic to aural-rhythmic imagining in Hemingway are as pronounced as those we saw in Crane. But while Hemingway's writing seems to resemble Crane's, the resemblance is only apparent. What we experience in Crane's fiction as a jumpy, sometimes drastic and self-canceling oscillation between the promise of realism and a sudden disinterest in that promise, becomes in Hemingway less a fluctuation than a continual action of merger and emergence. A phrasal unit or a single word (like *trout*, *pool*, *water*, or *bottom*, above) characteristically pedals its way out of and then back into Hemingway's sequences, recycling, receding, and then returning, with all the comforts of memory and recurrence. When that imagistic and rhythmic repetition spirals and loops back upon the forward drive of a realistic sequence, its visual dimensions seem to be both strangely enhanced *and* diminished. The visual potential of such passages is dimmed but not obscured, creating unusual effects that might be described, paradoxically, as visual resonance or cadenced clarity.

In this moment, the entire scene—stream and bridge and gravel and fish— begins to waver and swim before our mind's eye, like the pebbles of a streambed seen through clear but rippled water. The scene's imaginative presence is no longer solely generated by visual imagining, by our "seeing through" and moving off language toward life. Yet neither do we imaginatively lose sight of the "mist of gravel and sand" raised at the end of the second paragraph. The fact that one sort of imaginative energy and perception does not necessarily invalidate or permanently incapacitate another in Hemingway's writing is, I think, what often makes his fictional effects seem curiously limpid or tremulous. We both do and do not continue to see the imagined life of a trout stream or a line of marching troops or the plane trees on an African savannah; we both do and do not continue to "hear" our way through a given sequence.

Of course, there will always be some readers of Hemingway whose visual-intelligible orientation is so rooted that they continue to ascribe the repetition in passages such as those above to a character (or to the narrator as a character with personal dilemmas). Such readers typically see this kind of repetition as some version of a character's ritualistic banishment of thought.[43] In the case of "Big Two-Hearted River" these motivational ascriptions are not so much unwarranted as they are needlessly limiting. In other moments, however, when verbal performances like those above cannot be reasonably connected with a given character's psychology, they prove more prohibitive. Take, for example, the preliminary sentences of another story from *In Our Time*:

> There were big palms and green benches in the public garden. In the good weather there was always an artist with his easel. Artists liked the way the palms grew and the bright colors of the hotels facing the gardens and the sea. Italians came from a long way off to look up at the war monument. It was made of bronze and glistened in the *rain*. It was *raining*. The *rain* dripped from the palm trees. Water stood in pools on the gravel paths. The sea broke *in a long line in the rain* and slipped back down the beach to come up and break again *in a long line in the rain*. The motor cars were gone from *the square* by the war monument. Across *the square* in the doorway of the café a waiter stood looking out at *the empty square*. (*SS*, p. 167, my emphasis)

John Hollander has aptly remarked the tendency of Hemingway's sentences to move, almost effortlessly, from "the rhetoric of novelistic point of view into that of lyrical trope,"[44] which is what seems to happen here in "Cat in the Rain." There is an "American wife" looking out a hotel window in the second paragraph of the story. But the wistful emptiness of this moment is attributable not to her (she is concentrating on a cat crouched under an outdoor table) but to an echoing prose that begins to sound "empty." Once again we have a sequence that begins with short, brisk sentences whose accrued list of details (big palms, green benches, a bronze monument) help to engender and extend the visual substantiality of this seaside scene. But Hemingway's realistic imagining here, as I have tried to emphasize with italics, soon turns into a kind of chant: Rain, Rain, Rain, and an Empty Square. The repetition here starts to engulf and still the paragraph's narrative progression with an action of aural subsidence and return. The effect is spectral or apparitional, and it results not from the fact that the sea or a deserted garden looks ghostly in the rain but from the gradual loosening of this sequence's referential moorings. Words that seemed, a sentence ago, imaginatively solid enough to be big or bright or green or glistening, now cast no shadow. Their imaginative substance seems to fade as they are repeated, and their import becomes less visual and more rhythmic. They seem less like images than like the sounding of musical beats.

The effect of this moment resembles the one Jake Barnes remembers after being kicked in the head in a football game as a youngster: "my feet seemed to be a long way off, and everything seemed to come from a long way off, and I could hear my feet walking a great distance away" (*SAR*, pp. 192–93). After being knocked out by Robert Cohn, Jake reexperiences this same stunned sense of disengagement. Though he is empty-handed as he heads back to his Pamplona hotel, he feels as if he is holding the suitcase "full of my football things" he carried home after the earlier incident: "Going up the stairs took a long time, and I had the feeling that I was carrying my suitcase. . . . I went on up the stairs carrying my phantom suitcase. . . . I opened the door and went in, and set down my suitcase" (*SAR*, p. 193). The shift from realistic to aural imagining in sequences like the one above from "Cat in the Rain" verbally approximates Jake's state of mind here. What begins as a realistic narrative progression suddenly shifts, as it were, to hear its own feet walking a great distance away. A fictional movement that was making efficient imagistic head-way a moment ago, now seems to be picking up and carrying phantom suit-cases—and then setting them back down.

The kind of self-attenuating repetition and cadence I am pointing to here is less flamboyantly apparent than Hemingway's other uses of repetition. But it dramatizes the fact that a cognizance of the aural imagining in his work should revamp our notions of how to read it. The "hallmarks" of Hemingway's style will still remain intact, but they should be qualified by an awareness of stylistic motions and effects independent of them. No longer are we dealing solely with the laconic austerity of a tight-lipped understater who knows (in the face of political euphemism, fake emotionalism, and counterfeit depictions of life) that "the word continues to dematerialize and has to be made flesh all over again."[45] The impulse to dematerialize language—to lighten the historical loads of meaning and connotation that words bear, to turn them into verbal bobbers dotting a rhythmic current—is fully as strong in Hemingway as is the need for reticence and restraint. When Shelley Fisher Fishkin alludes to "the very solid and tangible nature of all [Hemingway] evokes" and finds that "as an artist he would settle for nothing less than communicating a new way of seeing," she is only half right.[46] The imaginative *in*tangibility of much of Hemingway's writ-ing communicates a new way of hearing as well as of seeing, one whose echoes are as strong as its ironies. When violence occurs within and because of these imaginative conditions, we can expect it to be as intriguing as the prose that depicts it is protean. We can expect some fairly unorthodox results when, to borrow one of Hemingway's own phrases, the "delicate anesthesia" (*FBT*, p. 51) of his writing treats of characters who need real anesthetics.

IT IS EASY ENOUGH to run across a less intriguing, less nuanced Hemingway than we might like to find. The spectacle of a sensitive writer imitating an attitudinizing public legend is not far to seek in his writing. "What would you

consider the best intellectual training for the would-be writer," George Plimpton once asked Hemingway, who replied: "Let's say that he should go out and
hang himself because he finds that writing well is impossibly difficult. Then he
should be cut down without mercy and forced by his own self to write as well
as he can for the rest of his life. At least he will have the story of the hanging
to commence with."[47] We might, if charitable, simply write off this "gallows
humor" not as bluff virility but as a good-natured mordancy in the face of
Hemingway's conviction that you have to "pay" for what you learn in writing.
("The fact that I am interrupting serious work to answer these questions proves
that I am so stupid that I should be penalized severely," he adds. "I will be.
Don't worry."[48])

Yet Plimpton is not entirely off base to push Hemingway about his self-
admitted affinity with Hieronymus Bosch, for there is a decidedly nightmarish,
sometimes gratuitous, quality to many moments in Hemingway's work: his
equivalent of, say, T. S. Eliot's "bats with baby faces" crawling "head down-
ward down a blackened wall." Take, for example, the lurid aftermath of the
shootout on Freddy Wallace's boat in *To Have and Have Not*. Out of gunshot
holes just above the waterline "something dark" drips and hangs "in ropy lines
against the new paint of her hull." There is no sign of life on board, for Harry
Morgan is in the cockpit hallucinating and slowly dying from a stomach
wound. One dead man, however, seems "to be leaning over to dip his hand
into the sea."

> His head and arms were in the sun and at the point where his fingers almost touched
> the water, there was a school of small fish, about two inches long, oval-shaped,
> golden-colored, with faint purple stripes, that had deserted the gulf weed to take
> shelter in the shade the bottom of the drifting launch made in the water, and each
> time anything dripped down into the sea, these fish rushed at the drop and pushed
> and milled until it was gone. Two gray sucker fish about eighteen inches long,
> swam round and round the boat in the shadow in the water, their slit mouths on
> the tops of their flat heads opening and shutting; but they did not seem to compre-
> hend the regularity of the drip the small fish fed on and were as likely to be on the
> far side of the launch when the drop fell, as near it. They had long since pulled away
> the ropy, carmine clots and threads that trailed in the water from the lowest splin-
> tered holes, shaking their ugly, sucker-topped heads and their elongated, tapering,
> thin-tailed bodies as they pulled. They were reluctant now to leave a place where
> they had fed so well and unexpectedly. (*HHN*, pp. 179–80)

Carlos Baker says this scene provides an effective contrast to the fury of the
previous night's gun battle and serves to remind us that "nature's quietude,
nature's continuum, nature's great age, when these are compared with the

149

fury and the mire of human veins, and the brevity of man's time on earth, are something like an echo of the passage from Ecclesiastes which was used as one of the headnotes to *The Sun Also Rises*."[49] If this is not what this passage reminds a reader of, it is probably because the ugly emphasis upon physiological mire here (upon "ropy, carmine clots and threads" and fish gobbling up gouts of blood) smacks more of an uncontrolled grotesque humor than of a redeeming sense of nature's quietude or even a darker Darwinian vision of nature red in tooth and sucker-tops.

There is a narrative fascination here, in other words, that borders upon the gratuitous. This moment strongly resembles one in Poe's *Narrative of Arthur Gordon Pym*, when a blood-spattered seagull that has gorged on a corpse with "its bill and talons deep buried," then drops "a portion of clotted and liver-like substance" that splashes at Pym's feet.[50] As we saw with Poe, violence or grotesque action seems gratuitous when it exceeds the dramatic justifications of its presence. We have to be cautious when deciding what is and is not justified in a novel, because one way to ignore the impact fictional violence has upon us is to transform our uneasiness in confronting it into a quick assertion of its irrelevance. But there is no implicit disgust in Hemingway's depiction of the dripping viscera in *To Have and Have Not*. There is no communicated perspective that suggests a creditable authorial justification for this particular rendition of marine life.

A "perspective" or some indication of narrative control seems necessary here because the descriptive function of this scene is not to neutralize Hemingway's authorial presence, as it would be in a successful realistic sequence. While the school of purple and golden fish embodies the instinctual force of brute, feeding life that might give glosses such as Baker's some intellectual respectability, the two sucker fish are not just "gray" but "ugly." With their demonically vaginal "slit mouths" "opening and shutting," these two gormandizing fish express a reluctance to dine where one might not eat "so well and unexpectedly." If all this were not bad (that is, uncontrolled) enough, the blood the fish feed on drips from the hand of a Cuban revolutionary who now has more fictional substantiality than he did when alive in the novel. One can only hope, for Hemingway's sake, that he does not intend these fish to provide a marine foreshadowing of the capitalistic bloodsuckers moored at the yacht pier at the novel's close.

There are other bizarre, unaccommodated examples of violence and its aftermath in Hemingway's work, like the "good German dog" that eats "a good [dead] German soldier's ass which had been roasted by white phosphorus" (*ART*, p. 257) in *Across the River and into the Trees* or the mock-clinical descriptions in "A Natural History of the Dead" of dismembered body parts or heat-bloated corpses "with a half-pint of maggots working where their mouths [had] been" (*SS*, p. 445). If this were all we found in Hemingway, we might be tempted to assert what Nemi D'Agostino does anyway, that Hemingway's early "disillusion and distrust of all values" degenerates, as he ages, into "a cultured and detached pleasure in the primitive and the barbaric," "a preposterous and unironical search for excitement for its own sake."[51] Yet while images such as those above form a not-unnegligible part of what a reader encounters, especially in Hemingway's later fiction, their imaginative power, as he seemed to know, was limited by their self-announced "graphic" status.

More characteristic of his work is violence and pain that appears so suddenly that it seems to startle the author almost as much as the reader. Take the narrator's memory, in "Now I Lay Me," of what he was once forced to use for fishing bait: "Once I used a salamander from under an old log. The salamander was very small and neat and agile and a lovely color. He had tiny feet that tried to hold on to the hook, and after that one time I never used a salamander, although I found them very often. Nor did I use crickets, because of the way they acted about the hook" (*SS*, p. 364). The sympathetic wince of pain involved in reading this passage has more to do with the writing here than with the very idea, as some might contend, of impaling bait. We could easily imagine a fisherman who routinely baits salamanders or crickets rewriting these sentences so as to make his own actions seem less brutal. What makes this moment disproportionately powerful is what Hemingway omits. Consider how little we are given here. We are spared the represented action of hooking the salamander as well as any depiction of the emotional transitions within the narrator. He simply moves from admiration of the salamander to an implicit cognizance of painful consequences to an indirect acknowledgment of remorse.

But Hemingway has not given up a thing here, just the opposite. He knows that our awareness of the salamander's pain will be heightened the more the representation of that pain does not declare itself—or rather, the more the reader, in the very motions of his response, is himself made to "declare" it. If we feel we know just how terrible the narrator feels about having inflicted this pain, all we have been told is that he will not hook a salamander again. We have been made to imagine the unbearable pain the salamander feels in being impaled, but we have only been offered the detail that his "tiny feet" tried "to hold on to the hook." The obstacles to our actually visualizing the salamander or conceiving of the narrator's emotions are so easily and so naturally overcome, we may fail to see how crucial they are in generating our response. The more the descriptive omissions here pose a resistance to our reading efforts, the harder we work to overcome them, to fill the imagistic gaps and visually translate or "rephrase" the sequence. We are invited by this kind of writing to move away from words and into imagined experience, and that action constitutes the imaginative substance of the pain we "experience" here. It is we as readers, as much as this salamander, who are "hooked" in this passage.

Because this kind of realistic effect is so common in Hemingway's fiction we might be tempted to define it as the norm in his scenes of violence. But as I have argued, the perceptual motives of his work shift so suddenly that such normative reading usually reduces and oversimplifies our responses to moments like the one in "Chapter 14" of *In Our Time*:

> Maera lay still, his head on his arms, his face in the sand. He felt warm and sticky from the bleeding. Each time he felt the horn coming. Sometimes the bull only bumped him with his head. Once the horn went all the way through him and he felt it go into the sand. Some one had the bull by the tail. They were swearing at him and flopping the cape in his face. Then the bull was gone. Some men picked Maera up and started to run with him toward the barriers through the gate out the passageway around under the grandstand to the infirmary. They laid Maera down on a cot and one of the men went out for the doctor. The others stood around. The doctor came running from the corral where he had been sewing up picador horses. He had to stop and wash his hands. There was a great shouting going on in the grandstand overhead. Maera felt everything getting larger and larger and then smaller and smaller. Then it got larger and larger and larger and then smaller and smaller. Then everything commenced to run faster and faster as when they speed up a cinematograph film. Then he was dead. (*SS*, p. 207)

The first aspect to strike us about this scene may be the way it gives the lie to the frequent complaint that Hemingway always glorifies his male characters as they heroically "take it," as they silently endure pain and abuse. Maera silently suffers here but he does not endure, he merely "lasts"; endurance becomes a simple matter of durational consciousness. As with the salamander, an outside narrator describes this situation and he only momentarily inhabits Maera's perspective—as he feels "warm and sticky" or feels the horn go through him and "into the sand." The pain consequent upon being gored by a bull remains to be imagined by the reader.

But what happens at the end of the sequence, when repetition and an established rhythm begin to sponge clean the visual aspects of the scene? According to Robert Scholes, the narrator becomes the dying Maera, a spectator at his own "last picture show": "the reel is empty, the screen has gone white; no more images, no more spectating, no more life. . . . After the word 'dead' we face blank white paper ourselves."[52] But in what sense does the narrator "become" Maera? Who is it that delivers the last line of the sequence—Maera's

ghost? Furthermore, despite the reference to a cinematograph in the penulti-
mate sentence, there is no screen to go white and no reel to empty at the
sequence's conclusion. There are "no more images" not because a film has
ended but because the sequence's conclusion is an indistinct blur. This imaginative "blurring" seems to occur in part because we cannot know or see what
it is ("everything") that commences to run faster and faster. More importantly,
it occurs because Hemingway's repetition plays to a reader's ear. The repeating words "larger and larger and larger and then smaller and smaller" convey
a sense of temporal modulation, not spatial expansion and contraction. The
words of the passage, not some imagined camera, go faster and faster and faster
and then slower and slower. They fill a cadence as a way of suggesting the
experience of expiring consciousness. The last line has the deadly jolt it does
not because we "face blank white paper" (we do at the end of any sequence) but
because it so suddenly halts and interrupts a rhythm that could go on indefi-
nitely, while Maera's life cannot. It is as if someone had abruptly turned off a
radio and left its sound hanging in the air (an effect we shall find in Faulkner's
writing as well). All that remains of Maera when we finish is the echo of a
truncated rhythm, the auditory equivalent of the afterimage left by a light bulb
when it has been turned off.

The imaginative power of this writing depends, that is, not just upon what
is or is not explicitly visualized (say, a horn slicing through flesh). It also
depends upon its rhythmic orientation at any given moment. That Hemingway
often blends visual detail with repetition or an overextended grammar that
subsumes and deemphasizes realistic imagining in scenes of violence would
seem to suggest that he knows visual definition can quickly turn gratuitous,
that it can turn into a morbid fascination with seeing someone gored. But it
also seems to suggest that he "knew," at least instinctively, that the imagination
of violence can be made all the more powerful and distressing by means of
aural imagining, which ordinarily lulls, calms, and deepens a realistic sequence. Critical claims that Hemingway "aestheticizes" violence usually ignore
the kind of imaginative depth and complexity I am pointing to here. Scholes,
for instance, contends that the scene above is an example of how Hemingway
turns "what for many is a repulsive, anachronistic slaughter" into "a sequence
of exquisite vignettes."[53] Aesthetic experience, as Scholes conceives of it here,
involves what he calls "the sleep of reason." His desire to exert his critical will
and agency over a sketch or a story is so assertive that any verbal layout that
suggests that such a desire may be unnecessary can be figured only as "emotional," as irrational and seductive in nature, as a capitulation to verbal sirens
tempting us to epistemological ruin. Scholes overlooks the fact that the imaginative power of aural imagining in Hemingway's work actually *increases* its

disturbing power rather than merely rendering it exquisite. Singing about violence, when it is done with Hemingway's unique mixture of motives, is often more powerful than simply letting someone else see it.

The fluctuations in Hemingway's work between narrative restraint and overabundance, between verbal reticence and rhythmic insistence, are often responsible for the characteristic psychological indeterminacy that both invites and restricts interpretation of his best work. As above, precise descriptions of pain and death can shade into powerfully imprecise evocations of what has happened. Take the climactic moment of "The Short Happy Life of Francis Macomber," for example, in which a newly revived Francis Macomber faces the charge of a wounded bull buffalo:

> Wilson, who was ahead was kneeling *shooting*, and Macomber, as he fired, unhearing his *shot* in the roaring of Wilson's gun, *saw* fragments like slate burst from the huge boss of the horns, and the head jerked, he *shot* again at the wide nostrils and *saw* the horns jolt again and fragments fly, and he did not *see* Wilson now and, aiming carefully, *shot* again with the buffalo's huge bulk almost on him and his rifle almost level with the on-coming head, nose out, and he could *see* the little wicked eyes and the head started to lower and he felt a sudden white-hot, blinding flash explode inside his head and that was all he ever felt. (*SS*, pp. 35–36, my emphasis)

"And that was all he ever felt": as with Maera's death, the conclusion here is final, indisputable in making its point, not only because Macomber is dead but because we cannot get beyond the irrevocability of this phrase.

The passage proceeds in some ways like a typical realistic sequence, affording a steady flow of imagistic variety and change. What I have not italicized in this remarkably long sentence are the linking "ands" that are often taken in Hemingway's work as establishing what Kenner calls the "texture of authenticity" in which a constant flow of serial sensation assures us "that nothing analytic is being smuggled in."[54] This accounts for one part of the effect here. But such moments emphasize not only what has been left out of Hemingway's writing (the analytic, the pejoratively literary) but what, in a given sentence, *falls out*. The verbal echoes in writing like this play across the syntax of sentences, and thus their tendency, as Guetti rightly suggests, is to elide.[55] As repetition begins to dominate a given moment of Hemingway's writing, whatever lies between the echoing rhetorical units seems to drop out or fade away. Thus we find ourselves reading not the sentence as it is written but "Macomber shot . . . and saw . . . and shot . . . and did not see . . . and that was all he ever felt." The similarities with Maera's death are obvious. Macomber definitely dies here but less because he has been hit in the head than because a rhythm full of momentum and renewal has abruptly ceased.

154

The effect is so abrupt, in fact, that Hemingway can only continue in this scene by restarting, by offering us a new perspective on the events we have just "seen":

> Wilson had ducked to one side to get in a shoulder shot. Macomber had stood solid and shot for the nose, shooting a touch high each time and hitting the heavy horns, splintering and chipping them like hitting a slate roof, and Mrs. Macomber, in the car, had shot at the buffalo with the 6.5 Mannlicher as it seemed about to gore Macomber and had hit her husband about two inches up and a little to one side of the base of his skull. (*SS*, p. 36)

Critics of this story (and there are dozens) have tended to divide themselves into pro-Margot or pro-Wilson factions. I do not intend to survey the range of opinions in either camp. Suffice it to say that those, like Kenneth Lynn, who wish to exonerate Margot Macomber note that she shoots "*at* the buffalo"; she tries to save her husband's life, not end it. Thus the story itself, in this view, belies Hemingway's comment years later that "Francis' wife hates him because he's a coward. But when he gets his guts back, she fears him so much she has to kill him—shoots him in the back of the head." "Macomber" is thus not "a fable about a soul-destroying bitch," Lynn argues, but "a fable about the perils of self-overcoming," about Macomber's "dangerous aspiration to be recognized as intensely masculine."[56] One fable usurps another and it is perhaps only expectable that Lynn's challenge of previous unambiguous readings of the story, which saw Margot as culpable, is itself now brandished as proof that the killing is unambiguously established as accidental.

The rush either to see the story as a misogynistic fable or to save it from being one has, in Nina Baym's words, reduced its "faceted narration . . . into a monologue"[57] If Margot is granted absolution, why is she crying hysterically, and what is the force of her saying "stop it" when Wilson tells her "of course it's an accident . . . I know that"? Any number of plausible answers could be adduced but none would be authoritative. (Young contends that Margot shoots her husband " 'by mistake on purpose,' as wise children say."[58]) If we examine the writing less with an eye toward rendering it "evidence" for or against Hemingway's misogynistic tendencies, however, we can see why interpretive uncertainty seems to be the inevitable result in the case of this story.

Margot, we are told, "hit her husband about two inches up and a little to one side of the base of his skull." Imagining so carefully how and where a bullet can enter a human head emphasizes Macomber's pathetic vulnerability. But this kind of surgical precision also represents a way of not talking about other aspects of the scene, such as what happened after the bullet entered Francis's head. It offers the imagistic equivalent of the rhythmic halt in "and that was all

155

he ever felt." The facts of death here offer such a severely narrowed and unchallengeable image that the question of whether Margot's actions were intentional actually seems beside the point: Macomber is dead, beastly dead, no matter what Margot was trying to do. Hemingway's description of the killing does not exactly indict her but it does not absolve her either. Wilson's comment, in a moment, that "that was a pretty thing to do" (p. 36) is spoken not in a triumphantly sarcastic voice but a "toneless" one. Hemingway effectively adopts that tonelessness throughout the story without thereby identifying himself with Wilson. As is typical of much of his work, the narrator's presence here is not clarifying but complicating and disquieting. The narrator replaces motive and emotion with stark physical details and noncommital tonal shifts, so that despite the realistic clarity of events, the narrator's feelings about these characters are obscured.

The narrative perspective shifts, at the moment of impact, from what Macomber sees to what he "feels": "a sudden white-hot, blinding flash explod[ing] inside his head." There is an example of this "inside" perspective earlier in the story when Macomber attempts to shoot a lion:

> The lion still stood looking majestically and coolly toward this object [the motor car] that his eyes only showed in silhouette, bulking like some super-rhino. There was no man smell carried toward him and he watched the object, moving his great head a little from side to side. Then watching the object, not afraid, but hesitating before going down the bank to drink with such a thing opposite him, he saw a man figure detach itself from it and he turned his heavy head and swung away toward the cover of the trees as he heard a cracking crash and felt the slam of a .30-06 220-grain solid bullet that bit his flank and ripped in sudden hot scalding nausea through his stomach. He trotted, heavy, big-footed, swinging wounded full-bellied, through the trees toward the tall grass and cover, and the crash came again to go past him ripping the air apart. Then it crashed again and he felt the blow as it hit his lower ribs and ripped on through, blood sudden hot and frothy in his mouth, and he galloped toward the high grass where he could crouch and not be seen and make them bring the crashing thing close enough so he could make a rush and get the man that held it.
>
> Macomber had not thought how the lion felt as he got out of the car . . . (SS, p. 15)

Again we are offered a flat, informed precision in hearing that "a .30-06 220-grain solid bullet" rips through the lion's stomach. But though the narrator never explicitly expresses it, this uninflected description establishes a strong sense of sympathy for the victim. The "sudden hot scalding nausea" the lion feels serves, on one level, to evoke only the physical sensations to which it is subjected. But imagining that nausea in the first place seems to be an act of sympathetic identification on the part of the narrator, if only because nobody within the story can adequately conceive of the lion's pain.[59]

Yet Hemingway's motives here go beyond simply juxtaposing uninflected precision and sympathetic recoil:

> That was the story of the lion. Macomber did not know how the lion had felt before he started his rush, nor during it when the unbelievable smash of the .505 [Wilson's gun] with a muzzle velocity of two tons had hit him in the mouth, nor what kept him coming after that, when the second ripping crash had smashed his hind quarters and he had come crawling on toward the crashing, blasting thing that had destroyed him. Wilson knew something about it and only expressed it by saying, "Damned fine lion," but Macomber did not know how Wilson felt about things either. He did not know how his wife felt except that she was through with him. (SS, p. 21)

This is a useful example of how unhelpful a preconceived conception of Hemingway's "tight-lipped" procedures can be. The "it" Wilson knows something about here is clearly the courage of the lion as well as the pain it suffers. A reader willing to defend Wilson might even go so far as to recall Hemingway's own chagrin at gut-shooting a sable bull in *Green Hills of Africa* ("I felt a son of a bitch to have hit him and not killed him. . . . I felt rotten sick" [GH, pp. 271–72].) But Wilson is not portrayed as merely a man who knows how animals feel if they are wounded rather than cleanly killed. His understatement above is expressly contrasted with Hemingway's abundance of narrative detail as the narrator goes on at length about the damage Wilson has just inflicted. The lion's pain is juxtaposed in such a way that Wilson's stiff upper lip about nasty matters ("damned fine lion") is implicitly shown up as an inadequate response. Hemingway now seems capable of more closely inspecting the British idioms he before evoked uncritically ("my word yes a most pleasant business"). We do not need to know, as Lynn tells us, that the caliber of Wilson's rifle renders its use on real, not fictional, safaris unsportsmanlike[60]—not when we are told that the rifle is a "short, ugly, shockingly big-bored .505 Gibbs" that emits a "blasting *carawong!*" (SS, pp. 13, 20). Hemingway does not simply admire Wilson, no matter how well he can quote the right passages from Shakespeare.

Apart from anything this passage may tell us about Wilson, however, it displays a certain surge of verbal adrenaline on Hemingway's part in the very act of imagining "the unbelievable smash" and "the second ripping crash" of Wilson's gun, with its "muzzle velocity of two tons." The description invokes sympathy for the lion at the same time that it expresses a fascination with the power of the gun. An expressed compassion for the pain "a .30-06 220-grain solid bullet" can cause is thus inextricably linked to an implicit pride in being able to use that phrase, in being able to imply that the narrator, in contradistinction to most readers, "knows something about it." Part of what makes this effect disquieting is the fact that we are more accustomed to sympathy for hunted animals coming from people who are unknowledgeable about hunting, people who do not feel that "blowing things' heads off is lovely." Hemingway does not "aestheticize" death here so much as he might be said, awkwardly, to technicize it. The narrator's compassion for the lion seems as dependent upon a technical expertise about guns as upon a sympathetic identification with pain. A sympathy for the animal being killed would be misplaced, his writing here implies, if it were not firmly enough grounded in an intimate knowledge of what maims and destroys it.

In locating these contradictory impulses in the "ballistic" sources of Hemingway's imagination here, I am not trying to dramatize the psychology of the narrator. Or rather, I am not trying to describe Hemingway's fictional effects in order to provide speculative psychological "answers" that "account" for them. We reduce the motivational complexity of the narrative voice in "Macomber" if we see the shifts in its descriptive energy—with the focus now on a dying animal, now on an involved depiction of what causes its death—as merely "endorsing" a particular character's behavior. We can always, with enough critical leverage, psychologically subsidize imaginative effects. But as we see in a sequence in which Jake Barnes watches the bulls run in Pamplona, attempting to psychologize either Hemingway or one of his characters does not always illuminate those effects:

> There was a great shout from the crowd, and putting my head through between the boards I saw the bulls just coming out of the street into the long running pen. They were going fast and gaining on the crowd. Just then another drunk started out from the fence with a blouse in his hands. He wanted to do capework with the bulls. The two policemen tore out, collared him, one hit him with a club, and they dragged him against the fence and stood flattened out against the fence as the last of the crowd and the bulls went by. There were so many people running ahead of the bulls that the mass thickened and slowed up going through the gate into the ring, and as the bulls passed, galloping together, heavy, muddy-sided, horns swinging, one shot ahead, caught a man in the running crowd in the back and lifted him in the air. Both the man's arms were by his sides, his head went back as the horn went in, and the bull lifted him and then dropped him. The bull picked another man running in front, but the man disappeared into the crowd, and the crowd was through the gate and into the ring with the bulls behind them. The red door of the ring went shut, the crowd on the outside balconies of the bull-ring were pressing through to the inside, there was a shout, then another shout. (*SAR*, pp. 196–97)

A man has been killed in this scene, a man, we find out in a page, who was twenty-eight years old. His name was Vincente Girones and he came "from near Tafalla" (p. 198). This and the other bits of information we are given about him seem to have an unusual function here. So does the manner in which Jake (who is headed for "a second coffee and some buttered toast" and does not seem shaken) answers a cafe waiter's query as to where Girones was impaled, just moments after this scene:

> "Here." I put one hand on the small of my back and the other on my chest, where it looked as though the horn must have come through. The waiter nodded his head and swept the crumbs from the table with his cloth.
> "Badly cogido," he said. "All for sport. All for pleasure." (SAR, p. 197)

Jake's explanatory efforts represent a visual amplification of a death that almost does not seem to occur our first time through the sequence. Girone's death is merely one more descriptive item on a grammatically extending skein: "There were so many people running ahead of the bulls that the mass thickened and slowed up going through the gate into the ring, and as the bulls passed, galloping together, heavy, muddy-sided, horns swinging, one shot ahead, caught a man in the running crowd in the back and lifted him in the air." No repetition is established here and there are plenty of what seem to be realistic details. We might even feel that the abrupt unreality of the goring works for a realistic effect: isn't that just the way it might have happened, just that quickly and unexpectedly? But an author seeking a realistic effect would have broken the sentence in two after "into the ring." Hemingway keeps its momentum going as much to fulfill a rhythmic obligation as to "tell it like it was." And that obligation seems to demand here that this incident not be granted a significance outstanding enough to derail an established cadence—it must be "dropped" in the interests of completing a verbal movement.

The man is not initially gored, only "caught" (as if playing tag) and "lifted in the air." The odd details that "both the man's arms were by his sides" and that "his head went back as the horn went in" evoke a powerful sense of both physical frailty and pathetic formality. That formality, as in "Macomber," originates in a perspective largely estranged from that of a given character (either Girones or, for that matter, Jake). It is the perspective of one helpless to do anything and yet not anxious about that helplessness. The waiter's sorrowful sarcasm seems, in a sense, to provide the moral outrage missing from Jake's description of Girone's death. The waiter's remarks are not the signs of an obtuse killjoy but, as Arnold and Cathy Davidson suggest, a quiet reminder that Hemingway himself is capable of critiques of his own "code." "The novel still insists," the Davidsons argue, "that the other side and the underside of the

159

ritual slaughter of the animal is pointless, quotidian human death and that the ritual cannot outweigh or cancel out this other death."[61]

Yet "insistence" seems too aggressive and volitional a notion here. The waiter, it is true, is given his say here and we are given the forlorn image of Girones's widow and two children "sitting, all three together, in an open third-class railway-carriage" (p. 198). But as the sequence continues, Girones's funeral becomes an extraordinary descriptive occasion, one that includes what Tom Stoppard calls "one of the greatest paragraphs ever written in English":[62]

> The train started with a jerk, and then ran smoothly, going down grade around the edge of the plateau and out into the fields of grain that blew in the wind on the plain on the way to Tafalla.
>
> The bull who killed Vicente Girones was named Bocanegra, was number 118 of the bull-breeding establishment of Sanchez Taberno, and was killed by Pedro Romero as the third bull of that same afternoon. His ear was cut by popular acclamation and given to Pedro Romero, who, in turn, gave it to Brett, who wrapped it in a handkerchief belonging to myself, and left both ear and handkerchief, along with a number of Muratti cigarette-stubs, shoved far back in the drawer of the bed-table that stood beside her bed in the Hotel Montoya, in Pamplona. (*SAR*, pp. 198–99)

Even the most aurally indisposed reader might intuit the rhythmic drive of these sentences by recognizing the utter superfluousness, in realistic terms, of adding "in Pamplona." There is a novel in the last sentence alone here, a sentence that "just to make the whole thing breathtaking," Stoppard says, "leaps forward in time way beyond the point we have reached in the story."[63] But temporal projection is only one element at work in this sequence.

Jake's presence, despite the phrase "belonging to myself," seems peripheral in this moment and is subsumed by the complete authority with which we hear Hemingway writing or, perhaps, once again listening to his feet walk at a distance. The augmenting phrasal repetition in the first paragraph—"*into* the fields of grain that blew *in* the wind *on* the plain *on the way*"—is so self-enclosed and self-sufficient that it effectively breaks off the story. It estranges the action of the novel, allowing only for a narrative summary of subsequent events. That summary seems less a fresh start than a willed focus, a determined effort to bring back the story from wherever it has just been and project it beyond where it has yet arrived.

We might say that the description of the train offers one way, one respectful ritual form, of burying the dead. But that would merely represent an attempt, as I see it, to "narrativize" its musical qualities, to make its evocativeness more accountable to its narrative moment. Hemingway's writing here seems to erase an interest in such accountability. Thus the sudden stress upon consequences and accounts paid (who killed the bull, when and where) seems to effect only a halfhearted return to narrative action. Hemingway's distance from the action in the second paragraph might in fact remind one of Crane's astral perspective near the end of "The Blue Hotel." But there is none of the grand hopelessness of seeing the earth as a whirling, space-lost bulb here, only a "record" of events whose meandering grammar and rhythmic certitude form a sad, almost Keatsian or Paterian acknowledgment of both Brett's alienated romanticism and her indifference to the life of the peasant who didn't run fast enough in front of the bulls. Hemingway does not use this scene to suggest that he, at least, is capable of mourning what Brett, in her cavalier disregard, cannot. The ability of anyone here, the author included, to assume a superior moral vantage, would vitiate this moment's emotional power. Its sadness is too unfocused to be specifically attached or attributed to Jake or to Vincent Girones, however much his death constituted its narrative opportunity. The last sentence's grammar of fate and inevitability is too pronounced for that kind of interpretive convenience. One of the most touching moments in Hemingway's fiction springs from an ostensible narrative refusal to mourn. It seems a testimony to the indelible effect of such a sequence that our attempts to account for its power seem inadequate, even a bit impertinent.

To assert that such verbal effects are typical of Hemingway's work would be to overstate matters. But they are not unusual, and that fact is still largely overlooked by many of his readers. His narrative voice (even when it is pretending to realistic voicelessness) fundamentally predetermines the interpretability of his characters' thoughts and actions in ways still too often inadequately described. Until we are ready to encounter his work with a critical flexibility unarmed by prior notions of an understated style, aestheticized violence, misogynistic tendencies, or anecdotes about his helping to kill four hundred jackrabbits or shooting sharks with machine guns, we are unlikely to describe the full range of his fictional abilities. Scenes of violence arise in his fiction out of the continual and complex mergings of verbal toughness and delicacy, of spare language and rhythmic energy. Adequate descriptions of that violence are inevitably bound to be stranger and more demanding that we might at first expect, for they will involve a richer understanding of what Hemingway himself would have probably referred to as only "good luck." "For a long time now I have tried simply to write the best I can," he once said. "Sometimes I have good luck and write better than I can."[64]

Faulkner

VIOLENCE IN THE REALMS OF HEARING

IN CONTEMPLATING how best to approach the author of *The Hamlet*, we might rephrase what a character in that novel asserts about Flem Snopes: William Faulkner don't even tell himself what he is up to. Not if he was laying in bed with himself in an empty house in the dark of the moon.[1] Such an avowal may or may not describe how Faulkner actually worked, and I do not mean to imply that his frequent self-depiction in interviews as what Joseph Reed calls a "gentleman dirt-farmer and guts-writer" who denied "he ever saw a theme or a symbol" is accurate or sufficient.[2] (The image of our prototypical artist as dumb American, Ronald Sukenick rightly contends, is one French critics like to promote: "you supply the energy, we'll supply the brains."[3]) But it can provide a way into a moment from *Sanctuary* that will serve as my starting point:

> Temple moved slightly; the dry complaint of mattress and springs died into the terrific silence in which they crouched. She thought of them, woolly, shapeless; savage, petulant, spoiled, the flatulent monotony of their sheltered lives snatched up without warning by an incomprehensible moment of terror and fear of bodily annihilation at the very hands which symbolised by ordinary the licensed tranquility of their lives. (*S*, pp. 286–87)

The woolly, shapeless creatures living the flatulent monotony of a sheltered life here are Miss Reba Rivers's two dogs, "Reba" and "Mr. Binsford," who are constantly "moiling" under the feet of their huge, breathless, tankard-wielding owner or "billowing into the rich pneumasis of her breast" (*S*, p. 277). The bodily annihilation that threatens them is the danger that Miss Reba will fling them out the window (as she has in the past) when she gets depressed thinking about her deceased "man," after whom Mr. Binsford is named. The language here seems comically inappropriate for its subject: too elevated, too portentous, too descriptively ambitious for its dramatic occasion. Its effect is like the impression left on Horace Benbow by a college boy's "squalling" on a train: "a series of cryptic, headless and tailless evocations" (*S*, p. 178). Yet nothing else about this moment of Temple Drake's imprisonment in a Memphis brothel— where the "spent ghosts of voluptuous gestures and dead lusts" linger "in the

wavy mirror of a cheap varnished dresser, as in a stagnant pool" (S, p. 286)—
seems particularly comic. What we have in this moment is a local example of
the "lack of proportion between stimulus and response" that Malcolm Cowley
complained of in reviewing Faulkner's novel Pylon.[4] It is a characteristic disproportion, one variously and repeatedly encountered in Faulkner's fiction.

We do not know what Temple actually thinks of these dogs here (whether,
for instance, she sees some analogy between herself and them), because we are
not given a language in which we can conceive of her thinking, or at least
thinking like this. Temple could no more talk or "think" like the voice in this
passage than Miss Reba (or most of us, for that matter) would recognize a "rich
pneumasis" if she saw one. We do not, that is, have the narrative situation we
encountered in Hemingway, where the verbal behavior of a narrator can be
construed as or confused with that of a character. Faulkner sweeps into or
intrudes upon his narratives with a verbal flamboyance unimaginable in Hemingway. Yet with both these authors a change in narrative conditions involves
a shift to aural imagining, to a sudden and unbidden emphasis upon the auditory substance of language. The shift to aural imagining does not involve, with
either writer, a wholesale cancellation of the realistic energies of a story, but
it certainly qualifies and reshapes the direction of those energies.

Hemingway's commitment to narrative action and a language and grammar
that realistically evoke it is deep and sustaining; his stories are held by the
gravitational pull of his realism, by an attention to character and action. That
imaginative "gravity," however, does not stop his writing from continually
rising clear of his narratives in compelling and intricate ways, and that verbal
disengagement typically evinces a quality of vagrancy and weightless motion.
With Faulkner, by contrast, the disconnection is usually effected by drafts of
willed rhetorical uplift. We might imagine him striking off the description of
Miss Reba's two dogs almost effortlessly, for instance, not because he actually
wrote it that way but because that is its communicated effect. Its self-involved
rhythm and adjectival volubility seem to spring, in a phrase from Sanctuary
about children making mud puddles, from "the intense oblivion of alchemists"
(S, p. 264). How we decide to "take" such surges of narrative energy in
Faulkner's work is fundamentally predetermined by where they take us and
how they redirect our readerly attention.

In terms of narrative progress, many of Faulkner's sentences and images
seem to default on their responsibilities. Yet as we saw with Hemingway, the
act of judging fictional language by the degree to which it promotes or increases dramatic action or psychological complexity often distorts and misconstrues its power and range. This is largely the case, as I have argued, because
the switch to language that plays to the ear is usually thought of in negative

terms, as a lapse or diversion from a narrative engagement with character, action, and psychology. The appropriateness of a given description is thus usually judged by its adherence to or deviance from a dramatic or descriptive standard of plausibility, from what a situation "calls for." This negative bias can be so strong as to prompt some readers to declare such "lapses" imaginative failures if they cannot be translated and fed back into the augmenting intelligibility of a story.

In a passage such as that above, where Faulkner's presence as an author is unabashedly revealed, the critical translation will be in terms not of a character but of the narrator. We might, on the one hand, see in Faulkner's writing a failure on his part to create a tragic dimension for material that neither requires nor supports it. We might see it as an example of what Delmore Schwartz calls Faulkner's "obsessive coaching" when he tries to compel, by style alone, emotions that cannot be compelled by dramatic action. ("One sometimes sees Faulkner shaking his characters to make them hysterical," Schwartz says, "jogging them up and down like a hysterical ventriloquist to gain the fury he wants."[5]) If on the other hand, we see his use of a descriptive high style as comically motivated, we might see it as an indication of Faulkner's weakened or weakening interest in his story, a sign of his willingness to forget about Temple, Reba, and Popeye for the moment and have some fun with these dogs. We might even go on to look for biographical reasons for Faulkner's intermittent disinterest in his own novel. Either way, the assumption would be that critics should work to make Faulkner's language intelligible in terms of his relation to and engagement with the story.

But what happens when we find a rhetorical disengagement such as that above not a temporary or unusual lapse from otherwise clearly delineated motives, but an exemplification of conditions more generally prevailing in Faulkner's fiction? In this light, the comedy of his description of Reba and Mr. Binsford might result less from conscious motivation on his part than from an inevitable clash of stylistic options always available to him. His readers will recognize in phrases like "terrific silence," "flatulent monotony," and "the licensed tranquility of their lives" (which may refer, in part, to dog licenses) what hostile critics have labeled "Faulknerese." Because Faulkner's "high" or "grand" style is, as George Garrett says, "hypnotically his very own, replete with its own special rhythms and its own rich and repetitive vocabulary," Faulkner's use of it for comic effects constitutes "a brave kind of self-parody, one result of which is to make the narrator more sympathetic and the style more acceptable, able to be used grandly precisely because it has also been used humbly and humorously."[6] Garrett stresses the "bravery" of Faulkner's motives because others have found his self-parody not knowing but unwitting.

Yet we have to walk a fine line here. Defenders of Faulkner's work are often eager to claim him as a High Modernist, one comfortably in the company of Bergson, Freud, Jung, Joyce, Frazer, and Cézanne. But this view frequently seems founded less upon attentive readings of his work than upon a desire to erase the image of Faulkner (one he himself helped promote) as a demon-driven, primitivistic hick who had a way with words. There seems to be a missing middle ground.

Faulkner's fiction is often ragged and unaccommodated in ways that cannot be neatly thematized and balanced. The example of Warren Beck writing, in 1941, on "William Faulkner's Style," serves as a cautionary tale in this regard. Admirably desiring to counter contemporary condemnations of Faulkner's writing, Beck could defend it, in effect, only by peripheralizing it. Faulkner's "profuseness of language" in his best novels, Beck says, "is always knit into the thematic structure," where his style effects "its persistent lyrical embroidery and coloring . . . of the narrative theme."[7] As we saw with Hemingway's critics, "theme" is seen here as preconstruing a style that can then be said only to ornament and embroider it. Beck later promisingly notes a "controlled dissonance" in Faulkner's descriptions that results from the insertion of "colloquial bits into the matrix of a more literary passage," but his emphasis is upon the control rather than upon the dissonance: "At times it seems as though the author, after having created an unsophisticated character, is elbowing him off the stage. . . . For the most part, however, the transcending of colloquial verisimilitude in the novels is a fairly controlled and consistent technique."[8] This notion of Faulkner's "control," which serves as a shield with which to protect his work from adverse criticism, too often fails to acknowledge the contradictory impulses of Faulkner's writing that are less controlled than merely juxtaposed or held in proximity. A candid acknowledgment that these interdependent impulses are not always balanced and subordinated need not entail a claim that Faulkner was an unsophisticated writer.

Because of the woefully belated attention to and rewards for his fiction, Garrett reminds us, Faulkner "was free, *liberated*, to be an explorer of the form, precisely because it didn't matter much to anybody, beginning with his publisher, what he did." Yet if "there is hardly any place where an American writer can go or would want to go today that William Faulkner hasn't been first," Garrett says, "as an artist, he didn't stay long in any one place."[9] This complex, often mercurial narrative restlessness forms not an aspect but the very substance of Faulkner's fiction. Its evocative power is less controlled than tensed and preemptive. The style of no other American novelist (except perhaps Thomas Pynchon) so exemplifies Ralph Waldo Emerson's notion that "every thing teaches transition, transference, metamorphosis: therein is human power, in transference, not in creation. . . . not in longevity but in removal. We dive and reappear in new places."[10]

The author who could begin one of his best stories by declaring that

Once (it was in Mississippi, in May, in the flood year 1927) there were two convicts . . . ("OM," p. 509)

has an obvious and entertaining hospitality for modes of imagining that would ordinarily contravene and modify each other. This kind of narrative hospitality does more than simply parody itself or "legitimate" in humble circumstances the grander uses of a high style. In *Sanctuary*, for example, the description of the dogs is also implicated, by its own verbal action, in the larger thematic concerns of the novel. The language describing the dogs resembles that which characterizes Horace Benbow's abstract conceptions of Truth, Honor, Justice, and their opponent, Evil. Horace's ethical vision (his commitment to fighting injustice or at least the "irony which lurks in events" [*S*, p. 261]) is repeatedly shown to be admirable but also hopelessly out of touch with the Memphis underworld and with Jefferson society. Miss Reba, Miss Jenny, and others tell Horace, as Olga Vickery rightly notes, that "his moral indignation and championing of the right is purely verbal," a matter of lifeless verbiage. Faulkner dramatizes the obvious inadequacy of Horace's innocence and his naive rationalistic faith in "conducting a mock battle with a phantom opponent [Evil]."[11] The nature of this inadequacy is obvious, however, only in light of the negative value by which "mere" words are seen as being lifeless and ineffectual. It is a value that underlies the division between "doing" and "talking" we so often encounter in Faulkner's fiction.[12] That division determines the shape and the nature of not only his characters' actions but of his writing itself. The various splits between doing and talking, motion and memory, narrative action and brooding consciousness in Faulkner's work all bear directly on his representations of violence. Faulkner was "able to get a subject to fight with about half the time," Delmore Schwartz said. The other half of the time he tried to get the fight going with "a stale version of the Swinburnian high poetic." "The distinction comes to the difference between boxing and shadow-boxing," he asserts.[13]

When drained of its derogatory implications, this seems a useful distinction, for part of what distinguishes boxing from shadow-boxing is the presence of an opponent with which one might "connect." What happens in Faulkner's writing is that boxing and shadow-boxing (realistic and aural imagining) alternate and sometimes even coalesce. Verbally dense, energetic, and self-involved passages give way to laconic dialect or a person spitting off a porch into the road. A particular kind of explicitly rhetorical sequence will often run headlong into some form of realistic life. Yet the rhythm and energy of Faulkner's "rhetoric" are usually so firmly established that they often seem difficult to contravene. They require the most recalcitrant personalities (Flem Snopes, Lena Grove, Percy Grimm) or melodramatic crudities (a rape with a corn cob, a boy drilling through a coffin into his dead mother's face) to stop them short or stand them up.[14] The result in violent scenes is frequently some kind of stunned (and often stunning) tableau of suddenly arrested motion. That result, as we shall see, is also not created without a cost, for the imaginative ground upon which this play of vectors takes place—the "opponent" who takes the blows in the boxing analogy—is generally a character. And when Faulkner's shadow-boxing suddenly "connects" with a character, it often turns him or her into a kind of punching bag, one designed to sustain memorable rhetorical "dents."

THE MOST IMPORTANT word in Faulkner criticism—insofar as that criticism concerns itself with something going on in the pages of his fiction—should probably be "excessive." The value of that term stems directly from its relation to its opposite, the presupposed norms by which a given "excess" (of racial guilt, sexual desire, italicization, unpunctuated syntax, or family genealogy) is measured and then evaluated. Critical strategies for expunging or "normalizing" his excesses—in order to satirize or to defend them—have proven not only similar but similarly inadequate in illuminating how embattled Faulkner's imaginative allegiances actually are. In matters of style, a perceived excess in Faulkner's work is often used as damning evidence that supposedly justifies distaste and even derision. The bad news in this respect might as well come from Wyndham Lewis, the Jason Compson of Faulkner criticism:

> [Hemingway's fiction] is almost purely an art of action, and of very violent action . . . Faulkner's is that too: but violence with Hemingway is deadly matter-of-fact (as if there were only violent action and nothing else in the world): whereas with Faulkner it is an excited crescendo of psychological working-up of a sluggish and not ungentle universe where there *might* be something else than high-explosive—if it were given a Chinaman's chance, which it is not. The latter is a far less artistic purveyor of violence. He does it well: but as to the manner, he does it in a way that any fool could do it.[15]

Faulkner's manner of representing violence, in this formulation, is somehow different from his "doing" it. Thus the fictional "high explosive" Lewis complains of here, which he finds inartistic, seems to refer to acts of violence, to the brutal rapes, castrations, and murders included in this fiction, rather than to their represented form. Psychology, not style, Lewis contends, is responsible for whatever effectiveness Faulkner's scenes of violence have, and he is not entirely inaccurate in that appraisal. His sense that Faulkner jump-starts his fiction with some spurious psychological wiring is in many ways justifiable. (How many real or even potential nymphomaniacs can there be in northern Mississippi?) But Faulkner's violence takes on a different and more intriguing imaginative valence if we think of it in terms of a rhetorical rather than a psychological crescendo, or in terms of both at once.

Lewis would probably have been unimpressed by such an idea, for he also pointed vigorously at the "wordy poetic padding" that made Faulkner's writing seem to him "second-rate":

> His characters demand, in order to endure for more than ten pages, apparently, an opaque atmosphere of whip-poor-wills, cicadas, lilac, "seeping" moonlight, water-oaks and jasmine—and of course the "dimensionless" sky, from which moonlight "seeps." The wherewithal to supply them with this indispensable medium is as it were stored in a *whip-poor-will tank*, as it might be called: and he pumps the stuff into his book in generous flushes at the slightest sign of fatigue or deflationary listlessness, as he thinks, upon the part of one of his characters.[16]

Characters, Lewis implies, do not need an "opaque" descriptive atmosphere in which to gain life, and an author who relies upon such an atmosphere is trying to resuscitate what he could not otherwise keep alive. With many authors this complaint about rhetorical life-support might be both apt and telling. It could refer, for instance, to the kind of Fine Writing we sometimes find in F. Scott Fitzgerald, when the descriptive extravagances of Nick Carraway (and, we suspect, his author) "leave their flavor of chocolate cream on the page," as Hugh Kenner puts it.[17] But with Faulkner the case is quite different. To imagine his narratives as being repeatedly flooded with an inappropriately "poetic" rhetoric is to presume they have a normative antediluvian shape, against which "flooded" distortions can be measured. It is also, more importantly, to assume that the narrative voice responsible for such floods must be restrained in order to be successful, that it must form a means rather than an end, subordinating its energy to evocations of character and psychology in such a way that it does not gain an imaginative status more vivid than the characters it creates.

Neither assumption proves particularly useful in the case of Faulkner's fiction, because the flood is often the norm there. James M. Cox has warned against the idea that we can discuss comic scenes in Faulkner's fiction as if they provided only a relaxation from some more general tragic intensity,[18] and the same holds true for his narratives as a whole. However "abstract, cerebral, time-and-space-obsessed, tortured and twisted" Faulkner's "special language" can be, Conrad Aiken says, it still offers "a life stream of almost miraculous adaptability," and there is always "a living *pulse* in it."[19] Faulkner's verbal current can be considerably stronger than what it momentarily carries, as we can see in a moment from "Old Man," a story about an actual flood.

The tall convict and his pregnant passenger have been in their skiff for only a matter of hours when a ten-foot wave suddenly appears ahead of them, curling "forward upon itself like a sheet of dough being rolled out for a pudding" and swirling "like the mane of a galloping horse":

> And while the woman huddled in the bows, aware or not aware the convict did not know which, he (the convict), his swollen and blood-streaked face gaped in an expression of aghast and incredulous amazement, continued to paddle directly into it. Again he simply had not had time to order his rhythm-hypnotised muscles to cease. He continued to paddle though the skiff had ceased to move forward at all but seemed to be hanging in space while the paddle still reached thrust recovered and reached again; now instead of space the skiff became abruptly surrounded by a welter of fleeing debris—planks, small buildings, the bodies of drowned yet antic animals, entire trees leaping and diving like porpoises above which the skiff seemed to hover in weightless and airy indecision like a bird above a fleeing countryside, undecided where to light or whether to light at all, while the convict squatted in it still going through the motions of paddling, waiting for an opportunity to scream. He never found it. For an instant the skiff seemed to stand erect on its stern and then shoot scrabbling and scrambling up the curling wall of water like a cat, and soared on above the licking crest itself and hung cradled into the high actual air in the limbs of a tree, from which bower of new-leafed boughs and branches the convict, like a bird in its nest and still waiting his chance to scream and still going through the motions of paddling though he no longer even had the paddle now, looked down upon a world turned to furious motion and in incredible retrograde. ("OM," p. 601)

Though *The Wild Palms*, in which this story was interpolated, came out after Lewis's essay, this moment seems to qualify quite literally as one of the "excited crescendos" to which he refers. Yet it can hardly be called a "*psychological working-up of a sluggish and not ungentle universe.*" The passage is apt for my purposes because it demonstrates that the "furious motion" of Faulkner's writing—here due less to actual flood conditions than to the "rhythm-hypnotised" sentences that evoke them—does not always have to be turned to psychological account. In fact, the desire for that kind of accounting too often takes shape as a reduction of narrative complexity to manageable proportions: manageability being synonymous with the production of psychological or dramatic "sense."

Broad as the lexicon of human behavior is in Faulkner, it is not half so intricate as the narrative innovations and stylistic testings that bring it to us. The *verbal* life and action of his narratives, in other words, often surpasses or runs counter to the interest and vividness of his characters' lives and actions. This counterlife, this wash of verbal phenomena in Faulkner's writing, is often richer and more disorienting than that to which it should, in Lewis's mind, be subordinated. The lines of dramatic action in his novels do not stand clear of their narratives in such a way that we can easily make out what is happening. "What happens" in Faulkner's fiction, to use Seamus Heaney's terms, is often overshadowed by "the music of what happens." The "drowned yet antic" animals on the wave above, for instance, reappear as an animated menagerie of birds, horses, porpoises, and cats a few moments later. The dead animals are resurrected in metaphor, and the resulting imagistic whirl makes the precise visual components of the scene difficult to absorb initially. The skiff is raised into an almost vertical position, sucked up the face of the wave (though not apparently capsized), and then thrown up and beyond the crest to land in a tree high enough to afford a view of a world "in incredible retrograde." We can, with concentration and several rereadings, fix the action of the boat in our minds, and the scene is not without realistic specificity. But the realistic details (a blood-streaked face, planks, drowned animals, new-leafed tree branches) seem themselves like so many wooden porpoises cavorting in a tidal grammar. Phrases like "aghast and incredulous amazement" and "weightless and airy indecision" can all be converted into increments of dramatic sense, but only by hovering over them in a way Faulkner's ever-accruing rhythm does not encourage.

The force and momentum of this writing is such that the convict's actions seem lodged within and against it, just as in "The Bear" Ike McCaslin remembers "the dogs and the bear and the deer juxtaposed and reliefed against" not only "the big woods" but within and against "the best of all talking" (*GDM*, p. 191). The convict's ex post facto recapitulation of events is framed in the story by Faulkner's own telling (a frame within a frame). The convict is not denied a voice, but like Natty Bumppo, his self-articulations are never as interesting or as sustained as the scenes in which he is described. Not only does Faulkner know everything the convict feels and experiences, he even makes a point of telling us what the convict does *not* feel or perceive. He entertains possible perceptions and behavioral motives on the part of the convict only to invalidate the authority of those perceptions with his repeated use of the "not [this] but [that]" construction. When the convict encounters a third huge wave in the story, for example, Faulkner says, "At first he refused to believe it, not that he felt that now he had served out and discharged his apprenticeship to mischance, had with the birth of the child reached and crossed the crest of his Golgotha and would now be, possibly not permitted so much as ignored, to descend the opposite slope free-wheeling. That was not his feeling at all" ("OM," pp. 673–74).

Whatever the echoes of T. S. Eliot's "Prufrock" a reader may hear in this moment, the last sentence seems less an allusion than an implicit chastisement of a symbol-minded reader. Faulkner first provides and then dispenses with a possible reason for the convict's refusal to believe. Yet we need not see this as only an example of Faulkner's perverse insistence on staying ahead of a reader by dropping false clues and speculative possibilities, as if fearing, in Donald Kartiganer's words, "the loss of energy that mars any stay against confusion."[20] To say that Faulkner has a temperamental affinity for evasiveness and irresolution is simply not sufficient. We have to examine the imaginative *substance* of that evoked evasiveness, whose effect may seem, as here, not irresolute but self-securing. The effect of this moment actually has less to do with denial and deprivation ("not" within "not") than with imaginative augmentation and expansion. Despite the disclaimer, the possibility rather irreverently entertained here—that of freewheeling down the back side of Golgotha—is not disavowed, at least not imaginatively disavowed. I do not mean to suggest that the image of Golgotha is particularly important to the story, only that *as an image* (given with one hand and taken with the other) it represents a typical feature of Faulkner's narration. We might be tempted to construe this complexity of hypothesized motives in Faulkner's writing as a constant reminder of the equivocal nature of human psychology and the fragility of a writer's authority in representing it. We might see it as yet another example of his continuing fascination with thought and perception that are instinctual and unformulatable. But such a reading does not seem justified here. Faulkner explicitly states that this is not an unresolved but an *incorrect* postulation. Psychological clarity or comprehension are not relative, the narrator implies, because the "not that" formula leads into a "correct" reading of what the convict feels: he cannot believe that the malevolent force responsible for the flood can be so "barren of invention and imagination, so lacking in pride of artistry and craftsmanship, as to repeat itself [the wave] twice" ("OM," p. 674).

Yet when a "correct" perception is so closely allied and grammatically tied to an incorrect one, the latter is not canceled but held in abeyance. This "explanation" of what the convict might feel is ostensibly negated but not stricken from the record. Despite its disclaiming syntax, it is offered as if it actually *did* form a plausible interpretation of the convict's consciousness. The plausibility of that explanation can be ostensibly negated, but not the image itself, which becomes a kind of interpretive down payment. It is less an explanation from which we actually learn anything than one by which we are, as readers, intriguingly led *past*.[21] Again, the act of offering up this image in the first place, rather than its potential explanatory relevance, is what seems important here. We are not encouraged to think of the tall convict as a Christ figure in any sustained way. But neither are the momentary similarities that the image suggests simply blotted from our minds because Faulkner steps in to say, "that was not his feeling at all." Those similarities become part and parcel of the descriptive amplitude Faulkner lavishes upon his character, and thus the imagistic activity and life of Faulkner's own voice can seem, for a time, more interesting than what the convict himself is doing or thinking. In the midst of Faulkner's writing in this story, the convict continues to seem more and more a descriptive potential whose exact dimensions are never entirely clear. This may be why he remains such a shadowy figure and why his endurance and stubbornness seem so perverse.

The "cosmic" perspective so frequently invoked in "Old Man"—like that from a helicopter gazing down upon a distant traffic jam—may have less to do with "the old primal faithless Manipulator of all the lust and folly and injustice" ("OM," p. 662) than with Faulkner's narrative voice. If we grow irritated with this voice it is probably, as Robert Garis suggests, because we grow tired of Faulkner's rhetorical will, which seems more interested in "dominating" the world than in "understanding and revealing it."[22] One palpable effect of this kind of rhetorical dominance is the diminishing distance at which the characters in the passage above are seen. The woman in the boat with the convict has almost completely vanished, and even he occupies only a tiny imaginative space in the rhythm and verbal motion of this sequence. At its finish he is "like a bird in its nest," ineffectually mimicking the motions of paddling and denied even the most primal of emotional releases—"his chance to scream." He seems, as Faulkner says of the maniacal Henry Armstid feverishly digging for gold at the end of *The Hamlet*, like "a mechanical toy . . . with something monstrous in his unflagging effort" (*TH*, p. 1074). The convict has seemed this all along. A hillbilly sad sack whose sheer intransigence reaches improbably heroic proportions, the convict ends up resembling the "fyce" in "The Bear," whose yapping valor is indistinguishable from its manic imprudence.

Faulkner partially admires the illogical stubborn streak the convict displays, but he also disdainfully invokes class distinctions in referring to the convict's "prolific and monogamous kind" ("OM," p. 595) as if they were some form of interesting insect. Likewise, when the woman sees that the convict refuses, out of an ill-conceived sense of protocol, to wear his prison jumper (and so turns his badly sunburned back into a mass of suppurating blisters), she does not say anything, Faulkner tells us, because "she too had stemmed at some point from the same dim hill-bred Abraham" ("OM," p. 667). Yet Faulkner cannot help but have a certain appalled respect for the convict's fiercely simple existence. When this man helps the Cajun hunt alligators, he does so "not to gain future security, a balance in bank or even in a buried soda can for slothful and easy old age, but just permission to endure and endure to buy air to feel and sun to drink for [a] little while" ("OM," p. 668).[23] Faulkner makes it clear that the convict is emotionally stunted in his fear of women, but his heart goes out to the convict (along with mine) when his "sweetheart" favors him not with a return visit in prison but with "a postcard, a colored lithograph of a Birmingham hotel, a childish x inked heavily across one window, the heavy writing on the reverse slanted and primer-like too: *This is where were honnymonning at. Your friend (Mrs) Vernon Waldrip*" ("OM," pp. 725–26).

Faulkner is less willing to brutalize his character for a stunning or comic effect than Poe, for instance, might be. But he does sometimes seem wryly amused at the convict's apparently limitless ability to endure savage, trying circumstances. Faulkner's response to the convict vacillates between concern and indifference. In this way he bears a striking resemblance to Crane; "Old Man" is Faulkner's "Open Boat." I say this not just because the dramatic situation in each story is similar or because the unnamed convict comes to us, like so many of Crane's characters, with a generic epithet. The stories share a much more fundamental affinity. They both display mixed conditions of fictional extravagance in which the fluctuations between self-consciously "literary" language and realistic imagining are constant and self-dramatizing. Both sustain a complex tension between fiction and reality, hearing and seeing. Both include sudden and continual shifts in perspective from realistic involvement to some kind of hypothetical "balcony" view that renders a scene "weirdly picturesque." But while Crane's realism typically replaces and interrupts his rhetorical imagination, rendering it suddenly and ironically inappropriate, the situation in Faulkner often seems to be reversed. The rhetorical-auditory bias of his imagination is so pronounced—his narrative voice is so energetic, so overbearing, and self-fertilizing—that his characters, in Warren Beck's terms, almost have to elbow their way back into their own stories.

Thus when the tall convict first falls out of the boat in which he and the plump convict have been sent out, he grasps onto the stern of the skiff, and we hear the following:

He was now in the channel of a slough, a bayou, in which until today no current had run probably since the old subterranean outrage which had created the country. There was plenty of current in it now though; from his trough behind the stern he seemed to see the trees and sky rushing past with vertiginous speed, looking down at him between the gouts of cold yellow in lugubrious and mournful amazement. But they were fixed and secure in something; he thought of that, he remembered in an instant of despairing rage the firm earth fixed and founded strong and cemented fast and stable forever by the generations of laborious sweat, somewhere beneath him, beyond the reach of his feet, when, and again without warning, the stern of the skiff struck him a stunning blow across the bridge of his nose. . . . With both hands free he now dragged himself over the stern and lay prone on his face, streaming with blood and water and panting, not with exhaustion but with that furious rage which is terror's aftermath. ("OM," pp. 592–93)

Once again Faulkner's narrative voice offers a mode of perception unavailable to the character it describes. The convict may indeed think, for an instant, of the flooded earth he is flying above. But he does not, we can be sure, think of it as "cemented fast and stable forever by the generations of laborious sweat." That language belongs to Faulkner, and the rhythm that carries it is so "fixed and founded strong" that only the smash of a boat hull seems capable of derailing it. The return to narrative action, in other words, carries the force not just of imaginative conversion but of reproach. Yet by the end of the last sentence the voice has again reestablished itself with another not-this-but-that formula, and a reader's sympathies may tend toward the character. Can't the poor convict just bleed, one might well ask, without two "reports" (one wrong, one right) on his consciousness?

It could be argued, I suppose, that Faulkner implicitly commiserates with the convict's plight by taking the time to represent his physical and mental states in the first place. But his descriptive amplifications of the convict's feelings and sensations do not all display an equal expression of narrative interest. As Albert Guerard puts it, Faulkner's imagination seems "both compassionate and ironic."[24] The hardships the convict undergoes serve to counteract any imputation that Faulkner feels sentimental toward his character. It is as if the convict's indestructible capacity for "taking it" must be tested to the point of black humor, lest that endurance seem somehow tenderized or too easily gained an attribute. As we will see in a different way in Pynchon's fiction, Faulkner's characters sometimes seem "imprisoned" in their own stories, at the mercy of the language and the imaginative ambitions of the novels in which they appear. Scenes of violence bring this latter issue into especially harsh focus, as our awareness of suffering consciousness within a novel is crucially predetermined by the ways in which characters are allowed to *be* conscious.

Whatever our compassion for the convict, his bruises and injuries form but one example of the ugly facts that momentarily dislodge the story's otherwise aloof oratorical voice. The convict's act of cutting the woman's umbilical cord with the jagged edge of an open can, the water moccasins that he throws out of the skiff with "thick solid plops" ("OM," p. 655), the clouds of mosquitos in the Cajun's shanty, the Cajun's rotting teeth: these graphic details and others like them are what alone seem capable of breaking into and temporarily anchoring the rhetorical momentum of the story. The sudden shifts from rhetorical imagining to gritty realism are often so startling in Faulkner's fiction that we may, as readers, come to feel a bit like the young boy Wall Street Snopes in *The Hamlet*. Unwilling to stay away from the auction of the Texas ponies, Wall peeks in at a knot-hole in the barn housing the ponies and is, when they explode out of the barn, "still leaning to the knot-hole in the door which in the next instant vanished into matchwood, . . . itself exploding from his eye and leaving him, motionless in the diminutive overalls and still leaning forward a little . . . unscathed, his eye still leaned to the vanished knot-hole" (*TH*, pp. 994–95). The violence we encounter in Faulkner's fiction often seems to leave us leaning to vanished narrative knot-holes and uncertain as to whether we should feel awkward in that stance.

"FAULKNER'S MISCALLED Mississippi Gothic," Hugh Kenner avows, "is more nearly a Mississippi aestheticism. The savageries his blood-saturated rustics ritualize are of frozen Art Nouveau sumptuousness."[25] This is, as we shall see, a just and justified discrimination, but there are still compelling reasons why critics have reached for the term "Gothic" in connection with Faulkner's work. Take, for instance, this moment during a fight that breaks out in *Sanctuary* during Red's funeral at the Grotto, a dance hall outside Memphis:

> [The bouncer] felled the first and whirled and sprang with unbelievable celerity, into the main room. The orchestra was playing. It was immediately drowned in a sudden pandemonium of chairs and screams. The bouncer whirled again and met the rush of the four men. They mingled; a second man flew out and skittered along the floor on his back; the bouncer sprang free. Then he whirled and rushed them and in a whirling plunge they bore down upon the bier and crashed into it. The orchestra had ceased and were now climbing onto their chairs, with their instruments. The floral offerings flew; the coffin teetered. "Catch it!" a voice shouted. They sprang forward, but the coffin crashed heavily to the floor, coming open. The corpse tumbled slowly and sedately out and came to rest with its face in the center of a wreath.
>
> "Play something!" the proprietor bawled, waving his arms; "play! Play!"
>
> When they raised the corpse the wreath came too, attached to him by a hidden end of wire driven into his cheek. He had worn a cap which, tumbling off, exposed a small blue hole in the center of his forehead. It had been neatly plugged with wax and was painted, but the wax had been jarred out and lost. They couldn't find it, but by unfastening the snap in the peak, they could draw the cap down to his eyes. (*S*, p. 351)

The first paragraph here jauntily describes a barroom (or auditorium) brawl that anticipates, in its lively action, innumerable Hollywood versions of the same scene. The action, as it is presented to us, is bloodless, even seemingly painless; the storytelling extravagance with which men rush, whirl, plunge, and go "skittering" across the floor comes right out of the conventions of antebellum frontier humor.[26]

The remainder of the sequence is no less amusing, though the humor turns mordant and provocative. The people awkwardly trying to cover up this "small blue hole" and reestablish decorum here are not unlike appalled or affronted readers who might wish to be done with this scene. The last awkward gesture of drawing the corpse's cap down to his eyes will only make him look as though he is trying to peer out from under it. Together with the image of Red's face pinned to the middle of a mortuary wreath, this forms an apt example of Faulkner's incorrigible sense of humor, which seems partially to delight, at moments like this, in the thought of squeamish, offended readers. "To me [Sanctuary] was a cheap idea," Faulkner wrote in an oft-quoted introduction to the novel. "I had to pay for the privilege of rewriting [the novel], trying to make out of it something which would not shame The Sound and the Fury and As I Lay Dying too much," Faulkner says, "and I made a fair job and I hope you will buy it and tell your friends and I hope they will buy it too."[27]

The violence in Faulkner's work, as this scene suggests, assumes multiple, often wildly variant shapes. Fights, killings, rapes, maimings, and domestic violence are commonplace in his work. In fact, it is difficult, as Schwartz says, to think of a crime not committed in Faulkner's work: "the stage has not been so loaded with corpses since late Elizabethan tragedy."[28] Yet when informed of the body count in an interview, Faulkner replied that complaining about an author's being obsessed with violence is "like saying the carpenter is obsessed with his hammer. Violence is simply one of the carpenter's tools."[29] Perhaps no moment better illustrates this "functional" role for violence than Popeye's rape of Temple Drake with a corncob. Surely the most notorious moment in all of Faulkner's fiction (at least among the public at large—many of whom know of the incident without ever having read Sanctuary), the rape is never actually shown in the novel. Faulkner knows that the mere idea of such a violation is potent enough to be the fictional hammer he wishes it to be.

Before we know precisely what has happened to Temple, we see her sitting "with her legs close together" in Popeye's car as they drive to Memphis, "feeling her blood seeping slowly inside her loins" (S, p. 273) and "saying dully to herself, I'm still bleeding. I'm still bleeding" (S, p. 274). This moment of pathetic vulnerability and humiliation proves more powerful in its unbearability than the account of the rape Temple later relates to Horace Benbow. It does so largely because we cannot quite make out, in the first instance, what has happened; we know very little about what Temple has been through or about

Popeye's "reasons" for hurting her. Her reference to "its" happening is part of a recounting she later tells Horace "with actual pride, a sort of naive and impersonal vanity, as though she were making it up" (S, p. 328): "It made a kind of plopping sound, like blowing a little rubber tube wrong-side outward. It felt cold, like the inside of your mouth when you hold it open" (S, p. 331).

This "image" does not ostensibly describe the rape itself (Temple says she went to sleep before "his hand got there" [S, p. 331]); it describes what happens when she thinks about and then mentally "becomes" a man. Nevertheless, the image actually does seem to describe the rape, and Faulkner may be using it as an indirect but withering example of Temple's self-degrading "pride" in what she has endured: she has thought about what the penetration sounded like.[30] The ugly evocation of "a kind of plopping sound" that is vaguely rubbery and cold may also, in its suggestions of crude, artificial sterility, seem appropriate for an act associated with the impotent Popeye, who exudes the "vicious depthless quality of stamped tin" (S, p. 181) and whose mother fed him, when he was three years old, on "eggs cooked in olive oil" (S, p. 390). Yet glosses such as these, while plausible, may simply represent a reader's uneasy attempt to understand an act of violence whose invisibility in the novel gives a dark, threatening quality to anything that might seem to refer to it.

It is often difficult to see Faulkner's depictions of violence as merely "functional" or self-effacingly instrumental in their emphasis of a particular theme. Even when his scenes of violence are primarily realistic, they often gain a kind of unusual depth and odd power, as we can see, for example, in the death of Old Ben in "The Bear." The final chase takes place in the "rain-heavy air" of a December morning (GDM, p. 240). A "streaming tide of dogs" and men chase the bear through cane brakes and across "a thick yellow river" (GDM, p. 239) before it is backed against a tree and attacked first by the giant dog, Lion, who drives in "leaping clear of the ground":

> This time the bear didn't strike him down. It caught the dog in both arms, almost loverlike, and they both went down. He [Ike McCaslin] was off the mule now. He drew back both hammers of the gun but he could see nothing but moiling spotted houndbodies until the bear surged up again. Boon was yelling something, he could not tell what; he could see Lion still clinging to the bear's throat and he saw the bear, half erect, strike one of the hounds with one paw and hurl it five or six feet and then, rising and rising as though it would never stop, stand erect again and begin to rake at Lion's belly with its forepaws. Then Boon was running. The boy saw the gleam of the blade in his hand and watched him leap among the hounds, hurdling them, kicking them aside as he ran, and fling himself astride the bear as he had hurled himself onto the mule, his legs locked around the bear's belly, his left

177

arm under the bear's throat where Lion clung, and the glint of the knife as it rose and fell.

It fell just once. For an instant they almost resembled a piece of statuary: the clinging dog, the bear, the man stride its back, working and probing the buried blade. Then they went down, pulled over backward by Boon's weight, Boon underneath. It was the bear's back which reappeared first but at once Boon was astride it again. He had never released the knife and again the boy saw the almost infinitesimal movement of his arm and shoulder as he probed and sought; then the bear surged erect, raising with it the man and the dog too, and turned and still carrying the man and the dog it took two or three steps toward the woods on its hind feet as a man would have walked and crashed down. It didn't collapse, crumple. It fell all of a piece, as a tree falls, so that all three of them, man dog and bear, seemed to bounce once.

He and Tennie's Jim ran forward. Boon was kneeling at the bear's head. His left ear was shredded, his left coat sleeve was completely gone, his right boot had been ripped from knee to instep; the bright blood thinned in the thin rain down his leg and hand and arm and down the side of his face which was no longer wild but was quite calm. Together they prized Lion's jaws from the bear's throat. "Easy, goddamn it," Boon said. "Cant you see his guts are all out of him?" (*GDM*, pp. 240–42)

Despite the terrific action and adrenaline of this sequence (which I have quoted at length partly because it is so difficult to break into), Faulkner's writing here is relatively restrained in contrast with the rest of the story. Outside of the words "houndbodies" and "loverlike," there is little neologistic extravagance, and the longer sentences are factored up into a realistic rhythm of itemized action. Old Ben is not without his mythic attributes in this moment, for he still rears up majestically and falls in death like a giant tree, facing the same woods Lion will face when he dies at sundown in a few pages. Still, the previous legendary and mythic evocations of the bear carry much of the drama here, and this basically realistic account of a mythic encounter creates a peculiar and indelible effect that seems other and more than realistic.

Faulkner once said that he preferred to read rather than to listen to music because "I prefer silence to sound, and the image produced by words occurs in silence. That is, the thunder and the music of the prose take place in silence."[31] Something like the opposite seems to happen here, for the mythic "music" of this sequence seems silenced within the imaginative space of the scene. The killing of Old Ben seems largely soundless. There are, of course, several dogs barking here; Lion no doubt snarls viciously as he fights; and surely there is some kind of crash as the entangled trio of man, bear, and dog topple over together. But none of this is communicated within the scene itself, as represented. The three of them do not crash when they fall, they "bounce," and all the action of clinging, surging, leaping, probing, and falling is reported as seen or watched by Ike, either directly or over the sights of his gun. Boon comes running up "yelling something, [Ike] could not tell what" and the effect is like the description of a man Ike and the others pass earlier in this chase sequence: "they passed the man who had fired—a swamper, a pointing arm, a gaunt face, the small black orifice of his yelling studded with rotten teeth" (GDM, p. 238). The physicality of this man's shouted directions is seen as if behind soundproof glass, though his rotten teeth, gaunt face, and gesticulating arm all seem realistically vivid and urgent. The effect is of frozen movement, of imagery, to borrow a phrase from Light in August, "motionless in midstride" (LA, p. 741). Neither dramatic action nor its imagistic immobilization seems to gain precedence. As with the image of the convict's skiff pulled up the wave and into a tree, realistic action and progress here seem not canceled but stilled and charged. The images of Lion and the bear "almost loverlike" and the "piece of statuary" the three participants "almost" resemble objectify the action in an attitude of electric arrest that resembles the moment Jake Barnes so admires when Pedro Romero becomes "one" with the bull as he kills it in The Sun Also Rises.[32] Yet this imaginative arrest is only partial; it forms but one part of the larger effect of this violence under a bell jar.

The action of the fight as presented is detailed and focused. We know who is on the bottom when the three fall over, who gets up first, how the bear staggers as he heads for the woods, and so on. Despite the statuary "images" here, the imaginative substance of Faulkner's writing is subordinated to and subsumed by the dramatic action of this scene. We imaginatively move into the actions of the fight with the ease and confidence characteristic of realistic imagining. But unlike most realistic sequences, the absence of sound here has an odd spectral effect. As I mentioned in discussing realism, the degree to which we imagine any kind of synchronized sound in fiction (the degree, for example, to which we imaginatively see a character's mouth moving when we read dialogue) seems fairly minimal. A writer can, of course, emphasize all manner of sound in a fictional world if he so wishes: the sound of breaking glass, a door opening, or a lawnmower droning. But our imagination of that "real" sound must take precedence over the sound of the words that evoke it for us, just as the silence of a realistically imagined world has to be "heard through" the words that describe it.

Throughout the course of "The Bear" the sound we are habituated to is not that of the nonverbal life squawking, honking, or roaring somewhere outside of language but "the best of all talking" (GDM, p. 191), the rich, rhythmic meandering of Faulkner's own narrative voice. Our accustomization to that voice is so pronounced, in fact, that its sudden disappearance into the one-dimensionality of realistic imagining is something like the experience one has when shutting the door to a room pulsing with music and entering a soundless one. The noise is cut off, as if with scissors, and the volume of the previous roar causes us to bring some of it with us into a new, abrupt quiet. The silence thus afforded seems buffered and distanced by a receding echo or "afterimage" of the music. In this scene, the loss seems to be first and foremost a loss of verbal richness, a sudden expressive emptiness when we have grown to expect more words. We noticed something of this same effect in Hemingway, but in his case the conversion from aural imagining nearly always moves back into realistic sequence. In Faulkner, at least in this moment, the process is reversed. His realism here causes only a temporary subsidence of the energetic resonance of his narrative voice, one that leaves the action and images of "real" life leached of sound.

The sense of deprivation and even anticlimax that attends the moment of Old Ben's death originates partly in the thought that the wilderness and a wild untouched form of existence are disappearing with him.[33] But in the immediate representation of his killing, the sense of loss we experience stems powerfully from the receding thunder of Faulkner's narrative voice. The poignancy of the bear's death, that is, springs as much from verbal as from symbolic sources, from the ebbing of the verbal energy and drive responsible for his imaginative life earlier in the story. Two kinds of soundlessness govern and shape the imaginative impact of Old Ben's death. The first consists of the absent sounds of the actual struggle; the second, of the absent sounds of Faulkner's narrative voice. The first condition focuses our attention on the visual aspects of the scene. The second, with the effect of a recessive echo, offers us the imaginative equivalent of "Sam Fathers lying motionless on his face in the trampled mud" after Old Ben has been killed (GDM, p. 242).

Soundlessness as an idea rather than an expressive condition figures in several of Faulkner's most explosive scenes of violence. One concerns the death in Sanctuary of Lee Goodwin at the hands of an outraged Jefferson mob convinced that it was he who raped Temple Drake. The mob, after apparently "raping" Goodwin, burns him alive in a vacant lot. We are given the scene through the eyes of Horace Benbow, who is still dazed and disoriented by the travesty of justice in Goodwin's trial. He runs on the scene and finds "a blazing mass in the middle of the lot":

It was now indistinguishable, the flames whirling in long and thunderous plumes from a white-hot mass out of which there defined themselves faintly the ends of a few posts and planks. Horace ran among them; they were holding him, but he did not know it; they were talking, but he could not hear the voices.

"It's his lawyer."

"Here's the man that defended him. That tried to get him clear."

"Put him in, too. There's enough left to burn a lawyer."

"Do to the lawyer what we did to him. What he did to her. Only we never used a cob. We made him wish we had used a cob."

Horace couldn't hear them. He couldn't hear the man who had got burned screaming. He couldn't hear the fire, though it still swirled upward unabated, as though it were living upon itself, and soundless: a voice of fury like in a dream, roaring silently out of a peaceful void. (*S*, p. 384)

Some readers might well feel like continuing this cycle of retaliatory, "scape-goat" violence by tossing the last bragging redneck here into the fire with Goodwin (though the screaming "man who had got burned" here is not Good-win but another man carrying an oil can, who apparently helped light the fire). Faulkner wants us, in part, to comprehend why the mob acts the way it does— they have no way of knowing Goodwin did not actually rape Temple. But it is also apparent from the voices of Goodwin's persecutors that however justified their motives may have initially seemed, these characters go at their job with a sadistic, vengeful relish exceeding not only seemliness but any justifica-tion. The scene is thus, among other things, an incisive dramatization of public morality and mob violence similar, in an abbreviated way, to Pilar's wrench-ing account of the lynching of the fascists in Hemingway's *For Whom the Bell Tolls*.

As so often with Faulkner, however, we are given more than an act of violence here. We are presented with a character's perception of that act or, in Horace's case, his insensibility. The psychological distraction and disconnec-tion Horace feels in this moment characterize him (as well as Temple) at several points in the novel.[34] Here they provide the perceptual buffer through which he experiences the scene; the fire is "soundless" to him because his shock, disgust, and disbelief have nearly incapacitated him. Yet in the last sentence Faulkner seems to lose all interest in what Horace can or cannot perceive. He no longer needs Horace's insulated perspective because the fire itself is dreamlike. It is "soundless" outside of Horace's apprehension, "roaring silently," "a voice of fury" in "a peaceful void." As Faulkner's rhythm begins to "live upon itself" here, the images turn into phrases that come to an imaginative rest. The startling incongruousness of that rhythmic stilling and balm, when they describe an event this disturbing, seems to feed back into the dramatic life of the scene. It emphasizes our terror, indignation, and helplessness in the face of this event. It also emphasizes Faulkner's penchant for horrible deeds, in Kenner's terms, sumptuously rendered. The represented form of his violence often owes as much to John Keats as it does to Erskine Caldwell.[35]

ONE OF FAULKNER'S most notable traits as a writer consists of his incongruous and testing juxtapositions (whether of social classes, morality, or forms of verbal imagining) that purposefully challenge our responsiveness as readers. The sheer transformative energy of his fictional voice often achieves its rhetorical power by the degree to which it can, by sheer verbal will, either suspend or renovate our moral judgment. Take Jody Varner's account of how one of Eck Snopes's horses broke its neck in *The Hamlet*:

> "I'll tell you what happened. Eck and that boy finally run it into that blind land of Freeman's, after a chase of about twenty-four hours. They figured it couldn't possibly climb them eight-foot fences of Freeman's so him and the boy tied their rope across the end of the lane, about three feet off the ground. And sho enough, soon as the horse come to the end of the lane and seen Freeman's barn, it whirled just like Eck figured it would and come helling back up that lane like a scared hen-hawk. It probably never even seen the rope at all. Mrs. Freeman was watching from where she had run up onto the porch. She said that when it hit that rope, it looked just like one of these here great big Christmas pinwheels. But the one you bought got clean away, didn't it?" (*TH*, p. 1030)

We can laugh here at Eck and Mrs. Freeman's analogies without thereby certifying ourselves as sadists, for there is no "horse" in this account to be violently upended, only a verbal entity that hells up an alley like a scared hen-hawk and spins like a pinwheel. Of course, in one sense there *should* be a horse here, and it was certainly there for Eck, who listens impassively to this version of what he himself saw. But the pleasure involved in reading such an account, as we saw in a different way in Poe's and Cooper's work, resides in Jody's storytelling ability to "de-realize" what would otherwise be an intolerable cruelty to animals. The negative characterization of this effect, however, is too weak to account adequately for its exuberance. Jody's verbal performance is engaging and entertaining not primarily because "reality" has been de-composed or de-constituted. Rather, his narrative voice is captivating and concentrated in its own right, so much so that its very consistency and self-sustenance seem independent of the "real" actions it might be said to represent. There may be reminders here of connections between life and this whirl of words, but they spark only an exhilarating recognition that such connections are, in the present case, either provisional or unbinding.

The visual equivalent of this effect is the slapstick routine of someone slipping on a banana peel. That action is amusing not because we know we are exempt from such accidents or because we know we are liable to them (and thus sympathize with the slipping victim because it is a "human" moment). Neither, I think, can we rightly construe ourselves as laughing "conscientiously" in such a moment, secure in the knowledge that the event is staged and that the actor has probably fallen on a padded floor or in some other way been protected from physical pain. Our response may in part be shaped by the comic vindication we feel in seeing pomposity humbled, if the person who slips, as is often the case in such gags, figures as a stuffed shirt. Thus in the passage above, part of the fun—the nastier part—would stem from what Caroline Gordon and Allen Tate call Jody's "Mephisphelean mirth over human credulity," his pleasure in demonstrating that Eck got just about what he deserved.[36])

But for the most part, our laughter at a slapstick routine is in response to the very image of the fall itself, whose abruptness and disruptive visual turbulence so occupy our attention that their self-substantiality becomes, for the moment, both exclusive and engrossing. The balletic athleticism of masterfully executed pratfalls are actually beautiful to watch, and like all intense performances, completely absorbing. Charlie Chaplin's "Proustian or Jamesian relationships with Murphy beds and flights of stairs and with vases on runners on tables on rollers," Stanley Cavell says, offer "the heroism of momentary survival." The "Olympic resourcefulness" of Buster Keaton's body makes him "perhaps the only constantly beautiful and continuously hilarious man ever seen, as though the ugliness in laughter should be redeemed."[37] The beauty and the hilarity coexist because at any moment a graceful physical negotiation can be abruptly compromised, with legs and arms fiercely flailing.

What is important for the contrast I am drawing here is that the "slip," the sudden frenetic fall or the comic deflation, does not amount to an acknowledgment of pain. It simply constitutes one more component of the performance, one that offsets the physical dexterity that seeks to avoid it. An actor's adroitness and timing (as well as his evocation of visual disintegration and chaos as he falls) can, in masterly slapstick, defy and banish any notion of normal physical restraints and consequences. This is partly a matter of expectation, for the conventions of slapstick require that the person who falls get back up again with only his or her ego wounded. But we often laugh at the pratfall itself, before we see how the victim recovers, and so once again we seem to respond, instantaneously, to the frantic performance of an actor falling down. We are not, in so responding, approving of someone else's pain, much less sympathizing with it. We are simply accepting the altered representational ground upon which an action is taken differently from the way it would be (or at least should be) in life. What makes such actions so compelling is their capacity to displace our otherwise authoritative sense of the pain that, say, landing hard on our back or our hip might occasion. It seems no accident that the most sophisticated examples of the slapstick mode are in silent black-and-white films. In those films stylized acting and costumes and a soundless atmosphere (we never *hear* anyone fall, unless as a riff on a whoopee whistle or a crash on a cymbal in an added soundtrack) all serve as supplemental distancing devices that help remove the consequences of certain cinematic actions from real consequences and pain.

We can always, of course, play Eck in these matters and insist on our ability to "talk back" to a text; we can always insist upon our right to reshape and flatten an imaginative texture in exerting our will and justifying our moral agency over it. "A dead horse is a dead horse," an unsympathetic reader might say about the passage above, "no matter what he looks like. Pain is pain—and never funny." All that can be emphasized here is that a reader who *does* give himself over to a voiced or "de-realized" depiction of violence (*even if it is not comic*) is responding to the depiction, not to the violence of the act depicted.[38]

Our sense of what actual violence is like may seem to serve a normative function in determining how we respond to such depictions (we know what *real* violence is like, which is why this violence, in not seeming real, can be funny). But as we saw in regard to realistic fiction, the primary reason a verbal sequence seems "real" is that we "normalize" it, we mis-take an imaginative sequence for our own experience and insist upon the priority of the latter. Thus the idea that a responsive "norm" determines our response to Eck's anecdote seems merely an ex post facto justification, a way of trying to explain why a reader might laugh in such a moment. Our response to "voiced" violence undoubtedly does involve a departure from an implicit norm, but that idea of "real" violence is so vaguely conceived as to serve only as a functional ground from which to depart. It forms an indispensable but almost imperceptible part of our imaginative experience, one useful only in the way a diving board facilitates a show of agility and control unachievable from a springless surface of departure. Once again a theory of deviation in such matters seems of little help. We laugh at Eck's account not so much because it is "not real" but because it so obviously *is* something else, and the verbal substance of that "something else" occupies most of our attention.[39]

I am stressing the transformative power of narrative voice here not in order to absolutize the conditions of its imaginative existence. In fact, the susceptibility of "voiced" accounts of violence to realistic seepage and rot seems all too apparent. We can easily imagine how Jody's account of Eck's horse might have quickly become, with a slight shift of intonation and focus, distasteful and even gratuitous in the way realistic violence so often can be. It thus goes without saying that the kind of verbal "purity" that sustains a wholesale relinquishment of realistic imagining in depicting violence is not usually encountered in an undiluted state. Nevertheless, Faulkner's fiction is one of the places in which remarkably pure examples of aural imagining are repeatedly encountered, and he seems firmly aware that the more unlikely or immoral the event displaced by a descriptive sequence, the greater the imaginative impact it may potentially have. It is a sign of Faulkner's strength as an artist that this awareness does not usually turn into mere sensationalism or diseased voyeurism, into a desire to see what the market will bear or what the censors will tolerate. He seems more interested in what our imaginations will bear, in how the conventionality of our responses to violence can be reimagined and revamped so as to be resensitized. This involves more than the limited pleasure of self-indulgent trespass, of shattering a convention just to see how it looks in pieces.

"The conflict between the idea of the Old South and the progressive actuality of the New South," Delmore Schwartz says, becomes in Faulkner's work "an obsession with values which cannot be realized with sufficient intensity except through violation and perversion":

> [Faulkner] can only seize his values, which are those of the idea of the Old South, by imagining them being violated by the most hideous crimes. Thus Temple Drake must be violated by a corn cob: mere rape is not enough. . . . how can one experience [the Old values] in modern life? How, except through the violence and abnormality which betrays them so brutally that, by a recognizable dialectic, their existence is recognized. The criminal helps one to remember the judge.[40]

One might object here to the overly convenient equation of Faulkner with the values of the Old South in uppercase, but Schwartz's comments are otherwise incisive. Still, I would locate Faulkner's "dialectic" of transgression and challenge at a more fundamental and less explicitly thematic level, one observable not only in certain actions and events but in the energetic life of individual sequences and sentences.

The triumphal instance of this transgressive impulse in Faulkner's work is, to my mind, the voice of Jason Compson as we hear it in *The Sound and the Fury*. I do not have room here to examine Jason's voice as fully and patiently as it deserves, but much of its imaginative force is on display in his first famous utterance: "Once a bitch always a bitch, what I say" (*SF*, p. 206). It is some time before we realize whom Jason is referring to here, but in one sense it does not really matter. His first statement, like those that pour forth after it, is to be judged not by its accuracy as a description of his niece Quentin but by its verbal adequacy to his own flagrantly immoderate imagination. The "what I say" here is Faulkner's stroke of genius. Without it the sentence would be considerably more menacing. With it, our attention is drawn not simply to a vicious opinion but to the blissfully isolated self-enclosure within which that opinion is expressed. Jason's opening line resembles the verbal tic of certain self-contained British speakers who "pose" a question ("it's a lovely day, *izzn* it?" or "he isn't much of an athlete, is he?") in order to foreclose on the need to answer it. In Jason's case, however, there is no need, indeed no *possibility* of answering back (at least in any way that would allow us to be heard). His psychological insularity is one with all his other unadmirable traits: hypocrisy, bigotry, prudery, sexism, and anti-Semitism, to name just a few. So it might at first seem only appropriate that critics have been quick to call Jason "bitter," "venomous," "hateful," "despicable," even "sick."[41]

But this is only half the story, for Faulkner obviously loves the verbal performance in which Jason engages. And he does not seem to relish it solely because it exemplifies a verbal pathology. Jason is for Faulkner more than simply a case study of how humor can function as a protective self-hypnosis in which someone projects onto others the responsibility for his own self-conceived martyrdom.[42] One critic, pursuing a "where there's smoke there's fire" line of argument, actually contends that we are "subliminally" seduced into sympathizing with Jason's view "because in some sense we share it."[43] This notion that Jason's rhetorical fury and versatility are to be judged by the degree to which they do or do not "seduce" us into accepting his point of view seems wrongheaded to me. Enjoying Jason's verbal performance does not necessarily entail a sympathy with his views. Faulkner never loses sight of Jason's remorseless and rancorous character, which he dramatizes by such examples of Jason's heartless behavior as his burning the extra circus ticket he might have given Luster. Still, from the moment Jason opens his mouth his paranoid verbal imagination is made to seem not just self-damning but entertainingly self-generative as well. Finding that he has accidentally put his hand in some poison oak while he chases Quentin, Jason says, "the only thing I couldn't understand was why it was just poison oak and not a snake or something. So I didn't even bother to move it" (*SF*, p. 278).

Jason's voice is to be judged by the extent to which it represents a "convinced"—not a convincing—performance. The psychology behind that performance seems less the source than an attribute of its energy. Thus the brilliance of Faulkner's evocation of this character is that our unfailing sense that Jason is paranoid, malevolent, and hypocritical seldom need impede our enjoyment of his evident verbal skills: an enjoyment that is not, as some would have it, tantamount to moral anesthesia. Those readers who have no tolerance for an immoral character, no matter how capable he is of expressing himself, are not in this instance morally superior or more perceptive than a reader who appreciates Jason's performance and Faulkner's behind it. In fact, an "intolerant" reader will miss more here than the fun of Jason's self-portraiture. He will also miss the daring and challenge of Faulkner's fictional methods. Jason's remarks offer a continual imaginative escape from the very psychological dimensions they also powerfully suggest. It is by making Jason's moral depravity inseparable from his remarkably inventive verbal skills that Faulkner allows us to appreciate a man we would otherwise morally condemn. Again, this admiration does not take the form of sympathizing with this character, but it does challenge us to rethink the relation of moral adequacy to verbal expression. Jason's character seems designed to unsettle our comfortable bestowals of compassion and respect and our concomitant recognition of the "appropriate" people and occasions that call it forth.[44]

The complications of expectation and effect involved with Jason Compson also characterize the life and the death of Joe Christmas in *Light in August*. Long and rightfully considered one of the loneliest, most enigmatic figures in American fiction, Joe Christmas is always seen from a distance. Faulkner's triumph in this novel, Alfred Kazin noted thirty years ago, resides in his "ability to keep his leading character a shadow, and yet to make us feel all his suffering."[45] As an illegitimate orphan of indeterminate racial origin but one who is supposed by others to be black, Joe's identity in the eyes of those around him is the result of whatever individual paranoia (about race, miscegenation, illegitimacy, or Calvinist damnation) they project upon him. As Warwick Wadlington rightly asserts,

> With his fixed mask [of a sneer], he is like a skeletal persona without a full-fleshed story, an abstract to be filled by tragedy. To be Joe Christmas is to have a story imputed to oneself. . . . He is figuratively as well as literally an orphan. The orphanage dietitian, Doc Hines, McEachern, Joanna Burden, Percy Grimm, and the community in general all try to adopt, and adapt, Joe to their explanatory fictions.[46]

But while Faulkner makes us aware of all these distorting projections on the part of other characters, he himself participates in something like the same process.

One of the most powerful images of Christmas occurs early in the novel and involves a literal projection onto his person. He stands, on the night before he murders Joanna Burden, beneath the "dark window" of her house, "cursing her with slow and calculated obscenity." Earlier in his life, we are told, he had once (for unexplained reasons) removed, "with the cold and bloodless deliberation of a surgeon" only those buttons that an unnamed woman had sewn onto his clothing (*LA*, p. 477). He now strikes off the one button on his "undergarment" and stands nude by the side of the road:

> The August weeds were thightall. Upon the leaves and stalks dust of a month of passing wagons lay. The road ran before him. It was a little paler than the darkness

of trees and earth. In one direction town lay. In the other the road rose to a hill. After a time a light began to grow beyond the hill, defining it. Then he could hear the car. He did not move. He stood with his hands on his hips, naked, thighdeep in the dusty weeds, while the car came over the hill and approached, the lights full upon him. He watched his body grow white out of the darkness like a kodak print emerging from the liquid. He looked straight into the headlights as it shot past. From it a woman's shrill voice flew back, shrieking. "White bastards!" he shouted. "That's not the first of your bitches that ever saw. . . ." But the car was gone. There was no one to hear, to listen. It was gone, sucking its dust and its light with it and behind it, sucking with it the white woman's fading cry. He was cold now. (*LA*, p. 478)

The image of an emerging photographic print (Joe watches his body "grow white") vividly suggests the racial attributions with which others endow him and with which he himself struggles throughout the novel.[47] Joe's obscurely motivated violence, his tough sexuality, and recalcitrant loneliness—all the qualities, in short, that make up his eruptive instability—are also exemplified in this image of a "developing" print. And these qualities are indelibly evoked without explaining why it is that Christmas behaves like this. Faulkner's presentation of Joe's behavior seems far more powerful, that is, than the ways in which we are encouraged to "account" for it.

Joe's external features may emerge from the darkness "like a kodak print" here but that initial invisibility only emphasizes the inaccessibility of his inner life. This lack of access remains a constant throughout the novel. The more psychological background we're given about Joe Christmas (and we are given quite a bit), the less his psychology seems "resolved." The more psychologically inclusive his portrait, the less definitive it seems. Yet through it all Christmas is presented via startling images like the one above, and their cumulative force has an imaginative impact of its own. Joe's fictional power as a character depends upon his always seeming to amount to more than the "evidence" Faulkner adduces to "explain" him. The more we feel we understand Joe Christmas, the more presumptive and fruitless that understanding comes to feel. The "truth" about Christmas, as Michael Millgate says, "is constituted precisely by the complexity of his presentation in the novel; it embraces, holds in suspension, all of those interpretations of his actions and insights into his psychology that have been offered along the way."[48] This seems not a failure on Faulkner's part but a satisfying reminder that knowing a great deal *about* a character is not always the same as "knowing" him.

The deliberate suspension of any single revelation that might make the full significance of a character's actions become clear is a well-known characteristic of Faulkner's work. But this effect in regard to Joe is very different from, say, the presentation of Popeye in *Sanctuary*, where certain biographical revelations that seem to help partly explain his earlier actions are postponed until late in the novel. In Christmas's case, the retrospective intelligibility we may grant his actions never seems adequate to the imaginative power with which those actions have been evoked. This in no way weakens the severity of Faulkner's criticism of the Southern social and religious forces responsible for the very possibility of a man like Christmas. Faulkner simply refuses to offer us final clarifications, in regards to Joe, which might themselves support the notion of a coherent, intelligible self upon which racial intolerance and religious bigotry depend. Some readers may even feel a bit like Christmas himself when he declares, in answer to the suggestion that he might not in fact be part black, "if I'm not, damned if I haven't wasted a lot of time" (*LA*, p. 586).

In light of Faulkner's narrative procedures, it seems no accident that critics have borne down heavily on the scene of Joe's death, for it would seem to offer the "answer to" or at least a catharsis or even "inoculation" from this character's violence and rootless tragedy.[49] The scene is framed by the narrative of Joe's killer, Percy Grimm. Grimm is introduced at this late stage in the novel (like Gavin Stevens before him, with his specious speculations about the promptings and counterpromptings of Joe's "white" and "black" blood) as one more "interpreter" of Joe's actions. But Grimm, who represents everything his name suggests (Faulkner once called him a "Fascist galahad"[50]), acts on his notion of who Joe is with the humorless intensity of a "blind and untroubled faith in the rightness and infallibility of his actions" (*LA*, p. 739) that Faulkner explicitly identifies as terrifying. The action of the chase, which is several pages long, resembles in some ways what we saw in "The Bear," even down to the dreamlike, imagistically frozen spectators Grimm passes: "faces blanched and gaped, with round, toothed orifices; they made one long sound like a murmuring sigh: 'There. . . . . . went that way . . . '" (*LA*, p. 738). The imagery is predominantly visual, with Christmas identified by the glint of the sun striking his handcuffed hands "like the flash of a heliograph" (*LA*, p. 740).

But as that analogy intimates (along with the next reference to the handcuffs "full of glare and glitter like lightning bolts, so that he [Joe] resembled a vengeful and furious god pronouncing a doom" [*LA*, p. 742]), Faulkner's narrative voice in this instance is full of the metaphoric thunder so noticeably absent at the death of Old Ben. Grimm's actions are conceived as being those of a "pawn" manipulated by a deterministic being called the Player, who seems to move Grimm and his "black, blunt, huge automatic" (*LA*, p. 738) with "unfailing certitude" to the kitchen in Gail Hightower's kitchen where Joe has sought refuge.

189

he ran straight to the kitchen and into the doorway, already firing, almost before he could have seen the table overturned and standing on its edge across the corner of the room, and the bright and glittering hands of the man who crouched behind it, resting upon the upper edge. Grimm emptied the automatic's magazine into the table; later someone covered all five shots with a folded handkerchief.

But the Player was not done yet. When the others reached the kitchen they saw the table flung aside now and Grimm stooping over the body. When they approached to see what he was about, they saw that the man was not dead yet, and when they saw what Grimm was doing one of the men gave a choked cry and stumbled back into the wall and began to vomit. Then Grimm too sprang back, flinging behind him the bloody butcher knife. "Now you'll let white women alone, even in hell," he said. But the man on the floor had not moved. He just lay there, with his eyes open and empty of everything save consciousness, and with something, a shadow, about his mouth. For a long moment he looked up at them with peaceful and unfathomable and unbearable eyes. Then his face, body, all, seemed to collapse, to fall in upon itself, and from out the slashed garments about his hips and loins the pent black blood seemed to rush like a released breath. It seemed to rush out of his pale body like the rush of sparks from a rising rocket; upon that black blast the man seemed to rise soaring into their memories forever and ever. They are not to lose it, in whatever peaceful valleys, beside whatever placid and reassuring streams of old age, in the mirroring faces of whatever children they will contemplate old disasters and newer hopes. It will be there, musing quiet, steadfast, not fading and not particularly threatful, but of itself alone serene, of itself alone triumphant. Again from the town, deadened a little by the walls, the scream of the [fire alarm] siren mounted toward its unbelievable crescendo, passing out of the realm of hearing. (*LA*, pp. 742–43)

This, in my opinion, is one of the most remarkable scenes of violence in American fiction. It is remarkable not only for its initial horror but for its rhetorical ambition as Faulkner attempts, by sheer verbal willpower, to create a final resting place for a character who could find none in this novel while alive. The energy of this moment resides not only in its transfiguring vision of a secular resurrection but in the ways it challenges the odds (also created by Faulkner) against that vision being entertained. That the catalyst for this evocation of Joe's imaginative "escape" is his brutal sacrificial appeasement of Grimm's (and his Southern white society's) sexual anxiety, that the "black blast" that ascends "like the rush of sparks from a rising rocket" is actually the blood spouting from his castrated groin, offers a defining example of the competing imaginative modes that characterize Faulkner's writing.

It seems to be almost a universal opinion in Faulkner criticism that Christmas accepts his death passively.[51] There is reason to entertain this notion and reason as well to be skeptical about it. "The town" wonders, at the start of the chapter this scene concludes, why when Joe is finally "run to earth" "he neither surrendered nor resisted. It was as though he had set out and made his plans to passively commit suicide" (*LA*, p. 727). So too, Gavin Stevens asserts that Christmas "crouched behind that overturned table and let them shoot him to death, with that loaded and unfired pistol in his hand" (*LA*, p. 731). But these are the speculations of people who did not see Christmas die. Faulkner encourages us, as he has throughout the novel, to take all such incomplete and speculative explanations of events (which are often later qualified or contravened) with a sizable grain of salt. In death as in life Christmas remains an unknown quantity and that may make him seem passive to those in the novel who are not granted the multiple perspectives of Joe that a reader is. Yet as I indicated, the multiplicity of ways in which we as readers "see" Joe amplifies rather than reduces the complexity of his fictional life, and thus we too are denied a decisive vantage from which to declare his passivity.[52]

If Christmas really accepts his death passively, why does he turn a table over? He is said to carry "a heavy nickelplated pistol" (*LA*, p. 740) in the chase and there may be no reason to doubt Stevens's contention that it was in his hand loaded when he died. Yet nothing establishes Stevens's account as authoritative. All we know for certain is that Joe's "bright and glittering hands" (his handcuffs? the pistol? both?) are "resting upon the upper edge" of the table. A case could well be made that Christmas actually *does* intend to fight back but that he has no chance in doing so. The fact that Grimm's five shots can be later covered "with a folded handkerchief" attests not only to the force of the firepower with which Joe is hit but to the speed with which the automatic's magazine is emptied. We are left not with answers here but with speculative possibilities. That enigmatic "something, a shadow" that plays about Joe's mouth as he dies may refer to his mouth filling with blood but it also seems, characteristically, to refer to a great deal more.[53]

At the very moment these final ambiguities are posed, however, Faulkner attempts nothing less than a resolution of *all* the tortured ambiguities of Joe's character he has so painstakingly evoked over the course of the novel. And he does this even while the evocative force with which those ambiguities are represented is such that any action or event capable of "resolving" them seems inconceivable. That Faulkner realized he could not achieve this imaginative reconciliation in anything other than a radically provisional form is partially evident in the fact that he does not end the novel with this scene. But to have attempted the feat at all is a testament to Faulkner's confidence in the transformative power of his language to test and alter the imaginative grounds upon which we can experience any fictional subject. And once again, the alteration has to do with the power of auditory imagining.

Joe's transformation is effected in part by metaphor, by "a trope transformed into the metaphoric truth embodied in that hope," as Carole Taylor puts it: "First, Joe 'seemed' to rise, and then 'seemed' changes to the 'are' and 'will be' of lyrical prophecy."[54] The rhythm as well as the imagery of this moment works to establish a calm that will seem permanent and reconciliatory. What is momentarily reconciled and quieted, however, are not the contradictions of Joe's life so much as the narrative complexities of this moment: the complications of our triple remove from the narrative "action" as we watch the men watch Joe die or, rather, as we listen to what Grimm's men will look back upon at some point in the future. Not only is Christmas's final "rest" granted in his physical release from the tortured tensions of his life; it also springs from the very description of that release. It stems from the displacement, by rhythm and imagery, of the complications of novelistic point of view: a displacement that is felt as a resolution.

Wadlington—who sees this scene, as I do not, as a "catharsis" for readers as well as for Grimm and his men—brings up the possibility that certain feminist readers may be so morally affronted by Christmas's previous misogynistic violence (or even by Faulkner's melodramatic portrayal of Joanna Burden's nymphomania) as to feel incapable of sufficiently sympathizing with him or being absorbed in the catharsis of his death.[55] Such an affronted response would, I take it, be on the order of thinking that we have to sympathize with Jason in order to find his monologue funny. Or to take a more contemporary event, it resembles the assertion that someone who refused to be pleased or (God forbid) gleeful about Ted Bundy's execution somehow indirectly condoned his brutal serial murders. A reader responding in this way would first have to think of this moment as tragically cathartic (and this seems a strange adjective here, even for Grimm and his men, as a catharsis is not usually thought of in retrospect as "musing, quiet, steadfast" and "not particularly threatful"). Second, this catharsis would also have to be taken as a sign that Faulkner somehow implicitly approves of Joe's prior actions in regards to women.

Joe's own history of humiliated victimization itself partially mitigates his later actions, even if it does not excuse them. Likewise, his brutal death seems designed to mobilize sympathy for Christmas. But Faulkner's attempt to provide an imaginative space or final image for Joe in the moment of his death does not have to be equated with sympathetic approval of his previous violence. This is especially true if this scene constitutes, as I see it, not a catharsis so much as an exertion of imaginative will on Faulkner's part that runs counter to his characterization of Christmas in the rest of the novel. "Joe has so often been described as a victim and so rarely as a character of tragic stature," Taylor aptly remarks, "partly because we habitually look for some recognizable catharsis in works aspiring to tragedy."[56] The possibility of an "affronted" response to Joe's death merely substantiates the larger point I am making here. It demonstrates that the alteration of fictional conditions by which Faulkner makes our normal modes of response to violence seem inadequate or even inappropriate is effective enough in its disorientation for some to find it disturbing and thus "unacceptable." This is not to suggest that such responses *are* in fact illegitimate, only that within the context of Faulkner's fiction they are made to seem so.

Joe Christmas's death offers something of a definitive exemplification, in both its bloody and its transformative aspects, of the variant, cross-currented forms of imagining that characterize Faulkner's fiction. The crude horrors of realistic violence do not stop or interrupt his rhetorical power in this scene, they actually serve to engender it. That does not necessarily make this a cathartic moment, but it does make it a largely "unfathomable" one. The sounds of "real" life enter at the end of this sequence in the form of a fire siren, only to ascend and pass "out of the realm of hearing" as the siren mounts "toward its unbelievable crescendo." In part, that silent scream seems meant to express Joe's intolerable agony, which the rest of the sequence seeks to metaphorically redeem and put to imaginative rest. But whatever its emblematic function here, the sound of the siren "disappears" only where it might exist—in the realm of realistic imagining that constitutes but half (maybe less) of Faulkner's fictional world. The rhythms of the sentence that describe its passing out of hearing stay very much within a reader's ear. The sounds of life in Faulkner's work, whether that of a ten-gauge shotgun or dogs moiling beneath a bed or even those of a rape, cannot be thought of as somehow separate from the often quite different sounds of the writing that entertains their "possibility": a writing filled with rhythms that often seem less like something poured than driven. We have to *listen* to the violence in Faulkner's work: both the scream from that upstairs bedroom and the music that fills the house.

Flannery O'Connor

VIOLENCE AND THE DEMANDS OF ART

ALICE WALKER is one of the few readers who openly declares that she likes Flannery O'Connor "because she could *write*." Wary about issuing bulletins concerning O'Connor's fiction, Walker says: "if it can be said to be 'about' anything . . . it is 'about' prophets and prophecy, 'about' revelation, and 'about' the impact of supernatural grace on human beings who don't have a chance of spiritual grace without it." Her impatient quotation marks here are meant to suggest that these topics grant rather than restrict O'Connor's scope; that, yes, writers can still write about religious subjects like spiritual grace, revelation, and prophecy with urgency and poignancy. "After her great stories of sin, damnation, prophecy, and revelation," Walker adds, "the stories one reads casually in the average magazine seem to be about love and roast beef."[1]

It has been too frequently assumed, however, that the "greatness" of O'Connor's fiction resides in her subjects—her use of sin, damnation, and prophecy—rather than in the writing that makes them take on an odd, foreboding life. An overemphasis upon the religious dimension of O'Connor's work (whether by those celebrating or dismissing it) has in many ways weakened our understanding of her fiction's capacity for making other writing seem like "roast beef." Criticism often simply seems incapable of acknowledging the full power of moments like this one, early in "The Lame Shall Enter First":

> That afternoon Norton was alone in the house, squatting on the floor of his room arranging packages of flower seeds in rows around himself. Rain slashed against the window panes and rattled in the gutters. The room had grown dark but every few minutes it was lit by silent lightning and the seed packages showed up gaily on the floor. He squatted motionless like a large pale frog in the midst of this potential garden. All at once his eyes became alert. Without warning the rain had stopped. The silence was heavy as if the downpour had been hushed by violence. He remained motionless, only his eyes turning.
>
> Into the silence came the distinct click of a key turning in the front door lock . . .[2]

Rain seldom simply falls in O'Connor's fiction: it slashes or splatters or in some way comes down in a befouling, thickened state more like paint than water and less like either than, say, varnish or creosote. But the unmistakable O'Connor touch here resides not in the verbs but in the surreal reach of the similes, which transform what might otherwise be a fairly innocent scene into one of humorous grotesquerie and impending violence. We are in a world where gothic clichés (flashing lightning, hushed silence, a turning key) are simultaneously used and parodied, a world where Poe's Roderick Usher meets Emerson's Transparent Eyeball in the form of a "large pale frog." The fact that we may not know, exactly, what a large pale frog looks like (except, perhaps, in an illustrated children's book), or that we seldom conceive of rain as being obligated to "warn" us that it is preparing to stop, seems to have little to do with the evocative power of this kind of writing. Or rather, such odd conceits do not depend for their power upon our knowing or even pretending to know what in the world they might "mean."

This passage is purely transitional, designed to set the scene for the entrance of the ominous, club-footed Rufus Johnson, who comes in out of the rain "like an irate drenched crow" and whose look goes through the motherless Norton "like a pin" (p. 603). But I have purposefully chosen a moment that is seldom quoted or felt to hold any special significance for this story, to emphasize how charged a metaphoric atmosphere everywhere permeates O'Connor's writing. Even in "off" moments, the images and analogies in what she once called her "one-cylinder syntax"[3] flop around like dangerous sparking wires. (She resembles not only Nathanael West in this respect, as many have noted, but, more interestingly, Stephen Crane.) Nearly every image in her writing seems to be a "potential garden" of Boschian delights.

Louise Westling has noted how the fictional "presence" of some of O'Connor's women characters often seems too strong and too troubling for the limited roles they play. Their unexpected violence and the "strange intensity" of their hatred "leave us with a shocked curiosity."[4] The disproportionate, mutinous energy of O'Connor's imagination, however, is not limited to particular characters or even aspects of their psychology. It expresses itself more indelibly sentence to sentence, in images and phrases whose recalcitrance resists narrative intelligibility. The solitary intransigence of O'Connor's metaphors actually comes to seem less a peripheral aspect of her style than the fictional source from which her characters themselves spring. Enoch Emery's vividness as a character in *Wise Blood*, to cite but one example, stems less from his emblematic "secularity" or his supposed symbolic descent into animality than from the fact that he eats a candy bar "as if he had something against it" (p. 98).

No one familiar with O'Connor's work would dream of denying the importance of her Catholicism, partly because of the way she herself tried to mortify

195

morally obtuse readers with narrative astringencies like the aside about Joy Hopewell in "Good Country People": "As a child she had sometimes been subject to feelings of shame but education had removed the last traces of that as a good surgeon scrapes for cancer" (p. 281). But while we may agree with Arthur Kinney's contention that O'Connor's letters "display everywhere a concern with her faith even more passionate than a concern with her fiction,"[5] his "even more" should alert us to what most theological readings of her work conveniently forget: just how exacting O'Connor's sense of what can and cannot be done in fiction was. Surely O'Connor herself would have been disheartened by Kinney's contention that "once we understand O'Connor, her fictions always seem transparent."[6] She was often leery, healthily so, of themes or symbols that could be too easily extracted from or detected in fiction. "The word *symbol* scares a good many people off," she once said,

> just as the word *art* does. They seem to feel that a symbol is some mysterious thing put in arbitrarily by the writer to frighten the common reader—sort of a literary Masonic grip that is only for the initiated. They seem to think that it is a way of saying something that you aren't actually saying, and so if they can be got to read a reputedly symbolic work at all, they approach it as if it were a problem in algebra. Find *x*. And when they do find or think they find this abstraction, *x*, then they go off with an elaborate sense of satisfaction and the notion that they have "understood" the story.[7]

Many of O'Connor's readers seem to have forgotten warnings like this and proceed to "understand" her fiction in abstract, translative ways. Should someone, with justifiable exasperation, ask of this author the question a black cook puts to the unnamed child in "A Temple of the Holy Ghost"—"Howcome you be so ugly sometime?" (p. 203)—the critical response is predictable. Violence or "being ugly" in her fiction (like just about everything else) is thematically positioned, religiously annotated, or inscribed within a genealogy of "the grotesque." O'Connor placed a premium upon violence in her work, Gilbert Muller asserts (and he is representative of a great deal of O'Connor criticism when he does), "because it is a natural corollary of the grotesque": "The violence in Miss O'Connor's fiction is real, yet it has a metaphysical dimension arising from man's loss of theological identity. If in terms of effect this violence partakes of exaggeration, sensationalism, and shock, it nevertheless raises problems which treat the moral and religious order of the universe."[8]

O'Connor's fiction in this formulation is not gratuitous, yet its effects partake of "exaggeration, sensationalism, and shock." Her fictional violence is both real and metaphysical, theological and grotesque, and it originates, we are told, in the "metaphysics of man's loss of theological identity." But *how* does it thus originate while "nevertheless" remaining real? How does a nod in the direction of "the moral and religious order of the universe" help us know what to make, for example, of what one commentator calls the Misfit's "cornpone nihilism"[9] in "A Good Man Is Hard to Find"? (The grandmother he has just shot three times through the chest "would of been a good woman," the Misfit claims, "if it had been somebody there to shoot her every minute of her life" [p. 153]). The word "spirituality," André Bleikasten reminds us, usually seems "too smooth, too polished, too blandly civilized to apply to the compulsions and convulsions" of O'Connor's tormented characters.[10]

To read O'Connor's work with the kind of agile attention I think it deserves we have to avoid the temptation either to simplify or to ennoble it. We have to resist the temptation to tame or explain away its tempestuous, eruptive power or to dull the sharpness of its humor. (And we have to forego these reductive explanatory tendencies, it should be added, even when they are adduced by O'Connor herself.) To read her fiction well involves attuning ourselves to constant shifts of authorial sympathy and distance, extensions and retractions of affection on the part of the author, which sometimes seem almost capricious. Why as readers do we sometimes feel like acting as defense attorneys for her characters? How much, we find ourselves asking, does one part of O'Connor like the characters that another part of her likes to wipe out?

O'CONNOR, TO ADAPT Robert Frost's description of Edwin Arlington Robinson, chose the old-fashioned way to be new. "There is such a thing," Frost asserted, "as being too willing to be different."

> And what shall we say to people who are not only willing but anxious? What assurance have they that their difference is not insane, eccentric, abortive, unintelligible? Two fears should follow us through life. There is the fear that we shan't prove worthy in the eyes of someone who knows us at least as well as we know ourselves. That is the fear of God. And there is the fear of Man—the fear that men won't understand us and we shall be cut off from them. . . . It has been said that recognition in art is all. Better say correspondence is all. Mind must convince mind that it can uncurl and wave the same filaments of subtlety, soul convince soul that it can give off the same shimmers of eternity. At no point would anyone but a brute fool want to break off this correspondence. It is all there is to satisfaction; and it is salutary to live in the fear of its being broken off.[11]

Both O'Connor and Frost publicly avowed that they valued human communication and "correspondence"—they knew what a brute fool fails to see—but they also seemed to value it most when it was in danger "of being broken off." In the work of both these writers there is a complicated relationship between the desire to be understood by and humanly connected to others and the wish to prove worthy in the eyes of God or a literary tradition. Both acknowledge the need for conventions, for orthodoxy, for the vitality of communal traditions of life and expression ("it is all there is to satisfaction"); yet both of them are also wary of the constraints and conformities which accompany the virtues of a community or a "home." The danger of being unintelligible is matched for them only by the danger of being too easily known. The only thing worse than an overeagerness to be different is an inability to be different enough.

In Frost's case, the cultural availability of his poetry, exemplified in his use of idiomatic speech, dissuades us, as Richard Poirier argues, from freely recognizing "his extraordinary capacity for *not* communicating." Frost "takes enormous pleasure in knowing all the ways in which the messages received by his readers are in fact never sent, never delivered, constantly detoured, interrupted, readdressed, returned unopened, or, especially, returned because of insufficient postage."[12] O'Connor's work reveals a similar tendency in her abiding affection for Southern vernacular. "The Southern writer's greatest tie with the South is through his ear," she insisted: "a distinctive idiom is a powerful instrument for keeping fiction social." "When one Southern character speaks, regardless of his station in life, an echo of all Southern life is heard" (*MM*, p. 199). Yet nothing is more characteristic of O'Connor's writing than her use of vernacular speech to ravage the very source from which it might be seen to arise. "The sourness, the angularity of the conceptions, the purity of the ear and style" in her work, Elizabeth Hardwick aptly contends, form "a southern literature that is a devastation of southernness."[13]

O'Connor believed strongly, as did Frost about poetry, in the "nature" of fiction, in its demands, inconveniences, necessities, and limitations—all words she repeatedly uses to describe it. ("You can do anything you can get away with" in fiction, she once remarked, "but nobody has ever gotten away with much" [*MM*, p. 76].) Wedded to this conviction was her equally firm sense of what Frost did not feel compelled to maintain—the fact that a "writer can choose what he writes about but he cannot choose what he is able to make live" (*MM*, p. 27). For O'Connor, such an assertion is meant to remind readers that the nature of fictional talent is more enigmatic than it may be convenient for them to recall. But it also offers a protective apologia for her own imaginative temperament, which others and often she herself felt needed justification.

It needed justifying largely because O'Connor could never quite rid herself of the specter of her potential audience. Her repeated chastisements of "the tired reader" who "comes home at night" and "wishes to read something that will lift up his heart" (*MM*, p. 47) represent not confident dismissals but an irritated testimony to the enduring presence of such readers for her. "You may say that the serious writer doesn't have to bother about the tired reader," she continues, "but he does, because they are all tired. One old lady who wants her heart lifted up wouldn't be so bad, but you multiply her two hundred and fifty thousand times and what you get is a book club" (*MM*, p. 48). In O'Connor's view, what opposed the artistic demands of fiction was the necessity of communicating to unbudged readers who wanted "Instant Uplift" (*MM*, p. 165), readers whose very presence compromised and vitiated those demands. This fierce ambivalence characterized her relationship with the Catholic Church as well. She respectfully acknowledged that "it is one of the functions of the Church to transmit the prophetic vision that is good for all time, and when the novelist has this as part of his own vision, he has a powerful extension of sight" (*MM*, pp. 179–80). But she also felt that the Catholic novelist "frequently becomes so entranced with his Christian state that he forgets his nature as a fiction writer" (*MM*, p. 170). "The final standard" for "the serious novelist" she avowed—in what might usefully serve as the compulsory epigraph for the next ten studies of O'Connor—will have to be "the demands of art, which are a good deal more exacting than the demands of the Church" (*MM*, pp. 183–84).[14]

O'Connor invokes the demands of both art and the Church when she addresses the presence of violence in her work, but the reader familiar with her fiction may not always find her remarks helpful:

> in my own stories I have found that violence is strangely capable of returning my characters to reality and preparing them to accept their moment of grace. Their heads are so hard that almost nothing else will do the work. This idea, that reality is something to which we must be returned at considerable cost, is one which is seldom understood by the casual reader, but it is one which is implicit in the Christian view of the world. (*MM*, p. 112)

"Violence is strangely capable of returning my characters to reality": O'Connor speaks of violence here as if she were diagnosing her characters and discussing the properties of a special fictional antibiotic. It is clear, even to the most "casual reader" (a dour, defensive phrase) that there is *something* in much of her fiction, whether we call it a "return to reality" or not, which exacts a "considerable cost." Atheism or spiritual indifference may destroy the soul, but probably not as efficiently as O'Connor disposes of some of her characters. Her God, Frederick Crews remarks, often manifests himself in "exercises of power less reminiscent of the New Testament than of Jahweh at his most dyspeptic."[15]

This does not necessarily represent a liability in her fiction. In moments when O'Connor asserts, for instance, that the South offers the Catholic novelist "exploitable benefits" (*MM*, p. 201) that other areas do not, she seems to me refreshingly free from squeamishness about acknowledging what Poirier has aptly called literature's "resourceful brutality," its "'use' of characters as merely one of many expressive, 'compositional' resources."[16] (Vladimir Nabokov was not averse, at times, to calling his characters "galley slaves.") Nevertheless, O'Connor was not always forthcoming about why the tribute of pain requisite for her moments of grace often seems as important, if not more so, than the "reality" it supposedly helps invoke. She frequently encouraged her readers, in effect, to read against the grain of their own response. In her remarks in 1963 at Hollins College, introducing her reading of "A Good Man Is Hard to Find," she told her audience that she was going to read them "the story of a family of six, which, on its way to Florida, gets wiped out by an escaped convict who calls himself the Misfit" (*MM*, p. 109). But "you should be on the lookout for such things as the action of grace in the Grandmother's soul," O'Connor tells them, "and not for the dead bodies" (*MM*, p. 113):

> I don't have any pretensions to being an Aeschylus or Sophocles and providing you in this story with a cathartic experience out of your mythic background, though this story I'm going to read certainly calls up a good deal of the South's mythic background, and it should elicit from you a degree of pity and terror, even though its way of being serious is a comic one. I do think, though, that like the Greeks you should know what is going to happen in this story so that any element of suspense in it will be transferred from its surface to its interior.
>
> I would be most happy if you had already read it, happier still if you knew it well. (*MM*, pp. 108–9)

This is but one of several moments in which O'Connor attempts to circumvent a fascination with her fiction that she obviously felt was all too likely to occur and that familiarity would help subvert. But in warning her listeners that the violence in her work is meant to be more than just gripping or sensational, she seems to suggest that it can be "more" only when it has been divorced from the dramatic intensity of the story. The type of reading encouraged here is the equivalent of the television broadcasts of Elvis Presley—contemporaneous with her writing—which rendered him less threatening by filming him only from the waist up. O'Connor often seems anxious to restrict in her readers the free will she readily grants and argues for in her characters. In viewing violence as a prelude to a redemptive act, she invokes a presumption of narrative order that over and over again she purposefully baffles in her fiction.[17]

O'Connor's terms here also seem unhelpful. What constitutes "interior suspense"? How are the "transfers" of suspense from surface to interior verbally effected? How does knowing what is going to happen in a story alter the qualities of its suspense? A footnote to "the Greeks" does not get us very far here, because knowing, for example, that Oedipus or the Misfit is going to perpetrate a violent act does not in itself ensure that his doing so will be any less terrifying (as opposed to startling). In these and other remarks, O'Connor in effect makes the "action of grace" one of the literary Masonic grips she warned her readers not to be intimidated by, and many critics have followed her lead. In admitting this, however, there has been an error in the opposite direction. Some critics seem to feel that they can somehow outsmart O'Connor by tearing her stories open to meanings she herself did not recognize. (This has been the strategy of the so-called sympathy-for-the-devil reading of her work initiated by John Hawkes's 1962 essay and expanded upon by Bleikasten and others.[18]) The effort to describe O'Connor's fiction accurately is not the same as encountering it only with a view to discovering what she is saying in spite of herself. What we need to confront, both in and out of her fiction, are her mixed motives in both encouraging readers to read stories in a certain way and then slapping their hands when they do.

VIOLENCE IS SO COMMON in O'Connor's work that we might be tempted to assert that like Mrs. Pritchard in "A Circle in the Fire," O'Connor "required the taste of blood from time to time to keep her equilibrium" (p. 246). What reaches her, we might ask (in adapting a line from one of Frank Bidart's poem); what reaches her except disaster? Yet the prevalence of violence in her fiction should not weaken our attention to the complicated imaginative contexts from which it emerges. Although O'Connor was an advocate of realistic imagining, she was not enamored of traditional realism in fiction, and she thought of herself as "a realist of distances" (*MM*, p. 46). She was quick to warn that the contemporary novelistic "orthodoxy" that demanded "a realism of fact" concerned with "social or economic or psychological forces" (*MM*, pp. 39, 38) narrowed rather than broadened the scope of fiction. (This conviction was partly behind her reluctance to portray much of the Civil Rights movement in her work.[19]) "The deeper kinds of realism" (*MM*, p. 39), she argued, while fully committed to sensory realism, "will always be pushing [their] own limits outward toward the limits of mystery" (*MM*, p. 41) and attempting to show that "the meaning of a story does not begin except at a depth where adequate motivation and adequate psychology and the various determinations have been exhausted" (*MM*, pp. 41–42).

That O'Connor was capable of uninterrupted passages of realistic violence is apparent in a moment from *The Violent Bear It Away*. Rayber, the rationalistic, "published" schoolteacher, takes Tarwater and his idiot-son Bishop to the natural history museum so he can stretch Tarwater's "mind by introducing him to his ancestor, the fish, and to all the great wastes of unexplored time" (p. 417). They stop in the city park before they get to the museum, and as they sit down on a park bench, Bishop—who Frederick Asals rightly asserts is an "intimate reminder" to Rayber "of the idiocy he perceives in the universe, and in himself"[20]—lies "sprawled and grinning" in Rayber's lap and conjures up "his hated love for the child":

> He held Bishop rigidly. Although the child started the pain, he also limited it, contained it. He had learned this one terrible afternoon when he had tried to drown him.
>
> He had taken him to the beach, two hundred miles away, intending to effect the accident as quickly as possible and return bereaved. It had been a beautiful calm day in May. The beach, almost empty, had stretched down into the gradual swell of ocean. There was nothing to be seen but an expanse of sea and sky and sand and an occasional figure, stick-like, in the distance. He had taken him out on his shoulders and when he was chest deep in the water, had lifted him off, swung the delighted child high in the air and then plunged him swiftly below the surface on his back and held him there, not looking down at what he was doing but up, at an imperturbable witnessing sky, not quite blue, not quite white.
>
> A fierce surging pressure had begun upward beneath his hands and grimly he had exerted more and more force downward. In a second, he felt he was trying to hold a giant under. Astonished, he let himself look. The face under the water was wrathfully contorted, twisted by some primeval rage to save itself. Automatically he released his pressure. Then when he realized what he had done, he pushed down again angrily with all his force until the struggle ceased under his hands. He stood sweating in the water, his own mouth as slack as the child's had been. The body, caught by an undertow, almost got away from him but he managed to come to himself and snatch it. Then as he looked at it, he had a moment of complete terror in which he envisioned his life without the child. He began to shout frantically. He plowed his way out of the water with the limp body. The beach which he had thought empty before had become peopled with strangers converging on him from all directions. A bald-headed man in red and blue Roman striped shorts began at once to administer artificial respiration. Three wailing women and a photographer appeared. The next day there had been a picture in the paper, showing the rescuer, striped bottom forward, working over the child. Rayber was beside him on his knees, watching with an agonized expression. The caption said, OVERJOYED FATHER SEES SON REVIVED. (Pp. 418–19)

O'Connor remains noncommittal and unobtrusive as an authorial voice here, and her distance from the actions she describes—even Rayber's moment of "complete terror in which he envisioned his life without the child"—creates an unnerving effect of uninvolved clarity. By remaining disquietingly unperturbed by and aloof from scenes most of us would find unbearable even to describe, O'Connor seems to display a hypercoldness some consider theatrical. Her narrators often seem to display the amorality of a hired gun. In this moment, unlike Rayber, O'Connor neither looks away nor experiences a change of heart. She seems more concerned with obliquely suggesting the fatuity of the newspaper's incongruous headline splash than she is with having us understand Rayber's resolve "to effect the accident as quickly as possible and return bereaved." There is little textual indication that we are to read this scene as one of figurative baptism. Bishop is neither a Little Father Time figure in this scene nor an emblem of primeval idiocy being conquered by rationalism. He is first an intolerably helpless child and then simply a "limp body" caught by an undertow. Joyce Carol Oates's more general comment about O'Connor's fiction is specifically applicable here: "there is nothing to be recognized—there is only an experience to be suffered."[21]

Yet there is an experience here for a reader to imaginatively suffer only because its realistic form has made sensory pain and our effort to feel its presence a crucial imaginative issue. I think Asals is mistaken in asserting that as Rayber "rushes out of the water with the body, the heroic ordeal dissolves into the farce of a mock pietà-and-resurrection."[22] The farce here (if such we call it) lies in the newspaper's treatment of the scene. The next day's picture, "showing the rescuer, striped bottom forward, working over the child," seems only incidentally amusing. It is a realistic detail attesting to the clumsy physicality of moments of emergency rescue, and we can turn it into a mock-religious icon only when we pull back from the motions of our reading experience.

The only comfort afforded by such a scene resides, ironically, in the very depth with which its violence is made disquieting, in the Jamesian degree of "felt life" its verbal illusion encompasses. The implicit affirmation here is that "to write at all," as Poirier has put it, "is to salvage, however reluctantly, some part of the existent humanity, the formulae and codes that belong to a shared human inheritance, even if your writing is an invitation to reject or disperse it."[23] What becomes an issue in reading O'Connor is whether or not this salvaging of "existent humanity" is so coldly executed as to seem merely perfunctory. Yet to accuse O'Connor of gratuitousness or cruelty in this moment is to indict not her but the nature of realistic imagining. Her distanced refusal to mitigate or condemn Rayber's actions, to grant us any felt sign of her authorial presence, establishes her commitment to the demands of realism. That commitment is not exclusionary, for the realism here is quickly surrounded by the novel's complicated context of baptismal imagery and biblical allusion. But the larger thematic concerns of O'Connor's fiction can never quite absorb or "explain" the startling power of its local effects.

MARTHA STEPHENS has noted "the tonal problem that exists in one degree or another in nearly all of O'Connor's fiction": the problem "of how to 'take,' how to react to, the disasters that befall her characters." Most of her short stories, Stephens says, "can be viewed as admonitory parables." But a reader is not without justification in finding the terms of the admonition disturbing:

> One does not mean to say that O'Connor's depiction of human suffering is . . . gratuitous [again, this word]; the reader's frustration comes from not being able to share, from being, indeed, sometimes repelled by, the authorial attitude towards the events described.
>
> There is a sense in which, as I have suggested, the O'Connor stories are designed as calculated affronts to humanistic thought. One often has the feeling . . . of being initially quite in harmony with the authorial viewpoint, of enjoying the story exactly in the way it seemed meant to be enjoyed, and then of being—often almost without warning—shaken violently off the track, so that one feels almost deliberately shut out from the final, and thus the overall experience of the story.[24]

Another, less "frustrated," way of putting this would be to say that we often feel an authorial presence in O'Connor's fiction, but not the controlling, directing presence of a writer beyond ourselves whom we can constantly acknowledge as the source of the story. We do not always feel the personalness of O'Connor's presence in her work, but nothing says she is required to provide it. Noting the lack of a personalized voice in her fiction is not the same as wanting her to be more personable.

O'Connor's story "Greenleaf," which won first place in the O'Henry Awards in 1956, involves violence that is kept plausible but that also strives for effects beyond the scope of plausibility. It provides a useful litmus test by which to measure the antihumanistic venom in O'Connor's fiction and her manner of verbally shutting readers out and shaking them violently off the track. The story structurally resembles the overly annotated "A Good Man Is Hard to Find." Both begin with domestic squabbles and the wry comedy of having various characters colliding with, baiting, and annoying each other. Both end with startlingly violent events that depend upon the comedy of manners preceding them for their darkened affective power, and both also end with female characters who may experience some kind of revelation in their moment of death. In "Greenleaf" many of the premonitory verbal gestures that precede Mrs. May's being gored by a scrub bull are recognized as foreshadowings only when we reread the story. Nothing reasonably ensures that a reader will remember Mrs. Greenleaf's previous cry, "Oh Jesus, stab me in the heart!" (p. 506), at the climax of the story or Mrs. May's wish to tell her seemingly heartless and needling sons that "you'll find out one of these days, you'll find out what *Reality* is when it's too late!" (p. 510). In fact, these seem like just the kind of details an earnest English teacher might be proud to point out to inattentive students. According the story that kind of coherence means ignoring other of its elements that compromise the convenience of such cross-referenced thematic parallelism.

The narrative floats in and out of Mrs. May's dreamings and her imaginations of what others might say and do, and her free indirect discourse tinges many of the descriptive passages in the story. As Carol Shloss, the most engaging critic of the story, points out, Mrs. May is not herself responsible for the mythical attributes with which the scrub bull is endowed. The omniscience that marks the story's opening informs us that the bull was "like some patient god come down to woo her" (p. 501), that it is "like an uncouth country suitor" (p. 502), and that the "hedge-wreath" caught in the tips of its horns looks "like a menacing prickly crown" (p. 502). These figurative annotations are lost upon Mrs. May and, to a certain extent, upon the reader. For while the bull is embellished with associations, it is not, Shloss notes, "just a symbol, but a farm animal." It has not been "metamorphized into something unsubstantial," and it is not "the key to an allegorical reading of the text."[25] The parallel circumstances of Mrs. May's death and Mrs. Greenleaf's plea that Jesus stab her in the heart cannot be ignored, but neither can the parallel be turned into a parable. To elevate that parallel into an exclusive interpretation would be to see the bull as Jesus and Mrs. May's goring as her encounter with God. Such a reading, Shloss rightly asserts, would "give final authority to what is incidental in effect."[26]

Shloss herself, however, tends to simplify Mrs. May, asserting that she subscribes to a narrow work ethic "of making gardens and washing clothes," as if these were self-evidently absurd activities. Mrs. May may be a "brittle, highly agitated widow"[27] but O'Connor does not entirely scorn her as a character or make her simply a reactionary paranoid we would just as soon see gored. Her two cynical sons Wesley and Scofield heap ridicule upon their mother, but O'Connor seems as distantly amused by their merciless baiting of their mother as she is by Mrs. May's smothering affection for her sons and her hapless status anxieties. After Scofield growls at his mother that "you're always yapping about when-you-die . . . but you look pretty healthy to me" (p. 511), we are privy to a paraphrase of Mrs. May's private musings:

> Her city friends said she was the most remarkable woman they knew, to go, practi-
> cally penniless and with no experience, out to a rundown farm and make a success
> of it. "Everything is against you," she would say, "the weather is against you and the

dirt is against you and the help is against you. They're all in league against you. There's nothing for it but an iron hand!"

"Look at Mamma's iron hand!" Scofield would yell and grab her arm and hold it up so that her delicate blue-veined little hand would dangle from her wrist like the head of a broken lily. The company always laughed. (P. 511)

From this moment alone, a reader might think that an author capable of describing Mrs. May's "delicate blue-veined little hand" dangling "like the head of a broken lily" might sympathize with her vulnerability and be eager to show up the cruelty of her son's mockery. But while O'Connor does not endorse Scofield's abrasive derision, she also remains glacially aloof from Mrs. May's self-pitying laments.

In another kind of O'Connor story it might be Scofield or the "thin and nervous and bald" Wesley, an intellectual on a salt-free diet, who would be gored. Part of the reason Mrs. May is singled out to be killed seems to be that she is a woman. The distasteful phallic implications of being gored would be lost were a bull to bury his head "like a wild tormented lover" (p. 523) in Scofield's or Mr. Greenleaf's lap. But another reason Scofield seems relatively "safe" in this story—and one could use worse terms in discussing O'Connor's fiction—is that he at least expresses his anger, while his anxious mother merely seethes in disapproving silence. It is always a bad sign when an O'Connor character slights religion or the workings of religious passion, no matter how clotted or twisted their expression—bad in the sense that the Lord exacts retribution. (In one of her book reviews O'Connor bemoaned the fact that contemporary children were forming their image of Christ not from "the stern and majestic Pantacrator" of medieval times but from "a smiling Jesus with a bleeding heart," "which neither mind nor stomach can any longer take."[28]) So when we learn that Mrs. May wishes her boys would go to church so they "would meet some nice girls" (p. 510) and that "she thought the word, Jesus, should be kept inside the church building like other words inside the bedroom" (p. 506), our sense is that these pious timidities may serve as invitations to a beheading.

Mrs. Greenleaf represents one of the more powerful embodiments of the unrestrained irrationality that seems to threaten Mrs. May. Mrs. Greenleaf's prayer healing consists of her moaning and flailing "her huge arms" over a hole in which she has buried "all the morbid stories out of the newspaper—the accounts of women who had been raped and criminals who had escaped and children who had been burned and of train wrecks and plane crashes and the divorces of movie stars [a wry, unexpected touch]" (p. 505). She is comically portrayed by O'Connor, but Miles Orvell rightly notes that the "the grotesque agony" of "her Job-like self-abasement, takes on the quality of an authentic backwoods devotion."[29] When Mrs. May hears Mrs. Greenleaf's "guttural agonized voice" groaning "Jesus! Jesus!" with "a terrible urgency," she "stopped still, one hand lifted to her throat. The sound was so piercing that she felt as if some violent unleashed force had broken out of the ground and was charging toward her. Her second thought was more reasonable: somebody had been hurt on the place and would sue her for everything she had. She had no insurance" (p. 506).

Mrs. May's lifting one hand to her throat here seems to be both a protective gesture and an attempt, as it were, to touch a sound that seems ominous in its conceptual "piercing." Mrs. May's second thought is apparently "reasonable" (and not vapid or mercenary), but only to *her*, the free indirect discourse indicates, not to O'Connor. Her first "thought"—that the cry "Jesus! Jesus!" is like "some violent unleashed force" charging toward her—is but one of several imaginations of piercing, invasive force. When inspecting O. T. and E. T. Greenleaf's clean, well-lighted milking room, Mrs. May is "conscious that the sun was directly on top of her head, like a silver bullet ready to drop into her brain" (p. 515). But in what sense is she "conscious" of this figurative possibility? Is she aware only that the sun is "directly on top of her head" or that it is also "like a silver bullet ready to drop into her brain"? If the mythical associations O'Connor ascribes to the bull are lost upon Mrs. May, how much else is? This uncertainty as to what capacity a character has for fashioning images for his or her own feelings remains a perplexing effect both in this story and more generally in O'Connor's fiction.

The vague conditional form of Mrs. May's feeling *as if* some violent unleashed force threatens her hearkens back to the first paragraphs of the story when "she had been conscious in her sleep of a steady rhythmic chewing as if something were eating one wall of the house. She had been aware that whatever it was had been eating as long as she had had the place . . . [and] would continue through the house, eating her and the boys, and then on, eating everything but the Greenleafs, on and on" (p. 501). The bull chews shrubbery outside an actual window as well as inside Mrs. May's drifting, apparitional dream-consciousness. Her "paranoia or fear of life impinging on and consuming the self" is paramount, Shloss notes, and the bull acts as a catalyst for her "most deep-seated anxieties," her "fear of defeat by some force that will destroy everything *except* the Greenleafs."[30] The degree to which Mrs. May is aware of this catalyst, however, remains ambiguous. She "*had been* conscious in her sleep" of the sounds of chewing: was Mrs. May dreaming of these sounds or more fully cognizant of them? O'Connor leaves open the possibility that Mrs. May does not remember her projected anxieties about the Greenleafs:

"When the munching reached her elbow, she jumped up and found herself, fully awake, standing in the middle of her room" (p. 502). But what Mrs. May quickly "identifies" is only the sound of a bull tearing at the shrubbery.

Various figurative elements of Mrs. May's fearful fantasies converge in a dream she has the night before going out to have the bull killed. Once again it is unclear whether what has become ominous foreshadowing for us has become so for her:

> Half the night in her sleep she heard a sound as if some large stone were grinding a hole on the outside wall of her brain. She was walking on the inside, over a succession of beautiful rolling hills, planting her stick in front of each step. She became aware after a time that the noise was the sun trying to burn through the tree line and she stopped to watch, safe in the knowledge that it couldn't, that it had to sink the way it always did outside of her property. When she first stopped it was a swollen red ball, but as she stood watching it began to narrow and pale until it looked like a bullet. Then suddenly it burst through the tree line and raced down the hill toward her. She woke up with her hand over her mouth and the same noise, diminished but distinct, in her ear. It was the bull munching under the window. Mr. Greenleaf had let him out. (P. 519)

The sound of "the sun trying to burn through the tree line" is described "as if some large stone were grinding a hole on the outside of her brain" and this then turns out to be the sound of the bull "munching under her window." Sound here is almost entirely conceptual, not sensory. It figuratively foreshadows Mrs. May's death (or so we know at the end of the story), but that foreshadowing is only for the reader, not for Mrs. May. Her dream serves not to weaken but to steel her resolve to get rid of the bull: "This is the last night I am going to put up with this, she said" (p. 519). Mrs. May's inability to attend to her dreams properly comes to seem like a self-indictment. Her problem, we are made to feel, is that she cannot properly interpret the story in which she appears.

This bears the subtle marks of a dramatic setup, as if O'Connor were giving her character every possible warning of impending violence but in terms she cannot possibly understand. Mrs. May is not entirely unlike certain "expendable" figures in movies who take risks that invite violence that then seems almost appropriate. John Fraser charmingly refers to these figures as "career victims," characters who presume a little too much on the world's treating them benevolently: "the over-sanguine homesteaders in Indian territory, for example, or the pea-brained blonde who inevitably goes prospecting in the cellars of the castle where she is spending the night, quite as if she herself had never seen a horror movie in her life."[31] O'Connor's foreshadowing sometimes seems so obvious that Bleikasten has called it "the fictional equivalent of pre-destination."[32] But precisely *what* is being foreshadowed is not made explicit as the story proceeds. O'Connor seems to realize that to make Mrs. May malignant enough for us to welcome her violent comeuppance would be to sponsor the coherence and comfort of a dramatic reprisal—one we could then confidently denounce or applaud. By merging a kind of psychological realism with what might be called unfinished allegory, O'Connor subverts simple terms of sympathy or victimization—which leads us to the end of the story.

As she drives out to the fields with Mr. Greenleaf (who is angry and agitated because, as he says "in a high rasping voice," it "ain't nobody ever ast me to shoot my boy's own bull!"), the prospect of getting rid of the bull sharpens Mrs. May's senses: "Birds were screaming everywhere, the grass was almost too bright to look at, the sky was an even piercing blue. "Spring is here!" she said gaily. Mr. Greenleaf lifted one muscle somewhere near his mouth as if he found this the most asinine remark ever made" (p. 520). O'Connor's narrative detachment here allows her to make the "screaming" birds, the "piercing" blue sky, and the grass that glares a bit desperately seem a little dangerous (as well as cheerful or asinine). At the same time, what passes for objective description here functions almost as a social rejoinder. O'Connor's description of Mr. Greenleaf's physical reaction to Mrs. May's remark suggests, in its flattened verbal indifference ("one muscle somewhere near his mouth"), that it might represent the most appropriate response in this instance. Mrs. May's gaiety obviously does not seem trumpery or malicious to her, but that is precisely what is wrong with it—or so O'Connor suggests by icily withholding any kindred sense of celebration.

While Mr. Greenleaf goes to search for the bull, Mrs. May lies back on the hood of her car, parked in the center of the pasture, and decides, with her eyes closed, that she is tired "because she had been working continuously for fifteen years." She has "every right to be tired" she feels, "before any kind of judgement seat, she would be able to say: I've worked, I have not wallowed" (p. 522). O'Connor emphasizes Mrs. May's bland self-congratulation by having her recall that she once "tactfully" told Mr. Greenleaf that his wife had "let religion warp her": "everything in moderation you know." Mrs. May dozes for ten minutes and then wonders, upon awakening, if perhaps Mr. Greenleaf has been gored by the bull in the woods: "The irony of it deepened: O. T. and E. T. would then get a shyster lawyer and sue her. It would be the fitting end to her fifteen years with the Greenleafs. She thought of it almost with pleasure as if she had hit on the perfect ending for a story she was telling her friends. Then she dropped it, for Mr. Greenleaf had a gun with him and she had insurance" (p. 523).

After apparently forgetting that the bull has previously attacked one of the Greenleaf boys' trucks, Mrs. May honks the car horn several times, and "the perfect ending for a story" begins with the bull coming "toward her at a slow gallop, a gay almost rocking gait as if he were overjoyed to find her again" (a possibility the narrator alone entertains):

> She looked back and saw that the bull, his head lowered, was racing toward her. She remained perfectly still, not in fright, but in freezing unbelief. She stared at the violent black streak bounding toward her as if she had no sense of distance, as if she could not decide at once what his intention was, and the bull had buried his head in her lap, like a wild tormented lover, before her expression changed. One of his horns sank until it pierced her heart and the other curved around her side and held her in an unbreakable grip. She continued to stare straight ahead but the entire scene in front of her had changed—the tree line was a dark wound in a world that was nothing but sky—and she had the look of a person whose sight has been suddenly restored but who finds the light unbearable.
>
> Mr. Greenleaf was running toward her from the side with his gun raised and she saw him coming though she was not looking in his direction. She saw him approaching on the outside of some invisible circle, the tree line gaping behind him and nothing under his feet. He shot the bull four times through the eye. She did not hear the shots but she felt the quake in the huge body as it sank, pulling her forward on its head, so that she seemed, when Mr. Greenleaf reached her, to be bent over whispering some last discovery into the animal's ear. (Pp. 523–24)

Louise Gossett argues that the violence of Mrs. May's death "welds together the hatred of the sons for the mother and the vulgar pride of the mother," but, she asserts, "such an emphatic treatment of the sensations of violence is uncharacteristic of Miss O'Connor's fiction, for the act is generally subordinate to the disturbed state of the person committing it."[33] But *how* have Mrs. May's "vulgar pride" and the hatred of her sons been "welded" together? Mrs. May's death, in the dramatic terms of the story, results from an accident she has unwittingly helped precipitate by honking the horn. The language of the scene implies that there may be more involved than such a bald summary suggests, but it does not provide us with the "emphatic treatment of the sensations of violence."

"She continued to stare straight ahead but the entire scene in front of her had changed—the tree line was a dark wound in a world that was nothing but sky": this is the only moment (aside from Mrs. May's obliquely seeing Mr. Greenleaf approach and feeling the "quake" as the dying bull sinks) in which we are given her perspective on the scene. We know nothing about her physical sensations in this moment. We know only what those sensations engender for her: a drastic alteration of her vision (though in one way she has only projected one more aspect of herself—now her wound rather than her anxiety about the Greenleafs—onto the exterior world.)[34] What we are given in place of Mrs. May's sensations is an external consciousness that tells us that she stares "as if she had no sense of distance," that she is immobilized not by fright but by "a freezing unbelief" (a suggestive but not exclusively religious phrase), that the bull "buried his head in her lap, like a wild tormented lover," that her expression changed to "the look of a person whose sight has been suddenly restored but who finds the light unbearable," that one of the bull's horns "sank until it pierced her heart," and finally that she seems "to be bent over whispering some last discovery into the animal's ear." The figurative endowments the narrator provides remain almost entirely abstract and conceptual. (What does a "wild tormented lover" look like? Is "the look of a person whose sight has been suddenly restored but who finds the light unbearable" an easily identifiable facial expression?) Yet these figurative glosses do not entirely invalidate the scene's realistic elements: the fact, for instance, that Mrs. May's shocked and loosening perception sees Mr. Greenleaf with "nothing under his feet" or that she does not hear the shot but feels the bull sag in death. Still, most readers will find Mr. Greenleaf's shooting the bull "four times through the eye" without hitting its victim an unlikely feat of marksmanship, and the language of the scene does not allow us to dismiss such complaints as misplaced demands for realism.

What epitomizes the mixture of realism and metaphor here is the fact that one of the bull's horns "sank until it pierced her heart [while] the other curved around her side and held her in an unbreakable grip." The word "sank" here evokes a distinctly sensory effect. But is Mrs. May's pierced heart an actual organ, a nest of ventricles, arteries, and aortas, or is it a figurative quantity, something a wild tormented lover might seek to pierce? The description is physically plausible—if the bull's head is in her lap, one horn could pierce her chest while the other held her side. But it still seems no mistake that the horn pierces her heart rather than, say, puncturing her lung.

The closing moments of the story are obviously meant to reach beyond the language and implications of naturalism alone (we have more here than simply the report of a tragic accident à la Theodore Dreiser or Frank Norris). O'Connor wishes to harvest the associative dimensions of "the perfect ending for a story," but that wish is precariously balanced against her desire to be realistically accountable. She must figuratively sidestep the visceral elements of Mrs. May's death while simultaneously implying their presence. The simple explanation for what happens here is set in a context that from the start of the story (when the bull is said to be "like some patient god come down to woo her") is meant to modify that explanatory simplicity. Here as elsewhere, O'Connor's desire for a larger symbolic reverberation, an "added dimension," was kept in check by what Shloss calls "a self-conscious discipline which had its origins in the Jamesian belief that the dramatic force of short-story writing would be dissipated by interpretive reflection."[35] Shloss goes on to argue, however, that "Greenleaf" embodies a familiar narrative pattern in O'Connor's fiction: "unexpected violence forces a farm widow to reevaluate her life." "It is clear that dying effects a change in [Mrs. May's] perspective," she says, and the import of her seeming to whisper "some last discovery" into the bull's ear is "unambiguously connected with a revelation." The problem "is not simply to identify the moment of insight, but to ascribe a more specific content to Mrs. May's final vision," and that content, she contends, is not necessarily religious: "calling the bull an agent of destruction and the catalyst for Mrs. May's awakening is totally different from contending that the bull is an example of spirit incarnate in flesh, a symbol of grace."[36]

Yet Shloss's contention is "totally different" in only one way, for she still assumes that Mrs. May has an "awakening" that is independent of, and more important than, the verbal means by which its possibility is entertained. She does not consider that Mrs. May's death effects a change less in her perspective than in *our* perspective on her. Instead of thinking that we should "ascribe a more specific content to Mrs. May's vision" (or discuss the difficulty of doing so), we might see the story as an exemplification of O'Connor's own powers of ascription.

Mrs. May's final moments are not, in fact, "unambiguously connected with a revelation": "She did not hear the shots but she felt the quake in the huge body as it sank, pulling her forward on its head, so that she seemed, when Mr. Greenleaf reached her, to be bent over whispering some last discovery into the animal's ear." "She *seemed* . . . to be whispering some last discovery," but it is not Mr. Greenleaf but the narrator who says she seemed to be doing this. Mrs. May seems to have had her sight suddenly restored, and she seems to have made some last discovery, but these narrative possibilities might be as lost upon her as were the metaphoric attributes with which the narrator earlier endowed the bull. To insist that Mrs. May has been granted a revelation (and then argue about what its content might be) is to miss the darker implications of O'Connor's hesitant realism.

There seems to be an "allegorical" or metaphoric dimension to the narrative action in the final scene, but it is not established in any incontestable way.[37] The allegorical possibilities are granted a flickering, conditional verbal life; they are neither firmly discounted nor confirmed. "The allegorist who admires realism [or vice versa]," E. M. Halliday reminds us, "is constantly pulled in two directions at once, and is very lucky when he can prevent one or the other of his meanings from unbalancing him."[38] O'Connor provides us, in Mrs. May's death, with a simultaneous impression of the accidental and of the inevitable and foreshadowed (Mrs. May was bound to "get" it). There is no clear choice in this story between two distinct modes of reading, one clarifying realistic, the other figurative or allegorical possibilities. It is the reader rather than Mrs. May who hesitates uneasily between these two ways of reading "Greenleaf." Mrs. May seems most valuable to O'Connor as a vehicle through which to suggest the possibility of last discoveries or restored sight. Such possibilities form the final standard by which to measure Mrs. May's social paranoia, the hateful tauntings of her sons, the petty triumphs of Mr. Greenleaf, even the comic excesses of Mrs. Greenleaf's fundamentalism. The suggestion of those possibilities, however, exacts a costly fictional price, for it comes at the expense of the very character through which they are conveyed. Mrs. May, O'Connor implies, cannot be trusted even in death to understand the metaphoric yield she makes available to a reader. She is the earthly term of an unearthly analogy, or rather she is the victim of O'Connor's desire for unearthly analogies.

JOYCE CAROL OATES has aptly argued that O'Connor's fiction is charged with a "curious sense of blunt, graphic impatience, the either/or of fanaticism and genius, that makes it difficult for even her most sympathetic critics to relate her to the dimension of psychological realism explored by the traditional novel": "Small obscenities or cruelties in the work of John Updike . . . have a power to upset us in a way that gross fantastic acts of violence in O'Connor do not, for we read O'Connor as a writer of parables and Updike as an interpreter of the way we actually live."[39] But how does reading fiction as a parable differ from reading it as a reflection of the way we actually live? Are these two ways of reading mutually exclusive? How does the fictional status of characters in a parable differ from that of realistic characters, and how is such a status established? How helpful, in other words, are available literary critical terms (such as "parable") in describing our experience of reading O'Connor's fiction? A consideration of the incident in *Wise Blood* in which Hazel Motes murders the rival preacher Solace Layfield may help shed some light on these questions.

"Murders" may be the wrong word here, for at least from Hazel's perspective (and perhaps from the narrator's) it seems too melodramatic, and the reader is put in the awkward position of sounding obtuse or self-righteous in insisting on having actions properly named. But that is part of the complication in our response for which we need to account. Hazel is approached by Hoover Shoats, a huckster-preacher and con man who goes under the pseudonym Onnie Jay Holy. Shoats tells Hazel that his idea for a Church Without Christ has promotional possibilities and that his "new jesus" is "up-to-date" (p. 90).

When Hazel tells Shoats, "in a barely audible voice," that he "ain't true," Shoats becomes the mouthpiece for some of O'Connor's wry, self-indicting satire: "'Friend, how can you say that?' Onnie Jay said. 'Why I was on the radio for three years with a program that give real religious experiences to the whole family. Didn't you ever listen to it—called Soulsease, a quarter hour of Mood, Melody, and Mentality? I'm a real preacher, friend.' Haze stopped the Essex. 'You get out,' he said" (p. 88). When Shoats continues to badger him, even after he has told him that the new jesus "wasn't nothing but a way to say a thing," Hazel slams the car door of the Essex on Shoats's thumb and the narrator informs us, with apparent neutrality, that "a howl arose that would have rended almost any heart" (p. 91). This is one of several moments in the novel where it seems impossible to characterize the narrative phrasing as either sarcastic or compassionate.

If Shoats's howl "would have rended *almost any* heart," does that mean "including the narrator's" or "except, of course, Hazel's"? In other words, O'Connor at least leaves open the possibility that her narrator is not entirely without sympathy for Shoats, no matter how religiously retrograde and accommodating the "Mood, Melody, and Mentality" with which he is associated. But there is also the equal possibility that the narrator is smirking at those whose hearts are rended a bit too easily, as if our ascription of pain to Hoover Shoats were a species of pathetic fallacy. ("Compassion," O'Connor wrote, "is a word that sounds good in anybody's mouth and which no book jacket can do without. . . . the kind of hazy compassion demanded of the writer now makes it difficult to be anti-anything" [*MM*, p. 43].[40]) Our uncertainty about how to take O'Connor's narrator in this small moment is to be expanded into one of the novel's most frightening scenes with the death of Solace Layfield.

Layfield serves, as several critics have noticed, as Hazel's double: he too drives a "rat-colored" car; he wears the same "glare-blue suit and white hat" as Hazel; he has a "loud, consumptive cough" that Hazel soon, as it were, catches; and there is even a suggestion that their facial features are similar. But at least as much as the sum of these similarities (which are subtly, not insistently suggested), Solace Layfield is defined and given to us as a name. It is as if Soulsease, Shoats's religious laxative, had assumed a physical presence. Although it is not implausible that Solace Layfield might be construed as an actual Southern name, it also seems to comprise, as Robert Coles notes, "an uncompromising jab" at what Americans "want out of religion: a bit of reassurance, maybe some sex therapy in the parish hall."[41]

The satiric aspects of Layfield's name indicate that he is more a caricature than a fully developed or three-dimensional character, not quite a cartoon but almost, and this holds true even—no, especially—if we think of him as Hazel's "double": a term from literature, surely, not life. There is a minimal amount of psychological depth or substantiality projected behind his name. "The Prophet" (capital P, as if this were how he thinks of himself or how Shoats thinks of him) "got three dollars an evening for his services and the use of his car. His name was Solace Layfield; he had consumption and a wife and six children and being a Prophet was as much work as he wanted to do. It never occurred to him that it might be a dangerous job" (p. 113). Solace Layfield does not seem to be an assumed name, like Onnie Jay Holy: it is just all there is to this character, or so we are being asked to believe. The narrator comically mechanizes and flattens our sense of Layfield by snidely telling us "he had consumption and a wife and six children" as if there were no qualitative difference between these items. There is no firm basis here for our disliking Layfield, even if he may conceive of "propheteering" as a profession. Yet in a fictional world where, in the words of another O'Connor character, "even the mercy of the Lord burns" (p. 342), a man named Solace Layfield seems doomed from the start. (It is something like being named Fortunato in a Poe story.) The limits of Layfield's fictional conception reveal just how puny and ineffectual he will seem before the grim perversity of Hazel, who sits in the Essex "watching him with the kind of intensity that means something is going to happen no matter what is done to keep it from happening" (p. 113).

Hazel drives out of town after Layfield's car at night, rams into it to force him to stop, and then, with "no sound but from crickets and tree frogs," he pushes Layfield's car off the road into a ditch and orders him to undress:

> "Take off that suit," Haze shouted and started the car forward after him. Solace began to lope down the road, taking off his coat as he went. "Take it all off," Haze yelled, with his face close to the windshield.
>
> The Prophet began to run in earnest. He tore off his shirt and unbuckled his belt and ran out of the trousers. He began grabbing for his feet as if he would take off his shoes too, but before he could get at them, the Essex knocked him flat and ran over him. Haze drove about twenty feet and stopped the car and then began to back it. He backed it over the body and then stopped and got out. The Essex stood half over the other Prophet as if it were pleased to guard what it had finally brought down. The man didn't look so much like Haze, lying on the ground on his face without his hat or suit on. A lot of blood was coming out of him and forming a puddle around his head. He was motionless all but for one finger that moved up and down in front of his face as if he were marking time with it. Haze poked his toes in his side and he wheezed for a second and then was quiet. "Two things I can't stand," Haze said, "—a man that ain't true and one that mocks what is. You shouldn't ever have tampered with me if you didn't want what you got."

The man was trying to say something but he was only wheezing. Haze squatted down by his face to listen. "Give my mother a lot of trouble," he said through a kind of bubbling in his throat. "Never giver no rest. Stole theter car. Never told the truth to my daddy or give Henry what, never give him . . ."

"You shut up," Haze said, leaning his head closer to hear the confession.

"Told where his still was and got five dollars for it," the man gasped.

"You shut up now," Haze said.

"Jesus . . ." the man said.

"Shut up like I told you to now," Haze said.

Haze gave him a hard slap on the back and he was quiet. He leaned down to hear if he was going to say anything else but he wasn't breathing any more. Haze turned around and examined the front of the Essex to see if there had been any damage done to it. The bumper had a few splurts of blood on it but that was all. Before he turned around and drove back to town, he wiped them off with a rag. (Pp. 114–15)

Layfield, largely a caricature until now, and denied even a name in this scene, is granted the illusion of realistic depth at his moment of greatest vulnerability, and our position as reader—a reader smiling at a caricature or enjoying the social comedy—changes to one of uncomfortable witness. We have suddenly been denied our previous grounds for considering Layfield an expendable commodity: the fact that he seemed merely fictional. We are no longer permitted to know the necessary degree of our implication (or O'Connor's) in what we have imaginatively witnessed. Hazel's running over Layfield is so suddenly unexpected it almost seems to be an accident. It is the cold deliberateness of Hazel's "backing" over him that makes this one of the most frightening moments in O'Connor's fiction.

Frightening first because O'Connor will not let the scene be melodramatic. The deliberate control of her omniscience here plays off against the depravity of Hazel's actions. She refuses to exoticize what is clearly extraordinary. Her neutrality is assiduous; there is an extravagance to the way she abnegates her descriptive presence in the scene. It is not entirely effaced, for she says that the Essex stands "as if it were pleased to guard what it had finally brought down," but this seems merely a neutral statement of fact, not a moral indictment of an automobile. Nevertheless, that phrase has an edge to it that suggests more than narrative neutrality, and this seems altogether typical. Indirection here allows O'Connor to imply an opinion (as when Mr. Greenleaf "lifted one muscle somewhere near his mouth") without being held responsible for it. "The man didn't look so much like Haze, lying on the ground on his face without his hat or suit on": this sentence can pass as objective description but it also sounds like what Hazel himself might proclaim in knowingly tight-lipped understatement. He seems totally without remorse or, for that matter, triumph. His "you shouldn't ever have tampered with me if you didn't want what you got" seems strangely flat and without heat, more an indifferent policy statement than a taunt. The murder seems of no real consequence to Hazel's spiritual pilgrimage. His ostensible reason for killing Layfield (that he "can't stand" "a man that ain't true and one that mocks what is") ironically rebounds on Hazel himself, for it as aptly describes the founder of the Church Without Christ as it does Layfield.

"All my stories are about the action of grace on a character who is not very willing to support it," O'Connor once wrote to her anonymous friend "A." But because the majority of her readers do not "know what grace is and don't recognize it when they see it," she says, "most people think of these stories as hard, hopeless, brutal, etc."[42] Yet a reader's sense of the hopelessness and brutality of this scene and others like it in O'Connor's work may originate less in some atheistic predisposition than in a legitimate response to O'Connor's fictional procedures. The terror of this scene stems from our inability to allegorize its action, for ideas (like that of the action of grace) don't bleed. Whatever we may be "learning" about Hazel here, his victim is suffering in disturbingly realistic detail. It is no longer "Solace Layfield" who lies in a puddle of blood moving one finger "up and down in front of his face as if he were marking time with it." It is no longer a two-dimensional fictional puppet or Hazel's depthless "double" who is before us but a man in his shoes and his underwear dying in the road with "a kind of bubbling in his throat." Layfield's condition, that is, becomes pitiable whether or not it deserves to be.

There are hints of Layfield's martyrdom (a halo-like puddle of blood around his head, and Hazel pokes his toe in Layfield's side like the spear in Christ's side). But any suggestion that perhaps *this* is Hazel's new jesus are forestalled by Layfield's pathetic "confession," a confession that makes Hazel, the murderer, a grotesque inversion of a priest granting absolution. The final mortuary touch is that Hazel himself administers the penance for Layfield's pitiful cry, "Jesus hep me": "a hard slap on the back" that kills him.

It is not at all clear in the novel why Hazel kills Layfield, though we grow to expect the unexpected from him. The last we see of Hazel before this scene, he intends to leave town with no apparent thought of Layfield, and most critics cite the destruction of his car and not this murder as the revelatory event that prompts him, for equally obscure reasons, to blind himself. Hazel's murder of Layfield has generally been interpreted as an attempt quite literally to crush his own conscience—his theological alter ego as represented by Layfield. Hazel seems convinced that Layfield actually believes in redemption, and thus O'Connor is seen as either darkly mocking Hazel's twisted religious beliefs or else dramatizing his earnestness and "super-integrity." ("The narrator asks for respect for Hazel's dilemma here," one critic asserts, if not "approval of the deed exactly," then at least "understanding" or even "pity."[43]) Both of these ways of reading the scene, however, reach for a thematic coherence O'Connor does not authorize, for her narrator remains as distantly unjudgmental about Hazel as about Layfield. The power of the scene resides precisely in its being rendered not as a "dilemma" but as a dramatic action, which unfolds with the weird inevitability of a dream. Whatever we think about a "truth" that exacts this kind of retribution, it is clear that we can least afford to forget what Hazel thinks about it.

We are given no perspective in this scene by which to limit or contain the narrative action. There is no behavioral norm (in the narrative or in the characters) that provides a respite from this sudden outbreak of grotesque nihilism. We are not, as Coles says, "allowed to turn Hazel into Good and Solace into Evil," nor, I would add, are we allowed to turn Solace into comic inconsequence. But Coles also avers that "we are reminded in this scene that there is something in Hazel that may save him, that may make him, at some future time, different from what he seems to be—another doomed heretic."[44] This too seems overly optimistic; for in what way are we "reminded" of this "something" in Hazel? I am less confident than Coles about an eventual change of heart in Hazel because O'Connor seems intent upon showing that Hazel Motes is Hazel Motes *malgré lui*. "I lent some stories to a country lady who lives down the road from me," O'Connor writes in an essay entitled "Writing Short Stories," "and when she returned them she said, 'Well them stories just gone and shown you how some folks *would* do,' and I thought to myself that that was right; when you write stories, you have to be content to start exactly there— showing how some specific folks *will* do, *will* do in spite of everything" (*MM*, p. 90).

The problem with seeing Layfield's murder as an example of what Westling calls "a typical O'Connor comeuppance" for the self-righteous, is that the narrator in this scene seems less vengeful than austerely aloof.[45] Neither do I see this, in Shloss's words, as one more "smirking challenge to the weak-hearted reader" that "the amoral, modern novel has helped to create."[46] O'Connor's unsmirking neutrality and amorality in this scene seem to me no less difficult to account for than her verbal behavior elsewhere in the novel. Over and over again the reader is made to feel, like the landlady Mrs. Flood in the book's last paragraph, "as if she were blocked at the entrance of something" (p. 131).

As often as not O'Connor withholds any account of why Hazel "*will* do in spite of everything," and the strangeness of what she offers in its place accentuates the unavailability of what it is that drives him. Throughout the novel O'Connor employs a language and imagery that we do not hear Hazel using but that we could imagine him thinking up, were he himself ever to write a novel:

> The reflection [of Hazel's face in a glass display case] was pale and the eyes were like two clean bullet holes. (P. 56)

> His face had a fragile look as if it might have been broken and stuck together again, or like a gun no one knows is loaded. (P. 37)

> His face behind the windshield was sour and frog-like; it looked as if it had a shout closed up in it; it looked like one of those closet doors in gangster movies where someone is tied to a chair behind it with a towel in his mouth. (P. 48)

"Discussing story-telling in terms of plot, character, and theme," O'Connor once wrote, "is like trying to describe the expression on a face by saying where the eyes, nose, and mouth are" (*MM*, p. 89). Instead of eyes, nose, and mouth, with O'Connor we get extravagant similes like these, which are themselves like unexpected bullet holes in the narrative and which ensure that our understanding of Hazel is to be granted only in an elaborately mediated fashion. Hazel's features tell of a personality, but that personality is untelling.

In what sense can a face be "like a gun no one knows is loaded" or, more implausibly, like "one of those closet doors in gangster movies where someone is tied to a chair behind it with a towel in his mouth"? What would it mean to say a face looked like an unloaded gun or a closet door outside of gangster movies? Would that get us any farther? Would that generate a higher figurative yield or offer more clues to Hazel's motives?

Steven Weisenberger has noted the "singular outrageousness" of many of the similes that make the novel seem as if it "had been furnished wall-to-wall with a variety of distorting mirrors." He claims that they form "the main source for that affective power of *Wise Blood*, which so many readers have felt but found it difficult to pin down." But Weisenberger goes on to suggest that the grotesquerie of the similes is meant to lay waste "the surface of things and eventually the order of all being": the entropic "effect of the similes is to *erase* all difference." The grotesque tropes, he contends, signify "the characters' perverse motives and their distance from true sanctuary."[47]

To assert that O'Connor's narrative behavior is at one with Hazel's "perverse motives," however, is to build a thematic sanctuary of our own against the vagaries of her style. It is to miss the eccentric playfulness of the novel that, while not a first-person narrative, often seems afloat in a first-person consciousness.[48] Far from erasing the difference in the "order of all being," O'Connor's similes often depend completely upon emphasizing the figurative incongruence between, say, a face and a closet door in order to suggest how little we know about Hazel Motes. This is the kind of character, it is implied, who inspires such an analogy.

O'Connor asserted more than once that modern fiction is characterized by a disappearance of the author, by which she meant the disappearance of an intrusive verbal intelligence initiating and directing our social and ethical evaluations. This is not entirely the case with *Wise Blood*. We can still hear O'Connor's "voice" in the novel but more as an echo than a certifiable presence. It keeps losing itself in various forms of free indirect discourse and it opulently absents itself by fashioning similes that often function like a safety catch being fingered on a gun. These images not only displace a voice, a locatable source of authorial control, they provide the violent undertow in the novel that seems somehow responsible for the violence done by and to various characters.[49]

The verbal intelligence telling us that the car horn of the Essex sounds "like a goat's laugh cut off with a buzz saw" (p. 91), or that its windshield wipers "made a great clatter like two idiots clapping in church" (p. 41), or that Hazel's "heart began to grip him like a little ape clutching the bars of its cage" (p. 34) is using its surrealism as protective armor. These similes are like so many "No Trespassing" signs; they seem to dare us to "understand" the motives of their maker. The grotesque disproportions in these images between figurative stimulus and response register, in miniature, the larger imbalances of the novel, such as that between the seeming inconsequence of Solace Layfield and the magnitude of the response he provokes in Hazel. The narrative voice in *Wise Blood* does, at times, assume what we might call Hazel's verbal temperament. But it seems truer to assert that what Hazel is longing for but cannot articulate throughout the novel is the chance to reach not spiritual sanctuary but the expressive condition of the narrator, who does not have to answer for her effects. Like Natty Bumppo and some of Faulkner and Pynchon's characters, Hazel seems to strain against the very writing by which he is imagined.

O'Connor's similes, like many of her other narrative tactics, confuse our sense of fictional security and tonal location by suggesting that there are very few safely deduced intentions in her work, especially about scenes of violence. This, it seems to me, is a large part of why critics may feel like calling her work "grotesque." If we are not overly reverential toward O'Connor's own remarks about her fiction, we can see that not even she is capable of gutting the darker, disturbing aspects of her stories. *In* rather than outside her fiction, O'Connor is often flamboyantly reticent to grant us the imaginative means by which we might glibly humanize (or etherialize) her violence and vitiate the true measure of its potency.

Robert Fitzgerald once aptly highlighted what he calls the "ascesis" of O'Connor's style, the strong sense that her "bald narrative sentences" convey of "how much has been refrained from, and how much else has been cut out and thrown away."[50] This undemonstrative reserve makes O'Connor's narrative detachment in moments of dramatic intensity and pain almost unbearable, and it makes her comic instincts seem perversely grim. Yet just as typical as such verbal "baldness" in her fiction is a tendency in the opposite direction, a propensity for invoking images that flaunt their figurative lack of restraint and stand clear of the narrative in memorably disorienting ways.

To insist upon careful characterizations of O'Connor's violence is to examine its problematic status in springing from a "realism of distances." This is not to say that the imaginative power of that violence is felt as a "problem," for that is criticism's way of distracting us from the violence itself, of assuring us it is not gratuitous, and, often, of panning for nuggets of "grace" in her work. What O'Connor's representations of violence confront us with is the imaginative intransitivity of both her characters and her narratives, her insistence upon setting fictional ground rules for herself. We may be able to identify, as Claire Katz has, the darker aspects of O'Connor's fiction: "her peculiar insistence on absolute powerlessness as a condition of salvation," her repeated location of the "means of grace" in the sexually perverse, and the fact that "she addresses rage and contempt to characters who at least partially represent herself."[51] But simply identifying these darker aspects will seldom be the same as imaginatively accounting for them. There is a quality as well as a weight to the impact they have on us, and we are not likely to highlight what her stories show as well as they show it. We are not likely to adequately describe the jarring, dolorous, angular qualities of O'Connor's fiction, or her barbed sense of humor, if we begin by attributing them to something other than what, in Hazel Motes's terms, "ain't nothing but words" (p. 29).

"The Late, Late, Late Show"

THOMAS PYNCHON'S VIOLENCE

> Restructuring of the riot goes on in other ways. All
> Easter week this year, in the spirit of the season, there was
> a "Renaissance of the Arts," a kind of festival in memory of
> Simon Rodia, held at Markham Junior High, in the heart of
> Watts.
>
> Along with theatrical and symphonic events, the festival
> also featured a roomful of sculptures fashioned entirely
> from found objects—found, symbolically enough, and in
> the Simon Rodia tradition, among the wreckage the rioting
> had left. Exploiting textures of charred wood, twisted
> metal, fused glass, many of the works were fine, honest
> rebirths.
>
> In one corner was this old, busted, hollow TV set with a
> rabbit-ears antenna on top; inside, where its picture tube
> should have been, gazing out with scorched wiring threaded
> like electronic ivy among its crevices and sockets, was a
> human skull. The name of the piece was "The Late, Late,
> Late Show."
>
> —*Thomas Pynchon, "A Journey into the Mind of Watts"*

THOMAS PYNCHON is "possibly the most accomplished writer of prose in English since James Joyce," Richard Poirier justly affirms, not because he is "the best novelist, whatever that would mean," but because "sentence by sentence he can do more than any other novelist of this century with the resources of the English-American language and with the various media by which it is made available to us."[1] Yet as Pynchon becomes the subject of numerous critical Baedekers, his verbal charisma—to borrow some of his favorite and borrowed terms—is in danger of being routinized; his narrative animation is rendered more and more inanimate. The unfortunate assumption of much Pynchon criticism is that his work is best footnoted or translated rather than directly confronted, best dealt with in essays (some sporting graphs and sine waves) about entropy, uncertainty principles, Apocalypse and Pentecost, and the death of modernism rather than in criticism that might attempt to detail the imaginative pressures of Pynchon's writing, which entertains and then disentitles these and all the other thematic elements that are no more than topical boarding platforms in his fiction.

Perhaps the aptest approach to Pynchon's narrative instincts is through his own note to the *Soho Weekly News* in response to an article stating that because Pynchon's emergence as a writer coincided with the disappearance of J. D. Salinger, Pynchon *was* Salinger simply using another name. "Not bad," he wrote; "keep trying."[2] Pynchon's personal elusiveness is intriguing in and of itself: his dossier at Cornell has mysteriously disappeared and there is a blank square where his photograph should be in the Freshman Register; his 1955–57 Navy service records were destroyed in a fire, and when he worked for several months after graduating from Cornell, preparing technical documents for Boeing aircraft in Seattle, his fellow workers report that "he often did his work in a cocoon he built around his desk with huge sheets of paper: he was a sort of aerospace Bartleby, as one commentator puts it."[3] But Pynchon's evasiveness as a person proves appetizing in a larger way because the culturally encyclopedic impulses of his fiction render him invisible behind all they encompass. The act of reading his work, as James Guetti suggests, "extends to that of reading the author, for the difficulties of the fiction, the dazzling and multiple incompleteness of its substance, sends us on toward the source of power, on to a more final intelligibility, to the fuller knowledge of it that we suppose its author must have."[4] Our difficulty in "finding" that author, I want to suggest, is more than just biographically important, especially in how it imaginatively shapes the forms of violence in Pynchon's fiction and how we respond to them.

PYNCHON'S FIRST novel, *V.*, provides a paradigm of how the "dazzling and multiple incompleteness" of his fiction helps us identify Pynchon by his unidentifiability. *V.* continually exemplifies the way a reader is always just catching sight of Pynchon's disappearing narrative coattails rather than reaching through scenes to shake the author's hand:

> Next evening, prim and nervous-thighed in a rear seat of the crosstown bus, Esther divided her attention between the delinquent wilderness outside and a paperback copy of The Search for Bridey Murphy. This book had been written by a Colorado businessman to tell people there was life after death. In its course he touched upon metempsychosis, faith healing, extrasensory perception and the rest of a weird canon of twentieth-century metaphysics we've come to associate with the city of Los Angeles and similar regions.

223

The bus driver was of the normal or placid crosstown type; having fewer traffic lights and stops to cope with than the up-and-downtown drivers, he could afford to be genial. A portable radio hung by his steering wheel, turned to WQXR. Tchaikovsky's Romeo and Juliet Overture flowed syrupy around him and his passengers. As the bus crossed Columbus Avenue, a faceless delinquent heaved a rock at it. Cries in Spanish ascended to it out of the darkness. A report which could have been either a backfire or a gunshot sounded a few blocks downtown. Captured in the score's black symbols, given life by vibrating air columns and strings, having taken passage through transducers, coils, capacitors and tubes to a shuddering paper cone, the eternal drama of love and death continued to unfold entirely disconnected from this evening and place.[5]

Thus begins a chapter entitled "In Which Esther Gets a Nose Job." It is a "functional" passage (little remembered, of all the events in this chapter) in that it seems sublimated to a narrative purpose: moving Esther from one place to another. But it is not where the reader is being taken that matters here but how he is being led, through what alien country the narrative is directing him. The narrator assumes the informational manner of, say, a book reviewer in order to joke wryly about a Southern California lifestyle. By the end of the next paragraph, however, this manner has been dropped in favor of what is, in a sense, just such a weird twentieth-century metaphysical conceit as has been laughed about. This self-pleasuring impulse in Pynchon's imagination seems to allow one part of a passage to inspire or at least suggest or provoke another imaginative and sequential reaction in the oddest and most complicated of all directions. A reader is best advised to seek, beneath every set of figures in Pynchon's work, not a meaning but a reflex. He must situate these tropes not only in the context in which they come to life but as a tactic of the narrative's imagistic libido.

The scene refers—and this is characteristic of Pynchon more generally—to what is largely invisible. There is a density of verbal fragments that, though charged with visual energy, are not confidently visualized by the reader. The effort of moving from one visual increment to the next involves an intensity of "almost seeing." This semi-invisibility makes the surreal a part of its created effect: "a faceless delinquent heaved a rock at it. Cries in Spanish ascended to it out of the darkness. A report which could have been either a backfire or a gunshot sounded a few blocks downtown." There is an intensified sense of the unknown, the literally but not imaginatively unseen. One of Pynchon's typical verbal habits surfaces in "a faceless delinquent." The phrasing makes a reader try to imagine a face in the very act of denying its existence. The use of words ending in "less" is continual in Pynchon's fiction and it predicates the expenditure of more imaginatively grasping energy on a reader's part.[6] Our effort to extract an image from a word that is ostensibly putting it under erasure deepens our sense that something is present but unidentified. Its resistance to visualization prompts us to try all the harder to see it. In this case the word forms a tiny rehearsal of the larger concerns of what is so oddly imagined here: the music, which both does and does not disconnect itself, verbally, from the scene. Of course, writing about a piece of music is a tricky business, for it depends in part upon the reader's ability to "hear" the composition invoked; the effort of extending the effect is foisted on the imaginatively manipulated reader. There can be few more tactically entrapping moments than when, at the end of the paragraph, the "entirely disconnected" aside, the active, the Pynchonesque reader attempts to reimagine the scene he has just "seen" by insinuating a soundtrack into it.

"The eternal drama of love and death" is incongruent with the "evening and place" into which it "flowed syrupy" to the same degree that the technical brilliance of its description disconnects itself from the narrative. By following an imaginative leap of association from the aching vitality "captured" in "the score's black symbols" (musical notes "caught" in a staff) and a visually modulated trace of the music's orchestral and then electronic beginnings, the conceptualization of the music itself forms a miniature drama of escape and extrication. The very act of assuming musical intelligibility cannot be imagined as separate from the medium that both imprisons and releases it. And all this is choreographed in vaguely sexual terms ("vibrating air columns," "a shuddering paper cone," both part of an "eternal drama of love and death") that add a resonant confusion. The virtuosity of a sentence that yields up such a sudden abundance of crosshatching effects tells us as much about how it gets written as about how the inanimate "participates" in the communication of human artistry.

The description of the radio can be taken as a figure for the novel as a whole. As many times as not, Pynchon's descriptive reflex takes him right out of a created world, like an overture "unfolding" through a radio, while thoroughly ensnaring the reader in its detail. As we watch Pynchon generate a new set of figures, the way a computer generates screen print or a telephone access network generates an open line, it is not clear what such figures are felt to be in contrast with. The fecundity of an unexpected image in his hands is so vital, even in the narrative's sotto voce tones, that it makes what preceded it seem limited and self-antiquating, though it too had felt vibrant enough when first encountered. Details and moments shine forth with a special clarity, as if escaping from the "repression" of the sentence before, only themselves to be later eclipsed by some further extension of a figure or by something newly minted. The metaphoric conductivity of his prose nearly always outdistances our means of accounting for it. He makes the act of investing an idea with complexity a way of skipping out of the difficulties it poses.

Pynchon's novels risk "ultimate ethical and aesthetic chaos," as one commentator puts it, in "their rage for an inclusive purchase on reality."[7] The imaginative dynamics of Pynchon's fascination with the vocabularies of pop culture, philosophy, and science, as well as with literary history, disorient and reshape our conventional responses to fiction. The alterations of pace and sensibility in *V.* are constant and dizzying. Like Vera Meroving, what is most unintimidated but itself intimidating about the language of the novel is the way it exemplifies Pynchon's "inability to come to rest anywhere inside plausible extremes, her nervous endless motion, like the counter-crepitating of the ball along its roulette spokes, seeking a random compartment but finally making, having made, sense only as the dynamic uncertainty she was" (*V.*, p. 238). This "dynamic uncertainty" consists in part of Pynchon's showing off; his flirtatious informational omnipotence often seems like that of some reference librarian run amok. But it also, often simultaneously, registers his fascination with "plausible extremes," with the ways in which the surreal or the parodically extravagant can come to seem oddly familiar or at least recognizable, while imaginable realities incline to the impulse of the enigmatic. Pynchon's realism, Guetti asserts, springs not only from his predominantly realistic imagination but also from "his dedication to plausibility, which is also his dedication to mystery: he is committed to the grid of knowing–not knowing and is fascinated with that sort of power."[8]

In the more extended scenes of violence in his work, Pynchon's informational precision and illusions of sensory immediacy are often so convincing (and thus so disturbing) that many readers find it difficult to complete them. The relentless anonymity of Pynchon's descriptive eye, which provides us, in the best realistic tradition, with an unrelieved stream of imagistic variety, change, and accumulation, can quickly become a source of terror in his fiction. The need for feeling from an author, as we saw with Flannery O'Connor, generally constitutes a desire for some sign of an author's presence. It usually exemplifies the hope that something—some hint of a moral vantage, some protective indication of disgust, tragedy, or at least sarcasm on an author's part—will imaginatively mitigate or cushion the stark sensory aspects of realistic violence. Like O'Connor, Pynchon usually denies the reader such hints but he does so in a very different fashion. His authorial presence evaporates in the wake not of cryptic similes or an extravagant sense of narrative aloofness but in the informational richness and density that characterize his prose.

Pynchon's assimilative instincts and his appetite for informational density are present even when he expresses what might be called a lyricism of marginality. Take, for instance, a well-known moment in *The Crying of Lot 49*. Oedipa Maas has "heard all about excluded middles," the logical axiom that if a proposition is false its contradictory must be true, and she knows that they are "bad shit, to be avoided" (*CL*, p. 136). So to reduce one's perspective (on love, America, Tristero, meaning), she realizes, is "like walking among matrices of a great digital computer, the zeroes and ones twinned above, hanging like balanced mobiles right and left, ahead, thick, maybe endless." Oedipa wonders, movingly, how the American land and all it sustains has been conditioned "to accept any San Narciso among its most tender flesh without a reflex or a cry," how such a situation "ever happened here, with the chances once so good for diversity" (*CL*, p. 136).

Yet however yearning and bereft the effect of this moment, Pynchon's ingenious image of an enlarged computer itself counteracts the drift of Oedipa's lament for diversity. Not only can Pynchon find a figure for a complicated perceptual problem but the verve with which he imagines it forms one kind of antidote to the crux it poses. This is why Oedipa's (or Stencil's or Slothrop's) dilemmas are never entirely Pynchon's. The thematic outlines of his novels, which we describe at a distance when we rise up out of our engagement with them, never entirely restrain or inhibit the surging energy that arranges and then disperses the narrative materials from which such outlines emerge. With their "complex patterns of iconography, allusion, and metaphor," Molly Hite avows, Pynchon's novels demonstrate that "meaning is not the exclusive property of narrative resolutions."[9]

Hite, in her excellent study of Pynchon, identifies in all his novels a structural principle she calls the "trope of the unavailable insight." His writing as well as his characters approach what one Pynchon narrator calls "holy centers," ready to receive the dispensation or gain access to the elevated vantage that promises, retrospectively, to bestow narrative coherence. This theocentric presumption of narrative, the expectation that experience accretes toward a terminal revelation, is encouraged and then parodied and disrupted by Pynchon. His novels, Hite argues, "promise to add up in order to call attention to the complex ways in which they do *not* add up." "Pynchon is able to sustain multiple emphases by loading the *promise* of insight to come with more connotations than any set of determinate meaning-statements could conceivably bear, and then deferring fulfillment of this promise beyond the conclusions of the books," which it haunts as something that is not there.[10]

Yet even Hite falls prey to the almost irresistible temptation in criticism (of Pynchon and more generally) to turn style into "stylistics," to attend carefully to the imaginative properties of style only when they can then be "thematized" and, too often, denatured. To extract a structural principle from Pynchon's fiction, even a principle that espouses evasiveness, is to double back on the writing and impose its theme as a statement about the evasions of perceptual impositions. Hite suggests that Pynchon's novels succeed in "foxing inevitability," but she attributes that success to larger factors like unanticipated plot developments, metaphoric structures of duplication and repetition, and gaggles of unreliable narrative voices.[11] These all comprise important elements of his novels, but they seem more fundamentally generated and governed by what Guetti calls "the realistic drive and pressure" of Pynchon's imagination, "an imagination always in a condition of testing itself." Pynchon's writing, he asserts, often becomes "a high wire act, as if he had continually to perform the unlikeliest feats far above us and show us that there is nothing and nobody that he cannot write about and no opening that he cannot follow."[12] Yet how is it that a writer who can perform the "unlikeliest feats" and write about blatantly fantastic or implausible subjects (the biography of a light bulb, for instance, in *Gravity's Rainbow*) can also be one of the most realistic novelists we have? George Levine rightly asserts that "the surreal takes on the immediacy of experience" in Pynchon's work.[13] But *how*? What is responsible for the mimetic evocativeness of his tomfooleries, and how does it affect our response to violence in his work?

PYNCHON'S PLOTS, characters, diction, and narrative techniques are instinctively parodic. Characters with names like Diocletian Blobb, Krinkles Porcino, Nicolai Ripov, Mike Fallopian, and Herbert Stencil (referring to himself only in the third person) involve themselves with such matters as "psychodontia," Banana Breakfasts, and Suck Hour at the Sailor's Grave Tavern. They watch for Giant Adenoids, dance "the dirty boogie," purchase land at Fangoso Lagoons, sing Rocket Limericks or logical-positivist love songs ("Let P Equal Me"), and join the likes of the Peter Pinguid Society or the law firm of Warp, Wistfull, Kubitschek, and McMingus. But Pynchon does not remain satisfied with parody or incongruity for long.

Peter Cooper, among others, has noted the fragile fictional status of characters in Pynchon's fiction. They seem, even when more developed, less like people "with a solid form" than "a locus of emotions" "refracted through remembered or fantasized events." Such characters, Cooper says, "are no more integrally cohesive or ontologically sound for being complex."[14] But what might ontological soundness consist of here? Characters who first appear to be little more than a bagatelle or a silly pun (Brenda Wigglesworth, Bloody Chiclitz) are then allowed to express, in however transient a gesture, convincing emotions that belie the cartoonish nature of their names. What seems "ontologically sound" about such characters is the vividness with which their shifting states of consciousness are rendered, but that evocation is not dependent upon a notion of a cohesive self. This will become an important factor in scenes of violence in *V.*, for how do we feel when we are witness to the lurid sensory pain of an ontologically unsound or cartoonish character?

Cooper attributes the fictional shape of Pynchon's characters to extratextual pressures. "Quasi-animate forces that seem to lurk inside social change, grinding individuals into anonymity and conformity" change his characters into "puny forms randomly colliding like subatomic particles—two-dimensional figures racing about chaotically against a four-dimensional backdrop" of "people-assimilating" cosmic and social forces.[15] This "four-dimensional" aspect of the novels that dwarfs and assimilates characters, however, might just as aptly be said to manifest Pynchon's verbal dynamics rather than social or cosmic ones. Cooper's assertion that characters often assume identities in Pynchon's fiction not in themselves but as members of groups that subsume individual personalities seems to me a perfect characterization of the writing itself and the sequential pressures that animate it: "These bizarre groups appear randomly scattered across the social landscape. Each seems to have an internal logic, consistent in its own terms but unrelated to those of other groups. There is no common context or set of terms, no informing whole that unifies the groups into a coherent society; they would be eccentric but there is no center from which to deviate."[16] The "internal logic" and consistency of smaller and smaller imaginative units in Pynchon's fiction impedes any larger social, psychological, or narrative coherence from taking shape. ("We do not walk ganged," Maijstral reminds Stencil, "all our separate selves, like Siamese quintuplets or more" [*V.*, pp. 424–25].) But the dispersal of such wider continuities (or conspiracies) takes place even as they are hauntingly suggested, for Pynchon invests the smallest moments and details with an animated immediacy that sends "simple dualism," in Maijstral's words, "into strange patterns indeed" (*V.*, p. 317).

Pynchon continually alters the dimensional scale of his fiction. His ability to infuse inconsequential details with a vivid illusion of referential precision forces us to rethink the perceptual classifications we normally invoke in reading fiction. It also modifies our notions of consequence. The precise visual or sensory qualities of the tiniest details displace our readerly attention as they satisfy what Nabokov called "certain camera-lucida needs of literary composition."[17] Details stand out from and free of the narrative like tiny spells of false spring or (to adopt one of Sidney Stencil's analogies) "like sequins on an old and misused ball-gown" (*V.*, p. 440). In Katherine Hayles's terms, Pynchon has recast the traditional difference between foreground and background in the novel. He takes "a radically egalitarian attitude toward his material" by obliterating the conventional distinction between "the meaningful event and the 'irrelevant' detail" and by collapsing background and foreground "into the same perceptual plane."[18] We cannot count on literary convention to keep the details populating Pynchon's fiction in place as self-extinguishing contrastive filler. With the traditional novel, Leo Bersani notes in discussing Roland Barthes's remarks on Robbe-Grillet,

> we skip from crisis to crisis, as if the rhythms of our eyes' movements while we read "were meant to reproduce the very hierarchy of the classical universe, endowed with alternately pathetic and insignificant moments." . . . [Pynchon deprives] us of that secure sense of general design which allows us to relax over specific passages. The sense of meaning which we bring to each sentence from our reading of previous sentences doesn't help us, so to speak, to get done more quickly with the sentence at hand.[19]

Pynchon's fiction is heir to Emerson's conviction that "an imaginative book renders us much more service at first, by stimulating us through its tropes, than afterward when we arrive at the precise sense of the author."[20] But his narrative sets and drifts do more than "stimulate" us. They provide the verbal conductors that convey Pynchon's larger fascination with subversive subcultures and signs of sentience in the inanimate, and they dramatize how perceptual restrictions can desensitize us to the presence of both. That latent sources of animation (and so, on another register, of menace) smolder just beyond our understanding is explicitly recognized by characters in *V.*, as when Benny Profane has "conversations" with the plastic test manikins SHOCK and SHROUD. But it is also intimated in subtler ways:

> And Rachel and Roony sat on a bench in Sheridan Square, talking about Mafia and Paola. It was one in the morning, a wind had risen and something curious too had happened; as if everyone in the city, simultaneously, had become sick of news of any kind; for thousands of newspaper pages blew through the small park on the way crosstown, blundered like pale bats against the trees, tangled themselves around the feet of Roony and Rachel, and of a bum sleeping across the way. Millions of unread and useless words had come to a kind of life in Sheridan Square; while the two on the bench wove cross-talk of their own, oblivious, among them. (*V.*, p. 275)

Pynchon's characters weave "cross-talk" (cross-talk he elsewhere affectionately records) while remaining oblivious not only to blowing newspapers in a city square but to the "kind of life" Pynchon gives them. We know nothing of what Rachel and Roony are saying here but we do not feel particularly deprived, for the descriptive force of what blows through this scene drowns out, in effect, what they are saying. Like two magnets coming together, Pynchon's characters never seem to bond in any lasting intimacy. His characters tend to swerve buoyantly past one another as a result of their private obsessions with manic plots and paranoias. Pynchon himself also tends to "lose" them in his continuing imaginative effort to digest and precisely render the exfoliating technologies, conventions, and encodings of the contemporary life that swirls around them. Stencil is the only character in the novel to practice the "forcible dislocation of personality," but he is not alone in being practiced upon.

Stencil forcibly dislocates himself into "a repertoire of identities," into "a past he didn't remember and had no right in, save the right of imaginative anxiety or historical care, which is recognized by no one" (*V.*, p. 51). A state of imaginative anxiety is also what Pynchon's repertoire of narrative identities often seems to ensure for a reader of *V.* The verbal flirtations and dodgings, the conceptual agility and realistic density we may admire elsewhere in the novel spill over into obscene or violent scenes in markedly inappropriate and disturbing ways. A small but telling example of this tendency occurs when Roony Winsome reflects that all he knows after five years of marriage to Mafia is "that both of them were whole selves, hardly fusing at all, with no more emotional osmosis than leakage of seed through the solid membranes of contraceptive or diaphragm that were sure to be there protecting them" (*V.*, p. 113). Is Pynchon actually interested in emotions here or only in the ways they can be imagined? Is he as concerned with the lack of "emotional osmosis" in Roony's and Mafia's marriage as he is with precisely visualizing the "leakage of seed" through contraceptive membranes meant to suggest it? This image suggests what their relationship has degenerated to, or failed from the start to rise above, but it takes on a descriptive life of its own that unnervingly preempts our attention from the rest of the analogy.

A larger instance of this preemptive impulse can be seen in chapter 14 ("V. in Love"), in which Pynchon details the life, memories, and dreams of Mélanie l'Heuremaudit, the fifteen-year-old ballerina who has had a "spell of incest" (*V.*, p. 382) with her father at a Normandy estate and with whom V. will have a fetishistic affair. In one of Mélanie's dreams she tells a German man ("He was Papa, but also a German"), who is trying to turn her over, to reach "between my thighs" (*V.*, p. 377). Pynchon also informs us that Mélanie "had always wanted to slide down the great mansard roof" of the family estate:

> . . . begin at the top and skid down the first gentle slope. Her skirt would fly above her hips, her black-stockinged legs would writhe matte against a wilderness of chimneys, under the Norman sunlight. High over the elms and the hidden carp pools, up where Maman could only be a tiny blotch under a parasol, gazing at her. She imagined the sensation often: the feeling of roof-tiles rapidly sliding beneath the hard curve of her rump, the wind trapped under her blouse teasing the new breasts. And then the break: where the lower, steeper slope of the roof began, the

point of no return, where the friction against her body would lessen and she would accelerate, flip over to twist the skirt—perhaps rip it off, be done with it, see it flutter away, like a dark kite!—to let the dovetailed tiles tense her nipple-points to an angry red, see a pigeon clinging to the eaves just before flight, taste the long hair caught against her teeth and tongue, cry out . . . (*V.*, pp. 370–71)

We might be tempted to chalk up the sensory attentiveness of the erotic details here (à la John Updike or Erica Jong) to what Poirier calls Pynchon's "taste for child-women," his novels being "heavily populated with barely pubescent bed partners."[21] But Pynchon himself anticipates such a response by inserting the writer Gerfaut into the scene, who "had two or three chins, sat erect and spoke pedantically" to Itague "on how for some reason the young girl—adolescent or younger—had again become the mode in erotic fiction" (*V.*, p. 377). This seems at first to be merely a whimsical dash of self-parody lost on the characters, for Gerfaut cannot possibly know about Mélanie's erotic dream of the German, which precedes his remarks on the page. But Pynchon extends the role of Gerfaut in this moment:

> Gerfaut had been describing the plot of his latest novel. The heroine was one Doucette, thirteen and struggled within by passions she could not name.
> "A child, and yet a woman," Gerfaut said. "And a quality of something eternal about her. I even confess to a certain leaning of my own that way. La Jarretière [Mélanie's stage name] . . ."
> The old satyr.
> Gerfaut at length moved away. It was nearly morning. Itague's head ached. He needed sleep, needed a woman. (*V.*, p. 378)

Itague's imagined remark here—"the old satyr"—is amusing both because of its incongruity with Gerfaut's unsatyrlike physique and because it indicates that Itague prides himself on deflating what has been Gerfaut's pseudoprofundity from the start. But the humor of the remark (especially coming from Itague, who himself "needed a woman," as if he could go grocery shopping for generic females) is also directed at the reader as much as at Gerfaut, at least the reader who might think seriously of indicting Pynchon himself as a satyr toying with his own versions of Doucette. Yet "directed at" may imply too intentional a motive on Pynchon's part for the force of this kind of elusive canniness resides less in its snickers at offended readers than in the way Pynchon's irreverent, self-consciously capricious narrative gestures release him from all responsibility for a reader's response.

Even when the narrator shows his cards it is done with a flourish that characteristically hides its confidence behind a screen of mock-modesty. Take, for example, Pynchon's revelation about his source of information concerning Father Fairing, a "topside" priest who decided, "in an hour of apocalyptic well-being. . . . early in Roosevelt's first term," to bring Roman Catholicism to the New York sewer rats residing "between Lexington and the East River and between 86th and 79th Streets" (*V.*, p. 105). (The exactitude with which the locale is identified attests to the narrator's veraciousness, his sensitivity to rat demography). "At no point in the twenty or so years the legend had been handed on did it occur to anyone to question the old priest's sanity. It is this way with sewer stories. They just are. Truth or falsity don't apply" (*V.*, p. 108). This is as close to an apologia as one is likely to get out of Pynchon. The sureness with which the pretense of impartiality is offered leaves a wary reader optionless; indeed it makes him appear presumptuous. He is dealing with an author who freely admits, with a grin, to writing and loving sewer stories because they just *are*.

This cockiness can begin to seem more gratuitous when it is not quite so merrily elusive. When Stencil hypothesizes, for instance, that the decadent Parisian lesbian hankering after Mélanie may be a thirty-three-year-old version of Victoria Wren ("the young entrepreneuse with all spring's hope in her virtù"), Pynchon notes that "we all get involved to an extent in the politics of slow dying, but poor Victoria had become intimate also with the Things in the Back Room" (*V.*, p. 386). A paragraph later, we are given a local Stencilian version of what one such "Thing" might be when he daydreams of V. as "an inanimate object of desire":

> Stencil even departed from his usual ploddings to daydream a vision of her now, at age seventy-six: skin radiant with the bloom of some new plastic; both eyes glass but now containing photoelectric cells, connected by silver electrodes to optic nerves of purest copper wire and leading to a brain exquisitely wrought as a diode matrix could ever be. Solenoid relays would be her ganglia, servo-actuators move her flawless nylon limbs, hydraulic fluid sent by a platinum heart-pump through butyrate veins and arteries. Perhaps—Stencil on occasion could have as vile a mind as any of the Crew—even a complex system of pressure transducers located in a marvelous vagina of polyethylene; the variable arms of their Wheatstone bridges all leading to a single silver cable which fed pleasure-voltages direct to the correct register of the digital machine in her skull. And whenever she smiled or grinned in ecstasy there would gleam her crowning feature: Eigenvalue's precious dentures. (*V.*, pp. 386–87)

Most of us will have but the vaguest notion of what "servo-actuators," "pressure transducers," and "Wheatstone bridges" are, but Pynchon's familiarity with this technology approaches the curatorial. His "great fondness for things

233

in their thingness," as Douglas Fowler puts it, forms not only "part of his astonishing ability to create a three-dimensional world" but "the excess of a loving god running his fingers through the riches of his own creation."[22] Our responses to Pynchon's fiction depend crucially upon how we feel about his always knowing, or seeming to know, more than we do and upon his continually anticipating possible moral objections to the metaphoric exuberance of his writing. "Stencil on occasion could have as vile a mind as any of the Crew": is this narrative insertion meant to assuage our offended sensibilities or is it falsely apologetic, a canny throwaway that actually mocks potential complaints about vileness under pretense of acknowledging them?[23]

Pynchon's suggestion that V. herself may be heading for what she fears Mélanie will become—the "foul-mind's darling of a male audience" (*V.*, p. 387)—is belied by the verve of Pynchon's descriptive precision. As with the analogy about the lack of emotional osmosis in Roony's and Mafia's marriage, the remarkable ease and attentiveness with which Pynchon details this sleazy "miracle of science" effectively displaces any qualms a reader may have about imagining a woman this way, grinning "in ecstasy." And this is true even if we dutifully decipher this as yet another sign of the entropic lassitude permeating the world of the novel—a lassitude Pynchon suggests by means of a quite indefatigable narrative animation.

"THOUGH A QUARREL in the streets is a thing to be hated," John Keats wrote to George and Georgiana Keats in 1819, "the energies displayed in it are fine."[24] To admire is not to condone: perhaps this seems the attitude we ourselves should critically adopt in reading Pynchon. But such a stance implies that we ourselves are doing something that Pynchon is not. It implies that by including vile and violent acts in his fiction Pynchon somehow "approves" of them. Levine contends that perhaps the "most disorienting and testing quality" of Pynchon's writing is "its almost sullen resistance to judging the various horrors it coldly narrates." Pynchon refuses "to protect us with his own disgust, or with ironies that don't cancel each other out."[25] This is another way of saying that Pynchon's writing fulfills the demands of its nature, the informational pressures of its sequences, by minding its own business, which is not necessarily ours. His fiction "has structures and plots based on his ideas of rockets, entropy, bondings, and paranoia," Roger Sale avers, "but he really runs on energy: these passages start out, go where they will, stop when they are tired. Thus he can be tasteless, vulgar, boring, indulgent, and inhumane because he runs out of fuel."[26] Pynchon's energy can take shape as the "approach and avoid" tactic Stencil uses in mapping out clues to V.'s existence (ibid., p. 44). It can also be seen in his highly self-conscious anticipation of responses to his own writing—responses that he himself variously formulates and follows through on before they have been evinced by a reader. This is why it seems mistaken to assert that Pynchon, in any sustained or preoccupied way, plays off his *reader's* responses. I know of no other writer whose fictional self-consciousness seems so unself-conscious or who so naturally assumes, in effect, the role of the black ghetto teenagers that Pynchon describes in "A Journey into the Mind of Watts." These young men have learned how to handle those wishing to account for their behavior:

> Usually [. . .] it's the younger cop of the pair who's more troublesome. Most Watts kids are hip to what's going on in this rookie's head—the things he feels he has to prove—as much as to the elements of the ritual. Before the cop can say, "Let's see your I.D.," you learn to take it out politely and say, "You want to see my I.D.?" Naturally it will bug the cop more the further ahead of him you can stay. It is flirting with disaster, but it's the cop who has the gun, so you do what you can.
>
> You must anticipate always how the talk is going to go. It's something you pick up quite young.[27]

One of the critics who has been bothered by Pynchon's vulgarity, tasteless-ness, and inhumanity when he is running on empty is Edward Mendelson. In discussing the "illegality of Pynchon's vision" in *Gravity's Rainbow*, Mendelson argues that

> critics who praise Pynchon tend to gloss over the uncomfortable fact that he writes quite a few stomach-turning pages. Slothrop's nightmare of a descent through the sewers, Brigadier Pudding's coprophilia, Mexico and Bodine's verbal disruption of officialdom at the dinner table—or Mexico's urinary dissolution of the solemnity of an official meeting—are all gross violations of literary and social decorum. When critics blithely quote such passages, as if they were as innocuous as Longfellow, they do Pynchon a disservice in ignoring the uncomfortable fact that his language retains an unmistakable power to shock and disgust, without ever allowing itself to be dismissed as infantilism or mere noise.[28]

Most of the critics who consider violence in Pynchon's work tend, predictably, to treat it metaphorically and thus to domesticate its unmistakable power to "shock and disgust." Consequently, Mélanie's death by impalement is seen as reflecting "the Western nexus of sex, art, and fatality,"[29] or violence in *V.* is read as a general gloss on the social and psychological dynamics of modern decadence and "Mass Man,"[30] or Pynchon himself is said to consider "purging violence" an answer to "benighted self-absorption."[31]

There should, conscientiously, be few generalizations about violence per se in *V.* or in Pynchon's fiction more generally, if only because it assumes and

235

emerges from so many different narrative stances with dramatically differing effects. Violence, like so much else in Pynchon's work, is less a subject than a theater of operations. Besides its extended sequences of violence, *V.* includes a plethora of violent details, like so many asterisks punctuating the historical scenes. Many of them seem designed to rupture what Kurt Mondaugen calls "the barren touchlessness" of the past (*V.*, p. 237): in German South-West Africa in 1904 a colonist's wife commits suicide and jackals eat her breasts, babies are "tossed in the air and caught on bayonets" (*V.*, p. 254); a Turkish pasha in 1565 floats a "death's flotilla" of beheaded English corpses into Malta's Grand Harbor (*V.*, p. 436); and a British intelligence officer is found mutilated and drowned off Malta in 1919, his genitals "sewn in his mouth" (*V.*, p. 456). Pynchon does not usually invoke such details for their sobering or plaintive aspects alone, however, for they often incongruously share the page (certainly the chapter) with parodic excesses or what Fowler calls "the kind of self-consciously smutty horseplay that used to be the staple of undergraduate humor magazines."[32] Pynchon often abdicates any lasting responsibility for having a "point of view" in scenes of violence.

At the scene of Mélanie's death, for example, we listen to a narrator who states that the account of "what happened then was available to Stencil in police records" (*V.*, p. 387) and who quotes from, among other sources, a 1913 French newspaper review of her stage performance. But as the scene progresses this source-citing narrative voice disappears into the details of its own account, and as readers we are left to imaginatively fend for ourselves. Mélanie is playing Su Feng in a ballet entitled "Rape of the Chinese Virgins" (*V.*, p. 371) at the Théâtre Vincent Castor. The composer of the piece is one Vladimir Porcépic. The night of the performance, "even as the pit orchestra tuned up," chaos ensues as an "anti-Porcépic faction" and friends of the composer who are "already calling themselves Porcépiquistes" (*V.*, p. 387) wrangle noisily in a typical Pynchon melee about "an international movement seeking to overthrow Western Civilization." It is only toward the end of the second act, with its "powerful, slow-building seven-minute crescendo," that "the attentions of the few serious onlookers [are] taken entirely by La Jarretière":

> Two of the male dancers, whom Itague had never left off calling Mongolized fairies, produced a long pole, pointed wickedly at one end. The music, near triple-forte, could be heard now above the roaring of the audience. Gendarmes had moved in at the rear entrances, and were trying ineffectually to restore order. Satin, next to Porcépic, one hand on the composer's shoulder, leaned forward, shaking. It was a tricky bit of choreography, Satin's own. He'd got the idea from reading an account of an Indian massacre in America. While two of the other Mongolians held her,

struggling and head shaven, Su Feng was impaled at the crotch on the point of the pole and slowly raised by the entire male part of the company, while the females lamented below. Suddenly one of the automaton handmaidens seemed to run amok, tossing itself about the stage. Satin moaned, gritted his teeth. "Damn the German," he said, "it will distract." The conception depended on Su Feng continuing her dance while impaled, all movement restricted to one point in space, an elevated point, a focus, a climax.

The pole was now erect, the music four bars from the end. A terrible hush fell over the audience, gendarmes and combatants all turned as if magnetized to watch the stage. La Jarretière's movements became more spastic, agonized: the expression on the normally dead face was one which would disturb for years the dreams of those in the front rows. Porcépic's music was now almost deafening: all tonal location had been lost, notes screamed out simultaneous and random like fragments of a bomb: winds, strings, brass and percussion were indistinguishable as blood ran down the pole, the impaled girl went limp, the last chord blasted out, filled the theater, echoed, hung, subsided. Someone cut all the stage lights, someone else ran to close the curtain.

It never opened. Mélanie was supposed to have worn a protective metal device, a species of chastity belt, into which the point of the pole fit. She had left it off. A physician in the audience had been summoned at once by Itague as soon as he saw the blood. Shirt torn, one eye blackened, the doctor knelt over the girl and pronounced her dead.

Of the woman, her lover, nothing further was seen. Some versions tell of her gone hysterical backstage, having to be detached forcibly from Mélanie's corpse; of her screaming vendetta at Satin and Itague for plotting to kill the girl. The coroner's verdict, charitably, was death by accident. Perhaps Mélanie, exhausted by love, excited as at any première, had forgotten. Adorned with so many combs, bracelets, sequins, she might have become confused in this fetish-world and neglected to add to herself the one inanimate object that would have saved her. Itague thought it was suicide, Satin refused to talk about it, Porcépic suspended judgment. But they lived with it for many years.

Rumor had it that a week or so later the lady V. ran off with one Sgherraccio, a mad Irredentist. At least they both disappeared from Paris at the same time; from Paris and as far as anyone on the Butte could say, from the face of the earth. (V., pp. 388–90)

Is Mélanie here for Pynchon the equivalent of Mrs. May for O'Connor: the fictional vehicle for registering larger cosmic ironies or entropic devolutions? Her "sacrifice" is gruesomely kept from seeming merely fantastic, yet Pynchon makes sure that it threatens to be, in order to satisfy the thematic ambitions of the novel. His infatuation with automatism, sexual excess, and the inanimate is fully exercised here. The automaton handmaiden "expresses" part of Mélanie's pain, "tossing itself about the stage," and the sexual aspects of the scene—the seven-minute crescendo, a "climax," an "erect" pole held by male dancers, impalement, "conception," the lack of a chastity belt for a Chinese Virgin—are all more than explicit. They also offer a lurid example of what Pynchon a few pages earlier called (as if for a graduate seminar) "the Porpentine theme, the Tristan-and-Iseult theme, indeed, according to some, the single melody, banal and exasperating, of all Romanticism since the Middle Ages: 'the act of love and the act of death are one'" (*V.*, p. 385). Here again Pynchon "interprets" a scene (this time *before* it occurs) but predictably the theme or "melody" he offers proves not more but less helpful in reading the sequence. It provides not an authoritative interpretation of the scene but one more subversion of the notion that the scene might or should be interpretable.

Robert Golden rightly asserts that Mélanie's death, along with the black masses, lesbianism, and incest in this chapter, forms part of "a Baudelairean atmosphere of decadence which is inseparable from the feeling of crisis, the feeling that the old order or the world itself is about to end." But Golden then goes on to say that Mélanie's death, surrounded by automata and viewed by a fetishist, makes her "the emblem of a new womanhood," the culminating example of how Pynchon often "equates Vheissu with vagina, the void of the inanimate with the sexual void of women."[33] Mary Allen, in a somewhat similar vein, has read the scene as "a powerful indictment" of lesbianism: "The heavy symbolism of this scene—her death, so utterly phallic a destruction—puts sex back into its violent but heterosexual place, freeing V. of the lesbian alliance and making her available to men again, her life cleansed. . . . Pynchon never damns male homosexuality with any such violence—it is more foolish than awful, not hideously out of order as in V.'s affair with Mélanie."[34] To accuse Pynchon (the old satyr) of "damning" lesbianism, however, is to hear him endorsing Stencil's comically vindictive feelings toward V. just before this scene occurs. "Let her be a lesbian," Stencil avows melodramatically, "let her turn to a fetish, let her die: she was a beast of venery and he had no tears for her" (*V.*, p. 387). Even Stencil is unlikely to take "so utterly phallic" a death as a recommendation of the heterosexuality it repulsively exaggerates. Neither is V.'s life cleansed of taint here, as Allen suggests, for she is not exonerated of her other connections with scenes of international crisis: her response, for example, as Victoria Wren in Florence, to the sight of "a rioter in a shirt of motley being bayoneted again and again by two soldiers":

She stood as still as she had at the crossroads waiting for Evan; her face betrayed no emotion. It was as if she saw herself embodying a feminine principle, acting as complement to all this bursting, explosive male energy. Inviolate and calm, she watched the spasms of wounded bodies, the fair of violent death, framed and staged, it seemed, for her alone in that tiny square. From her hair the heads of five crucified also looked on, no more expressive than she. (*V.*, pp. 192–93)

Mélanie's death forms a grisly expansion of Pynchon's habit of instilling parodic or incongruously named characters with believable life and emotions. He takes a fantastic event here and treats it realistically. He prevents Mélanie's death from becoming a sexual metaphor safely insulated from the visceral shock of her "spastic, agonized" writhings. The circumstances of her death are so bizarre and sexually charged that their very unlikeliness makes this particular form of violence inescapably metaphoric. Yet regardless of all his explicitly eroticized details, Pynchon offers no exclusively appropriate metaphoric context within which the scene might make sense. He purposefully resists the impulse to render her death intelligible as a metaphor even as he accentuates its metaphoric aspects. Fictional scenes of violence seem senseless (both gratuitous and unintelligible) if they lack a narrative, an explanatory context. More precisely, they seem senseless if they lack a narrative that offers us compensations or that shields us in some way from the liberties an author has taken with our imaginative weakness for visualizing pain and victimization. The senselessness of Mélanie's death can be interpreted, it can be forced to make sense (either as a suicide or, on another level, as an expression of Pynchon's sexual insecurities), but only by ignoring how one part of the passage giveth what another part taketh away.

Like Solace Layfield in *Wise Blood*, the most realistic aspect of Mélanie's characterization is her death. Her physicality as a character is made grimly apparent: she bleeds. The more we abstract Mélanie's fictional presence into part of a sexual image or analogy, the more we neglect or protect ourselves from the harrowing details of her impalement on a "wickedly" sharpened pole. To read her death as "phallic" (as Pynchon in part encourages us to do) is to treat it as symbolic rather than realistic, as represented rather than real. Mélanie dies in such a reading much less horrifically, on a "pole" made not of steel but of flesh. The word *phallic* is an interpretive term, the form of which applies not to life but to art and to representation. We speak of phallic configurations in terms of movies, cartoons, paintings, advertising, music videos, even architecture, but not usually in terms of actual occurrences. If, for example, we had witnessed or read a newspaper account of a car accident in which

239

a woman had been impaled on, say, a gear-shift (a morbid hypothesis to be sure), we would not consider it a "phallic" death. Yet that same event portrayed in fiction will almost automatically be considered by some in that light. Pynchon typically disorients his reader by depicting violence realistically while nevertheless incongruously suggesting that it can be read on another level. What purpose such other levels might serve he refuses to let us know, and in this way the metaphoric import of Mélanie's death remains as grotesquely provocative as it is indecipherable.

Pynchon also seems acutely aware of the conventions of victimization associated with women. Both because women have traditionally been seen as more physically vulnerable than men and because their being physically "pierced" in an act of represented violence often seems sexually overdetermined, images of violence done to women are usually more upsetting (though not necessarily more tragic) than images of the same act done to men would be. Mélanie's death thus becomes disturbing beyond its dramatic occasion, a violently charged image that disengages itself, in memory, from the story. Mélanie dies from the force of a steel bar, not from the implications of a sexual analogy. Yet in Pynchon's world, even metaphors seem capable of killing. The two ways of reading the sequence—as a realistic account of a ballerina's death or as a metaphor of the sexual violation of women; as the image of a victim or of a Victim—are contradictory, yet Pynchon generates and encourages them both. What makes his work so disorienting is that he achieves his realistic effects while simultaneously challenging them.

BECAUSE WE ARE GIVEN but momentary vertical perspectives on narrative events in Pynchon's fiction, he can seem to run unnervingly hot and then cold. He often fashions moving acknowledgments of human vulnerability that convey a numb leeriness or, in Sales's words, a yearning "raggedness and torn ness."[35] But he can also, in the next sentence, engage in enthralled renderings of the very technology that tears and maims people. His work thus offers, in part, the richest contemporary manifestation of a venerable American literary tradition in which, as Poirier has shown, "individuals are characterized less by their relation to one another than by their relation to conglomerations of power" such as "Nature, The City, Society, The Dynamo, The Bomb, [and] The Presidency," which "cripple the free articulation of individual consciousness."[36] Writers as otherwise radically different as Melville, Dreiser, Wharton, and Faulkner have all been fascinated with the brutalizing environmental forces that destroy characters they love or at least respect.

Such historical and scientific forces, so recurrently uncongenial to the traditional conceptions of self-affirmation and human value exemplified elsewhere in literature, provoke in American authors a fascination with their destructive potential. They also prompt sustained efforts by writers to create a style that incorporates and outstrips such destructive forces. This process often exerts its will by displaying (even flaunting) an indifference to human consequences, by treating the apologies and exonerations an understandably shocked or disturbed reader may expect, as mere bribes: bribes weighted with the kind of social contract and pressure of accommodation a writer may seek to evade. In Pynchon's case this indifference only rarely assumes the pseudoemancipated posture of unshockability, of watching comfortably, in John Fraser's words, "as other people are outraged in piquant ways."[37] Pynchon seems less interested in baiting his reader than in baiting himself, as he looks for the next lead to follow, the next sequence to write. *V.* offers us not so much a series of calculated affronts but the mobile, self-fertilizing workings of Pynchon's appetite for imagistic variety and parodic unrest.

One of the most disquieting examples of Pynchon's insistently noncommittal narrative impulses in *V.* is Esther's "nose job," a sequence that has become a kind of notorious set-piece discussed mostly outside of rather than within Pynchon criticism. The operation is performed by Shale Schoenmaker, M.D., whose professional sense of mission is sustained by "a number of bloodless theories about the 'idea' of the plastic surgeon."

> Schoenmaker's dedication was toward repairing the havoc wrought by agencies outside his own sphere of responsibility. Others—politicians and machines—carried on wars; others—perhaps human machines—condemned his patients to the ravages of acquired syphilis; others—on the highways, in the factories—undid the work of nature with automobiles, milling machines, other instruments of civilian disfigurement. What could he do toward eliminating the causes? They existed, formed a body of things-as-they-are; he came to be afflicted with a conservative laziness. It was social awareness of a sort, but with boundaries and interfaces which made it less than the catholic rage filling him that night in the barracks with the M.O. It was in short a deterioration of purpose; a decay. (*V.*, pp. 88–89)

The elaborate detailing of the physical price exacted by the "ideal of nasal beauty established by movies, advertisements, [and] magazine illustrations" (*V.*, p. 91) that inspires Esther to get a nose job will soon expose us to the consequences of Schoenmaker's "bloodless theories." Pynchon establishes enough of a provisional moral and professional norm here to accuse Schoenmaker of "conservative laziness" and "decay," yet he himself is about to offer us a scene full of narrative "boundaries and interfaces" that will make "catholic rage" at what we are presented seem almost anachronistic.

Pynchon may be appalled by the sheer physical damage perpetuated in the name of surgical vanity and bad taste (the "retroussé" Irish nose "they all wanted," Schoenmaker says, is itself "an aesthetic misfit: a Jew nose in reverse, is all" [*V*., p. 90]). But that can be inferred only from the energy with which he descriptively devotes himself to the sensory ravages of the scene (an energy that might also be construed as luridly and tauntingly indifferent). After a "two-inch" hypodermic needle has been pushed through Esther's nostrils "all the way up to the glabella—the bump between the eyebrows" (*V*., p. 92), Schoenmaker goes to work:

> "Let me know if you feel anything." He gave the chisel a few light taps with a mallet; stopped, puzzled, and then began to hammer harder. "It's a rough mother," he said, dropping his jocular tone. Tap, tap, tap. "Come on, you bastard." The chisel point edged its way, millimeter by millimeter, between Esther's eyebrows. "Scheisse!" With a loud snap, her nose was broken free of the forehead. By pushing in from either side with his thumbs, Schoenmaker completed the fracture. (*V*., pp. 94–95)

"Let me know if you feel anything": Schoenmaker's remark seems as apropos of the reader as of Esther, for Pynchon is determined that we as well as she "get an education" (*V*., p. 93) about the physical facts of plastic surgery. The chinking of chisel on bone we imaginatively hear behind the simple words "tap, tap, tap" adequately measures the explosive intensity of Pynchon's realistic effects.

The narrative eye in this scene is not entirely focused upon Esther's nose, however, and Levine is right to contend that the scene offers more than "a virtuoso extension of the tradition of naturalistic fiction": "It is not merely clinical, but clinical and vulgar, and not merely that but clinical vulgarity observed as though it were funny—which it almost becomes."[38] What makes the scene seem potentially amusing is the heightened incongruity between Esther's pain and the heartless jocularity of those who are operating on her. Immediately following the passage above, Schoenmaker says, "See? It's all wobbly now. That's act two. Now ve shorten das septum, ja." The self-consciously theatrical aspects of the scene and the distasteful implications of using mock-German accents in speaking to a Jewish patient seem purposefully designed to denigrate suffering consciousness. Yet both these elements form more than a mere critique of a bedside manner.

Trench, Schoenmaker's assistant, watches Esther's gyrating hips on the operating table ("all she had free to move for the pain") and "leered appreciatively": "The sexual metaphor in all this wasn't lost on Trench, who kept chanting, 'Stick it in . . . pull it out . . . stick it in . . . ooh that was good . . . pull it out . . .' and tittering softly above Esther's eyes. Irving would sigh each time, exasperated. 'That boy,' you expected her to say" (*V.*, p. 92). Irving, we have been told earlier, is Schoenmaker's mistress and his "secretary/receptionist/nurse with an impossibly coy retroussé nose and thousands of freckles, all of which Schoenmaker had done himself" (*V.*, p. 34). Her exasperation here is not that of moral outrage but of social indecorum, as if the problem with Trench is that he is so boyishly obvious rather than demeaning and crude. Irving's lack of a properly sympathetic response here is being offered for our unsympathetic scrutiny. But as a spectator herself, Irving functions as a projected image of those who watch *her*: a reader whose "exasperated" response to the scene has been made to seem not only inappropriate but easily anticipated and parodied.

Trench plays Aminadab to Schoenmaker's Aylmer in a grotesque updating of Nathaniel Hawthorne's "The Birthmark." His "tittering" implies that Pynchon sees his salacious chanting as both heartless and comically excessive. Pynchon implicitly asks us here to "consider the source." The least possibly titillating clinical occasion, smelling of iodine and antiseptics, is being inappropriately treated as if it were sexually arousing, which is why Trench's overactive libido seems grimly comic. (At least he seems comic, with such a name, as long as he remains a *fictional* attendant.)

After the operation, Esther (who during it seems completely victimized and degraded and who is described as "near delirium" and "teetering between here and hysteria") will herself add her own grotesque and incongruous response to what has happened to her:

> Passivity having only one meaning for her, she left the hospital Schoenmaker had sent her to after a day and a night, and roamed the East Side in fugue, scaring people with her white beak and a certain shock about the eyes. She was sexually turned on, was all: as if Schoenmaker had located and flipped a secret switch or clitoris somewhere inside her nasal cavity. A cavity is a cavity, after all. Trench's gift for metaphor might have been contagious. (*V.*, p. 96)

The mock-pedestrian explanations here—"she was sexually turned on, was all," "a cavity is a cavity, after all"—may come from Pynchon as narrator. But these quickly flipped switches of "common sense" might also be attributed, via free indirect discourse, to an Esther infected with "Trench's gift for metaphor." Pynchon's own irrepressible (and here fairly sophomoric) metaphoric instincts are thus exercised at the same time as they are disavowed and even located as a kind of imaginative contagion. Again the novel's imaginative energies are channeled into the surface of the narrative and away from the author. Pynchon disappears as effectively behind his evasive attributions of motive as he does behind his "tap, tap, tap."

Esther seems purposefully kept from engaging our continuing sympathy as a character. The chapter opens after the operation has taken place and she casts "a sentimental glance" at the operating table "on which her face had been altered" (*V.*, p. 84) before she beds down with Schoenmaker. A cross between a naif and a nymphette, she offers herself up for sexual exploitation with a self-victimizing thoughtlessness, and Schoenmaker is later said to have "spotted her at the outset as an easy make" (*V.*, p. 96). Esther suffers extreme pain during the operation ("nothing before in her experience had ever hurt quite so much" [*V.*, p. 92]), but even that does not provide a standard by which we are allowed to pity her. When Schoenmaker tells her, "gently, like a lover," that he is going to "saw off [her] hump,"

> Esther watched his eyes as best she could, looking for something human there. Never had she felt so helpless. Later she would say, "It was almost a mystic experience. What religion is it—one of the Eastern ones—where the highest condition we can attain is that of an object—a rock. It was like that; I felt myself drifting down, this delicious loss of Estherhood, becoming more and more a blob, with no worries, traumas, nothing: only Being. . . ." (*V.*, p. 93)

Pynchon mocks the dippy inappropriateness of Esther's psychobabble even as he allows the notion of her "loss of Estherhood" enough of the narrative spotlight to perk up those Stencils in the audience on the lookout for references to "the inanimate." Esther is denied the chance to feel helpless and thus compel our sympathy because Pynchon seems intent upon overturning fictional conventions of victimization. He does not replace them with new conventions so much as he sabotages the conditions under which our sympathies can be predictably engaged or outraged. He suggestively intimates that for certain readers as well as for certain characters, guilt can become an aphrodisiac.[39]

Levine contends that "by giving us no easy position from which we might judge" Esther's nose job, "Pynchon forces us into it beyond morality":

> The more we admire the prose that can make us feel the pain, the more it implicates us in it. The writer who makes us feel that something quite horrible has been routinized and socially accepted participates in the technical joys and power lust involved in the activity. Moral judgment becomes irrelevant, and the question is whether the prose, in facing the tyranny of its own skills, can release Pynchon or us from them.[40]

The question of imaginative "release" here, however, is not the same for Pynchon as it is for his readers. He seems concerned with a condition of moral relevance more for the sake of its immediate, temporary utility in furthering larger imaginative ambitions. The danger in reading Pynchon, as Robert Boyers has said of a very different writer (Jerzy Kosinski), is "that we will demand of a vision that it be pliable to our needs as [people] anxious for consolation, anxious as well for guilt and a complicity in guilt that cancels barriers, distinctions, realms, that would if it could make of imagination a mere handmaiden of behavioral imperatives."[41] If we do admire Pynchon's writing about Esther's nose job it is not because of what it tells us about a horrible, routinized social practice but, as Levine suggests, because of the ways in which the writing itself escapes routinization in so telling us.

Would we, to put it another way, want an "easy position from which we might judge" Esther's surgery as Pynchon presents it? His narrative high jinks seem calculated to imply that "judgments" of experience inevitably depend upon stable structures of selection and exclusion, relevance and irrelevance, comfort and guilt, which in themselves may well lead to the need for social remedies—for various forms of physical and psychological forms of reconstruction—the excesses of which we can then feel conscientious about bemoaning.

What is the difference, this scene prompts us to ask, between a traditional notion of narrative intelligibility that makes moral choice "relevant" and an ideal of nasal beauty that inspires such physical damage? Plastic surgery has always, Pynchon suggests, been a means of social normalization, whether in trying to help the "horrible postwar fraternity" (V., p. 87) of disfigured veterans or the hapless victims, like Esther, of socially inculcated self-loathing. We might contend that there are moral and immoral uses of plastic surgery. But even the positive uses of this science seem "positive" because of preestablished social agreements and norms based in part upon previous literary idealizations of beauty, agreements whose orderings and control Pynchon subverts and evades even as he suggests their inevitability. He continues to rob us of a ground from which we might feel safely judgmental or outraged, though many critics understandably feel impelled to provide that missing ground.

The yearning for inclusiveness that Pynchon's fiction more generally displays—the yearning for more images, more anticipated responses, more of what Itague calls "the jitterings and squeaks of a metaphysical bedspring" (V., p. 381)—implies that *any* acquiescence to a stable point of view or balance of narrative energies would be akin to imaginative heat death. The flux and drive of his imagination spill into scenes of violence that we are, as it were, dared to witness—"dared" both because they are shocking and testingly lurid and be-cause they are presented in ways that refuse to provide any guiding tone of response. We are denied any exclusive, exonerating perspective from which to locate ourselves in relation not only to narrative events but to any given sen-tence or sequence.

This is what makes Pynchon look, to some readers, like the Steven Spielberg of contemporary fiction: a figure frequently terrified of not giving us enough thrills and special effects. Pynchon's novels are often less "novels" than compe-titions: Pynchon versus Pynchon. His writing does become at times what Le-vine calls "a kind of litany aspiring to the infinite sequence."

> With such ambitions, the prose must also be self-consciously amoral, as if the
> ultimate morality is in a truly Whitmanesque embrace of everything, of copro-
> philia, sadism, masochism, gang bangs and daisy chains, genocide, incest, sodomy,
> fellatio, transvestitism, torture, physical decay, murder, pie-throwing, decomposi-
> tion, toilet bowls. But not only these. It is a prose that seems almost desperate in
> the tricks it will invent to keep from its own finitude, to find some sort of life in
> the very decadence and de-animation of which it is a symptom.[42]

Yet Pynchon's "embrace of everything" is not, it seems to me, ultimately Whitmanesque. It is ferociously inclusive only so as to get beyond the power of inclusiveness.

Pynchon feels compelled to exhaust, or seem to exhaust, every possible metaphoric resource open to him as a way of gaining a measure of freedom from them all. By availing himself of every possible contemporary idiom he seems to hope he will remain beholden to none. He can attempt such a task only by extraordinary expenditures of verbal energy that he alone seems capa-ble of sustaining and that render his fictional moments dynamic to a degree no comparable moment in life could be. Pynchon continues to be "the master of vanishing acts" (to borrow Salman Rushdie's phrase) in more than a strictly biographical sense.[43] The phantom movements by which he zigzags through the plotted fretwork of his novels, ceaselessly emerging from and vanishing into their complexities, make him a legatee, a shadow-legatee, of what Poirier calls "the distinctly American vision" of our great nineteenth-century fictional clas-sics. It is not a vision "of cultural deprivation, but rather of cultural inundation, of being swamped, swept up, counted in before you could count yourself out, pursued by every bookish aspect of life even as you try to get lost in a wilder-ness, in a randomness where you might hope to find your true self."[44] Pyn-chon's remarkable and disquieting strength, which we feel as if by induction, consists of counting himself in *as* he counts himself out. Nothing seems unassimilable to his imaginative appetite for illusions of precision, and he relishes them both because they are precise and because they are illusory.

The violence in Pynchon's work is realistic, but in such a way that it anticipatively evades our attempts to accommodate its imaginative power within an explanatory structure of significance—even as it suggests the presence of such structures. Realistic narratives always enact a resistance to our efforts to make sense of them. They invite us to read around words and misconstrue our experience of their verbal action as something beyond them. What Pynchon does, in effect, is make that imaginative resistance the basis of all his larger "themes": his fascination with mystery, paranoia, conspiracies, and political power, with everything that successfully evades our ordinary perceptual habits of making sense. With this imaginative dynamic so pervasive in his fiction, many readers may ultimately find Pynchon's writing in scenes of violence either too raw and unnegotiable or too warily knowing to bear rereading. When the fictional illusion of an authorless, unvoiced world becomes as potent and tricky as it does in his hands, it may find itself in a readerless world as well. But part of the reason that I admire Pynchon's work is that I doubt that this would bother him.

Style, Violence, American Fiction

THERE CAN BE a "violence of mirth, or wrath or suffering," Emerson reminds us in his late essay "The Tragic," a piece that alternately clouds and brightens as he muses on "the House of Pain."[1] Reflecting on the belief "in a brute Fate or Destiny," which he calls "the bitterest tragic element in life to be derived from an intellectual source," Emerson consoles himself by saying that this belief "disappears with civilization" and the introduction of "a better public and private tradition." He knows that only the *belief* in this "tragic element" can be "circumscribed," not the actual "laws of the world." No matter what the nature of our "private satisfaction," we cannot forestall "famine, fever, inaptitude, mutilation, rack, madness, and loss of friends." Yet despite these numerous reminders of the tragic in life, Emerson remains the apostle of imaginative power. He refuses to diminish the fact that "the intellect" and "the moral sense," at their purest, "ravish us into a region" into which "clouds of sorrow cannot rise." This ravishment occurs because a consoling intellect can put "an interval between a man and his fortune, and so convert the sufferer into a spectator, and his pain into poetry." The intellect "yields the joys of conversation, of letters, and of science. Hence also the torments of life become tuneful tragedy, solemn and soft with music, and garnished with rich dark pictures."

It is possible to imagine any number of responses to this vivid notion of "tuneful tragedy," but the most compelling might be: "that's easy for you to say, but keep *my* pain out of your poetry, brother." In other words, many might question whether the distance requisite to transform the "torments of life" into tragedy can be so easily achieved or yielded. But however Emerson's reflections may suit our designs on life (in every sense), they do seem particularly apt in describing the workings of literature. One intent of this study has been to show that generalized statements like "pain cannot be beautiful" (or rich or soft or tuneful or funny) are entertained only by way of an impoverished notion of art and its capabilities. This does *not* mean that those who admit this would somehow condone or endorse in life the violence they imaginatively experience in American fiction. Suggesting that they might represents, as Pauline Kael suggests, the means by which self-appointed guardians of morality inflict their own view of art on others. Condemnations of new and unexampled "uses" of violence in the arts, especially in film, stem from the conviction that art provides examples for imitation, which is why such guardians "think a good movie is one that sets 'healthy,' 'cheerful' examples of behavior, like a giant all-purpose commercial for the American way of life." Louis B. Mayer, Kael reminds us, "did not turn us into a nation of Andy Hardys," and "if, as has been said, we are a nation of mother-lovers, I don't think we can place the blame on *Oedipus Rex*." The accusation that the beauty of movie stars (like Warren Beatty and Faye Dunaway in *Bonnie and Clyde*) makes the antisocial acts of the characters they play seem glamorous or attractive forms a similar "clutching at straws": "After all, if they played factory workers, the economy might be dislocated by everybody's trying to become a factory worker. (Would having criminals played by dwarfs or fatties discourage crime? It seems rather doubtful.)"[2]

Violence in fiction can sometimes become "tuneful tragedy" because the life in fiction is life as it is imaginable in words (or as it is "structurable" or "narratable" or "tellable" in terms of other narrative elements), and words are capable of changing all they touch. Imaginative distance is always and already a feature of depictions of violence in fiction. Our experience of violence in fiction is always to some degree mediated. But the degree is all important. The truth of the notion that fictional violence is always secondhand will, in the case of realistic imagining, be almost inconsequential. Thus in studying the imaginative substance and "tunefulness" of particular instances of violence, I have been at pains to suggest that an exacting attention to individual verbal occasions seems best suited to counter the "all this is nothing but that" claims that now too often characterize literary criticism.

This book has been meant to serve as a kind of environmental impact study, an examination of the ways in which stylistic environments are created in fiction and of how their imaginative force fashions and reshapes what are later thought of as independent "topics" (like violence). The usefulness of such a study is to be tested more in its specific engagements with texts than in after-the-fact formulations. If a call for a particularistic attention to verbal performance is to have any force, it must fruitfully illuminate the life in language that forms its justification. Like Ike McCaslin in Faulkner's "The Bear," the best readers of American fiction, it still seems to me, are willing to surrender their perceptual equivalents of compass, watch, and gun (and maybe even the idea of a hunt) in entering the pages of a novel or a story. They are willing to be imaginatively lost before deciding it is better to be "found." They are encouraged—encouraged by the works themselves—to find the local pleasures, disappointments, and confusions of an author's engagement with his or her material more irreducibly valuable than the false clarifications by which those engagements might be made to seem more manageable.

Again, this does not mean that such readers have to be deferential to or ideologically hoodwinked by the texts they read. But it does mean that they encounter the verbal circumstances they find in those works with the least possible desire to make them stand to account. Readers never come to novels as blank slates; we cannot somehow "lose" our past and our past reading, which, to use Delmore Schwartz's image, stand behind us tugging "the hair on our heads, like the goddess Athena."[3] Neither can one reasonably assert that most readers read with no end in view. But the end of those readers whose work I admire is not reached by searching, pencil in hand, for signs of cultural hegemony or for semiological semaphores flashing between sentences. The end, insofar as it exceeds the desire to make it through this or that sequence or chapter, entails an account of what the trip was like. That the landscape traversed, not just the state of the traveler, fundamentally determines the shape of the journey should go without saying. And that the landscape in this case has all manner of social and historical conformations also makes that account more than merely a personal slide show.

Stanley Fish would undoubtedly see such temperamental tendencies as disguised ambitiousness and label them the foredoomed manifestations of "aggressive humility," of someone adopting the manner of a speaker at a temperance meeting who declares that he "will never interpret [texts] again but will instead do something else ('I mean to describe them')." This, however, is merely Fish's way of making sure that his own severely restricted notion of interpretation is, as he declares, "the only game in town."[4] Critical humility, as a value, does not have to preclude clear-eyed vision, so long as it is attended by Reuben Brower's conviction that "not knowing where one is coming out is an essential part of the experience of thinking."[5] To admit this is always to be open to ridicule by those who value conclusiveness and adhesion over flux and instability.

"The excitement of great literature is not that of being drunk or hypnotized," Christopher Ricks asserts,

> though it is no less vivid. The reader both enters into thoughts and feelings and codes of belief that are very different from his own, and yet simultaneously remains himself. A true reader and critic is open-minded but not vacuous; he does not surrender his own opinions, experiences, beliefs and knowledge, but neither does he clutch them desperately. He is both independent and accessible. He will not think that his way of discussing literature is the only acceptable one, but he will not slide into the easy sentimentality of thinking that any way of discussing literature is acceptable and as good as any other. A good critic will . . . ask, but not demand, that we agree with him.[6]

250

Some may find Ricks's agility here in delineating what a "true reader and critic" do positively aerobic, a form of excessive moderation. But he is clearly defining an ideal, and I find his evenhandedness both refreshing and a goal toward which to strive.

For Ricks, literary criticism and the act of reading itself are to be sharply distinguished: "Criticism is a discussion of literature. It is not a substitute for reading the work itself (though it can easily be mis-used as that), and it makes little attempt to reproduce the sensations of reading. No, its business is with, and only with, those elements in a work of literature which can profitably be discussed." Clearly, a great deal of weight falls upon Ricks's use of "profitably" here, and he goes on to use a less loaded term in asserting that "the critic's task is to discuss all those elements of the work which are amenable to discussion." But though his comments may at first seem restrictive and prohibitive, they actually work in an opposite direction:

> It would be satisfactory if the discussable parts [of a work] were always the more important, but that need not be so. . . . the critic must resist all the time the temptation to write as if the discussable things were the most important ones. Any critic is in danger of thinking that one poem is very good because he can discuss it a lot, and that another poem is bad because it does not at all lend itself to discussion.[7]

Attempts to reproduce "the sensations of reading" are not for Ricks somehow inconsequential. To the contrary, such "sensations" are usually so complex, evanescent, and powerful that they do not readily lend themselves to discussion. "Naturally the critic will hope to extend the area where rational argument about literature is possible," Ricks concludes, "and certainly the frontiers are always being pushed back."[8]

Yet despite (and too often, because of) some terminological heavy artillery, criticism still lacks an adequate vocabulary by which to characterize some of the most fundamental actions of our imaginations in reading fiction. This is especially true, as I have repeatedly suggested, in terms of aural imagining and the play of language to the ear. It has remained expedient for many critics to think of this aspect of our verbal imaginations as representing only an observable slippage and drift from other more dominant "conceptual" forms of imagining. (The denigration is usually enacted by recourse to metaphors of seduction, self-indulgence, solipsism, and capitulation in describing the aural imagination.) A full recognition and investigation of the power and influence of aural imagining in our verbal lives constitutes a fundamental challenge to several recent theoretical tendencies, especially those variously lumped under the term "deconstruction."[9]

Candid formulations of literary meaning and the role of the critic are certainly helpful in this regard. Millicent Bell has shrewdly and engagingly expounded what I take to be almost universally accepted critical standards, even if they are standards kept in place only so they can then be "deconstructed":

> Reading, it seems to me, is a continual process in which we strive to make meaning out of the materials of offered narrative. Even before the end is reached an ellipsis in the plot will *compel* us to a making-do, to the hypothesizing of design which dispenses with the omitted, and if the gaps are filled and those hypotheses *must be surrendered*, they have had a certain effect. When the gaps are permanent, our *meaning-hungry, plot-hungry* minds work passionately at still making a whole of what remains [my emphasis].[10]

Bell here is more forthcoming about her own motives than most critics would be, but her candor does not make her methods any less potentially manipulative or willful. We all try to make sense out of fiction, she asserts—we all make up stories about stories, even if our account is a deconstructive one that asserts, for example, that our implied definition or expectation of what a story should be was tendentious in the first place.

But how adequate is it to say that reading fiction involves a continual process of making meaning out of narratives (or haplessly striving to do so)? Bell's vocabulary of appetite and compulsion (along with the martial implications of "surrendering" our hypotheses) itself works hard to convince us of what should, it seems, be quite natural and honorable. It is as if we need to be forcibly reminded of our critical obligation to prowl texts for meaning and plot, forever famished, lest we accede to the temptation, in the lovely words of the movie title, to stop making sense. As I have tried to suggest in every chapter in this study, however, "making sense" of a text is by and large an extractive activity, one that excavates and refines (by translating, denuding, decoding, exhuming, deconstructing) various meanings from narrative materials that are themselves too often rendered mere waste products in a critical Bessemer process. "Because the motive of literary criticism is knowledge," James Guetti asserts,

> it is perhaps to be expected that the varieties of literature itself are most often described in terms of their intelligibility and imagined as various forms of knowing. The knowledge that literature communicates is of course supposed to be less obvious, or more complex or oblique or delicate, than is the case for nonliterary, or perhaps "ordinary," language, but it is held to be knowledge nonetheless, and its value as such is held the ultimate measure of the literary form that produced it. . . . far more frequently than they ask, of a poem or a narrative, what is it doing, what

is the energy of its action, critics, as well as general readers, want to know, what does it tell us and where does it get us—what do we know by it?[11]

The difficulties posed by such assumptions are not ephemeral. The fact that the terms for the ostenisble opposites of "intelligibility" and "knowledge" ("unintelligibility," "nonsense," "ignorance") carry overbearingly negative connotations always premarks the cards in advance and puts critics interested in investigating the energy of a poem or a narrative's action on the defensive. So does the notion that certain imaginative properties of fiction are explainable by rather than often merely *coincident with* certain social and historical conditions.

Recent explorations of what, in Ricks's terms, it is possible to discuss rationally in relation to literature have increasingly tended to base their authority on factors outside of texts themselves.[12] This tendency has generated, in part, a productive, enlivening ferment of interdisciplinary research and criticism. It has also, unfortunately, sponsored a willingness to flatten and simplify the imaginative conditions of texts in order that they might be more easily picked up by certain methodological tongs. That critics from both the Right and the Left seem liable to similar kinds of responsive inadequacies in this regard is evident in a recent essay on canonical debates by Gerald Graff. Pointing out the differences between "theorists" and "traditionalists" like Allan Bloom (who declares that "a liberal education means reading certain generally recognized classic texts, just reading them, letting them dictate what the questions are and the method of approaching them"), Graff claims that it is a fallacy to assume that "the intrinsic nature of a text predetermines what any reader can *say* about it":

> There's simply no functional relation between the intrinsic richness of a text, however you measure it, and the richness of the pedagogical discussion it can support. There's no upper limit to the potential thematizability of any text. . . . This explains how a critic who comes to a text equipped with a compelling set of issues can make something more of a James Bond thriller or a Harlequin romance than another critic may make of the greatest masterpiece.[13]

I would respect Bloom's position if he actually tried to enact what he says a liberal education means. But although it seems obvious to me that Bloom's pretense of letting books "dictate" a critic's questions and methods is merely a mask for his own polemical procedures (a way of "using Plato and Dante to flog current abuses," as Graff puts it), Graff's remarks here themselves serve a remarkably similar purpose. Like many critics today, Graff assumes that the measure of critical and pedagogical excellence resides in an ability to "thematize" a text, to approach it when one is "equipped with a compelling set of issues." This thematic equipment seems disembodied from particular novels, poems, and plays, and thus it can as successfully handle a book about James Bond as one by James Joyce. What concerns me here is not Graff's implied notion of what makes for a good teacher (someone who can ask engaging questions about *any* piece of writing) but the metaphorical model that supports that notion. Graff's very phrasing of what he takes to be a "functional" truth here—one nonpartisan and beyond debate—indicates his conviction that what critics *do* is thematize texts and that this is an external process, one in which we "come to" a book with issues and themes rather than learn as we go along. Graff is right to assert that no text can predetermine what a given reader can say about it (though the same holds true for a soup can or a lawn mower). But the intrinsic richness of a text, for him, seems less interesting than the richness of the discussion it can "support." This is not because we have no stable way of measuring what the richness of texts might consist of, but because criticism, Graff is convinced, involves coming to texts with preestablished compelling issues (as Bloom himself does).

What such a formulation inadequately acknowledges is the possibility that in our dealings with literature, as Robert Frost once said, the best way out is through. Studying literature *can be* a matter of exploring the life in works rather than of importing life into them from somewhere else, even if some feel that possibility is theoretically incoherent. There seems little room in Graff's view for being surprised out of our issues, or for setting aside the need to thematize texts in the first place. Even if the "issues" he refers to were to be coaxed out of a text—if a critic were to work from the inside out—my sneaking suspicion is that the novel, play, or poem under consideration (which is partly why it can be *any* novel, play, or poem) would be subsumed into mere "evidence" for a prior claim.[14]

"Some people have the notion," Flannery O'Connor once remarked with sour affability, that you read a story "and then climb out of it into the meaning." They "talk about the theme of a story as if the theme were like the string that a sack of chicken feed is tied with. They think that if you can pick out the theme, the way you pick the right thread in the chicken-feed sack, you can rip the story open and feed the chickens."[15] Walking out and away from the stories we discuss is not the same as staying within them as we talk. Picking out thematic strings in a novel (or bringing our own to it in order to tie it more tightly) is not the same as describing the weave of its imaginative cloth. If we grant this we are less likely to ignore the life of what falls outside our themes and issues. We will also have a better chance of locating energies in writing that the search for such "strings" inadvertently encourages us to disregard. What I miss in Graff's comments (and the kind of criticism it describes and

epitomizes) is any troubled or wondering awareness of how often good writing
refuses to fit the explanatory efforts critics exert upon it, how it evades the
orderings by which they attempt to account for it.

I am not sure whether I claim too much or too little in asserting that the
search for critical terms flexible enough to describe violence in American
fiction—or any occasion in that writing for expenditures of imaginative energy—seems parallel to the activity in which American authors themselves
have been perennially engaged. The best of those writers have sought to encompass and sustain the exhilarating variety of voices to be heard in the United
States at any given moment, without withering the life of any of them. The
terms I have in the end settled for are not meant to preclude others. They are
designed only to test the descriptive adequacy of other terms in describing a
particular verbal performance. They represent no more and no less, even in
regard to depictions of violence, than my attempt to articulate, in Robert
Frost's terms, when the "fun begins." "In the beginning was the word to be
sure, very sure," Frost says, and he is too serious to be anything but playful:
"and a solid basic comfort it remains in situ, but the fun only begins with the
spirited when you treat the word as a point of many departures. . . . Remember the future of the world may depend on your keeping practice with each
other's quips and figures."[16]

Notes

INTRODUCTION

READING VIOLENCE, MAKING SENSE

1. Ernest Hemingway, *The Sun Also Rises* (1926; reprint, New York: Charles Scribner's Sons, 1954), p. 148.

2. Ibid.

3. Ibid., pp. 114, 115.

4. T. S. Eliot, *Criterion* 12 (1933): 469. Quoted in Christopher Ricks, *T. S. Eliot and Prejudice* (London: Faber & Faber, 1988), p. 6.

5. Laura Tanner refers to the "noninterventionist dynamics of the reading process." But she inaccurately describes that process in order to indict it. She mistakes a reader's imaginative experience of violence in certain fiction for a complicitous endorsement of it. "Reading Rape: *Sanctuary* and *The Women of Brewster Place*," *American Literature* 62, no. 4 (December 1990): 567.

6. John G. Cawelti, "Prolegomena to the Western," in *Critical Essays on the Western American Novel*, ed. William T. Pilkington (Boston: G. K. Hall, 1980), p. 65.

7. Robert Warshow, "Movie Chronicle: The Westerner," in *The Immediate Experience: Movies, Comics, Theatre, and Other Aspects of Popular Culture* (Garden City, N.Y.: Doubleday, 1962), pp. 153–54.

8. Kenneth Burke, "The Imagery of Killing," *Hudson Review* 1, no. 2 (Summer 1948): 160.

9. Stanley Cavell, *The World Viewed: Reflections on the Ontology of Film*, enlarged ed. (Cambridge, Mass.: Harvard University Press, 1979), pp. 31, 32.

10. John Fraser, *Violence in the Arts* (Cambridge, Eng.: Cambridge University Press, 1974), p. 9.

11. W.J.M. MacKenzie, *Power, Violence, Decision* (Harmondsworth, Eng.: Penguin Books, 1975), p. 120. As Fraser puts it, "politically respectable violence is not considered to be violence at all and the term is reserved for actions that are denied political significance or are felt to possess the wrong kind" (p. 157).

12. Jane Tompkins, "Fighting Words: Unlearning to Write the Critical Essay," *Georgia Review* 42, no. 3 (Fall 1988): 585.

13. Quoted in N. Katherine Hayles, *The Cosmic Web: Scientific Field Models and Literary Strategies in the Twentieth Century* (Ithaca, N.Y.: Cornell University Press, 1984), p. 16.

14. Wendell Berry, "Writer and Region," *Hudson Review* 40, no. 1 (Spring 1987): 26.

15. Richard Poirier, *The Performing Self: Compositions and Decompositions in the Languages of Everyday Life* (New York: Oxford University Press, 1971), p. 117.

16. Ibid., p. 118.

17. Herman Melville, *Moby-Dick*, in *Redburn, White-Jacket, Moby-Dick*, ed. G. Thomas Tanselle (New York: Library of America, 1983), pp. 1098–99.

18. Joyce Carol Oates, *On Boxing* (Garden City, N.Y.: Dolphin/Doubleday, 1987), p. 107.

19. For a quite different example of such a moment, compare Ernest Hemingway's description of "that great [bicycle] rider Ganay," who takes a fall on the cement track of a French velodrome: "[I] heard his skull crumple under the crash helmet as you crack an hard-boiled egg against a stone to peel it on a picnic." *A Moveable Feast* (New York: Charles Scribner's Sons, 1964), p. 65. Hemingway almost seems pleased, first at having heard the sound of Ganay's death and then at having thought up a vivid analogy for it.

20. Oates, pp. 102–3. See also Ronald Levao's superb essay, "Reading the Fights: Making Sense of Professional Boxing," *Raritan* 5, no. 4 (Spring 1986): 59–76.

21. David Bromwich, "Without Much Hope," *Threepenny Review* 42 (Summer 1990): 32.

22. Robert Garis, *The Dickens Theatre: A Reassessment of the Novels* (London: Oxford University Press, 1965), p. 51.

23. See Leo Bersani, *A Future for Astyanax: Character and Desire in Literature* (New York: Columbia University Press, 1984), especially pp. 51–88; Leo Bersani and Ulysse Dutoit, *The Forms of Violence: Narrative in Assyrian Art and Modern Culture* (New York: Schocken Books, 1985); and Hayden White, "The Value of Narrativity in the Representation of Reality," *Critical Inquiry* 7, no. 1 (Autumn 1980): 5–27.

24. I am adverting here only to the violence such fans reperform, not the process of reenactment. Michael Goldman, in relation to drama, has noted the "powerful kinesthetic appeal" that acting holds for us: "As we leave the theater we may find ourselves walking or talking like one of the characters—a clear sign of the inner mimesis that acting induces." See *Acting and Action in Shakespearean Tragedy* (Princeton, N.J.: Princeton University Press, 1985), p. 10.

25. This temptation became a commercial money-maker on American television in the late 1980s, in the form of programs like *America's Most Wanted, High Risk*, and *Unsolved Mysteries*. Dubbed "reality television" by advocates and "tabloid TV" by detractors, these "reality-based" programs tended to blur the line between what is real and what is "Real," with the latter constantly threatening to consist only of events vivid enough in their charm, quirkiness, or violence to fill up a two-minute "take."

26. Arthur Krystal, "Ifs, Ands, Butts: The Literary Sensibility at Ringside," *Harper's*, June 1987, p. 64.

27. Richard Slotkin, *Regeneration through Violence: The Mythology of the American Frontier, 1600–1860* (Middletown, Conn.: Wesleyan University Press, 1973), pp. 564–65.

28. Denis Donoghue, "A Criticism of One's Own," *New Republic*, 10 March 1986, p. 33.

29. Helen Vendler, *The Music of What Happens: Poems, Poets, Critics* (Cambridge, Mass.: Harvard University Press, 1988), p. 31.

30. That Slotkin himself is partially aware of the methodological shortcomings I am emphasizing here can be seen in his "Prologue to a Study of Myth and Genre in American Movies," *Prospects* 9 (1984): 407–32, especially pp. 408–12.

31. The translative quality I identify here also characterizes the two most important studies of violence that do not focus upon American literature: René Girard's *Violence and the Sacred*, trans. Patrick Gregory (Baltimore, Md.: Johns Hopkins University Press, 1977), and Elaine Scarry's *The Body in Pain: The Making and Unmaking of the World* (New York: Oxford University Press, 1985). See also James B. Twitchell, *Preposterous Violence: Fables of Aggression in Modern Culture* (New York: Oxford University Press, 1989).

32. J. Hillis Miller, "Presidential Address 1986: The Triumph of Theory, the Resistance to Reading, and the Question of the Material Base," *PMLA* 102, no. 3 (May 1987): 283.

33. Noel Carroll, "A New Theory of Pictures," review of Norman Bryson, *Vision and Painting*, *Raritan* 6, no. 1 (Summer 1986): 138.

34. James Guetti, "Theory Troubles," review of *Literary Theory: An Introduction* by Terry Eagleton, *Raritan* 3, no. 4 (Spring 1984): 126–27.

35. Thomas R. Edwards, "Thinking about Sports," in *Over Here: Criticizing America, 1968–1989* (New Brunswick, N.J.: Rutgers University Press, 1991), p. 47.

36. William Gass, "Philosophy and the Form of Fiction," in *Fiction and the Figures of Life* (New York: Alfred A. Knopf, 1970), p. 25.

37. Ludwig Wittgenstein, *Remarks on the Philosophy of Psychology*, vol. 1, ed. G.E.M. Anscombe and G. H. Von Wright (Chicago: University of Chicago Press, 1980), p. 52.

38. Jean-Paul Sartre, "On *The Sound and the Fury*: Time in the Work of Faulkner" (1939), in *Literary and Philosophical Essays*, trans. Annette Michelson (New York: Criterion Books, 1955), p. 79.

39. Quoted in Hugh Kenner, *A Homemade World: The American Modernist Writers* (New York: William Morrow, 1975), p. 64.

CHAPTER I

INVISIBLE INK: VIOLENCE AND REALISTIC IMAGINING

1. Quoted in Peter Prescott, "Making a Killing," *Newsweek*, 22 April 1985, p. 63.

2. Walt Whitman, "Preface to *Leaves of Grass*," in *Walt Whitman: Poetry and Prose*, ed. Justin Kaplan (New York: Library of America, 1982), p. 14.

3. Warner Berthoff, "Literature and the Measure of Reality," in *Fictions and Events* (New York: E. P. Dutton, 1971), p. 58.

4. John Steinbeck, letter to Pascal Covici, 16 January 1939, in *Steinbeck: A Life in Letters*, ed. Elaine Steinbeck and Robert Wallsten (New York: Penguin Books, 1981), p. 178.

5. Wayne Booth, *The Rhetoric of Fiction*, 2d ed. (Chicago: University of Chicago Press, 1983), p. 8.

6. Ian Watt, *The Rise of the Novel: Studies in Defoe, Richardson, and Fielding* (1957; reprint, London: Chatto & Windus, 1974), p. 22.

7. Joyce Carol Oates, "Where Are You Going, Where Have You Been?" in *The Wheel of Love* (New York: Vanguard Press, 1970), p. 42.

8. Ibid., p. 47.

9. Mark Twain, "The Art of Authorship," in *Selected Shorter Writings of Mark Twain*, ed. Walter Blair (Boston: Houghton Mifflin, 1962), p. 226.

10. Roland Barthes, "The Reality Effect," in *French Literary Theory Today: A Reader*, ed. Tzvetan Todorov (New York: Cambridge University Press, 1982), p. 15.

11. A reader might, of course, have recourse to a biography of Oates or to her remarks in an interview about an actual person upon whom Friend is based. Such glosses, however, would not necessarily feed into the imaginative substance of the character we encounter within the confines of the story.

12. The most influential study of representation as mimesis is still Eric Auerbach's *Mimesis: The Representation of Reality in Western Literature*, trans. Willard Trask (Princeton, N.J.: Princeton University Press, 1953). Auerbach's subtitle reveals the differences between his approach and mine. He is concerned with the ways in which various authors and eras have represented their sense of reality. His treatment of the stylistic elements that make a representation seem "real" focuses more upon the nature and quality of evoked life (so that one era's perceptual devices can be compared and contrasted with another's) than upon the imaginative process of the evocation.

Auerbach argues, for instance, that the central impulse of the Homeric style (from which present-day realism largely derives) is to externalize phenomena that are fixed in their temporal and spatial relations. This takes place in a verbal foreground, a temporal present that avoids any impression of perspective, depth, or the past. Homer does not need to base his story on historical reality, Auerbach asserts, because "his reality is powerful enough in itself; it ensnares us, weaving its web around us, and that suffices him" (p. 13). The appeal of Homer's world per se interests Auerbach more than the imaginative status of that appeal. Auerbach's reader is fairly passive in this account (ensnared, woven around). He need not help create Homer's illusion of life, only fall within its irresistible orbit of appeal.

13. Carol Shloss—in *Flannery O'Connor's Dark Comedies: The Limits of Inference* (Baton Rouge, La.: Louisiana State University Press, 1980)—discusses the fact that any picture, verbal or visual, "contains a good deal less information than the object it represents would exhibit" (p. 2). "We construe the conventions of representation in fuller measure than is literally warranted," she says, "filling in [and] adding to what is literally unstated" in a text. And we do this, she claims, because of "prior knowledge." The idea that we "fill in" a character, adding detail above and beyond that with which we are presented in a text, seems problematic to me. If we are told that Lord Warburton in James's *Portrait of a Lady* (the example Shloss cites) has "a lively grey eye and the rich adornment of a chestnut beard," we probably do infer, as Shloss suggests, "that he is a normal human being with all parts intact" (p. 2). But that inference does not constitute a process of "filling in." What else do we "see," for instance, about Warburton's

face? Do we visualize his nose, lips, ears, or forehead? What do they look like? Could we sketch them if we were asked to do so? Would we reasonably expect that our sketch would closely resemble that of the next person asked to do the same thing?

Our imagination of actual objects or people in fiction often, as I have said, seems to constitute less a palpable visual image than a felt confidence that we could visualize such things if we took the time. This confidence might be defined as a sense that *further descriptive inference is possible*. And that possibility, in the run of our imaginative lives, usually seems sufficient. Wittgenstein's remarks about mental accompaniment in our imaginations bear importantly on my concerns here. For a useful summary of the theoretical implications of those remarks, see James Guetti, "Wittgenstein and Literary Theory, Part 2," *Raritan* 4, no. 3 (Winter 1985): 66–84.

14. James Guetti, *Word-Music: The Aesthetic Aspect of Narrative Fiction* (New Brunswick, N.J.: Rutgers University Press, 1980), p. 77.

15. James Guetti, "Aggressive Reading: Detective Fiction and Realistic Narrative," *Raritan* 2, no. 1 (Summer 1982): 134.

16. Ibid., pp. 152, 150, 153.

17. Noel Carroll, *Mystifying Movies: Fads and Fallacies in Contemporary Film Theory* (New York: Columbia University Press, 1988), pp. 43–44.

18. Amy Kaplan, *The Social Construction of American Realism* (Chicago: University of Chicago Press, 1988), p. 5.

19. Tom Wolfe, "Stalking the Billion-Footed Beast: A Literary Manifesto for the New Social Novel," *Harper's*, November 1989, p. 50. One can agree with Wolfe's assessment of the impact of realism without thereby accepting his patently frivolous notion that "no one was ever moved to tears by reading about the unhappy fates of heroes and heroines in Homer, Sophocles, Molière, Racine, Sydney, Spenser, or Shakespeare" (p. 50).

20. Hugh Kenner, *A Homemade World: The American Modernist Writers* (New York: William Morrow, 1975), pp. 125–26.

21. The most chilling contemporary example of such a "mistaken" aesthetic response may be that of John Hinckley, who saw the movie *Taxi Driver* and then shot Ronald Reagan as a "gift" to Jodie Foster.

22. Kaplan, p. 9.

23. Daniel H. Borus, *Writing Realism: Howells, James, and Norris in the Mass Market* (Chapel Hill: University of North Carolina Press, 1989), pp. 98, 94–95.

24. Richard Rorty, "Two Cheers for the Cultural Left," *South Atlantic Quarterly* 89, no. 1 (Winter 1990): 231.

25. The most intriguing model for this kind of research is Janice Radway's *Reading the Romance: Women, Patriarchy, and Popular Literature* (Chapel Hill: University of North Carolina Press, 1984).

26. Twain, p. 226.

27. Susan Sontag, "On Style," in *Against Interpretation* (New York: Farrar, Straus & Giroux, 1961), p. 18.

28. Paul West, "In Defense of Purple Prose," in *Sheer Fiction* (New Paltz, N.Y.: McPherson, 1987), p. 52.

29. George Levine, *The Realistic Imagination* (Chicago: University of Chicago Press, 1981), p. 15.

30. Cf. Robert Scholes, *Textual Power: Literary Theory and the Teaching of English* (New Haven, Conn.: Yale University Press, 1985), especially pp. 1–38, 70.

31. Bill Nichols, "The Voice of Documentary," in *New Challenges for Documentary*, ed. Alan Rosenthal (Berkeley and Los Angeles: University of California Press, 1988), p. 53.

32. Roger Sale, "The Golden Age of the American Novel," in *On Not Being Good Enough* (New York: Oxford University Press, 1979), p. 123.

33. See Kaplan, Borus, and Walter Benn Michaels, *The Gold Standard and the Logic of Naturalism* (Berkeley and Los Angeles: University of California Press, 1987).

34. William Empson, *Seven Types of Ambiguity*, rev. ed. (New York: New Directions, 1947), p. 245.

35. Ansel Adams, "A Personal Credo," in *Photography: Essays and Images*, ed. Beaumont Newhall (New York: Museum of Modern Art, 1980), p. 259.

36. Harriet Beecher Stowe, *Uncle Tom's Cabin; or, Life among the Lowly*, in *Harriet Beecher Stowe: Three Novels*, ed. Kathryn Kish Sklar (New York: Library of America, 1982), pp. 110–11. Further page references in the text are to this edition and cited parenthetically.

37. Robyn R. Warhol, "Poetics and Persuasion: *Uncle Tom's Cabin* as a Realist Novel," *Essays in Literature* 13, no. 2 (Fall 1986): 292, 290.

38. Stephen Railton, *Authorship and Audience: Literary Performance in the American Renaissance* (Princeton, N.J.: Princeton University Press, 1991), pp. 74, 82.

39. Lionel Trilling, "Reality in America," in *The Liberal Imagination* (New York: Anchor Books, 1950), pp. 10–11.

40. Frank Norris, "Simplicity in Art," in *The Responsibilities of the Novelist and Other Literary Essays* (New York: Doubleday, Page, 1903), pp. 244–45.

41. James Agee and Walker Evans, *Let Us Now Praise Famous Men* (1941; reprint, Boston: Houghton Mifflin, 1988), pp. 7, 11, 13.

42. Richard Wright, "How 'Bigger' Was Born," in *Richard Wright: Early Works*, ed. Arnold Rampersad (New York: Library of America, 1991), p. 873. All further page references in the text to this pamphlet and to *Native Son* will be to this edition and cited parenthetically.

43. Henry Louis Gates, Jr., *The Signifying Monkey: A Theory of African-American Literary Criticism* (New York: Oxford University Press, 1988), p. 184.

44. Guetti, *Word-Music*, p. 1.

45. William Gass, "The Concept of Character in Fiction," in *Fiction and the Figures of Life* (New York: Alfred A. Knopf, 1970), p. 51. Some words, mostly nouns, conjure up more imaginative visibility than others. But the same words that make for a realistic effect can be used in contexts that invalidate or deenergize their visual-realistic efficiency (a subject I will be investigating throughout this study).

46. Robert Alter, "Mimesis and the Motive for Fiction," in *Motives for Fiction* (Cambridge, Mass.: Harvard University Press, 1984), p. 19.

47. Jerry Bryant, "The Violence of *Native Son*," *Southern Review* 17 (Spring 1981): 304, 303.

48. Ibid., pp. 304–5. The novel for the most part supports Bryant's assertions, though it does seem questionable whether the "extremity" of Bigger's reaction to Mrs. Dalton is directly attributable to his internalization of the taboo of interracial rape. That taboo forms a factor, but only *one* factor. It represents the culminating confusion in the veritable saturnalia of social and psychological discomforts and disorientations to which Bigger is subjected during a night out slumming with Jan and Mary.

49. Robert Bone, *Richard Wright* (Minneapolis: University of Minnesota Pamphlets on American Writers, 1969), p. 21.

50. John Reilly, afterword to *Native Son* (1940; reprint, New York: Perennial Library, 1987), p. 395. Reilly says it is "clear" the white world is responsible for Bigger's actions because Mrs. Dalton is dressed in white, because a white cat "oversees" the dismemberment, and because it snows the next morning.

51. Bryant, pp. 310–11.

52. Robert James Butler, "The Function of Violence in Richard Wright's *Native Son*," *Black American Literature Forum* 20, nos. 1–2 (Spring–Summer 1986): 9–25.

53. James Baldwin, "Alas, Poor Richard," in *Nobody Knows My Name: More Notes of a Native Son* (New York: Dell, 1978), p. 151.

54. Laura E. Tanner, "Uncovering the Magical Disguise of Language: The Narrative Presence in Richard Wright's *Native Son*," *Texas Studies in Literature and Language* 29, no. 4 (Winter 1987): 419. Tanner rightly contends that there are two distinct narrative modes in the novel: the narrator's, which is characterized by a skillful use of metaphor and imagery and a complex facility with words, and that associated with Bigger's, which is halting and unsophisticated because his relation to language is "defined by alienation and distrust" (p. 417).

In locating this "tension between material and symbolic realities" in the novel, however, Tanner variously describes the former as "the material world" (p. 420), "the experiential world" (p. 421), and "literal circumstance" (p. 423), and she contends that Bigger "speak[s] from the force of the concrete, material world" (p. 427). Her characterization of what seems to oppose and subvert Wright's narrative interpretations, in other words, is made to seem *preverbal*—as if, somehow, "life" rather than Wright's realism were responsible for "Bigger as character" as opposed to "Bigger as symbol" (p. 419). *Native Son* is in many respects, Tanner says, "a novel about the insufficiency of novels . . . the insufficiency of words" (p. 428), which would make it a defining example of realistic fiction as I have been describing it. But the realism that convinces us that there is more to Bigger than how others "interpret" him is, of course, itself a verbal illusion, not something that can be set off as quantitatively different from the narrator's rhetoric and symbolic strategies.

55. See John Hersey, "The Legend on License," *Yale Review* 75, no. 2 (Winter 1986): 289–314.

56. Tom Wolfe, author's note to *The Right Stuff* (New York: Bantam Books, 1979), p. 368. All further page references in the text to the novel will be to this edition and cited parenthetically.

57. Morris Dickstein, "Introduction to the Penguin Edition: The 1960s Today," *Gates of Eden: American Culture in the Sixties* (New York: Penguin Books, 1989), p. vii.

58. Guetti, *Word-Music*, p. 77.

59. The movie version of *The Right Stuff* presents this scene largely in silence, from an omniscient perspective. When the jet spins uncontrollably back to earth we are given a dramatic montage that shifts between close-ups of Yeager's (Sam Shepard's) helmeted face, outside shots of the jet twisting and plummeting, and a wildly gyrating view, as if from Yeager's perspective, out over the instrument panel. When Yeager is blown free of the plane he is shown, from a distance, struggling with his helmet as smoke ribbons out of it. We are momentarily given a shot meant to suggest Yeager's perspective as he falls (the distant surface of the earth spinning vertiginously). But for the most part we watch as he falls "below" us through the clouds. The only sound outside of the explosive burst when he breaks free of the ejector seat is the amplified whistling of the wind.

60. Tim O'Brien, *Going after Cacciato* (1978; reprint, New York: Dell, 1979), p. 176.

61. Mark Twain, *Adventures of Huckleberry Finn*, in *Mark Twain: Mississippi Writings*, ed. Guy Cardwell (New York: Library of America, 1982), p. 676.

CHAPTER II

JAMES FENIMORE COOPER:

VIOLENCE AND THE LANGUAGE OF ROMANCE

1. D. H. Lawrence, *Studies in Classic American Literature* (1923; reprint, New York: Viking, 1966), p. 50. Mark Twain, "Fenimore Cooper's Literary Offenses" (1895), in *Selected Shorter Writings of Mark Twain*, ed. Walter Blair (Boston: Houghton Mifflin, 1962), p. 238.

2. Lawrence, p. 51.

3. Twain, p. 227. Richard Poirier, "Writing Off the Self," *Raritan* 1, no. 1 (Summer 1981): 122.

4. James Guetti, *Word-Music: The Aesthetic Aspect of Narrative Fiction* (New Brunswick, N.J.: Rutgers University Press, 1980), pp. 84–85.

5. Richard Chase, *The American Novel and Its Tradition* (New York: Doubleday Anchor Books, 1957), p. 21.

6. Harold Martin, "The Development of Style in Nineteenth-Century American Fiction," in *Style in Prose Fiction: English Institute Essays, 1958*, ed. Harold Martin (New York: Columbia University Press, 1959), p. 120.

7. Twain, p. 229.

8. James Fenimore Cooper, *The Deerslayer*, in *James Fenimore Cooper: The Leatherstocking Tales*, vol. 2, ed. Blake Nevius (New York: Library of America, 1985), p.

1030. All further page references to *The Deerslayer* in the text are to this edition and will be cited parenthetically.

9. Martin, p. 120.

10. Twain, p. 236.

11. Leslie Fiedler, *Love and Death in the American Novel*, rev. ed. (New York: Stein & Day, 1966), p. 180.

12. Allan Nevins, afterword to *The Deerslayer* (1841; reprint, New York: Signet Classics, 1963), p. 541.

13. Marius Bewley, *The Eccentric Design: Form in the Classic American Novel* (New York: Columbia University Press, 1957), p. 15.

14. Richard Poirier, *A World Elsewhere: The Place of Style in American Literature* (New York: Oxford University Press, 1966), p. 76.

15. Ibid., p. 33.

16. Ibid., pp. 76, 71–72.

17. Ibid., p. 72.

18. James Fenimore Cooper, *The Pioneers*, in *James Fenimore Cooper: The Leatherstocking Tales*, vol. 1, ed. Blake Nevius (New York: Library of America, 1985), p. 27.

19. Lawrence, p. 48.

20. Philip Fisher, *Hard Facts: Setting and Form in the American Novel* (New York: Oxford University Press, 1985), pp. 40, 41.

21. Ibid., p. 6.

22. Warren Motley, *The American Abraham: James Fenimore Cooper and the Frontier Patriarch* (New York: Cambridge University Press, 1987), p. 81.

23. Fiedler, p. 183.

24. Sydney Krause, *Mark Twain as Critic* (Baltimore, Md.: Johns Hopkins University Press, 1967), p. 128. Twain originally wanted to present himself in "Fenimore Cooper's Literary Offenses" as "Mark Twain, M.A., Professor of Belles Lettres in the Veterinary College of Arizona" publishing his lectures, "Studies in Literary Criticism." But instead "of giving himself professorial airs" and taking "the vinegar out of his reaction" by making "a buffoon of himself," Krause notes, Twain decided to assume the persona of "a wholesome plebeian" (pp. 140–41).

25. Twain, p. 237.

26. Krause, p. 128. Also see Lance Schachterle and Kent Ljungquist's "Fenimore Cooper's Literary Defenses: Twain and the Text of *The Deerslayer*," *Studies in the American Renaissance* (1988): 401–17.

27. Martin, p. 126.

28. Arthur Mizener, *Twelve Great American Novels* (New York: New American Library, 1967), pp. 4–5.

29. Richard Slotkin, *Regeneration through Violence: The Mythology of the American Frontier, 1600–1860* (Middletown, Conn.: Wesleyan University Press, 1973), pp. 499–500.

30. Henry James, preface to *The American* (1907), in *Henry James: European Writers and the Prefaces*, ed. Leon Edel (New York: Library of America, 1984), p. 1064.

31. Wayne Franklin, *The New World of James Fenimore Cooper* (Chicago: University of Chicago Press, 1982), p. 108.

32. Fisher rightly notes that Cooper uses terms of aggression, like *invasion*, in the novel in relation to the Indians rather than to whites. Cooper, he says, converts invasion "into rescue, offense into defense, clearing the land into rescuing innocent captives, surrounding into being surrounded" (p. 47).

33. Fiedler, p. 194.

CHAPTER III

POE'S VIOLENCE: GANGRENOUS PROTOCOL

1. Allen Tate, "The Angelic Imagination," in *Edgar Allan Poe: Modern Critical Views*, ed. Harold Bloom (New York: Chelsea House, 1985), p. 48.

2. Edgar Allan Poe, review of Cornelius Mathews's *Wakondah*, in *Edgar Allan Poe: Essays and Reviews*, ed. G. R. Thompson (New York: Library of America, 1984), p. 833. All further page references in the text to Poe's criticism will be to this edition and cited parenthetically. All further page references in the text to Poe's fiction will be to *Edgar Allan Poe: Poetry and Tales*, ed. Patrick F. Quinn (New York: Library of America, 1984). Julian Symons notes that Poe later told Mathews that his (Poe's) "savagely executed destruction of Mathews's poem was an 'impudent and flippant critique' done by somebody else." *The Tell-Tale Heart: The Life and Works of Edgar Allan Poe* (New York: Penguin Books, 1978), p. 186.

3. Symons, pp. 124, 92.

4. Edmund Wilson, "Poe as Literary Critic," in *Critics on Poe: Readings in Literary Criticism*, ed. David Kesterson (Coral Gables, Fla.: University of Miami Press, 1973), p. 74.

5. Leslie Fiedler, *Love and Death in the American Novel*, rev. ed. (New York: Stein & Day, 1966), p. 424.

6. Wilson, p. 76.

7. Joel Porte, *The Romance in America: Studies in Cooper, Poe, Hawthorne, Melville, and James* (Middletown, Conn.: Wesleyan University Press, 1969), p. 56.

8. Symons, p. 105.

9. James M. Cox, "Edgar Poe: Style as Pose," *Virginia Quarterly Review* 44, no. 1 (Winter 1968): 69, 75.

10. Harold Bloom, introduction to *Edgar Allan Poe: Modern Critical Views*, pp. 3, 3–4.

11. Ibid., p. 4. J. Gerald Kennedy similarly argues that Poe's "recurrent themes of vampirism, metempsychosis, spiritualism and spectral manifestation indicates [his] fixation with the fate of the body and the destiny of the soul. In effect, such motifs carry a significance independent of the narrative scheme in which they emerge; they constitute an esoteric ideography and *inscribe a parallel text* concerned exclusively with final questions" (my emphasis). "Phantasms of Death in Poe's Fiction," in *The Haunted Dusk:*

American Supernatural Fiction, 1820–1920, ed. Howard Kerr, John Crowley, and Charles Crow (Athens: University of Georgia Press, 1983), p. 39.

12. Walter Bezanson, "The Troubled Sleep of Arthur Gordon Pym," in *Essays in Literary History, Presented to J. Milton French*, ed. Rudolf Kirk and C. F. Main (New Brunswick, N.J.: Rutgers University Press, 1960), p. 173.

13. Symons, p. 234.

14. Tate, p. 39.

15. Gordon Weaver, "One Writer's Perception of the Short Fiction Tradition: How Would Edgar Allan Poe Make a Duck?," in *The Teller and the Tale: Aspects of the Short Story*, ed. Wendell Aycock (Lubbock: Texas Tech Press, 1982), p. 130.

16. Susan Sontag, "The Imagination of Disaster," in *Film Theory and Criticism: Introductory Readings*, 3d ed., ed. Gerald Mast and Marshall Cohen (New York: Oxford University Press, 1985), p. 455.

17. Judith Sunderland, *The Problematic Fictions of Poe, James, and Hawthorne* (Columbia, Mo.: University of Missouri Press, 1984), p. 20.

18. James Gargano, "The Question of Poe's Narrators," in *Critics on Poe*, p. 56.

19. Ibid., pp. 57, 61. Gargano argues that Montresor's "ironic appreciation of his own deviousness" in "The Cask of Amontillado" "seems further to justify his arrogance of intellect" (p. 60). But Poe does not simply condemn Montresor's arrogance of intellect, he also admires the latter's self-conscious deviousness. One can agree with Gargano's avowal that Montresor's crime remains, after fifty years, "the obsession of his life" without thereby concluding that Poe stresses only the "destructive inner consequences" it has had for Montresor. Poe also suggests in this story that in some respects *crime pays*.

20. Symons mistakenly asserts that the narrator kills for the inheritance (p. 211).

21. In addition to prolixity, Stanley Cavell also notes that "a series of imp words" (*impulse, impels, impatient, important*, and so on) recur insistently throughout the tale. "Being Odd, Getting Even," in *In Quest of the Ordinary: Lines of Skepticism and Romanticism* (Chicago: Univeristy of Chicago Press, 1988), p. 124.

22. Symons, pp. 177, 207, 211.

23. Brian Harding, *American Literature in Context, 1830–1865* (London: Methuen, 1982), p. 63.

24. Roland Barthes, "Textual Analysis of Poe's 'Valdemar,'" in *Untying the Text: A Post-Structuralist Reader*, ed. Robert Young (London: Routledge & Kegan Paul, 1981), p. 140.

25. Robert Irwin, *American Hieroglyphics: The Symbol of the Egyptian Hieroglyphics in the American Renaissance* (Baltimore, Md.: Johns Hopkins University Press, 1980), p. 69.

26. Sunderland, p. 26.

27. Cox also notes that Pym's forebears own property in "Edgarton" (p. 72).

28. Ibid., pp. 74, 73, 72.

29. Sunderland, p. 21.

30. Symons, p. 208.

31. Douglas Robinson, *American Apocalypses: The Image of the End of the World in American Literature* (Baltimore, Md.: Johns Hopkins University Press, 1985), p. 112.

32. The possibility of Zenobia's eyes "watching" her head fall is problematic because they seem to disappear after they roll out of the gutter.

33. Symons, p. 208.

34. John Fraser, *Violence in the Arts* (Cambridge, Eng.: Cambridge University Press, 1974), pp. 51–52.

35. Some might be tempted to see "A Predicament" as offering a parodic but still disturbing example of how images of violently silenced women fill Poe's stories. Such readings, however, usually begin from the premise that such images can never be amusing, no matter what their mode of presentation. For an even-handed discussion of images of women in Poe's fiction, see Cynthia S. Jordan, "Poe's Re-Vision: The Recovery of the Second Story," *American Literature* 59, no. 1 (March 1987): 1–19.

36. Bloom, p. 11. Evan Carton contends that "Man's inability to realize his spiritual identity . . . is the underlying joke of Poe's gruesome comic tales, in which individuals are negatively conceived as mere 'masses of Matter' that can impassively endure dismemberment, evisceration, and suffocation. The violence of these tales is largely self-directed, meant to puncture Poe's own metaphysical ideals and pretensions." *The Rhetoric of American Romance: Dialectic and Identity in Emerson, Poe, and Hawthorne* (Baltimore, Md.: Johns Hopkins University Press, 1985), p. 17.

37. Fraser, p. 69.

38. Harding, p. 58.

39. David Reynolds, *Beneath the American Renaissance: The Subversive Imagination in the Age of Emerson and Melville* (New York: Alfred A. Knopf, 1988), p. 526.

40. Ibid., pp. 524, 527.

41. T. S. Eliot, "From Poe to Valéry," *Hudson Review* 2, no. 3 (Autumn 1949): 333.

42. See Louis A. Renza, "Poe's Secret Autobiography," in *The American Renaissance Reconsidered*, ed. Walter Benn Michaels and Donald E. Pease (Baltimore, Md.: Johns Hopkins University Press, 1985), esp. pp. 61–65.

43. Paul Fussell, "The Persistent Itchings of Poe and Whitman," in *The Boy Scout Handbook and Other Observations* (New York: Oxford University Press, 1982), p. 16.

44. Edgar Allan Poe, letter to Thomas W. White, 30 April 1835, in *Letters of Edgar Allan Poe*, vol. 1, ed. John Ward Ostrom (New York: Gordian Press, 1966), pp. 57–58.

45. Fiedler, p. 497. See also Stephen Railton's chapter on Poe in *Authorship and Audience: Literary Performance in the American Renaissance* (Princeton, N.J.: Princeton University Press, 1991), pp. 132–51.

46. Weaver, p. 130. For Poe, Harold Martin asserts, "not simply the reference, but the sound, the location of stress, the 'color' of [a] word are all treated as if pregnant with meaning." "The concern is not for the *mot juste* but for the *mot resonant*." "The Development of Style in Nineteenth-Century American Fiction," in *Style in Prose Fic-*

tion: English Institute Essays, 1958, ed. Harold Martin (New York: Columbia University Press, 1959), pp. 136, 138.

47. Bezanson, p. 155.

48. J.R.R. Tolkien, "On Fairy-Stories," in *Tree and Leaf* (Boston: Houghton Mifflin, 1965), p. 50. Tolkien uses this term in describing a production of "Puss-in-Boots."

49. Sunderland, p. 26.

50. Wayne Booth, *The Rhetoric of Fiction*, 2d ed. (Chicago: University of Chicago Press, 1983), pp. 201, 203.

51. At least part of what makes "Berenice" an effectively unnerving story is that Egaeus's surgical removal of Berenice's teeth while she is still alive, happens offstage. The disturbing struggle that must have ensued is attested to only by the "impress of human nails" (p. 233) indented on Egaeus's hands.

52. Paul Elmer More, quoted in Cox, p. 69.

CHAPTER IV

VIOLENCE AND STYLE IN STEPHEN CRANE'S FICTION

1. Stephen Crane, "Harold Frederick" (1897), in *Stephen Crane: Prose and Poetry*, ed. J. C. Levenson (New York: Library of America, 1984), p. 986. All further page references in the text to Crane's work are to this edition and will be cited parenthetically.

2. Cf. Bettina Knapp's assertion that *Maggie* features "finely honed language" that is "bone-hard, incantatory, [and] deeply sensual in its rhythmic patterings and auditory effects," or her contention that the images in *The Red Badge of Courage* are "unforgettable for their thickly daubed pigmentations and also for their smooth and velvety hues." *Stephen Crane* (New York: Ungar, 1987), pp. 1, 2.

3. The most controversial new study of Crane is Michael Fried's *Realism, Writing, Disfiguration: On Thomas Eakins and Stephen Crane* (Chicago: University of Chicago Press, 1987). Many of the misgivings I have about Fried's methods are voiced by Raymond Carney in "Crane and Eakins," *Partisan Review* 55, no. 3 (1988): 464–73.

4. Amy Kaplan, "The Spectacle of War in Crane's Revision of History," in *New Essays on "The Red Badge of Courage"*, ed. Lee Clark Mitchell (New York: Cambridge University Press, 1986), pp. 100, 95. "The theatrical style of the narrator," Kaplan says, actually "becomes the focus of the spectacle, and [Crane's] composition of [a] scene provides the central heroic act" (p. 97).

5. Carney, p. 472.

6. Frank Bergon, *Stephen Crane's Artistry* (New York: Columbia University Press, 1975), pp. 134, 6. Bergon aptly terms Crane's style "shortwinded" (p. 2).

7. John Berryman, *Stephen Crane* (New York: William Sloane, 1950), pp. 287, 284. Berryman notes three stylistic "norms" in Crane's writing: the "nervous" style of *The Red Badge* and the "Baby Sketches," "the supple majesty" of "The Open Boat," and the "more closed, circumstantial" style of *The Monster*.

8. David Halliburton, *The Color of the Sky: A Study of Stephen Crane* (New York: Cambridge University Press, 1989), p. 241.

9. Kenneth Burke, *Attitudes toward History*, 3d. ed (1937; reprint, Berkeley and Los Angeles: University of California Press, 1984), p. 300. See also Kenneth Burke, *Permanence and Change: An Anatomy of Purpose*, 3d ed. (1954; reprint, Berkeley and Los Angeles: University of California Press, 1984), pp. 89–96.

10. Halliburton, pp. 9, 245.

11. Ibid., p. 242.

12. Donald Pease contends that "the exclusion of any coherent perspective" in Crane's work can, at times, actually begin "to function as a perspective." "Fear, Rage, and the Mistrials of Representation in *The Red Badge of Courage*," in *American Realism: New Essays*, ed. Eric J. Sundquist (Baltimore, Md.: Johns Hopkins University Press, 1982), p. 158. The imaginative dynamics of that exclusion, however, make this a complicated process. When Crane interrupts "intense narrative" with "trite generalizations" or "excessively mannered, slick, pithy, sententious, obvious, or silly sentences," Bergon notes, it creates "a distancing point of view" (p. 19). But that distancing is less a viewpoint than a momentary verbal effect that seems untargeted and perspectively unplaced. It is "sometimes difficult to know exactly who is talking in a Crane sentence," Bergon says, or "whose observations are being recorded" (p. 18).

13. James Guetti, *Word-Music: The Aesthetic Aspect of Narrative Fiction* (New Brunswick, N.J.: Rutgers University Press, 1980), pp. 126, 125.

14. John Ditsky notes the "absurd disproportionality" of some of Crane's remarks in "The Open Boat." But he conceives of the disproportion not in the sound of Crane's writing itself but in his use of metaphor and pathetic fallacy. For Ditsky, the "ominous soundscape" of the story results from sounds *within* the story (that of the ocean or the wind, for instance) and not, as I am arguing, from the verbal forms by which those "real" sounds are represented. "The Music in 'The Open Boat,'" *North Dakota Quarterly* 56 (Winter 1988): 119–30.

15. Crane's work was subject to editing, when he submitted it to periodicals, by the likes of Richard Watson Gilder, editor of *Century Magazine*, who found written phrases such as "B'Gawd" full of "an offensiveness beyond that of the actual word." Quoted in *Stephen Crane: Letters*, ed. R. W. Stallman and Lillian Gilkes (New York: New York University Press, 1960), p. 130.

16. Berryman, p. 288.

17. Andrew Lytle asserts that the narrator who assumes this balcony perspective is "so removed from the actual predicament as to imply an indifference to their fate, to make it unreal. It is almost as if they were already dead." "'The Open Boat': A Pagan Tale," in *The Hero with the Private Parts* (Baton Rouge: Louisiana State University Press, 1966), p. 66.

Jules Chametzky—in "Realism, Cultural Politics, and Language as Mediation in Mark Twain and Others," *Prospects* 8 (1983): 183–94—argues that Crane's reference to a balcony perspective is meant to show that "the picturesque" does not exist for the men in the boat, "nor should it have: Crane can dismiss it with a phrase" (p. 192). But the perspective is dismissed only for the men, not the narrator who continually occupies, vacates, and then reoccupies it in the story. Similarly, when Chametzky notes that "the view from the crest of a wave 'was *probably* splendid . . . *probably* glorious,'" he asks, "but to whom, and in what condition of removal from the real facts of life and death existence?" (p. 192). The answer (though Chametzky does not propose it) is *the narrator* or, rather, the narrator in certain moods.

18. "The right word, to [Crane's] context," Wright Morris says, "is the audacious word." "Stephen Crane," in *Earthly Delights, Unearthly Adornments* (New York: Harper & Row, 1978), p. 53.

19. Berryman, p. 285. For an interesting discussion of an analogously divided sensibility, see Sandy Petrey's remarks on Theodore Dreiser in "The Language of Realism, The Language of False Consciousness: A Reading of *Sister Carrie*," *Novel* 10, no. 2 (Winter 1977): 101–13. Petrey locates a permanent tension between the two rhetorical registers he refers to in his title. But Petrey finds Dreiser's "language of false consciousness" readily identifiable as sentimentality and "the verbiage of nullity" (p. 102) and he sees it as implicitly invalidated by the novel's realism. While the dissonance between Crane's realism and his rhetoric of fiction is not always as flamboyantly apparent as in *Sister Carrie*, its dramatization is more habitual and simultaneous than in Dreiser's novel. The varying contrasts that Crane's rhetorical imagination strikes with his realism are thus less easily categorized than they are in Dreiser.

20. Tony Tanner, *Scenes of Nature, Signs of Men* (New York: Cambridge University Press, 1987), p. 138.

21. Warner Berthoff, *The Ferment of Realism: American Literature, 1884–1919* (New York: Free Press, 1965), p. 229.

22. Stephen Crane, letter to Copeland and Day, June[?] 1895, in *Stephen Crane: Letters*, p. 59.

23. Berryman, p. 268.

24. Willa Cather, "Introduction to Stephen Crane's 'Wounds in the Rain'" (1926), in *Willa Cather: Stories, Poems, and Other Writings*, ed. Sharon O'Brien (New York: Library of America, 1992), p. 955.

25. Lee Clark Mitchell, *Determined Fictions: American Literary Naturalism* (New York: Columbia University Press, 1989), p. xii. Mitchell notes that the "dissociated sensibility" of Crane's characters is often "transformed into a physical fact" (p. 111). This helps to explain why Crane's characters often seem less coherent selves than assemblages of strangely unintegrated bodily organs or features: smiles, eyes, legs, countenances, and so on.

26. Crane's characters sometimes conceive of themselves or others as parts of speech. Two examples (among many) of this tendency are Henry Fleming's humiliated vision of himself as being scorned and leered at by the other soldiers ("He was a slang phrase" [p. 147]) and the Easterner's postulation, in "The Blue Hotel," that the gambler who kills the Swede "isn't even a noun. He is kind of an adverb" (p. 827).

27. Donald Pizer, *Realism and Naturalism in Nineteenth-Century American Literature*, rev. ed. (Carbondale: Southern Illinois University Press, 1984), pp. 144–45.

28. Berryman, p. 279. Cf. Bergon's contention that "simultaneous with every impulse to reduce, diminish, and deflate [in Crane's fiction] is the impulse to enlarge,
intensify, and even idealize. . . . There always remains in Crane a desire to rescue
something from the shambles left by his irony" (pp. 42, 43).

29. Morris, p. 57.

30. Alan Trachtenberg, "Experiments in Another Country: Stephen Crane's City
Sketches," in *American Realism: New Essays*, p. 148.

31. Bergon argues that Maggie is a victim both of her environment and of self-
deception. Middle-class morality and status anxieties are so interfused in the novel, he
says, that they do not oppose the amoral reality of the Bowery so much as they actually
help perpetuate it (pp. 66–76). Eric Soloman, on the other hand, contends that
Crane's "social view in *Maggie*" might be summed up in the repeated phrase "What
d'Hell!" "At once a cry of profanity, despair, disengagement, and unreason," the expression suggests that Crane lays direct blame for the world of the Bowery on "no
cause—not religion, nor class stratification, nor poverty, nor even those naturalistic
staples, coincidence and dark natural forces." *Stephen Crane: From Parody to Realism*
(Cambridge, Mass.: Harvard University Press, 1967), p. 33.

32. Bergon, p. 75.

33. Sydney Krause, "The Surrealism of Crane's Naturalism in *Maggie*," *American
Literary Realism* 16, no. 2 (Autumn 1983): 254.

34. George Monteiro, "Crane's Coxcomb," *Modern Fiction Studies* 31, no. 2 (Summer 1985): 300.

35. For an interestingly similar moment, see Carson McCullers's account of the
fight between Miss Amelia and Marvin Macy in *The Ballad of the Sad Café*, in *Collected
Stories of Carson McCullers* (Boston: Houghton Mifflin, 1987), p. 249.

36. Berthoff, p. 231.

37. Berryman, p. 280. The Easterner also, in the final section of the story,
finds "nothing accidental" about the Swede's death. For intriguing discussions of
his theory of social complicity, see Monteiro, pp. 301–3 and Halliburton, pp.
225–27.

38. Guetti, p. 129.

CHAPTER V

THE PURITY OF EXECUTION IN HEMINGWAY'S FICTION

1. Frederick Crews, "Pressure under Grace," review of *Hemingway* by Kenneth
Lynn, *New York Review of Books*, 13 August 1987, p. 35.

2. D. S. Savage, "Ernest Hemingway," *Hudson Review* 1, no. 3 (Autumn 1948): 381,
385–86.

3. Ernest Hemingway, *To Have and Have Not* (1937; reprint, New York: Charles
Scribner's Sons, 1970), pp. 7–8. All further page references in the text will be to this
edition (abbreviated *HHN*) and cited parenthetically. References to other of Hemingway's works quoted in the text are to the following editions: *Across the River and into*

the Trees (1950; reprint, New York: Charles Scribner's Sons, 1970), abbreviated *ART*; *Death in the Afternoon* (1932; reprint, New York: Charles Scribner's Sons, 1960), abbreviated *DA*; *A Farewell to Arms* (1929; reprint, New York: Charles Scribner's Sons, 1957), abbreviated *FA*; *For Whom the Bell Tolls* (1940; reprint, New York: Charles Scribner's Sons, 1968), abbreviated *FBT*; *The Green Hills of Africa* (1935; reprint, New York: Charles Scribner's Sons, 1954), abbreviated *GH*; *A Moveable Feast* (New York: Charles Scribner's Sons, 1964), abbreviated *MF*; *The Short Stories of Ernest Hemingway* (New York: Scribner's/Collier Edition, 1987), abbreviated *SS*; and *The Sun Also Rises* (1926; reprint, New York: Charles Scribner's Sons, 1954), abbreviated *SAR*.

4. Quoted in Julian Symons, *Bloody Murder: From the Detective Story to the Crime Novel, A History* (London: Faber & Faber, 1972), p. 141.

5. James Guetti, "Aggressive Reading: Detective Fiction and Realistic Narrative," *Raritan* 2, no. 1 (Summer 1982): 138–39. For a useful discussion of the "wise guy" element of Hemingway's early writing, see Delmore Schwartz, "The Fiction of Ernest Hemingway," in *Selected Essays of Delmore Schwartz*, ed. Donald A. Dike and David H. Zucker (Chicago: University of Chicago Press, 1970), p. 256.

6. Carlos Baker suggests that Harry is one of the novel's *haves* by dint of his possessing "a combination of social courage and personal integrity." *Hemingway: The Writer as Artist* (Princeton, N.J.: Princeton University Press, 1972), p. 216. By contrast, Kenneth S. Lynn refers to Morgan as "homicidal Harry," a character who acts out "a psychopathological view of life" that Hemingway never once identifies as a sickness. *Hemingway* (New York: Simon & Schuster, 1987), p. 462. One of Harry's less endearing accounts of violence, as Lynn notes, is his killing of a double-crossing Chinese crook named Mr. Sing: "I got him forward onto his knees and had both thumbs well in behind his talk-box, and I bent the whole thing back until she cracked. Don't think you can't hear it crack, either" (*HHN*, pp. 53–54).

7. Savage, p. 384.

8. Harry Levin, "Observations on the Style of Ernest Hemingway," in *Hemingway: A Collection of Critical Essays*, ed. Robert P. Weeks (Englewood Cliffs, N.J.: Prentice-Hall, 1962), p. 73.

9. E. M. Halliday, "Hemingway's Ambiguity: Symbolism and Irony," in *Hemingway: A Collection of Critical Essays*, p. 52.

10. Caroline Gordon and Allen Tate, "'The Snows of Kilimanjaro': Commentary," in *The House of Fiction: An Anthology of the Short Story with Commentary*, ed. Caroline Gordon and Allen Tate (New York: Charles Scribner's Sons, 1950), p. 421.

11. Ibid., p. 423.

12. Schwartz, pp. 256, 255.

13. Ibid., p. 259.

14. E. L. Doctorow, "Braver Than We Thought," in *Ernest Hemingway: Six Decades of Criticism*, ed. Linda W. Wagner (East Lansing: Michigan State University Press, 1987), p. 330.

15. Crews, pp. 35, 37.

16. Ibid., p. 30.

17. Lynn, p. 318; Crews, p. 35.

18. Lincoln Steffens, *The Autobiography of Lincoln Steffens* (New York: Harcourt Brace, 1931), p. 834

19. Richard K. Peterson, *Hemingway: Direct and Oblique* (The Hague: Mouton, 1969), p. 115. Peterson's study is still one of the best on Hemingway, especially his examination of how Hemingway creates "a 'literary' style with a built-in nonliterary sound" (p. 119). Yet even Peterson's investigation of Hemingway's style sometimes becomes programmatic in seeing its verbal expansiveness as merely a mask for a fear of undisciplined emotion.

20. Halliday, p. 65.

21. Cf. Jake Barnes's reflections upon the British in *The Sun Also Rises*: "What a lot of bilge I could think up at night. What rot, I could hear Brett say it. What rot! When you were with English you got into the habit of using English expressions in your thinking. The English spoken language—the upper classes, anyway—must have fewer words than the Eskimo. . . . The English talked with inflected phrases. One phrase to mean everything. I liked them though. I liked the way they talked" (*SAR*, p. 149).

22. Ernest Hemingway, "Interview: The Art of Fiction XXI," *Paris Review* 18 (Spring 1958): 88.

23. Hemingway sometimes compromises independent perception by becoming insistently prescriptive. Take for instance his account of how we respond to the sight of gored horses in the ring at a bullfight: "There is certainly nothing comic by our standards in seeing an animal emptied of its visceral content, but if this animal instead of doing something tragic, that is, dignified, gallops in a stiff old-maidish fashion around a ring trailing the opposite of clouds of glory it is as comic when what it is trailing is real as when the Fratellinis give a burlesque of it in which the viscera are represented by rolls of bandages, sausages and other things. If one is comic the other is; the humor comes from the same principle" (*DA*, p. 7). Too often, Hemingway seems to assume that what "we really feel" is only what outrages some moral standard to which a supposedly deluded or timid person adheres.

24. Peterson, pp. 171–216.

25. Hugh Kenner, *A Homemade World: The American Modernist Writers* (New York: William Morrow, 1975), p. 156. Schwartz notes that the values of courage and sacrifice remain ideals of human behavior for Hemingway when properly enacted. Those values can be vitiated only in their verbal expression, he argues, not in their substance (p. 261).

26. Outside of his fiction Hemingway was not as conscientious about lying as is Krebs. The most notorious example of his tendency to falsify or distort his past experience concerns his numerous accounts of his World War I wound in Italy (see Lynn, pp. 75–86).

27. Levin, p. 77.

28. My references to Hemingway's "early" and "late" work are meant to be provisional. Though I generally agree that there is a gradual lapsing of imaginative subtlety

and force in his work after 1930, too schematic a rise-and-fall charting of his career seems to me unhelpful.

29. Ernest Hemingway, "Interview: The Art of Fiction XXI," p. 84. Paul Smith's article, "Hemingway's Early Manuscripts: The Theory and Practice of Omission," *Journal of Modern Literature* 10, no. 2 (June 1983): 268–89, provides a useful overview of Hemingway's various espousals of this "theory" and their practical implications in some of his manuscripts. Smith rightly contends that "it takes some stretch of imagination" to conceive of some of the subjects Hemingway claimed he omitted (especially the suicide that was supposedly deleted from "Out of Season") "as having been 'there' at 'first,' wherever and whenever that was" (p. 271). His assertion that Hemingway's comments about omission represent "the literary equivalent of the law of gravitation," however, seems to me mistaken. To contend that such remarks simply rehearse "the commonplace that the structures of literature, like the sentences of the language, imply more than they state and make us feel more than we know" (p. 271), raises more questions than it settles. What "structures of literature?" How do *all* sentences "imply more than they state?" What would it mean to say they "make us feel more than we know?" "Know" about what?

30. See Millicent Bell's discerning discussion of the "loss of larger meaning" attendant upon repairing the gaps in Hemingway's stories "with grafts from other parts of his work." "Narrative Gaps/Narrative Meaning," *Raritan* 6, no. 1 (Summer 1986): 96–99.

31. Kenner, pp. 150, 156.

32. Ibid., pp. 151, 152.

33. Ibid., p. 123.

34. Ernest Hemingway, letter to John Dos Passos, 26 March 1932, in *Ernest Hemingway: Selected Letters, 1917–1961*, ed. Carlos Baker (New York: Charles Scribner's Sons, 1981), p. 354.

35. James M. Cox, "*In Our Time*: The Essential Hemingway," *Southern Humanities Review* 22, no. 4 (Summer 1988): 312.

36. Cf. Edmund Wilson, "Hemingway: Gauge of Morale," in *The Portable Edmund Wilson*, ed. Lewis M. Dabney (New York: Viking, 1983), pp. 396–418; Philip Young, *Ernest Hemingway: A Reconsideration* (University Park: Pennsylvania State University Press, 1966), pp. 43–47; Kenner, pp. 150–52; Shelley Fisher Fishkin, *From Fact to Fiction: Journalism and Imaginative Writing in America* (Baltimore, Md.: Johns Hopkins University Press, 1985), pp. 152–55; and Lynn, pp. 103–4. Lynn rightly contends that "Big Two-Hearted River" raises "more tantalizing questions than any other Hemingway story" (p. 103) and that "first and last, Nick remains an enigma" (p. 104). But the lack of textual evidence with which he faults the "war-wound" readers of this story just as obviously marks his own biographical speculations about Nick/Hemingway's state of mind.

Many critics who would now be reluctant to invoke a "war-wound" reading of Hemingway's stories simply locate the missing subsurface elements as disguised versions of homophobia and sexism. (See Judith Fetterley, "Hemingway's 'Resentful Cryptogram,'" in *Ernest Hemingway's "A Farewell to Arms"*, ed. Harold Bloom [New York: Chelsea House, 1987], pp. 61–75; and Arnold E. and Cathy N. Davidson, "Decoding the Hemingway Hero in *The Sun Also Rises*," in *New Essays on "The Sun Also Rises"*, ed. Linda Wagner-Martin [New York: Cambridge University Press, 1987], pp. 83–107.) These "new" readings (in which a "resisting" critical truculence simply masks an implicit lament that Hemingway was not a kinder, gentler guy) seem as unpromising as the earlier interpretations they seek to revise. The new vocabulary of "decodings," "cryptograms," and "sublimations" represents only a new issue of a dated coinage. The conception of a submerged iceberg still licenses these recent approaches; an underlying "subject" is still taken to rule our ability to construe the ice at waterline.

37. Levin, p. 77.

38. James Guetti, *Word-Music: The Aesthetic Aspect of Narrative Fiction* (New Brunswick, N.J.: Rutgers University Press, 1980), pp. 4–14, 139–49.

39. Wyndham Lewis, "Ernest Hemingway: The 'Dumb Ox,'" *Men without Art*, ed. Seamus Cooney (1934; reprint, Santa Rosa, Calif.: Black Sparrow Press, 1987), pp. 27, 28; Young, p. 46. Lewis complains of the supposed passivity of Hemingway's characters and of his unawareness of political context. Hemingway "is interested in the sports of death . . . [and] war," Lewis claims, "but *not* in the things that cause war, or the people who profit by it, or in the ultimate human destinies involved in it" (pp. 19–20).

40. Lewis, pp. 26, 24.

41. William Pritchard, "The Trouble with Ernest," review of *Hemingway* by Kenneth Lynn, *Hudson Review* 41, no. 1 (Spring 1988): 223.

42. Young, p. 44.

43. Richard L. McLain is more helpful than most in describing Nick's "ritualism," because what he sees as ritualistic are not Nick's actions but "the semantic pattern" that underlies their description. This pattern, McLain asserts, "has a great deal in common with the function and nature of ritual involvement: agency, prescribed activity, individual accomplished fixities, stages toward some vague satisfaction of an emotional state." "Semantics and Style—With the Example of Quintessential Hemingway," in *Ernest Hemingway: Six Decades of Criticism*, p. 160.

44. John Hollander, "Hemingway's Extraordinary Reality," in *Ernest Hemingway: Modern Critical Views*, ed. Harold Bloom (New York: Chelsea House, 1985), p. 213. In an analogous vein, Daniel J. Schneider discusses the repetition of image clusters in *A Farewell to Arms* that form what he calls a musical key. He does not examine the imaginative status of the images as they are repeated, however, and thus their communicated impression for him is always one of "endless sameness and weariness." See "The Novel as Pure Poetry," in *Ernest Hemingway's "A Farewell to Arms,"* pp. 9–24.

45. Levin, p. 83.

46. Fishkin, pp. 147, 155.

47. Ernest Hemingway, "Interview: The Art of Fiction XXI," p. 69.

48. Ibid., p. 81.

49. Baker, p. 220.

50. Edgar Allan Poe, *The Narrative of Arthur Gordon Pym*, in *Edgar Allan Poe: Poetry and Tales*, ed. Patrick F. Quinn (New York: Library of America, 1984), p. 1086.

51. Nemi D'Agostino, "The Later Hemingway," in *Hemingway: A Collection of Critical Essays*, pp. 153, 152.

52. Robert Scholes, *Textual Power: Literary Theory and the Teaching of English* (New Haven, Conn.: Yale University Press, 1985), pp. 69–70. Lynn too asserts that Hemingway "becomes" the matador in this sketch, but he eroticizes Hemingway's projection into the consciousness of Maera. Lynn argues that this sketch resembles "Up in Michigan" in imagining "the sensation of lying helpless beneath an unstoppable male assault" (p. 213).

53. Ibid., p. 71. Scholes's discussion of this moment seems to me both mistaken and willfully tendentious. Hemingway's "reader is invited" Scholes says (which here means "let's invite ourselves in") to string together the bullfighting vignettes in *In Our Time* so that we see (on the basis of virtually no textual evidence) that the crowd is actually saluting *Hemingway* as Maera dies. "As the matador kills the bull," he contends, so Hemingway kills Maera "with a grace and beauty equivalent to that of Villalta as he kills his last bull and raises his triumphant hand to the crowd," leaving "criticism" with no apparent option but to "emit a bloody roar and collapse in admiration" (p. 70).

Scholes wishes to find a critical stance "sufficiently antagonistic to Hemingway's to bring his 'untold' presuppositions to light" and thus to "free" us "from the power of his text." He can do this, however, only by misrepresenting what Hemingway has written in order to call it a "presupposition" (p. 70). If the "whole function of criticism," as Scholes asserts, is to learn how to "loosen the bonds of the textual powers in which we find ourselves enmeshed" (p. 73), perhaps we might first liberate ourselves from the reductive methods he himself depends upon here.

54. Kenner, p. 126. See Levin's more suggestive comment that a "key word" for Hemingway "is *and*, with its renewable promise of continuity, occasionally varied by *then* and *so*" (p. 79). Hemingway himself was not above fatuity in discussing this aspect of his writing. "In the first paragraphs of *Farewell*," he once told Lillian Ross of the *New Yorker*, "I used the word 'and' consciously over and over the way Mr. Johann Sebastian Bach used a note in music when he was emitting counterpoint. I can almost write like Mr. Johann sometimes—or, anyway, so he would like it." Quoted in Lillian Ross, "How Do You Like It Now, Gentlemen?" in *Hemingway: A Collection of Critical Essays*, pp. 17–39.

55. Guetti, *Word-Music*, p. 143.

56. Lynn, p. 436.

57. Nina Baym, "Actually, I Felt Sorry For the Lion," in *New Approaches to the Short Stories of Ernest Hemingway*, ed. Jackson Benson (Durham, N.C.: Duke University Press, 1990), p. 115.

58. Young, p. 73.

59. Baym asserts that the viewpoint of the dead lion is somehow "transferred to Margot Macomber" and that she knows "almost everything" about its death (pp. 114,

119). There is no textual evidence for such a claim. Margot's acidic remark to Wilson that he was "lovely this morning. That is if blowing things' heads off is lovely" (*SS*, p. 9) shows that she sees, as Baym says, that "what is a matter of life and death for the animal becomes a wasteful war game for men" (p. 119). But Margot herself, in dismissing the brutality of hunting, remains incapable of imagining the pain the lion feels in the ballistic terms in which the narrator presents it. Margot is also not as untainted by war games as Baym implies, preferring, as she does, Wilson's "gimlet" to Macomber's "lemon squash." See Lynn's discussion of the erotic valences of these drink choices (pp. 431–32).

60. Lynn, p. 434.

61. Arnold E. and Cathy N. Davidson, p. 100. The Davidsons overstate matters in speculating about Girones's life: "You can embrace a wife, children, a simple life on the farm; you can also embrace the life of the fiesta, a thrust of the bull's horn. Vincente Girones made his choice and died to be celebrated by 'all the members of the dancing and drinking societies of Pamplona, Estella, Tafalla, and Sanguesa'" (p. 100). One might think from such a description that Girones purposefully ran onto the bull's horn rather than having been gored from behind.

62. Tom Stoppard, "Reflections on Ernest Hemingway," in *Ernest Hemingway: The Writer in Context*, ed. James Nagel (Madison: University of Wisconsin Press, 1984), p. 24.

63. Ibid.

64. Ernest Hemingway, "Interview: Art of Fiction XXI," p. 81.

CHAPTER VI

FAULKNER: VIOLENCE IN THE REALMS OF HEARING

1. William Faulkner, *The Hamlet* in *Faulkner: Novels 1936–1940*, ed. Joseph Blotner and Noel Polk (New York: Library of America, 1990), p. 991. All page references in the text to this novel (abbreviated *TH*) and to "Old Man" (abbreviated "OM") will be to this edition and cited parenthetically. References to other of Faulkner's works quoted in the text are to the following editions: *As I Lay Dying*, *Light in August*, and *Sanctuary* (abbreviated *ALD*, *LA*, and *S*, respectively) in *William Faulkner: Novels 1930–1935*, ed. Joseph Blotner and Noel Polk (New York: Library of America, 1985); *Go Down, Moses* (New York: Vintage Books, 1942), abbreviated *GDM*; and *The Sound and the Fury* (1929; reprint, New York: Vintage Books, 1987), abbreviated *SF*.

2. Joseph W. Reed, *Faulkner's Narrative* (New Haven, Conn.: Yale University Press, 1973), p. 2.

3. Ronald Sukenick, *In Form: Digressions on the Act of Fiction* (Carbondale: Southern Illinois University Press, 1985), p. xx.

4. Quoted in Robert Penn Warren's introduction, "Faulkner: Past and Present," to *Faulkner: A Collection of Critical Essays*, ed. Robert Penn Warren (Englewood Cliffs, N.J.: Prentice-Hall, 1966), p. 7.

5. Delmore Schwartz, "The Fiction of William Faulkner," in *Selected Essays of Del-*

more Schwartz, ed. Donald A. Dike and David H. Zucker (Chicago: University of Chicago Press, 1970), pp. 279–80.

6. George Garrett, " 'Fix My Hair, Jack': The Dark Side of Faulkner's Jokes," in *Faulkner and Humor: Faulkner and Yoknapatawpha, 1984*, ed. Doreen Fowler and Ann J. Abadie (Jackson: University Press of Mississippi, 1986), pp. 221–22.

7. Warren Beck, *Faulkner* (Madison: University of Wisconsin Press, 1976), pp. 36, 37.

8. Beck, pp. 147, 148.

9. Garrett, pp. 228, 226.

10. Ralph Waldo Emerson, journal entry, June 1847, in *Emerson in his Journals*, ed. Joel Porte (Cambridge, Mass.: Harvard University Press, 1982), p. 372.

11. Olga Vickery, *The Novels of William Faulkner: A Critical Interpretation* (Baton Rouge: Louisiana State University Press, 1964), pp. 113, 112.

12. For but two of the innumerable examples of this conceptual divergence in Faulkner's fiction, see Addie Bundren's vision of "how words go straight up in a thin line, quick and harmless, and how terribly doing goes along the earth, clinging to it" (*ALD*, p. 117) and Joe Christmas's contemptuous conviction that when a woman "finally [comes] to surrender completely, it's going to be in words" (*LA*, p. 576).

13. Schwartz, p. 280.

14. See James Guetti's discussion of *As I Lay Dying* in *Word-Music: The Aesthetic Aspect of Narrative Fiction* (New Brunswick, N.J.: Rutgers University Press, 1980), pp. 149–56.

15. Wyndham Lewis, "Ernest Hemingway: The 'Dumb Ox,'" in *Men without Art*, ed. Seamus Cooney (1934; reprint, Santa Rosa, Calif.: Black Sparrow Press, 1987), p. 20.

16. Ibid., pp. 37, 39.

17. Hugh Kenner, *A Homemade World: The American Modernist Writers* (New York: William Morrow, 1975), p. 133.

18. James M. Cox, "Humor as Vision in Faulkner," in *Faulkner and Humor*, p. 1.

19. Conrad Aiken, "William Faulkner: The Novel as Form," in *Faulkner: A Collection of Critical Essays*, p. 49.

20. Donald M. Kartiganer, "William Faulkner," in *Columbia Literary History of the United States*, ed. Emory Elliott (New York: Columbia University Press, 1988), p. 888.

21. See Richard Poirier's discussion of Faulkner's "grammar of refutation" in *A World Elsewhere: The Place of Style in American Literature* (New York: Oxford University Press, 1966), p. 80. Poirier notes that Faulkner's negatives sometimes discard what the narrative itself will later entertain.

22. Robert Garis, *The Dickens Theatre: A Reassessment of the Novels* (London: Oxford University Press, 1965), p. 33.

23. Faulkner also admires the convict's refusal to take lying lightly: "his hill-man's sober and jealous respect not for truth but for the power, the strength, of lying—not to be niggard with lying but rather to use it with respect and even care, delicate quick

and strong, like a fine and fatal blade" ("OM," p. 682). I find it difficult, however, to credit Albert J. Guerard's notion that the convict embodies "monastic integrity" or that he is "one of [Faulkner's] least equivocal heroes," *The Triumph of the Novel: Dickens, Dostoevsky, Faulkner* (New York: Oxford University Press, 1976), p. 109. David Minter, for his part, takes an almost opposite stance, seeing the convict as a psychologically "diminished" man. But Minter says that diminishment makes "Old Man" as a whole seem "slight and overextended." *William Faulkner: His Life and Work* (Baltimore, Md.: Johns Hopkins University Press, 1980), pp. 174, 173. As I am suggesting, psychological complexity need not form the only criterion for judging the story's depth and effectiveness.

24. Guerard, p. 222. Faulkner, Guerard contends, evokes "a general vision of *the absurd* (or, in Faulkner's word, *outrage*): the sudden shifts in circumstance, the backfiring of reasonable plan, the thwarting of obsessive expectation." Yet this pessimistic vision, he says, is "essentially comic" for "particular absurdities of every kind are energizing." *How* such "absurdities" are energized, however, differs dramatically in Faulkner's work, as does the fictional status of the person at whose expense such comedy is invoked.

25. Kenner, p. 196.

26. See Thomas L. McHaney, "What Faulkner Learned from the Tall Tale," in *Faulkner and Humor*, pp. 110–35. Guerard also rightly notes that the "wild anti-realist fun" of Red's funeral resembles moments in Nathanael West's *The Day of the Locust* (p. 134).

27. William Faulkner, introduction to *Sanctuary* (1931; reprint, New York: Vintage Books, 1987), p. 339. In its mix of grotesquerie and humor, Red's funeral resembles the considerably grimmer spectacle of how a "countryman" (Hamp Waller) attempts to move Joanna Burden's nearly completely decapitated corpse from her burning house in *Light in August*. Byron Bunch tells Gail Hightower of the incident:

> The man said . . . how he was afraid to try to pick her up and carry her out because her head might come clean off. And then he said . . . he run back into the house and up the stairs again and into the room and jerked a cover off the bed and rolled her onto it and caught up the corners and swung it onto his back like a sack of meal and carried it out of the house and laid it down under a tree. And he said that what he was scared of happened. Because the cover fell open and she was laying on her side, facing one way, and her head was turned clean around like she was looking behind her. And he said how if she could just have done that when she was alive, she might not have been doing it now. (*LA*, pp. 465–66)

At least part of a reader's laughter at the unearthly obtuseness of Waller's last remark seems to spring from the relief it provides from the otherwise repulsive physicality of this moment.

28. Schwartz, p. 277.

29. William Faulkner, "William Faulkner," in *Writers at Work: The Paris Review Interviews (First Series)*, ed. Malcolm Cowley (New York: Penguin, 1977), p. 134.

30. Stephen M. Ross points out that Temple is portrayed through the novel as a listener, "an *écouteur*" who is severely estranged from the phenomenal world and who

"cannot be judged in simple moral terms." *Fiction's Inexhaustible Voice: Speech and Writing in Faulkner* (Athens: University of Georgia Press, 1989), pp. 47, 48.

31. William Faulkner, *Paris Review* interview, p. 134.

32. Ernest Hemingway, *The Sun Also Rises* (1926; reprint, New York: Charles Scribner's Sons, 1954), pp. 218–19.

33. James Guetti suggests that the "flavor of anticlimax" in Old Ben's death partly exemplifies the danger of certain rigidified attempts to apprehend the "reality" of the wilderness. *The Limits of Metaphor: A Study of Melville, Conrad, and Faulkner* (Ithaca, N.Y.: Cornell University Press, 1967), p. 160.

34. Both Temple and Horace frequently observe themselves or a part of their anatomy as if it belonged to somebody else: "[Temple] saw her hand lying on the stove. She snatched it up with a wailing shriek . . ." (*S*, p. 243); "[Horace] still held the cold pipe, and he discovered his hand searching his pocket for a match" (*S*, p. 301); "Popeye was gripping her wrist, shaking it, and she found that her mouth was open and that she must have been making a noise of some sort with it" (*S*, p. 343); "[Horace] watched himself cross the porch and then tread the diffident snow of the last locusts" (*S*, p. 382).

35. See, for example, the death of Jack Houston at the hands of Mink Snopes in *The Hamlet* (pp. 933–34).

36. Caroline Gordon and Allen Tate, "'Spotted Horses': Commentary," in *The House of Fiction*, 2d ed. (New York: Charles Scribner's Sons, 1960), p. 334.

37. Stanley Cavell, *The World Viewed: Reflections on the Ontology of Film*, enlarged ed. (Cambridge, Mass.: Harvard University Press, 1979), p. 37.

38. It might be objected here that individual readers, for different reasons, may find it difficult or impossible to respond to voiced depictions of certain violent or demeaning actions and events: that there are moments in which pain will not, so to speak, allow for art. By separating "pain" and "art," such readers assume that the former must always precede the latter and that art is obligated to represent pain accurately or mimetically. Faulkner often simply refuses to accept this premise. His fiction constantly reminds us of how art can spin free of its ostensible subject and assume an orbit of its own, whether readers choose to respond to that new imaginative trajectory or not.

39. For an interestingly similar example of voiced violence, see Ike McCaslin's recounting of Boon Hogganbeck's shooting abilities in "The Bear" (*GDM*, pp. 235–36).

40. Schwartz, pp. 284, 287, 284–85, 286. Claude-Edmonde Magny makes a similar point from a theological perspective when he asserts that "one might say that in Faulkner's world sanctuaries assume their sacred character only through the profanation which despoils them forever." "Faulkner or Theological Inversion," in *Faulkner: A Collection of Critical Essays*, p. 71.

41. These are all terms used by Edmond L. Volpe in *A Reader's Guide to William Faulkner* (New York: Farrar, Straus & Giroux, 1964), p. 119.

42. Jason's conception of himself as a martyr is not entirely inaccurate—not in a household in which Mrs. Compson rules as a dark queen whose rallying cry is "I'll be gone soon" and not with his headache-racked physiology, which is another Compson

legacy. But in no way, Faulkner makes clear, does Jason's family situation or his physical condition adequately "explain" his malicious verbal gifts.

43. William N. Claxon, Jr., "Jason Compson: A Demoralized Wit," in *Faulkner and Humor*, p. 30.

44. See Cox, pp. 1–20.

45. Alfred Kazin, "The Stillness of *Light in August*," in *Faulkner: A Collection of Critical Essays*, pp. 153, 152.

46. Warwick Wadlington, *Reading Faulknerian Tragedy* (Ithaca, N.Y.: Cornell University Press, 1987), p. 155.

47. Eric Sundquist mistakes this image of a photographic print for that of a photographic negative and calls it "a figure of simultaneous concealment and revelation." *Faulkner: The House Divided* (Baltimore, Md.: Johns Hopkins University Press, 1983), p. 71. Even if this were the image of a negative, what, as the vehicle of the analogy, could a negative's polarized images be said to "conceal" and "reveal"?

48. Michael Millgate, "'A Novel: Not an Anecdote,' Faulkner's *Light in August*" in *New Essays on "Light in August,"* ed. Michael Millgate (New York: Cambridge University Press, 1987), p. 43.

49. Wadlington contends that Faulkner rhetorically "contains and transmutes" the violence of Joe's death "into a kind of immunization" or "inoculation" (p. 167).

50. William Faulkner, letter to Malcolm Cowley, 20 September 1945, in Malcolm Cowley, *The Faulkner-Cowley File: Letters and Memories, 1944–1962* (New York: Viking, 1966), p. 32.

51. Sundquist goes so far as to say that Joe, in his "seemingly insane passivity" "allow[s] himself to be shot and castrated" (p. 73).

52. A further complication is that Faulkner's emphasis upon the "black blast" of Joe's "black blood" rushing out of his "pale body" seems troublesome because it partially reanimates the duplicitous black blood/white blood distinction Gavin Stevens proposes. Faulkner refers elsewhere to the blood of whites, when it flows, as "black." But in the racially charged atmosphere of the novel, it seems an odd contrast to strike here, especially in light of other descriptions such as that in which Joe puts on a pair of brogans he has stolen from a black woman:

> the black shoes, the black shoes smelling of negro . . . looked like they had been chopped out of iron ore with a dull axe. Looking down at the harsh, crude, clumsy shapelessness of them, he said "Hah" through his teeth. It seemed to him that he could see himself being hunted by white men at last into the black abyss which had been waiting, trying for thirty years to drown him and into which now and at last he had actually entered, bearing now upon his ankles the definite and ineradicable gauge of its upward moving. (*LA*, p. 643)

There is the possibility that the "black blast"/"pale body" contrast might characterize what Grimm's men see, but that possibility seems tenuous.

53. Some critics overstate the nature of what we know about Joe's consciousness in his final moments. See for instance Carole Anne Taylor's "*Light in August*: The Epistemology of Tragic Paradox," in *William Faulkner's "Light in August"*, ed. Francois

L. Pitavy (New York: Garland, 1982), pp. 203–24. Taylor says that Joe, in dying, "achieves the fullness of paradoxical understanding that is tragic," an understanding that entails "contradictory intuitions about the nature of knowledge," "the certainty of uncertain knowing," and "the timelessness (within the mind) of events which happen in time" (p. 222). But how can we be certain that this is what Joe feels when all we are shown is the enigmatic "shadow" about his mouth and the knowledge that his eyes are "empty of everything save consciousness"?

54. Ibid., p. 218.

55. Wadlington, pp. 167–68. For one version of the kind of reading Wadlington refers to, see Joyce Carol Oates, "'At Least I Have Made a Woman of Her': Images of Women in Twentieth-Century Literature," in *The Profane Art: Essays and Reviews* (New York: Persea, 1983), pp. 35–62. Oates claims that Joanna Burden is judged as "rightly dead, and her murderer as 'innocently' guilty" (p. 62). Her quotation marks around *innocently*, however, suggest the strain of this reading. There is little textual evidence that Faulkner thinks of Joanna's death as in any way "right," though he may see it as inevitable.

56. Taylor, p. 224.

CHAPTER VII
FLANNERY O'CONNOR: VIOLENCE AND THE DEMANDS OF ART

1. Alice Walker, "Beyond the Peacock: The Reconstruction of Flannery O'Connor," in *In Search of Our Mothers' Gardens: Womanist Prose* (San Diego: Harcourt, Brace, Jovanovich, 1983), pp. 46, 53, 57.

2. *Flannery O'Connor: Collected Works*, ed. Sally Fitzgerald (New York: Library of America, 1988), p. 602. All further page references in the text to O'Connor's novels and stories will be to this edition and cited parenthetically.

3. Flannery O'Connor, letter to John Hawkes, 27 July 1958, in *The Habit of Being*, ed. Sally Fitzgerald (New York: Farrar, Straus & Giroux, 1979), p. 292.

4. Louise Westling, *Sacred Groves and Ravaged Gardens: The Fiction of Eudora Welty, Carson McCullers, and Flannery O'Connor* (Athens: University of Georgia Press, 1985), p. 148.

5. Arthur F. Kinney, "Flannery O'Connor and the Fiction of Grace," *Massachusetts Review* 27, no. 1 (Spring 1986): 74.

6. Ibid., p. 85. Lewis A. Lawson argues, in a similar vein, that "given O'Connor's many statements of her intentions, we must assume that she would have expected her work to be judged by its communicability." See *Another Generation: Southern Fiction since World War II* (Jackson: University of Mississippi Press, 1984), p. 32.

7. Flannery O'Connor, *Mystery and Manners: Occasional Prose*, ed. Sally and Robert Fitzgerald (New York: Farrar, Straus & Giroux, 1969), p. 71. All further references in the text to the these essays will be to this edition and cited parenthetically, with the abbreviation *MM*.

8. Gilbert Muller, *Nightmares and Visions: Flannery O'Connor and the Catholic Grotesque* (Athens: University of Georgia Press, 1972), pp. 78, 77.

9. Ralph C. Woods, *The Comedy of Redemption: Christian Faith and Comic Vision in Four American Novelists* (South Bend, Ind.: University of Notre Dame Press, 1988), p. 95.

10. André Bleikasten, "The Heresy of Flannery O'Connor," in *Les Américanistes: New French Criticism on Modern American Fiction*, ed. Ira D. Johnson and Christiane Johnson (Port Washington, N.Y.: Kennikat Press, 1978), p. 59.

11. Robert Frost, *Selected Prose of Robert Frost*, ed. Hyde Cox and Edward Connery Lathem (New York: Collier Books, 1968), pp. 60, 61.

12. Richard Poirier, "Frost, Winnicott, Burke," *Raritan* 2, no. 2 (Fall 1982): 124.

13. Elizabeth Hardwick, "Southern Literature: The Cultural Assumptions of Regionalism," in *Southern Literature in Transition, Heritage, and Promise*, ed. Phillip Castille and William Osborne (Memphis: Memphis State University Press, 1983), p. 26.

14. O'Connor's stricture here is *not* the same as Bleikasten's assertion that "the truth of O'Connor's work is the truth of her art, not that of her church" (p. 69) or that "as a writer she belongs to no other parish than literature" (p. 70). We do well to remember O'Connor's sense, as she articulates it to her friend "A." in a letter of 25 November 1960, that "you do not write the best you can for the sake of art but for the sake of returning your talent increased to the invisible God to use or not use as he sees fit. Resignation to the will of God does not mean that you stop resisting evil or obstacles, it means that you leave the outcome out of your personal considerations. It is the most concern coupled with the least concern. This sermon is now ended" (*The Habit of Being*, p. 419).

15. Frederick Crews, "The Power of Flannery O'Connor," *New York Review of Books*, 26 April 1990, p. 52. Crews sees O'Connor's absolutist theology and her emphasis on a severe, uncompromising redemption as "dubiously Christian in spirit." Bleikasten also emphasizes the pain and suffering in O'Connor's fiction. But his assertion that O'Connor takes an "almost sadistic glee" in reducing "the human to the nonhuman" and that her Catholicism may represent merely "an alibi for misanthropy" (p. 57) seem to me overstated. Woods argues, in a more balanced way, that O'Connor's fiction, at its worst, expresses "her dubious conviction that the iron fist of negation must smash all human pretense before the glad hand of grace can lift up" (p. 125) and threatens "to turn redemption into a baleful cornering by the Hound of Heaven" (p. 281). At its best, however, her work suggests that "the Kingdom of Heaven is not borne violently away by frustrated atheists; it is gratuitously given to the unsuspecting children of God" (p. 82).

16. Richard Poirier, *The Performing Self: Compositions and Decompositions in the Languages of Contemporary Life* (New York: Oxford University Press, 1971), p. 76.

17. James Mellard notes that O'Connor denies her readers "the very principle of free will that is opened up by her own sense of Catholic theology." But it does not necessarily follow that we can thereby assume, as Mellard does, "that O'Connor's readers are in fact free to read as they will." "Flannery O'Connor's *Others: Freud, Lacan, and the Unconscious*," *American Literature* 61, no. 4 (December 1989): 626. For a detailed critique of Mellard's position, see Crews, pp. 49–50.

18. For a discerning discussion of this approach, see Crews, pp. 52–53.

19. For differing perspectives on O'Connor's relations to race relations in the South, see Crews (pp. 53–55) and Robert Coles, *Flannery O'Connor's South* (Baton Rouge: Louisiana State University Press, 1980), pp. 3–55.

20. Frederick Asals, *Flannery O'Connor: The Imagination of Extremity* (Athens: University of Georgia Press, 1982), p. 184.

21. Joyce Carol Oates, "The Visionary Art of Flannery O'Connor," *Southern Humanities Review* 7, no. 3 (Summer 1973): 246.

22. Asals, p. 184.

23. Richard Poirier, "Writing Off the Self," *Raritan* 1, no. 1 (Summer 1981): 106. An expanded version of this essay appears in *The Renewal of Literature: Emersonian Reflections* (New Haven, Conn.: Yale University Press, 1987), pp. 182–223.

24. Martha Stephens, *The Question of Flannery O'Connor* (Baton Rouge: Louisiana State University Press, 1973), pp. 18, 39, 40.

25. Carol Shloss, *Flannery O'Connor's Dark Comedies: The Limits of Inference* (Baton Rouge: Louisiana State University Press, 1980), p. 70. The bull, Shloss says, is endowed with "sexual associations, intimations of classical divinity (Jupiter, the bull as disguised god-lover) and of the Christian passion (Jesus' crown of thorns at the time of his persecution) . . . and the multiplicity of references has independent conceptual implications. Far from calling for a selection of one comparative term (for example, the Christian one), the complexity of the narrative suggests that cumulative definition is necessary. . . . It does not seem to matter, then, whether the bull is a suffering Christ, a Roman divinity, or a country lover, for these terms commonly contribute a sense of life forces that impinge on and threaten a mind closely programmed to exclude the irrational" (pp. 70–71).

26. Ibid., p. 72.

27. Ibid., pp. 73, 66.

28. Flannery O'Connor, *The Presence of Grace, and Other Book Reviews by Flannery O'Connor*, ed. Carter Martin (Athens: University of Georgia Press, 1983), p. 100.

29. Miles Orvell, *Invisible Parade: The Fiction of Flannery O'Connor* (Philadelphia: Temple University Press, 1972), p. 24.

30. Shloss, pp. 68, 69.

31. John Fraser, *Violence in the Arts* (Cambridge, Eng.: Cambridge University Press, 1974), p. 71.

32. Bleikasten, p. 62.

33. Louise Gossett, *Violence in Recent Southern Fiction* (Durham, N.C.: Duke University Press, 1965), p. 86.

34. The imagery of one of her dreams has also been literalized, for the tree line is now the "dark wound" that the sun, "like a bullet," had previously burst through as it "raced down the hill toward her."

35. Shloss, p. 65.

36. Ibid., pp. 65, 66, 72.

37. Westling says O'Connor never suggests that Mrs. May has the slightest understanding of the bull's figurative significance and that her "revelation" introduces prob-

lems "which prevent a wholly satisfactory resolution of the story" (p. 164). She sees the shock of the final scene, however, as attributable to reversals and denials of mythological female associations with the earth rather than to conflicting narrative modes.

38. E. M. Halliday, "Hemingway's Ambiguity: Symbolism and Irony," in *Hemingway: A Collection of Critical Essays*, ed. Robert P. Weeks (Englewood Cliffs, N.J.: Prentice-Hall, 1962), p. 56.

39. Oates, p. 242.

40. O'Connor did assert on another occasion that she did not want to "defame" the word *compassion*: "There is a better sense in which it can be used but seldom is—the sense of being in travail with and for creation in its subjection to vanity. This a sense which implies a recognition of sin; this is a suffering-with, but one which blunts no edges and makes no excuses. When infused into novels, it is often forbidding. Our age doesn't go for it" (*MM*, pp. 165–66).

41. Coles, p. 80.

42. Flannery O'Connor, *The Habit of Being*, p. 275.

43. Stephens, p. 77. Frederick Asals argues that O'Connor is mocking Hazel in this moment, p. 27.

44. Coles, p. 81.

45. Westling, p. 153.

46. Shloss, p. 51.

47. Steven Weisenberger, "Style in *Wise Blood*," *Genre* 16, no. 1 (Spring 1983): 78, 80, 81.

48. This narrative playfulness belies Crews's assertion that O'Connor's stories "adhere to the classroom formula of her day," which dictated that one "keep the narrative voice distinct from those of your characters" (p. 49).

49. Claire Katz rightly argues that O'Connor often displaces our readerly attention by investing inconsequential details with a "special intensity." But it does not necessarily follow that this happens because "the source of imaginative power" in her work "lies in her ability to evoke fearful primitive fantasies" or "archaic fears." "Flannery O'Connor's Rage of Vision," *American Literature* 46 (March 1974): 54–67.

50. Robert Fitzgerald, "'Introduction' to *Everything That Rises Must Converge*," in *Women Writers of the Short Story*, ed. Heather McClave (Englewood Cliffs, N.J.: Prentice-Hall, 1980), p. 133.

51. Katz, pp. 55, 66.

CHAPTER VIII
"THE LATE, LATE, LATE SHOW": THOMAS PYNCHON'S VIOLENCE

1. Richard Poirier, "Humans," review of *Slow Learner* by Thomas Pynchon, *London Review of Books*, 24 January 1985, p. 18.

2. Cited by Tony Tanner, *Thomas Pynchon* (London: Methuen, 1982), p. 18.

3. Poirier, p. 20.

4. James Guetti, *Word-Music: The Aesthetic Aspect of Narrative Fiction* (New Brunswick, N.J.: Rutgers University Press, 1980), p. 94.

5. Thomas Pynchon, *V.* (Philadelphia: Bantam Books, 1964), p. 83. All further page references in the text will be to this edition and cited parenthetically. Page references to *The Crying of Lot 49* (abbreviated *CL*) and *Gravity's Rainbow* (abbreviated *GR*) will be to the Bantam paperback editions (1967 and 1974, respectively); references to *Slow Learner* (Boston: Little, Brown, 1984) will be abbreviated *SL*. All unbracketed ellipses in quoted passages are Pynchon's. Any bracketed ellipses represent my own editing.

6. Pynchon uses all of the following in *V.* alone (and this is by no means an exhaustive list): "gloveless," "dimensionless," "twitchless," "windowless," "raidless," "roofless," "walless," "parishless," "tearless," "noteless," "wheelless," "bra-less," "pillowless," "tenantless," "featureless," "lustless," "ageless," "shoeless," "expressionless," and "contraceptivelessness." Pynchon's use of these words is a local symptom of his larger impulse to stage soundless scenes in his fiction, scenes where fictional sound has been banished from the narrative. Examples of this include the murder at the summer theater in the Ezbekiyeh Garden in *V.* (pp. 81–82), Oedipa Maas's ballroom dance among "deaf-mute delegates in party hats" in a hotel lobby (p. 97) in *The Crying of Lot 49*, and the moment in which Meatball Mulligan and his friends telepathically pursue the jazz art of Gerry Mulligan in "Entropy" (*SL*, pp. 94–96).

7. Max Schulz, *Black Humor Fiction of the Sixties* (Athens: Ohio University Press, 1973), p. 13.

8. Guetti, p. 98.

9. Molly Hite, *Ideas of Order in the Novels of Thomas Pynchon* (Columbus: Ohio State University Press, 1983), pp. 14, 50.

10. Ibid., pp. 25, 26. In this respect as well, Pynchon's fiction oddly resembles O'Connor's, however different their other motives and imaginative procedures. O'Connor frequently ends a story with a character who at last seems capable of acknowledging the transformative actions of Catholic grace. But whether the character actually *does* realize this transformation seems not irrelevant but indeterminable. The dramatic outcome of such moments—like the various forms of resolution Pynchon might temporarily invoke—is postponed beyond the end of the story (or, as in "Greenleaf," rendered indecipherable). O'Connor's stories tend to end with a theological (rather than an epistemological) opportunity whose fulfillment, because it is so consistently deferred, seems unrepresentable.

11. Hite, p. 45.

12. Guetti, p. 107.

13. George Levine, "Risking the Moment: Anarchy and Possibility in Pynchon's Fiction," in *Mindful Pleasures: Essays on Thomas Pynchon*, ed. George Levine and David Leverenz (Boston: Little, Brown, 1976), p. 113. See also Brian Stonehill, *The Self-Conscious Novel: Artifice in Fiction from Joyce to Pynchon* (Philadelphia: University of Pennsylvania Press, 1988), pp. 146–49.

14. Peter Cooper, *Signs and Symptoms: Thomas Pynchon and the Contemporary World* (Berkeley and Los Angeles: University of California Press, 1983), p. 182.

15. Ibid., pp. 45, 182.

16. Ibid., p. 54.

17. Vladimir Nabokov, *Speak, Memory: An Autobiography Revisited* (1951; reprint, New York: Capricorn Books, 1970), p. 92.

18. N. Katherine Hayles, *The Cosmic Web: Scientific Field Models and Literary Strategies in the Twentieth Century* (Ithaca, N.Y.: Cornell University Press, 1984), p. 174. For different discussions of this point, see Levine, pp. 123, 127; Cooper, pp. 220–22; and William Vesterman, "Pynchon's Poetry," in *Mindful Pleasures*, pp. 102–3.

19. Leo Bersani, *A Future for Astyanax: Character and Desire in Literature* (New York: Columbia University Press, 1984), p. 51.

20. Ralph Waldo Emerson, "The Poet," in *Ralph Waldo Emerson: Essays and Lectures*, ed. Joel Porte (New York: Library of America, 1983), p. 462.

21. Poirier, p. 19.

22. Douglas Fowler, *A Reader's Guide to "Gravity's Rainbow"* (Ann Arbor, Mich.: Ardis, 1980), p. 175.

23. The situation is complicated by our continuing uncertainty as to whether we are ever, in the Stencil chapters, listening to a narrator or to the reconstructive voice of Stencil himself, playing narrator to his own life by using the third-person mode of address.

24. John Keats, *Letters of John Keats*, ed. Robert Gittings (London: Oxford University Press, 1970), p. 230.

25. Levine, p. 119.

26. Roger Sale, "The Golden Age of the American Novel," in *On Not Being Good Enough* (New York: Oxford University Press, 1979), p. 114.

27. Thomas Pynchon, "A Journey into the Mind of Watts," *New York Times Magazine*, 12 June 1966, p. 80.

28. Edward Mendelson, "Gravity's Encyclopedia," in *Mindful Pleasures*, p. 173.

29. Catharine Stimpson, "Pre-Apocalyptic Atavism: Thomas Pynchon's Early Fiction," in *Mindful Pleasures*, p. 38.

30. Robert Golden, "Mass Man and Modernism: Violence in Pynchon's *V.*," *Critique* 14, no. 2 (1972): 5–17.

31. Cooper, p. 96.

32. Fowler, p. 28.

33. Golden, pp. 11, 11–12.

34. Mary Allen, *The Necessary Blankness: Women in Major American Fiction of the Sixties* (Urbana: University of Illinois Press, 1976), p. 45.

35. Sale, p. 116.

36. Richard Poirier, *A World Elsewhere: The Place of Style in American Literature* (New York: Oxford University Press, 1966), pp. 237, 252.

37. John Fraser, *Violence in the Arts* (Cambridge, Eng.: Cambridge University Press, 1974), p. 116.

38. Levine, p. 119.

39. Rachel Owlglass refers to this notion in discussing Esther (*V.*, p. 35).

40. Levine, p. 121.

41. Robert Boyers, "Language and Reality in Kosinski's *Steps*," in *Excursions: Selected Literary Essays* (Port Washington, N.Y.: Kennikat Press, 1977), p. 73.

42. Levine, p. 116.

43. Salman Rushdie, "Still Crazy after All These Years," review of *Vineland* by Thomas Pynchon, *New York Times Book Review*, 14 January 1990, p. 36.

44. Richard Poirier, "The Importance of Thomas Pynchon," in *Mindful Pleasures*, p. 29.

POSTSCRIPT

STYLE, VIOLENCE, AMERICAN FICTION

1. Ralph Waldo Emerson, "The Tragic," in *Ralph Waldo Emerson: Lectures and Essays*, ed. Joel Porte (New York: Library of America, 1983), pp. 1289–95.

2. Pauline Kael, "Bonnie and Clyde," in *Kiss Kiss Bang Bang* (Boston: Little, Brown 1968), p. 56.

3. Delmore Schwartz, "The Fiction of William Faulkner," in *Selected Essays of Delmore Schwartz*, ed. Donald A. Dike and David H. Zucker (Chicago: University of Chicago Press, 1970), p. 287.

4. Stanley Fish, *Is There a Text in This Class? The Authority of Interpretive Communities* (Cambridge, Mass.: Harvard University Press, 1980), p. 355.

5. Reuben A. Brower, "Reading in Slow Motion," in *In Defense of Reading: A Reader's Approach to Literary Criticism*, ed. Reuben A. Brower and Richard Poirier (New York: E. P. Dutton, 1962), p. 8.

6. Christopher Ricks, *Poems and Critics* (New York: Harper & Row, 1972), p. 23.

7. Ibid., pp. 9, 10–12.

8. Ibid., p. 10.

9. See James Guetti's essay "Wittgenstein and Literary Theory": part 1, *Raritan* 4, no. 2 (Fall 1984): 67–84; and part 2, *Raritan* 4, no. 3 (Winter 1985): 66–84.

10. Millicent Bell, "Narrative Gaps/Narrative Meaning," *Raritan* 6, no. 1 (Summer 1986): 101–2.

11. James Guetti, *Word-Music: The Aesthetic Aspect of Narrative Fiction* (New Brunswick, N.J.: Rutgers University Press, 1980), p. 33.

12. The perhaps foreseeable extreme here is the use of "text-centered criticism" as a derogatory term by certain reader-response critics.

13. Gerald Graff, "Jargonarama: What We Talk about When We Talk about Lit," *Village Voice Literary Supplement* 71 (January–February 1989), pp. 24, 28.

14. My suspicion is borne out by another essay by Graff in which he questions the term "special interests" in politics and education. "Who gets to determine," he asks, "which values are deemed 'common' and 'universal' and which merely 'special'"? In Graff's own "teach the conflicts" philosophy, however, it remains fairly evident which

interests are "special" and deserving of his attention in debates about the canon. He proposes to put "highbrow and lowbrow traditions back into the dialogical relation in which they have actually existed in our cultural history." Once again, larger entities like "highbrow and lowbrow traditions" and "dialogical relations" precede the texts that are, in Graff's model, then belatedly brought in to "prove" what has already been assumed. See "Teach the Conflicts," *South Atlantic Quarterly* 89, no. 1 (Winter 1990): 53, 54.

15. Flannery O'Connor, *Mystery and Manners: Occasional Prose*, ed. Sally and Robert Fitzgerald (New York: Farrar, Straus & Giroux, 1969), pp. 73, 96.

16. Robert Frost, "A Romantic Chasm," in *Selected Prose of Robert Frost*, ed. Hyde Cox and Edward Connery Lathem (New York: Collier Books, 1977), p. 78.

Index

180–81, 189, 279nn. 26 and 27, 280n.30–
281n.30, 281n.34
Sartre, Jean-Paul, 22
Savage, D. S., 131, 133
Scarry, Elaine, 259n.31
Schloss, Carol: on O'Connor, 205, 207, 212, 218,
285n.25; on representation, 260n.13–261n.13
Schneider, Daniel J., 276n.44
Scholes, Robert, 36, 152, 153, 277n.53
Schwartz, Delmore: on Faulkner, 164, 166, 176,
185, 250; on Hemingway, 134–35, 137,
274n.25
seeing, imaginative. *See* visual imagining
self-consciousness: in Poe, 85, 97, 103; in Pynchon,
234–35
self-parody: in Faulkner, 164; in Hemingway, 97;
in Poe, 91, 94, 96
sensory imagining: in Cooper, 69–70, 76; in Crane,
107, 113, 114, 126, 129; and fictional violence,
in general, 42–43, 51–52, 60; in Hemingway,
145, 146; in O'Connor, 201, 203; and voice,
75–76; in Tom Wolfe, 53–56, 59, 264n.59; in
Wright, 42–43, 47, 48, 50–51. *See also* auditory
imagining; visual imagining
Shadow over the Promised Land (Karcher), 19
Shakespeare, William, 14
"Short Happy Life of Francis Macomber, The"
(Hemingway), 154–58, 159, 277n.59–278n.59
"Simplicity in Art" (Norris), 40
Sister Carrie (Dreiser), 271n.19
Slotkin, Richard, 17–18, 74, 259n.30
smell, in sensory imagining, 53–54
Smith, Paul, 275
social contexts of fiction, 19–20
Soho Weekly News, 223
"Soldier's Home" (Hemingway), 138
Soloman, Eric, 272n.31
Sontag, Susan, 35, 85
Sound and the Fury, The (Faulkner), 185–87,
281n.42–282n.42
Southern Literary Messenger, 97
Spielberg, Steven, 246
Steffens, Lincoln, 136
Stein, Gertrude, 143
Steinbeck, John, 25, 39
Stephens, Martha, 204
Stoppard, Tom, 160

Stowe, Harriet Beecher, 37–38, 39
style: in general, 22–23; in Cooper, 66–67, 69–74,
76, 77, 79; in fictional violence, in general, 4, 5,
8, 25–27, 40, 249; in O'Connor, 194–95, 198,
219–21, 286nn. 48 and 49; in romance, 65;
satirization of, 91, 94, 96, 123; in Tom Wolfe,
53, 57, 58–59; in Wright, 41–42, 43–44, 45,
263n.54. *See also* Crane, Stephen, style in;
Faulkner, William Cuthbert, style in; Hemingway, Ernest, style in; Poe, Edgar Allan, style in;
Pynchon, Thomas, style in; style in realism;
voice
style in realism: in general, 25–27, 29–30, 34,
260n.13–261n.13; in Crane, 106–10, 112,
271n. 19; in fictional violence, in general, 25–
27, 40; in Oates, 27–29, 30, 260n.11; and
reader's response, 31–33, 261nn. 19 and 21; and
realistic imagining, 35. *See also* mimesis
Sukenick, Ronald, 162
Sullivan County tales (Crane), 113
Sun Also Rises, The (Hemingway), 3–4, 8, 138, 147–
48, 150, 158–61, 274nn. 19 and 21
Sunderland, Judith, 85, 90, 102
Sundquist, Eric, 282nn. 47 and 51
symbolism: in Cooper, 70; in Faulkner, 171–72; in
Hemingway, 141–42, 275n.36–276n.36; in
O'Connor, 195, 196, 212; in Poe, 102; in Pynchon, 238; in Wright, 263nn. 50 and 54
Symons, Julian, 82–83, 84, 87, 90, 95, 266n.2,
267n.20
syntax, 45, 73, 84, 106, 167, 171

Tanner, Laura, 49, 257n.5, 263n.50
Tanner, Toby, 112
Tate, Allen: on Hemingway, 133–34, 137; on Poe,
82, 84
Taxi Driver (film), 261n. 21
Taylor, Carole Anne, 192, 193, 282n.53–283n.53
television, violence on, 258n.25
"Tell Tale Heart, The" (Poe), 87
"Temple of the Holy Ghost, A" (O'Connor), 196
themes: in Cooper, 69–71; in Crane, 106, 122,
272n.31; critical approach to, in general, 6, 19,
254; in Faulkner, 165, 166, 185, 189, 281n.40;
in Hemingway, 135, 138, 274n.25, 276n.39; in
O'Connor, in general, 194, 204, 219, 254; in
Poe, 83–84, 85–87, 266n.11; in Pynchon, 222–